DIVERSITY SUCCESS STRATEGIES

DIVERSITY SUCCESS STRATEGIES

NORMA CARR-RUFFINO, PH.D.

An Imprint of Elsevier

Boston   Oxford   Auckland   Johannesburg   Melbourne   New Delhi

Butterworth–Heinemann supports the efforts of American Forests and
the Global ReLeaf program in its campaign for the betterment of trees,
forests, and our environment.

Library of Congress Cataloging-in-Publication Data
Carr-Ruffino, Norma.
        Diversity success strategies / Norma Carr-Ruffino.
                p.   cm.
        Includes bibliographical references and index.
        ISBN 0-7506-7102-5 (pbk. : alk. paper)
        1. Diversity in the workplace.   2. Personnel management.   I. Title.
        HF5549.5.M5C388   1999
        658.3'008—dc21   98-48868
                                                                CIP

British Library Cataloguing-in-Publication Data
A catalogue record for this book is available from the British Library.

The publisher offers special discounts on bulk orders of this book.
For information, please contact:

Manager of Special Sales
Butterworth–Heinemann
225 Wildwood Avenue
Woburn, MA 01801–2041
Tel: 781-904-2500
Fax: 781-904-2620

For information on all Butterworth–Heinemann publications available, contact our
World Wide Web home page at: http://www.bh.com

10 9 8 7 6 5 4 3 2

Printed in the United States of America

Contents

1

How to Succeed in a Diverse Workplace

American workplace diversity can be a major source of innovation, global savvy, and profitability—or a source of conflict and chaos. It all depends on us: on how we respond to workplace changes, and on our ability to build productive relationships with people from many cultures and lifestyles. The increasing diversity you encounter in your workplace may pose challenges to your ability to do your job, but that diversity can also be the source of amazing career success. You're about to learn the diversity success strategies that make all the difference.

HOW THE AMERICAN WORKPLACE IS CHANGING

The workplace is changing in most every way. The kinds of people we see in high-powered jobs are more diverse. The way people work together and what they do are changing. And the way business is done throughout the world is changing almost month by month. The terms we use for various groups are changing, too, as we'll discuss a little later.

New Faces in New Jobs

People with university degrees and technical expertise come from all types of backgrounds these days. Since the 1960s, more and more African Americans, Latino Americans, Asian Americans, and women have been entering college programs and technical areas that were formerly dominated by Euro-American ("White" or European American) men. As a result, these "minorities" have been moving into managerial, executive, technical, and professional careers formerly closed to them.

The workplace is becoming more diverse in other ways, too. A survey of the disability research literature reveals that persons with disabilities have been finding ways to use the many abilities they do have as productive employees. Many gay persons no longer try to hide their sexual orientation and want to be dealt with as employees who have rights equal to those of straight employees. Older employees now have the right to refuse mandatory retirement and can work as long as they are still productive. Obese persons are beginning to expect and gain some rights to be treated fairly and equally in the workplace. And people are becoming aware of the unfairness of "appearance bias" in general, especially when it is not essentially related to job productivity.

These dramatic changes in the workplace are producing some interesting challenges for everyone, from entry-level employees to top management. All must face the misunderstanding, communication breakdown, conflict, and even failure that can result when people from widely diverse backgrounds must pull together as a team or at least complete some sort of business transaction together. But these changes also offer bountiful opportunities for new levels of growth, innovation, expansion, and productivity. This book is about successfully meeting the challenges and prospering from the opportunities.

More Women and Immigrants

Since the 1960s, more and more women have worked outside the home for most of their adult lives. Some are there because they want careers, even though they may be wives and mothers as well; some because their family needs their income; and most for both reasons. More and more ethnic minorities are in the workforce because immigration quotas were expanded in the 1960s, allowing more Latinos and Asians to become citizens. In 1940 more than 85 percent of people who had come to the United States as immigrants were European, while in 1995, 75 percent were from non-European countries. Most are from Latin American (47 percent) and Asian countries (22 percent). These immigrants tended to be younger on average and to have more children than the Euro-American population, further expanding their numbers.

Figures 1.1(a) and 1.1(b) show the ethnic makeup of the population and the workforce in 1990, as well as the proportions of major American ethnic groups in the better-paying middle- and top-level management jobs. Although Euro-American women and minorities made up 65 percent of the workforce, they held only 30 percent of middle management jobs and 5 percent of top management positions.

Income for these groups reflects the glass ceiling that is still in place and blocking access to higher-level jobs in corporate America. In 1990, according to the U.S. Census Bureau, median incomes for full-time workers were:

	Men	*Women*
Median income, all workers	$20,409	$10,371
Euro-American	22,065	10,747
African American	12,950	8,825
Latino American	13,501	8,354
Asian American	19,396	11,986
American Indian	12,180	7,310
Other Americans	12,493	7,876

Figures 1.1(a) and 1.1(b)   *Ethnic and Gender Segments of the Workforce and of Management, 1990.*

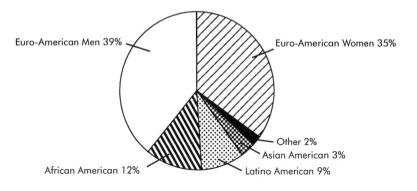

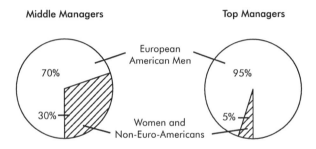

Source: U.S. Census Bureau, 1993; U.S. Dept. of Labor, 1991

The trend toward a more diverse population and workforce is expected to continue. Of the 26 million new workers coming into the workforce between 1990 and 2005, about 85 percent are expected to be women and non-Euro-Americans. A handy way to remember the proportions is to think in terms of sixths: women will account for about four-sixths, minority men more than one-sixth, and Euro-American men one-sixth, as depicted in Figure 1.2.

Historically, men of European ancestry have run virtually all the major American organizations. They have set the rules of the game in the American culture as well as in corporate cultures. Other types of employees were tradition-ally excluded from mainstream leadership roles. They worked on the periphery of our organizations as the workers who were told what to do and how to do it, and as temporary employees and part-timers. Some were kept out completely—the unemployed and unemployable.

In the past, most American businesses functioned primarily within U.S. bor-ders. Now even very small businesses may do much of their business in global

Figure 1.2 *New Workers Entering the Workforce, 1990-2005.*

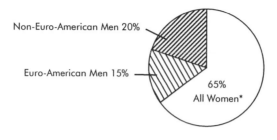

Non-Euro-American Men 20%

Euro-American Men 15%

65%
All Women*

*45% Euro-American Women, 20% Non-Euro-American Women

Source: U.S. Bureau of Labor Statistics

markets. Corporate success now depends on building positive, productive relationships with people from many cultures around the planet. Corporate cultures that are open, flexible, appreciative, and savvy about cultural and lifestyle differences have a competitive edge. Having diverse employees at all levels in all functional areas of a corporation enhances that edge—and is becoming ever more crucial for success and profitability as reliance on global transactions increases.

New Terms that We Use for People

Not only is workplace diversity growing and changing, but the terms we use for various groups has been changing. People who resist such change say the new names are a demand for "political correctness." Others say they're a sign of common courtesy. People are very sensitive about the labels that others attach to them. Most prefer no labels at all. Yet how do we discuss the issues of cultures and subcultures, of diverse groups in a pluralistic society, of prejudice and discrimination based on group stereotypes? Obviously, verbal communication requires the use of descriptive terms. Such terms tend to change over time in response to social and cultural changes and interactions.

African Americans were properly called "Negroes" during the 1800s, politely called "Colored" during the first half of this century, then took the term "Black" for themselves. Women were politely called "ladies" before the women's movement of the 1960s. When group labels are continually used in a limiting, demeaning, scornful, or hostile way, they eventually are resented by some of the people of that group. Therefore, if you want to show respect and appreciation for others, you'll naturally want to use the terms they prefer. This can be difficult, since members of a particular group rarely have unanimous opinions about preferred terms.

The terms used here are those adopted by The President's Task Force on Multiculturalism in the Curriculum at San Francisco State University, one of the most diverse campuses on earth. This campus claims the only College of Ethnic

Studies in the world, one with separate departments for African American, American Indian, Asian American, and Latino American studies. The task force met weekly for many months to work out terminology and basic policy concerning diverse groups. The terms for the largest ethnic groups are listed below and reflect the preferences of activists and leaders from those groups.

- African Americans
- Asian Americans (such as Chinese Americans, Asian Indian Americans)
- Euro-Americans (or European Americans) referring to "White" persons
- Jewish Americans
- Latino Americans (such as Mexican Americans, Puerto Rican Americans)
- American Indians (such as Navajo, Hopi)

If you got a sense of equality as you looked at these terms, you're on the right track. The major rationale for these particular terms, rather than some others, is that we're all Americans, and most of us are native Americans. If we go back far enough, all of us have ancestors who came from somewhere else. And how long we or our ancestors have been here is not a valid measure of our worth or our right to be here.

If your ancestors were immigrants from Europe, you're a Euro-American and you're a member of the dominant majority in American culture. The terms *Asian American* and *Latino American* are used for convenience in discussing certain cultural and statistical commonalties. Most Asian Americans don't think of themselves as Asian Americans so much as *Chinese Americans* or *Filipino Americans* or one of the many Asian subcultural groups. The same is true for Latino Americans, many of whom don't appreciate the term "Hispanic," because it brings up painful visions of Spanish conquest and colonialism.

The terms used for other major groups are based on discussions with various leaders of those groups and on a review of current literature. These groups are:

- Persons with disabilities
- Gay, lesbian, and bisexual persons
- Older persons
- Obese persons

Because Euro-American men have traditionally been in charge in the American workplace, others are often called minorities. Some feel the term "minorities" trivializes the fact that, taken together, ethnic subcultures are the majority in most metropolitan areas and in many workplaces. The Task Force did not resolve this terminology issue.

"Minorities" is the term I will use for all groups that are not Euro-American men, that is, all those groups that are generally considered disadvantaged in the workplace, even though we know that taken together they are a large majority. The alternate terms are persons from various cultures and lifestyles, persons of diverse backgrounds, and non-Euro-American employees or persons.

When you relate one-to-one with people from any of these groups, you rarely need to use group names. You're dealing with the individual. When you need to discuss group issues with others, consider asking them questions about what terms they prefer to use for their own group. Reach some agreement about appropriate labels. Become sensitive to language that some consider racist and sexist, and weed it out of your vocabulary. Every time you use such terms, you may reinforce the prejudicial patterns, even though you don't intend to.

Diverse Backgrounds = Diverse Issues

Whether you're an entry-level trainee, a team leader, or a top manager, your career success and enjoyment increasingly depend on how well you understand and relate to a diverse range of people. If you can mentally slip inside their skin for a time and see the world through their eyes, you'll gain great power in understanding the way others think and feel and the issues most important to them. Here's a brief preview of some of the issues you'll soon learn about. These issues have been extensively explored by a wide variety of researchers from many fields, such as business, sociology, and anthropology. For example, Geert Hofstede has done major comparative studies of corporate employees across many countries and cultures; M. L. Hecht has done extensive research on African American cultural and communication patterns; and Paul Longmore is a leading activist on disability issues and has done much well-respected research in that field.

Career women often find themselves in catch-22 situations. For example, many people assume that women are more emotional, indecisive, and vulnerable than men. But business leaders are expected to be in control of their emotions, decisive, and able to roll with the punches. If women project the traditional feminine image, they're not seen as potential leaders. But if they project the business leader image, they're often seen as too hard and masculine, even abnormal.

Men are expected to be aggressive, ambitious, and proud. But many corporate cultures are changing in ways that call for leaders who are cooperative and who focus more on inspiring and supporting others than on personal achievement. Many men are confused about what companies expect of them, just as they're confused about what the women in their lives expect. The dramatic changes in women's roles have had a major impact on men's lives.

African Americans who have a problem with a "brother or sister" typically take the bull by the horns and confront the issue directly. They go straight to the person, "tell it like it is," and try to work it out immediately. To them this approach is real and honest. But to many other people in a workplace, it may seem threatening and imply anger that might erupt into violence. They may feel threatened by African American "confrontation, rage, or violence" because they misinterpret these cultural behavior patterns.

Asian Americans are taught that one of the highest values is to control one's reactions and to become mature enough to put relationships before personal concerns. As a result, they may be very indirect about expressing criticism or disagreeing. Often, they don't show or express strong emotion, especially outside the family circle. When coworkers conclude that Asian Americans are closed, secretive, inscrutable, and even cold, it's usually because they're unaware of Asian cultural values.

Latino Americans are often assumed to have a *mañana* (literally "tomorrow") attitude, which implies that they're not the ambitious, productive go-getters that most Euro-Americans admire. Actually, most Latino Americans are hard workers, but they tend to wait for orders from the boss. Their cultural beliefs include greater respect for authority than most Euro-Americans hold—and greater acceptance of themselves as subordinates to a powerful boss. Also, Latinos tend to be more accepting than Euro-Americans of undesirable circumstances, often seeing such situations as God's will. When Euro-Americans judge Latino Americans as lacking initiative, it's usually because they don't understand these aspects of their cultural background.

Gay persons are sometimes avoided by coworkers on the assumption that gays don't have "normal" relationships. Coworkers have made such comments as, "I just don't feel comfortable socializing with Joe [a gay man]. Maybe he'll come on to me sexually," or "Maybe he'll get jealous of my friendship with a guy he's attracted to, when to me we're just hanging out." Joe would probably say, "Hey, I'm *me* first and foremost, just a person. My sexual orientation is just one slice of the whole pie that's me. What's more, I'm very sensitive to the discomforts and fears of straight guys." Studies indicate that people in the gay community have a whole range of relationships, as people in any community do, and that overall they're as likely to have "normal relationships" as people from any cultural group.

Persons with disability are thought to be a small minority by most people and are often seen as distinctly "different," even abnormal. Actually, most people have some type of disability, usually fairly minor. Persons classified as "disabled" simply have a disability that affects their ability to perform one or more major life functions, such as walking, reading, or hearing. They're not really "different" from the person who limps around occasionally with back trouble, the person who wears contacts, or the person who doesn't hear too well out of one ear. It's just a matter of degree. Even persons with a severe disability, such as paralysis from the neck down, can learn to live and work independently and to make significant contributions through their careers.

Obese persons are often as healthy as most adults, depending upon the extent of their obesity and their age. Many cruel myths and stereotypes surround obesity in our culture. The type of discrimination obese employees experience has an element of appearance bias and is related to skin-color discrimination. Obese persons also experience discrimination based on assumptions about what they cannot do, similar to that experienced by persons with disability. Recent court rulings that support the employment rights of obese persons are based on their rights to "reasonable accommodation" under laws that protect the disabled.

Older persons are often assumed to be rigid, dogmatic, and forgetful. Their younger coworkers may avoid them and may wonder why these "old folks" haven't retired or when they're going to retire. Research indicates that aging itself does not cause any significant loss of intelligence, memory, or learning capacity. However, with age one's habits tend to come home to roost. People who abuse or neglect their bodies start paying the price in their later years, while people with good eating and exercise habits tend to remain healthy and vibrant. People who habitually spend much of their time in negative thinking tend to become even more negative with age, while those who work on a positive outlook and self-growth become more delightful to be around.

Other groups that have distinct issues include American Indians, Arab Americans, Jewish Americans, and bi-ethnic persons (those whose parents are from two distinctly different cultural backgrounds). For example, the person whose mother is Euro-American and whose father is African American tends to experience a unique type of cultural conflict growing up. Because of the limitations of time and space, these and other groups are not explored here.

Every cultural subgroup has its own unique set of values, habits, customs, life circumstances, and issues to resolve. Understanding the key cultural themes and issues of each group can give you great insight and power for building good work relationships and helping other team members do the same.

NEW WAYS OF WORKING TOGETHER

In the new technologically oriented companies, employees are more highly skilled and educated than ever. Old hierarchies and authoritarian bosses who dictate orders are fading into the archaic past. More common are:

- self-managing work teams
- leaders who facilitate team meetings and help teams to reach consensus
- consultants and technical experts who function more as professionals than as traditional employees

Relationships with teammates, customers, and suppliers, and the information that flows among them, are the lifeblood of the organization. Corporations are increasingly built upon trust, collaboration, cooperation, and teamwork. In such organizations, it's more obvious than ever that people are the most valuable resource, that how we work together creates energy and innovation or decay and demoralization, that our interactions spark the knowledge and information that fuel organizational growth and success. In summary, key trends that point to the need for new people skills are:

- A shortage of qualified, educated workers means companies must be more responsive to workers' needs and expectations.
- The U.S. workforce is becoming dramatically more diverse at all levels. Workers expect more accommodation to their needs and identities than in the past. Fewer workers are willing to compromise their unique cultural characteristics for the sake of "fitting in" with corporate cultures built on narrow, exclusive values and norms.
- The global marketplace that now affects most American corporations is intensely competitive, making qualified employees more crucial than ever for providing the quality, innovation, and productivity companies need to compete.

- The growth of these subcultural groups means a growth of subcultural market segments. Companies need a workforce that "looks like America" to project a multicultural company image, contribute to marketing insights, and relate well to multicultural customers.
- Success in the global marketplace depends on building profitable relationships with people in all the countries where an organization does business. Diverse people skills are as powerful in the global marketplace as they are in the American workplace—and can be readily expanded to include other cultures and environments.

NEW APPROACHES TO MANAGING DIVERSITY

Business leaders are changing the way they manage diversity, as indicated in Figure 1.3. Most realize now that the melting-pot approach was a myth so far as people of color and women are concerned. They also realize that the legal approach, which relies on meeting equal opportunity and affirmative action requirements, has been an effective tool for opening doors to all, but it does not provide an adequate basis for managing diversity. What is emerging is an action-oriented approach that values diversity and also works toward creating a corporate culture that reflects the cultures of all employees. This culture has values, heroes, heroines, myths, rituals, and customs from all the cultures and lifestyles of its employee groups. It creates a climate that welcomes and nurtures all types of employees.

Business leaders who use an active, change-oriented multicultural approach are discovering a surprising wealth of benefits for their organizations. Benefits accrue at all levels: personal, interpersonal, and organizational. They include:

- attracting and retaining the best available human talent
- increasing organizational flexibility
- gaining and keeping greater market share—locally and globally
- reducing costs
- improving the quality of management
- creating and innovating more powerfully
- solving problems more effectively
- increasing productivity
- contributing to social responsibility
- bottom line: increased profits

We'll explore briefly why and how each of these benefits is important.

Attracting and Retaining the Best People

Attracting and retaining the best people as employees is more essential to profitability than ever. Tom Peters and other management gurus say "the name of the game these days is finding talent." This means that organizations meet potential employees' needs, show respect for them as individuals, and use similar multicul-

Figure 1.3 *Evolution of Approaches to Workplace Diversity*

Approach:	assimilation	→ legal	→ valuing diversity	→ managing diversity
Basis:	melting pot myth	→ EEO/AA	→ differences as assets	→ multicultural corporate cultures

tural skills in working with them. Researchers such as A. S. Tsui and L. W. Porter find that good diversity management leads to retaining qualified employees.

Attracting Qualified People

As qualified employees become more scarce, employers must become more flexible. They can no longer afford to convey the implicit message, "This is what we offer and how we do things. Fit in or leave." Now they must adapt to potential employees who say, "These are my needs and goals; they must be met if I am to stay."

Retaining High-Potential Employees

To retain good employees, firms must be truly committed to treating all employees fairly and to valuing diversity. Employers who appear to favor some personal orientations and stifle others risk paying the price of low productivity due to a restricted pool of applicants, employee dissatisfaction, lack of commitment, turnover, and even sabotage. Dr. J. H. Sheridan of Vanderbilt University has done research that indicates that professionals (both strong and weak performers) stay an average of fourteen months longer in firms whose main focus is "interpersonal orientation" values than in firms whose focus is "work task" values. Sheridan estimates that the work-task-value firms incurred opportunity losses of $6 to $9 million more over the six-year period studied than the interpersonal-value firms. Sheridan concludes that it makes more sense to foster an interpersonal orientation culture rather than to try to find individuals who will fit into a work task culture.

Meeting Employee Needs and Expectations

Nearly five-sixths of new employees now and in the coming decade will be women and non-Euro-Americans. Most are from a new generation who expect something extra from their careers, namely, meaning and a sense of making a contribution. And most, especially career women, expect to have a personal and family life and are less willing than previous generations were to sacrifice all for career success. And most, especially ethnic minorities, are more resistant to fitting into a corporate culture that requires them to squelch important parts of their persona.

These better educated employees want their individual and group needs recognized and met. They want more control over their own destiny, a say in decisions that affect them, and more flexibility in the terms and rewards of employment. They want a fair, open, flexible, responsive, and responsible work environment where they can enjoy the workday as well as be productive. They want to experience the excitement and stimulation of meeting challenging opportunities and problems as well as the security and serenity that come from being appreciated and supported.

Word gets around quickly about how companies treat diverse employees and which companies are the best to work for. People are less likely to stay with employers who don't meet their needs.

Communicating Respect for Others

One of the basic principles of effective multicultural leadership is to signal respect for the unique characteristics of another's culture. Small gestures can communicate respect, such as greeting persons in their native language, taking time to chat and learn more about a person, and keeping their cultural and personal viewpoints and values in mind as you work together. Doing this effectively requires learning about diverse subgroups and building skills in relating to them. People do work together more cooperatively after receiving training in viewpoints and values that are important for success in the organization, according to Dr. Jennifer Chatman's research.

Increasing Organizational Flexibility

Companies are teaming up, forming alliances to pool their resources and to tighten relationships with suppliers and customers. An alliance may require that two teams or units from two different companies blend together to act as a link between the firms involved. The most frequently cited source of problems with alliances is "different corporate cultures," according to a *Harvard Business Review* survey. Multicultural skills can be applied to working in various corporate cultures as well as working with individuals from various cultures, according to Dr. Rosabeth Moss Kanter.

Gaining and Keeping Greater Market Share—Locally and Globally

The spending power of African Americans, Latino Americans, and Asian Americans was about $424 billion in 1990 and is expected to grow to $650 billion by the year 2000. In California, these three groups make up 40 percent of the population and are expected to make up 50 percent by 2000. It is estimated that by 2000 about half of all business travelers will be women. Diverse employees can help to attract and retain minority customers. Researchers such as Ann Morrison find that good diversity management increases global competitiveness as well as workplace harmony and productivity.

The experiences and perspectives of a diverse workforce can certainly be valuable in building sales. Such diversity is the best way to be sure the organization remains flexible enough to capture diverse markets and to provide adequate customer service. Having African American women on the team, for example, may motivate management to respond to growing market niches involving such customers. This happened to Avon in the cosmetics market. Also, customers tend to perceive that someone of their own ethnicity or sex is better able to serve their needs, and this can influence them in choosing one service or product over another. Using diversity to improve marketing skills within ethnically diverse domestic markets can help a company market itself more effectively internationally. Learning how to be responsive to such markets and to project the right image to them will help the company sharpen its skills for the international marketplace.

Diverse employees can prevent many awkward public relations problems. They can also help in those one-on-one provider-customer interactions that are becoming increasingly common as companies focus on providing services, information, and custom products to customers. It makes sense for a company to employ a workforce that mirrors its customer base. Women have a special edge in tuning into women's needs and expectations and meeting them, just as African American men have an advantage in understanding and communicating with one another. Diversity can help prevent the following types of problems:

- An advertisement for a major telephone company featured a drawing of animals making telephone calls from various continents. A gorilla was making the call from Africa. Many African Americans were incensed.
- General Motors launched a major marketing campaign in Mexico to sell its Chevrolet Nova. In Spanish "no va" means "doesn't go." Almost no one bought the car. And Dr. Gregory Stephens' research indicates that many American ventures in Mexico since NAFTA have suffered because people didn't understand the cultural differences involved.
- A major bank instructed its tellers, all women, to wear straw hats with a band reading "Free and Easy Banking." The word "Banking" was hidden under the turned-up brims. When women realized why customers were snickering, they were upset.

Reducing Costs

A multicultural approach saves money in the long run and often even in the short run, according to such researchers as John Hinrichs. For example, diversity efforts reduce the high turnover rate of nontraditional employees and the costs that go with it. The cost of turnover per person has been estimated at $5,000 to $10,000 for hourly workers, and from $75,000 to $200,000 for an executive at the $100,000 salary level. When a nontraditional manager is included in a development program or gets a promotion, other nontraditional employees at lower levels tend to feel more committed to the company. Such companies are more likely to be sought out by nontraditional recruits, which reduces the costs of recruiting. They also may save money in defending grievances, complaints, and lawsuits regarding discrimination, sexual harassment, and similar problems. In addition to lost time and legal fees for dealing with such problems, other costs are job-related stress, lowered morale, lowered productivity, and resulting absenteeism and turnover.

Improving the Quality of Management

Knowing they must compete with all comers can encourage the more competent Euro-American men to perform even better, while the less competent ones are screened out. Diversity can prod managers to learn fresh approaches to business problems, to see issues from new perspectives, and to add new contacts to their business networks. Exposure to diverse colleagues can help managers develop breadth and openness. Perhaps this explains why Euro-American men who graduate from universities where African American students comprise 8 to 17 percent of the student body earn roughly 15 percent higher wages than whose who graduate from "lily-white" schools, according to Dr. Jonathan Marshall's research. Also, much of what an organization learns in trying out a special training program for diversity purposes may later be broadly applied to all employees.

Creating and Innovating More Powerfully

Traditional assembly-line industrial organizations required creative thinking from only a few, but postindustrial virtual organizations with their self-managing work teams require it of many. If people from diverse backgrounds are truly respected, supported, and appreciated, they will be willing to contribute their ideas to group sessions. This in turn gives the group a broader range of diverse ideas to choose from, increases group synergy, and prevents "groupthink."

The conclusion that creativity is fostered by diversity is supported by research showing that the tolerance of diversity, defined as judging relatively few behaviors as deviant from norms, is a defining characteristic of innovative organizations, according to research by Dr. S. Siegel and W. Kaemmerer.

For best results, relationships among team members must be predominantly harmonious. In any group, people will naturally have different viewpoints and will sometimes disagree about how situations should be handled. This can enhance creativity and result in better decisions, if relationships are basically strong. When group members have not learned how to value and respect their differences, the result can be group conflict that interferes with productivity, closes down communication, wastes energy, and even causes people to leave. On the other hand, when people nearly always agree on everything, this can be a sign of complacency, repression, or old approaches to addressing new problems, according to Dr. S. E. Jackson's research. The challenge is to bring differences into play in ways that respect individuals and maintain goodwill—which you will learn to do in this book.

Solving Problems and Increasing Productivity

Culturally diverse workforces have the potential to solve problems better because of several factors: a greater variety of perspectives brought to bear on the issue; a higher level of critical analysis of alternatives; and a lower probability of groupthink and, therefore, a higher probability of generating creative solutions.

All the benefits mentioned so far work together to generally increase organizational productivity. Specifically, an effective approach to managing diversity helps diverse teams and individuals to be more productive, according to research reported in *Fortune* magazine.

Learning about each employee's unique values, expectations, and goals is essential to effectively working with diverse team members on team projects. It's also essential for leaders in helping others with job objectives, job performance, and career plans. Job performance, dedication, and attendance are boosted when employees perceive they are valued and cared for by their organization. Employees are more productive when they enjoy coming to work, feel happy to be working where they're seen as worthy and competent, and can relax into being themselves. In addition, such employees are more innovative, even without any direct reward or personal recognition. Research by Dr. R. Eisenberger indicates that groups that are diverse in terms of ethnicity, age, values, background, and training are more productive and innovative than homogeneous groups.

The Center for Creative Leadership identified twelve companies that showed exceptional leadership in encouraging diversity. All the companies were in the top half of Fortune magazine's "most admired" corporations, and 80 percent were in the top 20 percent. Dr. Rosabeth Moss Kanter found that companies with a reputation for progressive human resource practices had more profitability and financial growth than their competitors over a twenty-year period.

Contributing to Social Responsibility

When we see the growing crime and violence almost everywhere, and the continued divisiveness and prejudice, we begin to understand the price we must pay when we don't find ways to balance diversity with unity and harmony. Unity with diversity has always been an ideal in our nation, as has equality of opportunity. Our challenge in the workplace today is to make these ideals a reality.

The organization can become an agent for change, for making the world a better place. If one organization can thrive by creating an environment where diverse people can work effectively together, this can serve as a model for the entire world. A Los Angeles executive, as quoted in the *Los Angeles Times*, said, "In this area the situation is so desperate and so in need of role models, that if we in corporations can't advance minorities so they can turn around and do what needs to be done in their communities, I don't see any of us surviving. The bigger picture we have to deal with is the minority situation in this country."

The problems we're facing in our business organizations and metropolitan areas reflect the problems we're facing at all levels: personal problems, family problems, national problems, and global problems. As we grow in our understanding of diversity in the workplace, of the major roles of beliefs, values, stereotypes, prejudices, relationships, and access to information, we grow in understanding ourselves, our family dynamics, and our national and global priorities. As we gain skill in establishing and nurturing relationships with the whole spectrum of diverse people in the workplace, we gain skill as a national culture in working out the problems now dividing us: violent crime, ethnic conflict, inner-city decay, and failing schools. If we learn how to find greater unity and harmony as a nation, we can bring this knowledge to the arena of global culture, where as a community of nations we can apply it in meeting global challenges, prospering from global opportunities and creating global harmony and abundance.

Bottom Line: Increased Profits

Global competition is an established fact of life now. The reengineering, restructuring, and downsizing of the 1990s reflect the reality that United States business can no longer afford bureaucratic, hierarchical structures with a homogeneous group running the show. We can no longer afford the luxury of paying big salaries to layer upon layer of managers to carry information back and forth between workers, managers, and staff experts, information that everyone can now access through their computers. We can no longer afford to pay tiers of high-salaried managers to set goals and make plans for workers and then try to motivate them and keep them productive, when work teams and individuals can do the job better. We can no longer afford to exclude people with the talents and skills we so desperately need for business success. All the benefits they bring to the workplace add up to increased profits—provided we learn to build productive working relationships with each other.

No wonder workplace diversity has become a hot topic! It symbolizes the key to our power in meeting challenges and creating the world we want—at every level of existence. It symbolizes the new world beyond the year 2000 and the changes we need to make in order to meet its challenges and rise to its opportunities.

CAREER SUCCESS: HOW TO BUILD DIVERSE PEOPLE SKILLS

Yes, the work world is a dynamic place, and it's changing more rapidly every day. It's becoming more diverse, more technical, more global, and at the same time more dependent than ever on productive working relationships. You can become a better business leader—whether you're the new entry-level worker or the CEO—by developing leadership attitudes and acting in responsible ways toward *all* your associates. You can gain the skills that help to create a multicultural work environment—in fact, your career success depends more and more on building multicultural skills. That's the purpose of this book. In working through the book, you'll use the following five-step learning process.

Process for Building Multicultural Skills

Step 1. Becoming aware of culture and its pervasive influence.

Step 2. Learning about your own culture—and if you're not of Euro-American background, learning how the dominant American culture differs from others.

Step 3. Recognizing your own patterns of stereotyping—the ways in which you assume, judge, and discriminate, why you do this, and the impact it may have on you and others.

Step 4. Learning about other cultures you encounter in the workplace, so you can recognize when cultural differences may be at the root of problems, and so you can appreciate the contributions people from diverse cultures can make to the work situation.

Step 5. Building interaction skills and practicing new behaviors by working through case studies and other skill builders.

You'll begin building and practicing these skills right away, and you can continue building them throughout your career. Let's review the part that each chapter plays.

Laying the Groundwork

In the next three chapters, you'll work through steps 1, 2, and 3. In Chapter 2, "How Cultural Differences Affect Job Success," you'll start becoming aware of culture's pervasive influence, and learn some key cultural patterns that will help you compare cultures. In Chapter 3, "Understanding the Dominant Culture: Euro-Americans," you'll become more aware of key aspects of the American culture and of typical corporate cultures. In Chapter 4, "Beyond Stereotypes to Profitable Collaboration," you'll begin to recognize your own biases and learn about the nature of prejudice. These chapters lay the groundwork for building your skills. They're the necessary background you'll need.

Building the Framework for Seeing through Another's Eyes

In Chapters 5 through 12 you'll work through steps 4 and 5. Here you'll focus on learning about other cultures and lifestyles by seeing the world through the eyes of people typical of each cultural group, based on what scholars from each of those communities have discovered. According to Daniel Goleman, author of *Emotional Intelligence*, empathy and compassion are essential ingredients of a high level of emotional intelligence. Empathy and compassion come from seeing the world as another might see it, to feel as another might feel in a particular situation. This process of learning to see the world through another's eyes is based on asking the right questions, and these chapters are structured to give you some answers.

Process for Learning about Other Cultures

Key Questions	*Chapter Structure*
What are the key barriers to career success for this group?	Myths versus reality—that reflect stereotypes, prejudice
How did it get that way?	Background or evolution of situation
What's going on now?	Current profile
What makes these people tick?	Cultural themes, patterns, issues
What skills do I need to interact with these employees?	Leadership challenges and opportunities
How can I apply my new knowledge and practice multicultural skills?	Cases and other skill builders

In Chapters 5 through 12 you will learn about various cultures, ranging from the ways men and women live in parallel worlds within a culture, to African American, Asian American, and Latino American subcultures, to the culture-like aspects of life experienced by such groups as gay persons, persons with disabilities, and older persons. While the latter are not *ethnic* subcultures, most members rely heavily on their own networks and communities, forming a subculture in the process.

In this way you will build a multicultural skills framework, a structure for housing the new skills you'll continue to develop in the everyday work world.

Making Your Skills Count

But what can one person do? Whether you're the brand new, entry-level employee, the CEO, or somewhere in between, your skills can make a difference. You can take whatever leadership role your situation allows. To begin with, you can notice the contributions of employees from groups that seem to be excluded in some way, and you can talk up their positive qualities. You can tell the stories of those who succeed, helping to make them stars in the company grapevine of myths and legends. You can visibly support them in any way that seems right. You can unfailingly respect their dignity and speak out against disrespect in the form of wisecracks, jokes, put-downs, exclusion, and similar behavior. If you have the power, you can provide information and training for other employees to help them understand and appreciate people from excluded groups.

2

How Cultural Differences Affect Job Success

You may have noticed that the new coworkers and business associates you encounter in your daily business dealings are from increasingly diverse backgrounds and lifestyles. To succeed in today's workplace, you need to master the people skills that help you build productive relationships with your diverse customers, coworkers, and other business associates. And by learning about the cultures of most of the people you encounter in your workplace and the marketplace, you'll build a framework for understanding and identifying with each person you meet. You'll see more facets of people's differences. This will help you appreciate the roles they can play in expanding the team and corporate idea pool, increasing innovation and problem solving, and boosting productivity and profit. You'll recognize more of the common values you share with others, providing a basis for bonding and building profitable relationships.

You'll complete the first step of the five-step process for becoming a diversity-savvy person: Becoming aware of culture and its pervasive influence.

In this chapter you'll learn about:

- What we mean by culture and how it affects our lives
- The nine basic ways that cultures differ: (1) I control or I'm controlled; (2) me-first or us-first; (3) tight ties or loose ties; (4) achievement-first or people-first; (5) equality or not; (6) take risks or play it safe; (7) time—step-by-step or dive-right-in; (8) space—come close or back off; (9) communication—direct or indirect
- An underlying cultural theme: How we make money and how that affects our dependence upon each other

First, complete the Self-Awareness Opportunity.

Self-Awareness Opportunity 1—What's Your Cultural Orientation?

Purpose: To determine your personal orientation regarding key cultural factors.

Instructions: For each of the following numbered pairs of statements, circle a or b according to which statement best reflects your orientation. See the feedback at the end of this chapter for an interpretation of your responses.

1. a. I create my life by what I do and by what I allow.
   b. I'm just a cog in the wheel of life. Most of what happens to me is outside my control.
2. a. My top priority is to achieve my personal goals.
   b. My top priority is to be a good son/daughter, wife/husband, boss/worker, mother/daughter, that is, to fulfill those roles expected of me.
3. a. I'm happiest when I'm ahead or winning.
   b. I'm happiest when I'm working or playing with friends, family, or coworkers.
4. a. My top priority at work is getting the job done.
   b. My top priority at work is maintaining good relationships with people.
5. a. If a top manager asked me to discuss my ideas, I'd be comfortable.
   b. If a top manager asked me to discuss my ideas, I'd be nervous and uncomfortable.
6. a. People who have talent and work hard can become very successful.
   b. People need the right family background and connections to become very successful.
7. a. My motto is "Nothing risked, nothing gained."
   b. My motto is "Stick with the tried and true."
8. a. I believe that "the exception makes the rule."
   b. I believe that we must stick to the rules of the game or we'll have chaos.

WHAT IS A CULTURE?

Culture is the environment you live in. Because it's like the air you breathe, you're probably unaware of most of its content. You learned it from your parents, teachers, the media, everyone and everything you knew as you grew up. Culture is what a particular group agrees is reality. It becomes the backdrop for the ways people think, feel, speak, and act. For every aspect of culture that we're aware of, there are about 1,000 aspects that we're unaware of. Anthropologists such as Ashley Montagu agree on three characteristics of culture, according to researcher Thomas Pettigrew:

- Culture is learned, not innate.
- The various facets of culture are interrelated. If you touch a culture in one place, everything else is affected.
- Culture is shared, and it defines the boundaries of different groups.

Culture is far more than mere custom that can be easily changed from the outside, even though it's always changing and evolving naturally from the inside.

Surface aspects may change rapidly, but core aspects tend to be very resistant to change.

Cultural Levels

Cultural groups are found at many levels of society:

World culture = humanity; common values and customs found in all cultures
Major culture = a regional or national group that represents a common culture
Subculture = a cultural group within a major culture
Corporate culture = an organization within a major culture

Cultural Elements

As a cultural group, people decide what to believe about the world, which beliefs are most important (values), who their heroes and heroines are, what stories or myths are important to express their values, how to do things—the rituals by which they act out their values, the networks of people connections, and which symbols will serve as shortcuts to remind people of these cultural bonds. All these elements of culture underlie how the people in a major culture decide to handle their families, schools, churches, government, housing, business, and science. They're expressed in a culture's art forms, food, dress, play, and every other aspect of life.

Values

A value is an enduring belief that one way of acting or being is preferable to another. A value system is an organization of such beliefs along a continuum of relative importance, a prioritizing of beliefs into a set or cluster. Norms are cultural do's and don'ts about how to act. Some values and their related norms may be talked about, but most are just understood.

Heroes and Heroines

Heroes, heroines, and role models may also be called champions, stars, or big wheels. They're often seen as fearless leaders or courageous adventurers. They personify the core values and the strength of the organization or group. They become symbolic figures whose deeds are out of the ordinary—but not so far out that people can't identify with them. People like to think, "Maybe I can do that too." Such leaders become great motivators, the people everyone will count on for inspiration when things get tough. They tend to be intuitive, to envision the future, to experiment, and to appreciate the value of celebrations and ceremonies.

Myths and Legends

A myth is a story or saying whose function is to bind together the thoughts of a group and promote coordinated social action. It may be a legend that symbolizes a central belief of the culture. It's often more symbolic than factual, but may be either. Some myths are based on powerful truths; some on manipulative, hurtful lies; still others on harmless little white lies.

Rituals

Rituals are "the way we do things around here." They include the customary day-to-day actions people take, their expected actions and responses. Core values would have no impact without ritual and ceremony. The unwritten rules of personal communication and the rituals of social interaction govern relationships between bosses and workers, professionals and support staff, men and women, old and young, insiders and outsiders.

Work rituals spell out standards of acceptable behavior and how such procedures as strategic planning or budgeting or report writing should be carried out. Recognition rituals, such as awards, are more formal. They acknowledge achievements that are valued and signal that the person belongs to the culture. Rituals meet people's need to belong. They help establish and maintain some common values and goals that connect people in the group. A true ritual is always connected to a myth that represents some basic group value. Otherwise, it's just a habit that does nothing but give people a false sense of security.

Networks

Networks, such as the grapevines, are the primary means of communication within an organization. It ties together all parts of the company without respect to the organization chart. It not only transmits information, it also interprets its significance. In most organizations, only about 10 percent of business takes place in formal meetings and events. The real process of making decisions, gathering support, developing opinions, and so on, happens before or after the meeting. Of course, formal networks are important too. They include the formal organization chart, task forces, work teams, professional and trade associations, and similar groupings.

Symbols

Symbols are shortcuts that remind people of those cultural elements that bind them together. A song, banner, flag, logo, picture, motto, or brand name may bring up corporate values. A nickname or motto may recall a heroine or star. A figure of speech may recall a key myth or ritual. A good symbol can serve to trigger communal thoughts and feelings about a common cause or goal.

HOW DO CULTURES DIFFER?

Cultures differ in thousands of ways, and categorizing the major differences into nine areas gives us a practical basis for comparison. These categories deal with the ways people view themselves in relation to others and to the world, and how they act out those viewpoints. Taken together, these differences reflect one of three underlying themes—dependence, independence, or interdependence—that are connected to whether a culture's economy is mainly agricultural, industrial, or information/service-based.

The following differences were found by researchers Geert Hofstede, Gary Althen, J. Szapocznik, O. E. King, A. Ramirez, E. T. Hall, and M. R. Hall.

Cultural Difference #1—I'm Controlled or I Control?

The most basic beliefs we have are about who or what creates our environment and causes the events within that environment. How much is caused by our own attitudes and actions? How much by a Supreme Being? How much is just chance or coincidence? Beliefs about the cause of life events dramatically affect every other aspect of culture.

I'm Controlled

People from I'm-Controlled cultures might say, "Things happen to me and I have little control over my life. It depends on my boss, my customer, fate, luck, God's will." Most cultures fall into this camp, including most African, Asian, Arab, and Latino cultures. Women in all cultures are more likely than men to hold this viewpoint.

I Control

People from I-Control cultures might say, "What happens to me is up to me. It depends on what I do or don't do. God helps those who help themselves." Most Western cultures, in particular Euro-American, hold this viewpoint, especially men.

Cultural Difference #2—Us-First or Me-First?

This is the most important cultural difference for understanding how people interact with others. Cultures that focus on us-first are called collectivist cultures, because individuals are seen first as members of a family or cohesive group. Cultures that focus on me-first are called individualist cultures, because they believe that each individual must first take responsibility for her or his own life and should have the freedom to succeed or fail. It's similar to looking at a bouquet. Do you focus first on the whole bouquet with the attitude that one flower alone would be out of context and lost? Or do you focus first on each individual flower and then notice how the group forms a bouquet?

Us-First

"I should first integrate my goals, thoughts, and actions with those of my group. Working within what the group wants and needs, I can try to get what I want and need. People should always stay close to their parents and relatives and never stray far." Hofstede's research indicates that most cultures fall into this camp, including most African, Asian, Arab, and Latino cultures. Certain families, religious groups, and subcultures within individualist cultures have collectivist values. Women in all cultures are likely to hold collectivist viewpoints.

Me-First

"I must first focus on my personal goals. When people grow up, they have to cut the apron strings and make their own way in the world. I work toward better things for my family and work team and community, but my personal goals must come first. I'll stay with a group as long as it doesn't block my efforts to meet my own wants and needs." Euro-cultures fall into this camp, with Euro-Americans being the most individualistic.

Cultural Difference #3—Tight Ties or Loose Ties?

Cultures vary by how much alike people are, how homogeneous or diverse. This in turn helps determine whether people feel bound together by many ties or only loosely connected with few ties.

Many Ties That Bind = Us-First

"I see people first as part of a particular family or organization or community, and they see me that way. If I fail, the others in my group will 'lose face' and feel shame, so I should try to cover up my failure. If I succeed, the glory goes to my group, not to me." This mind-set predominates in Eastern cultures, and is held by a majority of the world's people.

"As I grew up, I thought of myself as part of 'we' rather than 'I.' It's important to me to protect my family and close friends and to be loyal to them. I expect them to protect and be loyal to me. Who I am is a member of my family, work group, and community. The ideal way to live is in close relationship with them. I belong to several groups and organizations. I depend on those relationships. We make decisions together, and I believe in those decisions. Who my friends are depends a great deal on the groups I belong to. My status and prestige comes from these relationships. The groups I belong to provide what I need—expertise, order, duty, and security. I'm loyal first to my parents and immediate family, then my relatives, and then the clan or nearby community. Success and satisfaction in life comes from living up to those loyalties. If I gain material success, I'll share it with my family and close friends."

"When I was a university student, I studied hard to pass exams in order to acquire the status of a degree. Now I seek the satisfaction of a job well recognized. It's very important for me to preserve face, or respect, from my family and friends, and to avoid shaming them through my failure. My job life and private life are inseparable. It's okay if my boss inquires about my private life, and I expect the boss to help out with family or personal problems. On the job, relationships are even more important to me than getting tasks done. I must develop a relationship with the people I work with and become adopted into the work group before I can do a good job on my tasks."

Loose Ties = Me-First

"I am unique, one of a kind. Growing up means becoming my own person. If I fail in life, it's strictly my fault, and I would probably feel guilty and want to be by myself till I got over it. What I value most are autonomy, self-reliance, self-identity, emotional independence, and individual initiative."

"When I was a university student, I worked hard in order to master the subject matter for my major. It's important to me to maintain my self-respect and avoid guilt. On the job, I value challenges, individual achievement, and personal ambition. I want the satisfaction of a job well done, especially by my own standards. I keep my job life and private life sharply separated. Getting tasks done is more important than spending time on work relationships." These are typical views of people from Western cultures. The United States is one of the most loosely knit cultures of modern times.

Cultural Difference #4—Achievement-First or People-First?

Most cultures place greater value on building and maintaining strong interpersonal relationships than on getting things done. Others value most highly a person's (or group's) achievements. People-first values are found most often in us-first cultures, while achievement-first predominates in me-first cultures. A people-first orientation reflects feminine values, while an achievement orientation reflects masculine values. However, in both types of cultures men dominate the political and workplace arenas, as research indicates that no country or culture is dominated by women in these areas.

People-First = Connecting, Cooperating = Feminine Aspect

"I focus on building and maintaining positive, personal relationships. The type of life I build is more important than the things I accumulate. I value my hunches and intuition. What motivates me is contributing to my family, workplace, and community. I work in order to live rather than live in order to work."

The Scandinavian cultures are the most people-focused. The roles and viewpoints of men and women are not as separate as in most cultures. Neither men nor women need to be ambitious, competitive, or focused on material success. Men and women may respect whatever is small, weak, and slow. Values within political and work organizations center around interpersonal relationships and concern for the weak.

Achievement-First = Focus on Competition, "Things" = Masculine Aspect

"I am very ambitious, and I believe I'm here to work. Hard work will bring me independence. Men should be assertive, ambitious, and competitive. They should work for material success, and respect whatever is big, strong, and fast. Women should serve and care for the intangible qualities of life, for the children, and for the weak."

The most masculine culture by far is Japan's, while the United States culture is moderately masculine. Such cultures define very different social roles for men and women, with a focus on clear gender roles. They tend to be patriarchal, materialistic, performance-oriented, and factual. Political and corporate values stress material success and assertiveness. While Euro-Americans, especially men, tend to be highly competitive in social interaction and in task performance, Latino Americans, African Americans, and Asian Americans favor a more cooperative approach.

Cultural Difference #5—Equality or Not?

Some cultures, primarily Western ones, are based on the ideal that all persons have equal value and status as human beings. People are therefore entitled to equal opportunity to achieve and advance in the society. Other cultures accept the idea that some people are naturally more powerful, affluent, and privileged than others. They therefore accept the inequality of rank and status in a hierarchical or stratified society. In these cultures people from different levels feel a greater sense of "power distance" than do people who live in more egalitarian cultures.

Inequality = Rank/Status Cultures

"My company's organization chart looks like a pyramid, with a few autocratic leaders at the top and many ordinary workers at the bottom. If my country had an organizational chart, it would look that way too. Our leaders are very strong and powerful. We depend on them to make the right decisions. We expect them to control things. If they asked us what to do, we would assume they were weak and should step down. The leaders we admire are good people, similar to good fathers who take care of things. Of course they live well, with people to take care of menial tasks for them. Such leaders should have the trappings of wealth that go with the territory. I expect my boss to make the decisions, give me clear orders, and to take a personal interest in me and my family. I do not speak up to my boss unless he tells me to. I would never contradict my boss, either at work or elsewhere. My status depends on the status of my boss and my company."

Nearly all so-called underdeveloped and developing countries have such vertical societies. When people from these cultures move to Western countries to work, they often initially feel lost because their leaders are not as authoritarian and patriarchal. For example, people from Latino and Asian cultures pay more homage to the boss than do people from Western cultures. They may be appalled at the idea of arguing a point with the boss or seeing the boss pitch in to help out in a pinch. They are much less likely to point out potential problems with their manager's decision, and may have difficulty speaking up when team decisions need to be made. To them, bosses do the bossing and employees do the work, and deviations from that norm imply that one or the other can't do their jobs properly.

Equality = Democratic Cultures

"My company's organization chart looks sort of like a low box. The organization chart of my daughter's company looks like a web within a circle, with the executive team at the center. I believe that my boss has power because he's worked his way up to boss, not because he's better than me. I appreciate it when my boss consults me about decisions that affect me and my job. I like it even more when he lets me or the team make the decisions. I like being independent, but I don't mind choosing to be interdependent with my work team."

In moderately egalitarian cultures—such as the United States, Japan, and most European countries—consultation is usually appreciated but not necessarily expected. Participative environments are initiated by the participative leader, not by subordinates. Ideal leaders are pragmatically democratic. Moderate status differences and privileges for leaders are acceptable. Rules and laws are expected to apply to superiors and subordinates alike. Change normally starts with the top leaders, but key people throughout the organization must buy into the change if it is to be effective and lasting.

In very egalitarian cultures—such as in Scandinavian countries, Israel, and Austria—subjecting yourself to the power of others is seen as undesirable. Everyone should have a say in everything that concerns them. Status differences are suspect. Ideal leaders are democratic and loyally carry out the will of their groups. Change comes about through group consensus. Leaders must persuade and influence the group. Former leaders are usually comfortable with accepting new, less powerful roles, for the power differential is in the roles, not the people who fill them. In general, women are more likely than men to value equality in relationships and to manage in a democratic way.

Cultural Difference #6—Take Risks or Play It Safe?

In cultures that value playing it safe, people like to play it safe and avoid uncertainty. People are not comfortable with unstructured, unclear, or unpredictable situations, so they adopt strict codes of behavior and a belief in absolute truths in order to avoid such uncertainty.

Play It Safe

"We keep things under control in my culture. We do it by:

- making sure that everyone knows the rules and not allowing people to break the rules without punishment;
- making sure that people know what's expected by designating precise relationships, assignments, and schedules; and
- arranging life so that everyone knows what to expect."

"Since change creates many unknowns and uncertainties, we don't like change and try to prevent it by sticking with tradition."

People in play-it-safe cultures are also generally more active, aggressive, emotional, security-seeking, and intolerant. Greece is the most certainty-oriented culture, followed by Japan. Most European and Latino cultures fall into this pattern.

Take Risks

"'Nothing ventured, nothing gained' is my motto. Rules have their place, but there are exceptions to every rule. I like change and new adventure. I like investing in the future and looking forward to possible payoffs. For a business to be successful, people must come up with new ways of doing things, new products and services, and new technology."

People in risk-taking cultures tend to be more contemplative and tolerant, and less aggressive and emotional than those in play-it-safe cultures. The United

States has a moderately risk-taking culture, and Singapore is by far the most risk-taking culture researchers have studied.

Cultural Difference #7—Time: Step-by-Step or Dive-Right-In?

Some cultures see time as a series of points along a line in which people do one task at a time. Others see time as a circle in which they jump in doing many tasks at one time.

Dive-Right-In Time

"Time is like a circle, and I use points of time within the circle. Several things may be happening at once in this circle, because several people may need my attention at any one time. After all, it's more important to maintain good relationships with others and to complete transactions with others than to do one thing at a time on a preset schedule. Each point in time is sacred but only because I give myself fully to the moment, to the relationships, events, or activities of the moment. An activity simply takes as much time as is needed for its completion, so if the activity is important, the time it takes is irrelevant."

Circular-time cultures include Latino, Middle Eastern, and some Asian and African cultures. In the U.S. workplace, it is likely that many African Americans, Asian Americans, and Latino Americans are circular-time people. While they may necessarily adapt to the Euro-American time orientation when they work in U.S. organizations, they tend to return to their own time orientation for social and family events.

Euro-Americans sometimes feel they don't really have the full attention of a busy circular-time person. They worry that the person may never get around to the most important business at hand. Some feel that nothing seems solid or firm with circular-time people, particularly regarding the future. Often there are changes in the most important plans, right up to the very last minute. In circular-time organizations, systems need a much greater centralization of control, because the top person deals continually with many people.

In some cultures, time is determined by repeated cycles of activities, such as the agricultural cycles of planting, cultivating, and harvesting. People in such cultures do not see time as stretching into the future, but focus on the past and present. This orientation is dominant in Cuban, Mexican, and many African tribal cultures.

Step-by-Step Time

"Time is made up of the past, the present, and an infinite future. I pay most attention to the future. Time can be separated into units or steps with fixed beginnings and endings for events. I measure my time and budget it as I schedule appointments, decide on the starting and ending times for events, get to things on time, meet my deadlines, and plan ahead. The best way to use my time is to focus on one task, appointment, or event at a time." This view is prevalent in Western countries, especially the United States.

Cultural Difference #8—Space: Come Close or Back Off?

Cultures differ in how much personal space individuals expect to occupy, how close they stand or sit to one another, and how much physical contact they have. In the workplace, this translates into different perceptions about comfortable office sizes and layout, and requirements for privacy in work stations.

Come-Close Space

"I'm from the Middle East. When I talk with business associates and friends, we stand close enough to be able to feel each other's breath on our face and to be able to catch each other's scent. We touch each other a great deal as we interact. My male business associates often embrace instead of shaking hands."

People in Latino cultures prefer slightly more distance than those in Middle Eastern cultures, but they like to stand closer and to touch more than do people in Western cultures. Asian cultures like the most space and least public touching of all.

Back-Off Space

"I'm a Euro-American. When I talk with business associates and social acquaintances, it's usually at arm's length, about two or three feet away. Of course, I'm closer to my lover as well as family members and close friends. I notice that I stand farther away when I want to protect myself or to stay uninvolved. If someone moves too close into my space, I usually feel uncomfortable and back up till I feel comfortable. It really bugs me if a person keeps moving in even after I back off."

Western cultures are basically noncontact societies, according to Hall. In most Asian cultures, perhaps because of dense populations, people maintain an even greater distance for all but family and close friends.

Cultural Difference #9—Communicating Directly or Indirectly?

While there are many variations in communication style, two that stem directly from the key cultural patterns we've discussed are directness and indirectness.

Using Go-Betweens and Implied Messages

"I try to maintain harmony and to get along with people, so I never say things that would offend them. Saying no directly would be offensive, so I try to gently let them know that I'm not terribly enthusiastic about something. To make an initial overture or bring up a sensitive topic, I usually ask someone close to the other person to feel them out first."

People in most cultures use an indirect style of communication, especially in those cultures identified as us-first, people-first, rank/status, and play-it-safe. In us-first cultures with many close ties, many messages can be implied because people have been socialized alike and are on "the same wavelength." And in many cultures, go-betweens are used to broach sensitive topics. In all cultures, women are likely to use an indirect style, such as hinting, implying, keeping quiet in order to keep peace, and mentioning problems or desires to associates of the decision-maker in the hope that they'll "put in a good word."

Going to the Person; Getting to the Point

"I try to build trusting relationships based on honesty and sincerity. It's important to be up-front and genuine in my dealings with people. If I have a problem with a person, or a proposal, I go directly to that person first and try to work it out."

The direct style is typical in Western cultures, especially those that focus on I-control, me-first, achievement-first, equality, and risk taking. Within those cultures men are more likely then women to use a direct communication style.

Underlying Theme: How We Make Money

Cultural values and customs are greatly affected by a group's dominant way of making a living, whether it's primarily agricultural (the economically underdeveloped countries of the world), industrial (the developing countries), or postindustrial (the developed countries), according to John Nierenberg's research.

Agricultural Economy = Dependent Worldview

In many countries that are primarily dependent upon an agricultural economy, the value system of the masses in the peasant class is quite different from that of the elite ruling-class. The masses are quite dependent on the extended family and village groups. They are likely to believe they're controlled, put the group first and have many close ties, focus on cooperative relationships, accept status differences, avoid change and risk, view time as circular, like physical closeness, at least with family, and use an indirect communication style. All this adds up to a worldview that's primarily dependent on external forces, the family, and village groups.

The dependent pattern is traditionally typical of most women in all cultures and of men and women in most Asian, Latino, and African cultures, in fact of most of the world's peoples.

Industrial Economy = Independent Worldview

As a culture moves into a manufacturing-based economy, values shift to a more independent focus that's needed for success in the workplace. People are likely to believe they're in control, put their own goals first, have looser ties with others, focus on competitive achievement, demand equality, take calculated risks to bring needed change, view time as points on a line, keep most people at arm's length, and use a direct communication style. An independent worldview is traditionally typical of men in Western cultures.

Post-Industrial Economy = Interdependent

As a culture moves to an information- and service-based economy, it begins to shift to an interdependent focus. Some values and customs seem similar to dependence on the surface. But a major difference is that people are aware of their individuality and independence. Instead of feeling dependent upon local groups for survival, they choose to join workplace groups that may be local or global. The purpose is a higher level of achievement through working together. One key difference, then, is that group members bring to the group the strength of their individuality and independence. A related difference is that group members choose to be interdependent—it's a preference rather than a need.

People in post-industrial economies are likely to believe they're in control. They may embrace elements of both the me-first and us-first orientations: as autonomous people they choose to put the work team first in order to achieve greater things together. They focus on cooperative relationships in order to achieve greater success. They're also likely to demand equality, take calculated risks, be flexible in how they use time and physical closeness, and use a direct communication style.

Skill Builder 1—Identifying Some Perceptions

Purpose: To learn more about your way of thinking.

Step 1. Relax and focus on the words listed below, one at a time. Notice what mental picture, what words, and what feelings you experience when you focus on the words. Jot down the word and note your reactions and associations with it. Do this for all the words.

Stranger, Foreigner, Immigrant, Native, People, Family, Home, Work, Nature

Step 2. Now go back and review your list. For each word, note any judgment, attitude, or belief that came to mind when you first saw the word or that comes to mind now. Do this for all the words.

Step 3. Go back again and review your judgments, attitudes or beliefs. Where do you think each of these originally came from?

Step 4. Write down any thoughts, feelings, and insights that occur to you now that you've completed working with the list of words. What, if anything, did you learn about yourself?

Skill Builder 2—Your Sense of Time

Purpose: To increase your awareness about how you and others view and use time.

Instructions: Describe briefly at least one instance when you and someone from a different cultural background experienced conflict, misunderstanding, or problems about time. Use the following list to help you remember your situation.

- Being on time
- Meeting deadlines
- Feeling hurried, rushed
- Using time efficiently
- Using time effectively
- Being "out of sync"
- Feeling impatient over others' slowness
- Focusing on past events, tradition
- Living for the moment, short-range view
- Focusing on the present moment
- Focusing on the future, what might happen
- Focusing on planning, or long-range view
- Other issues about time

Skill Builder 3—Your Boundaries

Purpose: To increase your awareness about how you and others view and use personal space.

Instructions: Describe briefly at least one episode when you (or others) experienced conflict, misunderstanding, or problems about personal space, touching, or boundaries. Use the following list to help you remember your situation.

- Invasion of privacy, yours or others
- Discomfort because of lack of privacy
- Invasion of personal body space
- Someone in your face
- Feeling crowded or claustrophobic
- Too much touching
- Invasive touching
- Too much coldness and distance
- Other issues about space, boundaries, or touching

Skill Builder 4—Your Values

Purpose: To learn more about yourself and what you want in life.

Instructions: Before you begin, remember that the purpose of this Skill Builder is for you to learn more about you. Don't evaluate, judge, or analyze what comes up; just notice what comes up.

Step 1. Brainstorm. Relax, close your eyes for a few moments, and think about these questions:

- What are the aspects of my life that I treasure the most? That I wouldn't want to lose? That I would fight to keep?
- What are those aspects of life that I don't yet have and want most to have? That I would work hard to have?
- What are my values?

Step 2. Write. Don't try to evaluate or analyze the thoughts that occurred to you. Just write them down in whatever sequence you remember them. As more ideas come up, write them down.

Step 3. Categorize. Look over what you've written. Do the items fall into any patterns or categories, such as:

family, friends	money, power	intelligence, emotions
work, leisure	beauty, truth	spirituality

You'll find your own categories, not necessarily these. Work with your list till you see some logical categories; then rewrite your list of values by category.

Step 4. Personalize terms. What would you call the items on your list if you didn't call them values? (desires? goals? beliefs? issues? other?)

Skill Builder 5—Cultures You've Known

Purpose: To recognize the hidden aspects of your own and other cultural groups.

Instructions: Perhaps reviewing some obvious rites, rituals, heroes, and symbols of the cultures you've belonged to will help you recognize more subtle rites, rituals, etc., in the cultures you encounter. Remember, rites and rituals relate to the need for belonging. A rite is any formal practice, custom, or procedure. A ritual is any detailed method of procedure that is regularly followed. Be aware that in every organization, the stronger the rules, rituals, symbols, and heroes, the stronger the effect and influence the organization has on its members' lives.

For each category that is relevant to your own life, such as your nation, school, religious community, family, or workplace, identify examples of cultural practices, as exemplified in the National Symbols category below.

Step 1: National Symbols
   Rites and Rituals: (What rites and rituals gave you a feeling of national unity—an overall community with common purpose? For example, the national anthem.)
   Heroes: (What heroes personify key national values?)
   Symbols: (What symbols serve to unify, to express values? For example, the flag.)
   Values: (What values are expressed by the above?)

Step 2: Pick at least one other area of your life—such as your workplace, school, family, religious community, or social organization—and give examples of important rites, rituals, heroes, symbols, and values.

Feedback on Self-Awareness Opportunity 1—What's Your Cultural Orientation?

1. a. Internal source of control, individualism, independent
   b. External source of control, collectivism, dependent
2. a. Me-first, individualism
   b. Us-first, collectivism
3. a. Achievement first, competitive, individualism
   b. Relationships first, cooperative, collectivism
4. a. Achievements and tasks first, linear time orientation
   b. Relationships first, circular time orientation
5. a. Focus on equality, democratic orientation, direct communication
   b. Focus on class differences: status, rank, deference to authority, indirect communication
6. a. Risk-taking orientation; focus on future change, independence, individualism
   b. Security-seeking orientation; focus on tradition, hierarchy and the status quo, dependence, collectivism
7. a. Equality, risk-taking orientation
   b. Security-seeking, avoid-uncertainty orientation
8. a. Risk-taking, equality
   b. Security-seeking, deference to authority

3

Understanding the Dominant Culture: Euro-Americans

The American culture in the United States was founded by Euro-American men, and their values and customs are still the most dominant. Though American culture contains many elements of Western culture, meaning European, it has a unique flavor of its own. The pioneering, independent spirit of the founding fathers is an important element, as is the belief in the basic equality of people and their right to be free to pursue the American Dream.

Nearly all U.S. corporations and corporate cultures were founded by Euro-American men, and they are still 95 percent of the top managers who run the corporations. Therefore, corporate cultures are also a reflection of Euro-American male values. But corporations are changing because the marketplace is now global and the workplace is culturally diverse. Corporate cultures must become open and flexible enough to profit from that diversity. For example, management researchers such as Taylor Cox and Roosevelt Thomas have discovered that corporate cultures are increasingly moving away from the old attitude that "We're just one big happy family," which usually implies a one-way approach meaning, "New employees must adapt to our corporate culture if they want to stay." They're moving toward a new attitude: "We're learning what it's like to walk in other people's shoes so we can fully appreciate what they need and what they can contribute," which implies a two-way approach that means, "Our corporate culture is broad enough and flexible enough to adapt to new employees from a diversity of backgrounds, just as they adapt to us." To succeed in today's increasingly global marketplace and diverse workplace, you need to understand these corporate culture trends so you can help your organization profit from diversity.

The term "American" as used in this chapter refers to those qualities of the U.S. culture generally agreed upon by such scholars as Gary Althen, R. L. Kohls, P. R. Harris, R. T. Moran, and D. J. Boorstin, who look at American values and customs as compared to those of other world cultures. The crosscultural research of Geert Hofstede further confirms their work. While American culture is based on the values and customs of the dominant group, Euro-Americans, it also includes some aspects of its subcultures, such as African American and Latino American. Although culture changes slowly, the American culture is changing to reflect more elements of its subcultures as they become greater in number and larger in size.

In this chapter you'll complete the second step of the five-step process for becoming a diversity-savvy person: Learning about your own culture—if you're a U.S. resident. If you're not, you'll be learning about another culture: American, which is primarily Euro-American. If you're a U.S. resident who is not of Euro-American background, you're aware that you become somewhat bi-cultural when you function for an extended period within a dominant culture that contrasts with your own.

Specifically, you'll learn in this chapter:

- How Americans view the world and how that differs from other cultures
- What Americans value the most and how that differs from others
- How Americans relate to others and how that differs from others
- How cultural differences affect your company and your job; how corporate acculturation approaches are changing; and what works and what does not
- How you can use knowledge of cultural differences to build your people skills and to boost team and corporate achievement

THE AMERICAN CULTURE: HOW IS IT DIFFERENT?

Americans think of themselves as individuals first, view the world as basically inanimate and nature as something to be conquered, and consider material success as the major goal and "doing" as the preferred state. Most value self-improvement and hard work as the way to ensure a better future for themselves and their families. Americans believe in scientific and technological "progress," and view the world in rational, linear, cause-and-effect terms. People from other cultures usually see Americans as pragmatic, factual, and future oriented, with a tendency to view things in either-or terms rather than the shades between. A summary of American values and customs is shown in Figure 3.1.

Conquering Nature

Making progress often requires conquering nature. Americans tend to implicitly assume that the external, nonhuman world is physical and material, like a complex machine with many parts, and therefore does not have a soul or a spirit. Nature, or Mother Earth, is not seen as a living entity. Americans, probably more than any other group, believe the physical environment is there to be used, even exploited, for human purposes. This contrasts with views common in Asia and among American Indians that stress the unity among all forms of life and inanimate objects. According to these views, people are part of nature and the physical world instead of in opposition to them.

Figure 3.1   *The American Culture*

World View	Personal Values	Relationships
Conquering nature	Individualism	Friendliness
Progress	Achievement	Generosity
Change	Self-reliance	Many casual friends
Rationalism	Assertiveness	Arms'-length closeness
Scientific method	Work hard—play hard	Competition
Facts, practicality	Material success	Cooperative achievement
Measuring things	Freedom	Fair play
Quantifying things	Self-improvement	Specialized roles
Either-or thinking	Keeping busy	Directness
Change oriented	Staying young	Informality
Future oriented		

Making Progress and Welcoming Change

Americans believe in and value progress, scientific and technological developments that improve their material world. Americans often use their concept of progress to evaluate themselves and others. This concept is unknown by many in the non-Western world and may be rejected by them. Americans have traditionally believed that the basic problems of the world are technological, that science can solve them, and their solution will bring about economic abundance. The final measure of what's good and desirable is how economically feasible or lucrative it is. Progress is usually tied to their struggle to increase their physical comfort, health, material possessions, and standard of living. Also tied to their concept of progress is a feeling of general optimism towards the future, that their efforts can bring about a better future in which there is enough for everyone.

Progress implies change. Americans have their fair share of resistance to change, yet have pursued institutionalized change to a greater degree than any other society. "New" and "improved" are seen as "better." This acceptance of change shows up in their willingness to relocate. The United States is the most mobile society in the world, changing addresses more often than people in any other nation.

Using a Rational, Linear, Cause-and-Effect Approach

Americans believe that everything has a cause-and-effect relationship, as in the operation of a machine. The notion of a natural "happening" has not been familiar or acceptable to most Americans, who see the world as rational in the sense that they believe the events of the world can be explained and the reasons for particular occurrences can be determined. Effective performance in the real world is based on experience, training, and education, which should be practical.

Americans believe in the scientific method. This means focusing on facts, figures, and techniques as the means to solve problems that represent obstacles to achieving goals. This action orientation leads Americans to look for a simple cause of an event, in order to plug this cause into the problem-solving process and decide on a course of action. Americans like to develop alternative courses of action, anticipate their future effects, compare them, and choose the one that seems best for the purpose at hand. Americans like action plans that are practical, with results that are visible, measurable, and materialistic. They see action (and the world itself) as a chain of events, a connection of causes and effects projecting into the future. To people from other cultures, Americans may seem to sacrifice the end result for the means of getting there, for the scientific method is the only means they trust.

Management scholar Margaret Wheatley reports in *Leadership and the New Science* that recently some quantum physicists and business leaders have been collaborating to move beyond the traditional scientific method to more holistic approaches to science and management. Based on new discoveries about the interdependence of the web of life, how the mere act of observing a phenomenon can change it, how random events tend to self-organize into coherent patterns, and similar breakthroughs, leaders are focusing more on the importance of intuition, emotional intelligence, human relationships, and similar factors.

Getting the Facts, Putting Them to Work

Most Americans don't pay much attention to theories that do not seem to have a practical application. The role of concepts and ideas in American life is to provide direction for purposeful activity. Theories are judged and tested according to their usefulness in daily life. Americans have not followed in the European tradition of evaluating ideas or systems of thought according to the "intellectual consistency" or "aesthetic appeal" that researcher D. J. Boorstin identified.

Americans love facts. Their thinking process generally begins with facts and then proceeds to ideas, an inductive process. How good the ideas are depends on how well they work and whether people can bring them into the way they do business. Americans are somewhat unique in their insistence on practical applications: the continual need to organize their perceptions of the world into a form that enables them to act. They will accept a certain amount of pure science (research for the sake of curiosity), but expect most research to result in technology or products they can use, something that represents "progress." This operational style of thinking leads to an emphasis on consequences and results. "So much for the hypothetical. What's the bottom line?"

Americans especially resist systems of thought that lose sight of the individual. For example, despite their many programs of governmental responsibility and care for the individual, Americans resist unifying them into a system of ideology, some sort of modified socialism. Instead, they cling to the ideal of individual enterprise.

Measuring Things

Americans prefer qualities that can be measured and like to see the world in dimensions that can be quantified. Even quality and experience can be at least partially quantified, if only as first or last, least or most. Or we can assign them arbitrary values, such as "on a scale of 1 to 7." In business, government, and academia, Americans tend to use statistics to measure success and failure, amount of work, ability, intelligence, and overall job performance.

Americans have managed to create unparalleled economic abundance with the combined focus on externalized achievement and on exploitation and control of the physical environment. Further, they tend to believe in unlimited physical resources and that there's enough to go around for everyone. This expansive view of achievement in a world of economic abundance contrasts sharply with the perception of limited wealth that prevails throughout most of the world. Only recently have large groups of Americans, such as environmentalist groups, begun to question the sustainability of their abundance worldview. Now, with satellite television carrying pictures of their abundant lifestyle to every corner of the globe, billions of people are beginning to clamor for similar affluence. If the way of life of 250 million Americans is damaging the planet, what will happen if billions choose this way? Will Americans have to change their beliefs and their ways?

Thinking in Either-Or Terms

When you value the scientific method, objectivity versus subjectivity, and measurable outcomes, this allows you to set a numerical cutoff point for whether something is one way or another. This may be one reason Americans tend to focus on either-or viewpoints rather than many subtle differences. Americans draw a clear distinction between the subjective or personal and the objective or impersonal.

Americans often ask such questions as, "Who's your best friend?" or "What's your favorite color?" People outside the culture would generally have difficulty answering such questions, because the answer would depend on knowing additional factors, such as work friends or social friends, color for a room or color for a suit. Americans often make judgments or justify actions based solely on personal preference. This tendency is related to the tendency to see the world in terms of either this or that, and it's related to a predisposition to action. Americans set up unequal dichotomies, with one element valued more than the other: for example, right/wrong, good/evil, work/play, peace/war. These polarities simplify their view of the world, prime them for action, and provide them with their typical method of evaluating by means of comparison.

When it comes to evaluating people, however, Americans allow more shades of gray. Most Americans are unlikely to give much thought to religious views that humans are flawed or evil by nature. They're more likely to see humans as a mixture of good and bad or as creatures of their environment and experience. Most important, Americans stress the ability to change.

Using Time to Change the Future

Americans see time as an abstract quality, separate from self. "Time moves fast. It's important to cope with time slipping away. You've got to keep up with the times." Time is something to organize, schedule, use, and save. In business, time is money, so being on time and using time efficiently are critical.

Americans are future oriented, believing they can improve on the present and that action and hard work pays off in creating a better future for themselves. They see any unpleasantness in their work, or any stress due to incessant activity, as necessary intermediate steps for change and as a way to progress toward the future. In contrast, Latinos, who have a present orientation, focus on immediate events. Chinese, who have a past orientation, focus on traditions.

AMERICAN VALUES: HOW DO THEY DIFFER?

Becoming an achieving individual is the name of the American game. As the most individualistic culture on the planet, Americans value responsible, autonomous individuals who make their own decisions and go out and achieve in the world. They admire people who work hard, play hard, get rich, and stay young.

Becoming an Individual

Americans love their freedom to be autonomous individuals. Closely related are the values of competition and assertion. They admire people who decide what they want and go for it, who are willing to compete and don't easily give up. They generally don't place as much faith in fate or luck, as do people in many other cultures. The meaning of their brand of self-reliance is neither translatable nor self-evident in other cultures.

Making Their Own Decisions

Americans encourage their children, from the earliest age, to decide for themselves, to make up their own minds. They encourage children to believe that they're the best judge of what they want and what they should do. Therefore, as adults, Americans are likely to view bankers, teachers, counselors, and other experts as people who can give them advice, not as people who should make decisions for them. Americans expect to choose their own mates, careers, homes, and, to some extent, lifestyles. By contrast, in many other cultures, all or part of these decisions are made by parents.

Americans believe in democratic processes that are fair, give everyone an equal say, and help groups make action decisions. Most believe in majority rule and that people are capable of helping to make good decisions, although many men still accept the chain of command and autocratic decision-making found in military, government, and business organizations. In contrast, some Asian cultures, such as Japan, reach group decisions by feeling around or groping for a voice, preferably that of the chairman, that will express the group's consensus. It's offensive for any one person to urge the group to accept his own opinion about what to do.

Americans believe that personal motivation should come from within. They don't like it when others, such as managers, impose their motives on them, especially when managers issue orders and threats. Americans value persuasion as the method of coordinating people in organizations. The subtle threat of failure is always in the background, which empowers the manager's persuasive appeals to self-interest and reason. Americans want to believe that they decide what they must do.

In rank/status cultures, people accept a personal bond between subordinate and superior, which makes the authority figure an acceptable source of motivation. Direct orders, explicit instructions, and demands for personal conformity may be acceptable, and even desirable, in such cultures. For people from these cultures, the American preference for persuasion may be seen as weakness on a leader's part, and self-determination may be viewed as egotism and a threat to the organization.

Valuing Achievement

Americans tend to think they can achieve just about anything, given enough time, money, and technology. Externalized achievement has traditionally been the dominant motivation of American men, and they use competition as the primary method for driving themselves and others to achieve. Competition is seen by many as the keystone of American culture.

In many non-Western cultures, and traditionally among American women, affiliation is the primary motivation and way of relating to others. A communal feeling toward others excludes the incentive to excel over others, either as a member of a group or individually. American values seem to be evolving, however. For example, many women are learning to accept their need for individual achievement and success. Some men, who formerly felt compelled to be competitive, are becoming more group-oriented and less autonomous in their behavior, as demonstrated in self-managing work teams and other alliances.

Working Hard and Playing Hard

Americans are known to be work-oriented and efficient. They act upon persons, things, or situations. Others may see Americans as living at a fast pace and incessantly active. Americans are likely to fill their waking hours primarily in a doing mode, seldom asking if getting things done is worth it. They like the kind of activity that results in accomplishments, that are measurable by standards that the culture says are valuable. Americans believe hard work is rewarded by success, and failure usually means you didn't know how to do it right, you didn't try hard enough, or you're too lazy to care. In contrast, people in some Asian cultures fill their waking hours with a "being" rather than a "doing" mode. Their focus is on valuing the spontaneous expression of themselves as humans, or on developing all aspects of the self toward a higher-level of integration as a whole person.

Americans are somewhat unique in categorizing activities as either work activities or play activities. Work is pursued for a living. You may not necessarily enjoy it but you must do it and you put it first. In contrast, many non-Westerners rarely allow work to interfere with the amenities of living. For Americans, play is relief from the drudgery and monotony of work and is enjoyable in its own right. However, Americans often pursue play with the same seriousness of purpose as they pursue work. They tend to admire the person who "works hard and plays hard."

Americans currently in their 30s and 40s are more likely to look to both work and play for personal enlightenment and fulfillment, and are now looking for ways to balance their career goals with family and personal priorities. Those in their 20s are the most insistent on balance, being less willing to sacrifice family and personal life for careers or employers. They're most likely to insist that play be fun and carefree and to make it whatever they want it to be.

Achieving Material Success

Americans consider it almost a right to be materially well-off and physically comfortable. People should have shelter, clothing, warmth, and all the other necessities for material comfort. An important part of the good life is each household unit having its own house, car, and other physical possessions. Americans spend great time, effort, and money acquiring such comforts. They expect convenient, rapid transportation, preferably under their control, a variety of clean and healthful foods, and comfortable homes equipped with many labor-saving devices, certainly including central heat and hot water. They assume that cleanliness is nearly identical with health, if not with "Godliness."

The American stress on material things is related to the achievement value and to the European belief in private property, one that is highly valued and upheld by an entire legal system. It's difficult for many Americans to imagine, but some cultures don't even have a concept of private property, and some Asian cultures value a person's "state of grace" much more highly than their material wealth.

Americans under age 40 are more likely than older Americans, however, to look to other determinants of status, success, and accomplishment, specifically:

- personal satisfaction with their lives
- control of their own lives
- the respect of other people
- a good marriage

Staying Young

America is a youth culture. It often seems that everyone wants to look and act about 25. In most cultures, such as Asian and Latino, older persons are nearly always catered to, honored, and even revered. In the United States, they're often ignored, and even shunned.

Extensive research by the polling firm Yankelovich Partners, Inc. points to possible changes in this value, based on generational differences. They predict a shift toward these beliefs about youth and beauty:

- Age will be beautiful.
- Comfort will be beautiful—people will be less willing to sacrifice comfort to look stylish.

- Beauty will come in many skin tones and ethnicities.

Only time will tell how strong these new value trends will become.

THE AMERICAN WAY OF RELATING: HOW DOES IT DIFFER?

Americans are seen by those in other cultures as friendly and informal, direct and casual. They have many casual friendships and few deeply committed ones. Their ideal is equality of all people, but in practice they often violate this ideal. Americans believe in cooperation and fair play, in specialized roles, and in positive change.

Making Many Casual Friends

Americans are known to be friendly, informal, and generous. They tend to reject the idea of someone being special or privileged merely because of birth. They're more likely to defer to those who have achieved power and affluence through their own merit. The way they dress and greet each other tends to be informal relative to many cultures. Americans are known to be generous, willing to come to the aid of people, and to embrace a good cause.

To Americans a "friend" may be a passing acquaintance or a lifetime intimate, but they're likely to have many personal relationships that are friendly and informal, and to form few deep and lasting friendships, according to research by Harris and Moran. In contrast, people from many other cultures are slow to form friendships, but once committed, they're friends for life. They will do almost anything for a such a friend, such as loan them money or help them move their household. In these situations, Americans would prefer to hire professional help rather than inconvenience friends (or be inconvenienced, if the situation were reversed). Americans' immediate friendliness, forming of instant friendships, and lack of deep commitment are confusing to people from cultures that form deep friendships.

Americans change friends and membership groups more easily than most. Though Americans spend a great deal of time in social activities, they generally avoid personal commitments and intense involvement except with one or two "best friends." Their exchange of invitations and gifts is within a loose, informal framework. The quality of their social interactions tends to stress equality, informality, impermanence, and personal detachment. Many Americans need to express friendship and to be popular in order to feel self-confident. They often judge their personal and social success by popularity, almost literally by the number of people who like them.

Preferring Arm's-Length Space

Americans' personal boundaries are about an arm's length. When someone breaks through that boundary, they may feel invaded, and such an act often carries sexual or belligerent overtones. The way Americans use space reflects the desire to have privacy and to maintain some distance in their personal lives. Traditionally, the more space and privacy a person has—both in the workplace and at home—the higher their position. Americans are more willing than others to sacrifice such benefits as shorter commute times in order to have homes with more floor space and yard space.

Fitting into Specialized Roles

As a primarily industrial economy, American workplace roles have been developed and filled with specialists who deal with specific functions and problems. The organizational hierarchy has been like a machine with interchangeable parts, that is, people with specific skills. Until recently, Americans never thought of an organization as growing out of the unique qualities that people brought to it and their ability to respond to unique opportunities that unfolded in the environment. Instead, they focused on specialized roles in business, the military, and government, particularly where technical skills and complicated equipment are involved. Associates from other cultures often find it difficult to understand the traditional American insistence on separating planning from implementing. That's changing with the movement toward self-directed teams, which merge these two functions.

The same tendency towards specialization of roles often occurs in interpersonal relations. American friendships are likely to be based on their role activities, such as work, hobbies, sports, children, charities, games, and political or religious interests. They tend to think of others as coworkers, fellow tennis players, club associates, old school chums, neighborhood friends, PTA parents, and so on. This specialization of friends often reflects their reluctance to become deeply involved with more than one or two friends and a wish for privacy. Americans' separation of occupational and social roles, of work and play, is different from that of other cultures.

Valuing Equality

An important theme in American relationships is equality. Ideally, just the fact of being human gives each person a certain irreducible value, and interpersonal relations are typically horizontal, conducted between presumed equals. However, big business and big government have traditionally been hierarchical and authoritarian, run by able-bodied, heterosexual, Euro-American men, who in practice generally considered themselves the only true equals. When one of them needed to confront another who was a subordinate, he was more likely to establish an atmosphere of equality than the bosses in rank/status-oriented cultures. However, this value has often not extended to employees who were "too different," such as African Americans or women.

In addition to these contradictions, Americans have further reservations about total equality: Not everyone is presumed to have equal talent and ability, even though they're entitled to equal rights and obligations. Americans generally believe, however, that in any group there will be people of ability and leadership potential. They emphasize equality of opportunity more than equality of results or equality of individuals per se. During their history, they have blatantly violated their belief in equality, as they have modified their understanding of it. But the belief remains a pervasive cultural value and the keystone for building an inclusive, profitable workplace.

Cooperating and Playing Fair

Although Americans value competition, they usually compete against a backdrop of cooperation, for competition requires a considerable amount of coordination among individuals and groups. Americans can do this because they don't commit themselves as wholeheartedly to a group or organization as those from most other cultures. Americans pursue personal goals while cooperating with others who, likewise, pursue their own. They tend to accept the goals of the group, but if their expectations are unfulfilled, they feel free to leave and join another group. Americans can adjust their goals to those of other group members for carrying out joint action. This compromise is practical to them, allowing them to achieve a benefit they couldn't attain on their own. Americans cooperate in order to get things done, but that doesn't imply that they're giving up their personal goals or principles.

Americans believe you don't have to accept other persons in totality to be able to work well with them. Part of being practical or professional is the ability to work effectively with anyone who can do the job, even if you disapprove of a coworker's politics, lifestyle, or religious beliefs. It's this trait that allows Americans to cooperate with a diversity of people in order to achieve specific goals. This is a strength Americans can build upon to overcome the systemic and subtle discrimination that still exists in the workplace.

Communicating Informally and Directly

The American communication style is known for being informal and direct. Americans stress a simple vocabulary, a relative disregard for style, and the use of slang to show they (and the other person) are "one of the gang." As a loose-knit, diverse culture, Americans must rely more on the specifics of verbal communication, while tight-knit cultures can rely more on vague, nonverbal signals.

Americans' informal, direct approach to interacting with others can seem brusque, rude, or confusing to people of other cultures. Compared to others, Americans tend to make fewer discriminations among people—quickly moving to a first- name basis with all and relating with breeziness, humor, and kidding. Their friendly, personal way of treating everyone, even enemies, contributes to a depersonalization.

While Americans tend to avoid confrontation, once they decide that a situation with another person must be resolved, they're likely to deal directly with the person. This contrasts with the idea of "saving face" and using a go-between or other indirect approaches that are valued by many other cultures.

HOW DO AMERICAN CORPORATE CULTURES HANDLE DIVERSITY?

In the past few years, most organizations have been in flux. People have been changing their views of the workplace—from the traditional melting pot of people from many backgrounds, to a place where civil rights laws must be observed, to a place where people's differences are not just tolerated but appreciated, to an inclusive corporate culture that welcomes and supports people of many backgrounds (see Figure 1.3). All these views are still held to some degree by some people.

The Melting Pot Myth

Most Americans still believe in the idea of the melting pot. "Let's just ignore our differences, get the work done, and it will all work out." The American workplace melting pot was something of a miracle for a couple of hundred years. The founding fathers escaped a European aristocratic caste system with its long history of wars among the nations. The melting pot did work well for Euro-American men but was a cruel myth for others. People of color and women simply don't look and act like the men who run the workplace, so they have never really melted in. American society has actually been a series of melting pots, representing groups of people who relate closely to those within their own "pot" and only superficially with others, as the following vignette exemplifies.

> *Vignette: Growing Up Among Many "Pots"*
>
> A group of friends who grew up in a North Texas city during the 1940s were reminiscing about their "all-WASP" childhood. Ralph said, "You know, I never knew a Mexican American when I was growing up; never talked to one except for the man who sold tamales from a cart on the street. But I know there had to be a Mexican American community somewhere." Others agreed that this was a common experience. Andrea said, "I never had any African American friends either. Of course, that's easier to understand, with the severe segregation and all. The only African Americans I knew were the cleaning women who came to our home sometimes."

What about American unity? What glue holds Americans together as a nation? Certainly, two primary values that have pulled immigrants to these shores and kept them here are freedom and opportunity: the freedom to pursue one's own lifestyle and religion, and the opportunity to make a decent living. A whole set of values formed around this American Dream, shaped the society, and is remarkably strong in holding it together. Americans have rallied round a common consumer market and media. Their political system lets them participate and have influence, and their political and legal system effectively sets the rules of the making-money game and referees conflicts. Their many interest groups get to have their say through members' votes and whatever influence they can wield within the system.

The Legal Approach

Beginning in the late 1960s, companies opened new doors to women and persons from ethnic minority groups in order to meet the requirements of the new civil rights laws. Most still embraced the melting pot approach, expecting everyone to adapt to the corporate culture. The Euro-American male way of viewing things and doing things was the right way, the only way to achieve success. Many "minorities" didn't fit. Some who managed to fit in didn't like the price they paid: giving up big chunks of who they were and "selling out" for corporate bucks.

Meanwhile, the men who had traditionally run things—and their families and supporters—did not necessarily open their hearts and minds to the newcomers, just the job doors required by law. Even persons from the diverse groups often don't understand why the laws are needed or how they've opened job doors. Even so, outward actions have an eventual effect on inner habits of thought and feeling and can open up views of limited, stereotyped roles. Most people were startled the first time they encountered an African American manager or Latino American judge. They are no longer startled. For this reason, legal action has been one of the major methods of reducing private prejudice as well as public discrimination.

Valuing Diversity

The increase in work-force diversity, the need for close teamwork in the workplace, and the pressures of global competition on those teams, all work together in calling us to build bridges across cultural differences. Some corporate leaders have seen the payoffs for moving beyond tolerance of diverse people to fully appreciating them. For example, Microsoft, Hewlett-Packard, Apple Computer, Levi-Strauss, and many others have made continuing efforts to promote a diverse workforce. They see this as an asset that can increase the degree of corporate innovation, networking, marketing savvy, and other achievement—an asset that's becoming a business necessity if they want to attract and keep enough talented employees.

Creating Inclusive Corporate Cultures

Some of these corporate leaders have recently advanced to a more action-oriented strategy. Still valuing a diverse workforce, they're going further to find ways to shift the corporate culture itself, to make it more welcoming and inclusive for people of all backgrounds.

HOW TO RECOGNIZE AN INCLUSIVE CORPORATE CULTURE

American culture, diverse subcultures, and corporate culture each play important roles in the ability of your company to hire and retain the diverse talent it needs, because people must fit in if they are to stay and contribute. You and each employee play an important role in making your corporate culture the type that welcomes people from diverse backgrounds and includes them in the "inner circle." Your ability to build profitable workplace relationships with these people may determine your job success.

The first step is learning what qualities an inclusive corporate culture tends to have, so that you can recognize whether or not your organization has these qualities. Then you can do your part to bring them into existence. We'll discuss how to recognize such inclusive qualities as the following:

- two-way company-employee cultural adaptation process
- interdependent
- strong and participative
- flexible in adapting to a diversity of employee needs and talents
- tolerant of reasonable nonconformity
- appreciative of the contributions diverse employees make to organization success and profitability

First, complete this Self-Awareness Opportunity.

Self-Awareness Opportunity 1—Who Are the Insiders?

Purpose: To get a picture of how well "minorities" are included in your company.

Step 1. Think about which employees are involved in the Inner Circles of your company, in the learning, decision-making, and other activities that directly affect the success of the organization and its bottom-line results.

Step 2. Place symbols, such as triangles or circles, that represents corporate insiders within the Inner Circle. You might use a different symbol, incorporating colored ink or pencil, for each employee, or a different symbol for each work team, unit, or department that's in the Inner Circle.

Step 3. Which employees are not included in the Inner Circle, are not involved in activities that make a real difference? Draw symbols for those employees in the area outside the Inner Circle.

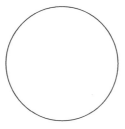

Step 4. What does this picture say to you about your organization?
- About its effectiveness in managing diversity?
- About its effectiveness in utilizing all its human resources?
- About its effectiveness in developing all its employees' potential for contribution?

Is Two-Way Adaptation the Goal?

Acculturation is a cultural orientation process that occurs when new employees join an organization. They learn not only about company procedures and employee benefits, but also about the organization's culture: its values, do's and don'ts, legends, champions, and rituals—the "way we do things around here." Here's where the unspoken, unwritten, and sometimes most important information about getting along and succeeding should be learned. The values and norms may be more difficult for diverse employees to learn, because they are usually not part of the Euro-American cliques and grapevines.

Informally, acculturation happens through hearing stories that express key values and norms, through watching the role models, and through learning the rituals and jargon. Formally, it happens through training, performance appraisal, and promotion decisions. There are four types of acculturation processes that new employees may encounter:

1. *Exclusion*—New employees stay relatively isolated because of (1) being ignored and left out of key groups and events, (2) weak corporate culture values, and (3) either little opportunity or weak motivation to cluster with others of their own diversity group.
2. *Clustering*—New employees relate primarily with others of their own diversity group and hold onto ethnic identity, often for the same reasons that cause exclusion.
3. *Assimilation*—One-way inclusion, melting-pot style, in which new employees give up much of their own ethnic identity and ways of working, adopting the Euro-American male culture and ways at work.
4. *Inclusion*—Two-way adaptation, a learning and change process carried out by both the new employees and the people already in the corporation. The focus is on appreciating and valuing diversity and on inclusion of all new employees in the "inner circle."

When two-way adaptation is the primary acculturation process, the corporate culture is likely to be seen as inclusive.

How Interdependent Are People in the Corporate Culture?

The evolution from independence to interdependence is reflected in the American business culture generally and in the corporate cultures of leading organizations specifically, as the discussion of this underlying cultural theme in Chapter 2 indicated. Just as the culture at large ties people together and gives meaning and purpose to their everyday lives, corporate culture is the glue that holds corporations together, according to such researchers as T. E. Deal and A. A. Kennedy, as well as E. H. Schein.

Most U.S. corporations are postindustrial information- or service-based, where interdependence is the most effective style. This movement toward group-centered cooperation is not a case of the pendulum swinging back to an old agricultural-style pattern of dependence. It is an evolutionary spiral of interdependence that's grounded in personal autonomy and choice. The most effective corporations have a dual emphasis that ties individual performance to group-centered cooperation, linking the desires to compete and cooperate into very powerful team achievement. And they add a crucial factor for productive teamwork—trust.

Many demographic experts agree that the United States is probably the most diverse culture on earth. For example, in several metropolitan school districts the students represent over 100 different language backgrounds. It's also the country with the highest level of personal independence, according to the research of Geert Hofstede and others. This gives the United States tremendous potential power to lead the world in cooperative enterprise. Every employee can be a leader in this area by appreciating the assets that diverse coworkers bring to the workplace, and by using these assets to provide more innovative, effective, competitive products, processes, and services—a unity that capitalizes on diversity.

How Strong and Participative Is the Culture?

The stronger and more participative the corporate culture, the more success it is likely to experience in shifting toward inclusion. In weak corporate cultures, leaders do not clearly communicate a set of core values that are reinforced by role models, myths, rituals, and symbols. Employees naturally stick with their own culture group's viewpoints, norms, and values. Employees have more freedom to determine how to act, but if the culture is too weak, they go off in all directions and have great difficulty coordinating their work with others. Frequently, chaos and crisis occurs. Some essential values must be shared by members if an organization is to be able to achieve its goals. In fact, to survive and thrive over time, an organization needs a strong culture.

In strong corporate cultures, leaders clearly define and enforce values and norms, giving more direction to how people should act, more reinforcement about what they should do, and perhaps higher penalties for not conforming. The result is that people are more likely to view a situation in the same way, to respond similarly, and to expect similar results—in other words, to march to the same drumbeat. In strong authoritarian corporate cultures, management expects people to conform to values and norms that encompass most all of their activities. Such cultures tend to be rigid and have difficulty shifting to the inclusive two-way adaptation that welcomes diverse employees.

Strong participative cultures are more democratic. Leaders clearly communicate a few core values that define their mission—why the company is in business and what makes it successful. They require all employees to buy into these values and to observe them in their decisions and actions. On most other matters, they allow a great deal of freedom and constructive nonconformity in the name of diversity, creativity, and "just getting the job done." Strong participative cultures have the power and flexibility necessary to adapt to diverse employees.

Figure 3.2 *Conformity Comparisons*

Managers in Low-Conformity Cultures	Manager in High-Conformity Cultures
See many behaviors as O.K. unless they violate a few core values, such as integrity and quality	Have a narrow view of behavior that's O.K.
Don't judge ideas until they clearly · understand them	Evaluate, judge, and criticize others who have questionable ideas
React to new ideas as possibilities, interesting, something to play with	New ideas are either good or bad
Take calculated risks; encourage others to do so	Avoid taking risks
View failure, within limits, as part of innovation, a learning opportunity	Are intolerant of mistakes Focus on mistakes
Pay more attention when people exceed standards than when they don't	Ignore many positive contributions
Encourage people to create new approaches that work	Prescribe the details of how to do things See one right way to do most things

How Flexible Is the Culture in Adapting to Diverse Needs?

Employees who come to the organization with quite different viewpoints, values, needs, and work approaches are most likely to feel valued and to succeed in a corporate culture that's flexible enough to provide a welcoming niche for them. Here's what corporations are doing to increase their flexibility.

- Customizing mentoring programs.
- Making job assignments that ensure a progression of sympathetic and supportive superiors.
- Assigning newcomers to a series of problem-solving task forces so they can form a series of peer relationships that sustain them through the early years.
- Developing explicit guidelines for all employees about working with "minorities" and a procedure for making everyone aware of these guidelines.
- Specifying standards for social behavior in relationships with "minorities."
- Removing ritualistic cultural barriers to the acceptance of "minorities."

How Much Nonconformity Is Allowed?

How comfortable do people generally feel about differences, uncertainty, debate, and other forms of nonconformity? In inclusive cultures these are all viewed as normal and potentially useful rather than as dysfunctional and threatening. Figure 3.2 compares attitudes of managers in such cultures with those in high-conformity cultures.

Do People Recognize How an Inclusive Culture Pays Off?

Companies who are creating inclusive corporate cultures recognize and experience a surprising wealth of benefits at all levels—personal, interpersonal, and organizational. These benefits include:

- Increasing personal skills for relating to customers, suppliers, and others in a global marketplace
- Attracting and retaining the best available human talent
- Increasing organizational flexibility
- Improving the quality of management
- Creating and innovating more powerfully from a diverse idea pool
- Solving problems more effectively
- Increasing productivity
- Gaining and keeping greater market share
- Reducing costs
- Contributing to social responsibility by providing success opportunities for people from all groups

HOW TO HELP CREATE AN INCLUSIVE CORPORATE CULTURE

To begin with, you can examine and overcome any resistance you have to learning about other cultures and making the company more inclusive. You can encourage others to do the same. You can help create a sense of unity that also values diversity, and you can learn more about stereotypes and other American subcultures and communities. Armed with new attitudes and information, you can keep learning about diverse communities and people.

Overcome Resistance—Your Own and Others

Check out some typical reasons that employees resist diversity efforts. See if they apply to you. If so, overcome them and encourage others to do so.

- Lack of motivation—not understanding the business rationale for diversity, how it will affect their personal skills resume, their innovative problem-solving skills, and the organization's ability to compete and to profit.
- Ignorance about culture and its potential as an effective tool for empowering employees.
- Stereotyped, prejudiced beliefs about groups of people.
- Affirmative action backlash, and suspicion that any new diversity approach is an effort to sneak more such programs through the back door.
- Risk aversion and an unwillingness to risk the experimentation and changes required for adapting to new cultural ways and shifting the corporate culture to include them.
- Lack of power, knowledge, or skills in creating inclusion on the part of those employees and managers who want to become change agents.

- Responsibility overload—employees believing they don't have the time or energy for another initiative, and not seeing how it can help them achieve their goals rather than pose a distraction.
- Belief in the melting pot, that people should adapt and be one big happy family—paying attention to group differences is divisive.
- Belief in individualism, that we are each unique so we just treat people as individuals—paying attention to group differences is divisive.

Some variations on the divisive rationale are, "We shouldn't put labels on people. We're all just people, just Americans. Using such labels as 'African American' or 'Euro-American' just sustains racism and other 'isms.'"

These rationalizations are common and can erect rigid barriers to even discussing cultural and lifestyle differences. This in turn makes it impossible to develop deeper understanding and empathy. These myths are so common that we'll discuss a few in more detail so you can be prepared to counter them. Basically they all amount to holding on to the status quo—resisting change that would increase the opportunities for people of diverse backgrounds.

Myth #1—Learning about Differences Is Divisive.

Some people think that if we look at how people from various cultures differ, we won't see how they're alike, and therefore we won't find a common ground of unity. But learning about other cultures and valuing cultural differences need not be a barrier to unity.

- Anthropologists assure us that humans are more alike than they are different.
- Psychologists point out that we all have needs for survival, security, belonging, recognition, and self-actualization. We differ only in the ways we go about fulfilling these needs.

Our common ground is the set of needs and desires that touch every aspect of our lives. Learning about diverse ways of fulfilling those needs and desires can enrich our lives and our organizations.

Many employees from the diverse groups we've described probably do feel "divided"—that is, excluded from the mainstream of exclusive cliques, inner circle, and corporate power, especially when differences are ignored. They don't have the luxury of ignoring the differences. They must deal with them every day. They know that many misunderstandings are based on cultural differences, and that ignoring them keeps us from getting at the root of problems, which in turn tend to fester and grow.

Myth #2—Learning about Differences Causes Stereotyping.

For an opinion to be a stereotype, it must be rigid, not taking into account individual differences within a group. We can use knowledge of a community's cultural values and customs as flexible general guidelines to help us understand what makes people act the way they do. That helps us find some questions to ask people when problems arise. We must always keep in mind that each person adopts some of the culture's values and customs wholeheartedly, some partially, and some not at all. When we learn about a culture or community, that is only the starting point for getting to know a person from that culture.

Treating each person as a unique individual is the next step in building profitable relationships. Even if you had time to start from scratch and ask all the persons you meet how their culture differs from yours, they probably would not be able to tell you. Unless they have studied cultural differences, they assume their ways are the natural ways. On the other hand, if you already know something of their culture, you're a giant step ahead in the process of learning each person's unique pattern of values and customs. When you keep the individual in the forefront of your mind, with the culture in the background as shown in Figure 3.3, you can quickly reach a deeper level of understanding and empathy.

Myth #3—Focusing on Differences Is Racist or Sexist.

This implies that if we ignore our differences and pretend we're all alike, then we're not prejudiced. Actually, not admitting differences is more likely to result in support for a discriminatory status quo than is exploring and respecting differences. After all, if we're all alike, who are we like, which culture? What culture represents the norm to which we all should conform? The unconscious assumption is that it is our own, of course. This a way of saying, "People are basically alike—like me." Since the dominant cultural group in the United States is Euro-American, this means going along with the status quo—and we learned earlier what that means in terms of glass ceiling issues.

Myth #4—Focusing on Similarities Is Easier.

Life seems easier, in the short run, if we ignore differences and assume that everyone is alike. Dealing with diversity means dealing with complexity and uncertainty, and it may seem easier to settle for "we're all basically alike, one big happy family." As workplace diversity increases and as the business game increasingly depends on finding and keeping talented people, ignoring differences will block company goals in the long run.

Knowing about these resistances can help you plan for overcoming them. This knowledge can also help you analyze why change efforts are not working as well as expected. The resistances list can become a checklist for figuring out why.

Create a Sense of "We" That Also Values Diversity

Diverse organizations often have unity problems, and therefore building a strong corporate culture is essential to overcoming these problems. Typical issues are finding common ground, maintaining group cohesiveness, and communicating through cultural barriers.

Figure 3.3 *Stereotypes Versus Background Information*

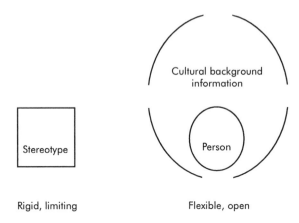

Find Common Ground

Too much diversity in work teams, management groups, or any type of problem-solving group can be especially dysfunctional in traditional corporate cultures where appreciation of diverse inputs is not valued. When communication barriers, style conflicts, and points of view lack even a core of commonality, decision-making may become impossible. Leaders can provide that core of commonality by fostering a corporate culture that's strong enough for all groups to feel connected to common values, heroes, myths, rituals, and other cultural anchors. Building a strong culture that focuses on corporate niches and also values diversity must be a complex, ongoing effort. This means that some values and rituals should be expressed in terms that speak to people from each cultural group. Heroes and myths should be diverse enough to "look like" the entire workforce. Some of the legend-type stories that people repeat should be about women or African Americans or Asian Americans, or others, who did great things.

Common goals are important common ground. While group cohesiveness has many advantages, cohesiveness alone rarely improves group productivity. Highly cohesive groups will be more productive only if they adopt values that center around achieving goals, know how to develop clear, specific goals, and get adequate rewards for achieving them.

Avoid Communication Breakdown

When a group becomes diverse, misunderstandings may increase, conflict and anxiety may rise, and members may feel less comfortable with being in the group. These effects may combine to make decision-making more difficult and time-consuming. In these respects, culturally diverse work groups are more difficult to manage effectively than homogeneous work groups. The challenge is to manage in such a way that you maximize the potential benefits of diversity while minimizing the potential difficulties.

Use Self-Managing Teams

Being in contact with persons from other cultures does not lead to better relationships unless that contact is between equals and is substantive enough to really get to know each other. Superficial contact is likely to reinforce stereotypes. Self-managing teams are a perfect vehicle for getting to know people in depth. When team goals require members to depend on each other and to work together in order to succeed, members must get to know each other well. They must understand that trust is crucial—building it, maintaining it, and never betraying it. Under such circumstances, stereotypes and prejudice tend to vanish and deep bonding takes place.

Become a Culture Catalyst

You can become a leader, a role model who vividly shows by actions and words what the company stands for. The role of leaders is to focus on creating sparks in the corporate culture. You can make cultural change happen without forcing it. You can help to build, enunciate, and promote a strong culture that bonds people together, giving people a changed core of common values, a sense of common purpose, and new heroes, rituals, and symbols that reflect the changes.

Learn about Stereotypes and Cultures

How can you accelerate the process of getting to know people as unique individuals and also identify common values you share with them? A constructive approach is to find out what it is like to be a person from a particular cultural or experiential background. You have already completed the first two steps in a positive five-step process for building multicultural skills:

Step 1. Become aware of cultural differences.

Step 2. Learn about the American culture (and any subcultures you belong to).

Step 3. Recognize your own stereotypes and prejudices from a cultural awareness perspective. Chapter 4 will help you with this.

Step 4. Learn about cultures of people you encounter in the workplace—what it's like to be a person from that background. You'll find help in the chapters on African Americans, Asian Americans, Latino Americans, persons with disabilities, gay persons, older persons, obese persons, and men and women (bridging gender gaps).

For each group, you will learn about the stereotypes and prejudices members face; their past and current socioeconomic status; the values, customs, and issues most important to them; and how you can help them overcome barriers and make optimal contributions to the work team and the organization.

Step 5. Build your people skills by applying your new cultural knowledge to real-life situations and by continuing to learn about issues important to each group. This chapter gives you a chance to get started, with self-awareness opportunities and case studies. You can continue the process on your own.

Keep Learning about Diverse Communities and People

Once you have a framework for better understanding others' behavior that was formerly a puzzle, continue to learn by interpreting with new eyes and ears the media presentations, news stories, work situations, and nonwork situations you encounter.

If you are Euro-American, join a couple of organizations in which you are distinctly in the minority—to see what it's like. Don't fool yourself that it's the same as actually being an ethnic minority. You still have the implied privileges and power of the dominant group. But the experience should give you some insights and at least increase your comfort level for being with "minorities."

In the workplace, the more you learn about each person, the greater your skills for collaborating with that person as an individual and as part of a work team or business alliance. Remember, what you don't know may keep you from doing your own job effectively. Here are some suggestions that may help.

Avoid Appearance Stereotypes

Don't assume race or ethnicity from appearance alone. Many Latinos have Asian features, and many Blacks have Latino, Jamaican, or other origins and strongly distinguish themselves from African Americans. The cultural backgrounds of bi-ethnic persons are not easy to determine from appearance only. Asking, "What is your cultural heritage?" implies respect and appreciation for all ethnicities.

Avoid Ethnic Stereotypes

Don't assume that foreign or minority workers are impoverished, deprived, have poor language skills, and so on. Get to know the background of each employee. You can ask tactful questions, such as, "What do you see as your major challenges and opportunities here?"

Put Emotions in Perspective

Don't take emotional outbursts personally. Ask, are emotional outbursts a normal way of responding to the situation in that person's culture? Remember, also, that newcomers often experience a phase of frustration and anger as they adapt to the corporate culture. On the other hand, don't assume that no show of emotion means lack of emotion.

Discover Other People's Values

Watch how they behave. When someone behaves consistently in similar circumstances, it suggests a value at work. Identify precisely which values are at play in a given situation. For example, it is one thing to know that a person values family ties more than you do. It is more difficult to recognize that the family ties value is at stake when that person is absent from work for what would seem like a trivial family matter to you. Your tendency may be to judge that person by your standards for consistent attendance at work rather than by his or her standards of family loyalty.

Apply Employee Values to Work Enhancement

Look for the positive side of the other person's values: not only how that value is positive in the other's culture, but also how that same value could be applied in ways that are consistent with organization values and goals. Apply the value to the job at hand. How can you bring the person's value into play so that it helps achieve job goals? For example, when you need teamwork to accomplish something previously done by individuals, persons from tightly-woven, group-oriented cultures are likely to rise to the occasion.

Apply Relevant Training

If you are in a supervisory role, determine each new employee's knowledge of the system, and train each one accordingly. Has this employee faced the complexities of the U.S. corporate system before? You may need to train some employees in very basic ways.

Determine Each Employee's Primary Thinking and Learning Pattern

If you see that abstract and hypothetical thinking is not familiar to them, try using examples, stories, and hands-on experience. Be patient while employees are in the process of gaining necessary knowledge and experience. Be aware of how cultural differences in perceptions, beliefs, and customs may affect an employee's learning style in ways that enhance or block their grasp of new information.

Reinforce Successful New Behavior

Choose reinforcers, recognition, and rewards that people value as such. Give them in a way that is in line with that person's values.

Understand Cultural Style Differences

For example, some cultures use compliments and flattery as a normal, polite way of interacting. You may need to learn to accept compliments gracefully and without suspicion.

Skill Builder 1—Learning More about an Organization's Culture

Purpose: To learn more about a target organization's culture, perhaps the one you work in or one you're thinking about joining, and to place it into a frame of reference for understanding what's going on.

Name of Target Organization: _____

Step 1. Investigate. Visit the organization and observe or ask the following questions.

1. *Observe the physical setting.*

- What's your initial impression?
- What does the physical layout seem to communicate?
- Is the image consistent in all divisions and facilities?

2. *Collect and analyze written materials*, such as annual reports, newsletters, news releases, manuals.
   - What does the company say about itself?
   - What type of culture do written materials reflect?
   - Do you see signs of diversity at all levels in the materials?
3. *Observe reception area procedures.*
   - Formal or informal?
   - Relaxed or busy?
   - Elegant or plain?
   - What is the receptionist doing? How does she or he interact with visitors?
   - What procedures or processes are used with visitors?
   - Do visitors wait?
   - Do you see signs of diversity so far?
4. *Ask employees questions such as these:*
   - Tell me about the history of the company. (Notice what facts seem accurate, what myths surface.)
   - What has made the company successful? (Look for company values. Do people generally agree on which company values are most important?)
   - What kind of people work here? Who gets ahead? (Look for signs of diverse role models, descriptions of role models; look for clear agreement about how to succeed. Are role models constructive, serve the company well? Do women and minorities often succeed?)
   - What's it like to work here? How do things get done? (Look for important rites, rituals, meetings, or bureaucratic procedures; do all departmental or team subcultures have some unifying values? Do rites, rules, and procedures encompass or respect the diversity found within the organization?)
5. *Observe and ask*, how do people (really) spend their time?
6. *Ask about career paths:*
   - Who gets ahead? What departments were top people once in? What positions did they hold? Do people from diverse groups get ahead?
   - What do people have to do to get promoted?
   - What does the company reward? Competence in key skills? Performance against objective criteria? Seniority? Loyalty? Good team player? Other?
7. *Find out how long people usually stay in jobs.* (Short terms usually mean people are motivated to make their mark quickly and to steer clear of longer-term, slower payback activities. They also can mean that people from diverse groups became discouraged, felt they couldn't reach their career goals, and left.)
8. *Find out what people are talking about and writing about.*
   - What are memos and reports about in their actual content?
   - What are meetings about? What is actually discussed, and who talks to whom?

Step 2. Review and Analysis. Go over the results of your survey to determine how strong or weak, how conformist or flexible, you think the company is. Use it to help identify companies that are in danger of failing. Look for the issues in the following categories.

1. *Patterns and Themes*   Think about patterns that emerged from the stories and anecdotes that people volunteered. What are the key points? Do most stories revolve around customers? Political infighting? Individual initiative that was rewarded or punished?

2. *Inward Focus*   People don't pay much attention to what's going on outside the company with customers, competitors, new trends. They focus on placating the boss, looking good, getting one up on the people around them. They seem to overemphasize budgets, financial analysis, or sales quotas.

3. *Short-Term Focus*   If people spend most of their time and energy meeting short-term goals, then sustainable business receives no support and the company is headed for problems.

4. *Declining Morale*   Is turnover high or trending upward? Look at the whole company and at subcultures within the company. Look at the track records of employees from diverse groups, such as minorities. Poor morale often begins with a lackadaisical attitude, moves on to loud complaints, and culminates with people starting to leave.

5. *Weak Culture*   When a culture is weak or in trouble, people get frightened and anxious. This fright shows up in emotional outbursts in the workplace, such as condemning company policy at a meeting or getting angry with coworkers or bosses. Did you hear any stories that indicate that stress, anger, or other emotions are building up? If so, did you get any clues about the causes?

6. *Fragmentation or Inconsistency*   When a division is unhappy about how headquarters is handling things or tells jokes about what goes on there, it's usually a sign that the parts of the culture are not integrated into a coherent whole. Signs that normal variations in different functions of the firm are becoming a problem:

- Subcultures (within departments, or sometimes within ethnic groups) are becoming ingrown. Regular interaction among subcultures is declining.
- Subcultures are clashing, publicly trying to undermine each other. The healthy tension among two subcultures has become destructive.
- Subcultures are becoming exclusive. One or more subcultures is acting like an exclusive club. People are feeling left out and resentful, not pulling together toward company goals.
- Subcultures act as if their values are more important than company values, not giving key overriding company values top priority.

Skill Builder 2—Assessing Corporate Culture Fit

Purpose: To raise your awareness about how various corporate cultures fit the needs of diverse employees.

Begin with how a target corporation fits your needs. Select an organization you want to study or to work in. After you have conducted a survey of the corporate culture (Skill Builder 1), complete the following Skill Builder using this scale.

Target Org.	My Root Culture	Values: What's Most Important	
A or B? 1, 2, or 3?	A or B? 1, 2, or 3?	A Values	B Values
		Doing the work	Building relationships
		Living for the present	Working for future rewards
		Being aggressive	Being passive
		Promoting myself	Being modest
		Competing	Cooperating
		Being unemotional	Expressing emotions
		Individual goals	Team goals
		Taking risks	Avoiding risks
		Other	Other

1 = moderately important, 2 = very important, 3 = extremely important

Step 1. Assess the organization's values. In the Target Organization column, assign either an A or B for each value, to best represents that organization's value, and a number from 1 to 3 to represent whether moderate to extreme importance is placed on that value by the firm. Add any other organization values you think will affect you significantly.

Step 2. Assess your values. In the My Root Culture column, repeat Step 1 for your own values, modifying your root culture's focus, where necessary, to reflect your own values. Add any other workplace values that are important to you.

Step 3. Estimate cultural fit. Compare the target organization's profile of values with your root culture's profile, and write a brief paragraph about what this means in terms of cultural fit between someone from your culture and this organization.

Step 4. Assess another person's cultural fit. Think of someone from another culture that you know well. Do Steps 1-3 substituting that person's profile for your own. In the paragraph write-up in Step 3, include comparisons between your own fit and this person's fit and any insights that occur to you regarding cultural fit.

4

Beyond Stereotypes to Profitable Collaboration

As Americans, we have inherited a legacy of prejudice. But we have also inherited a legacy of equality, and the mainstream has grown to accept more and more people as basically equal and therefore entitled to equal opportunity in the workplace. "Minorities" as a whole will soon outnumber Euro-Americans in some states. Leading-edge businesses know they need people from all the diverse groups—as customers and as talented employees who work in all corporate functions and levels.

This legacy of prejudice means that no one grows up without developing some degree of stereotyping and prejudice. They are woven into the very tapestry of our culture: springing up from the grassroots of family; filtering down from the top levels of government, business, and society; and feeding back on themselves at all levels in between. The first step to breaking out of this web is for each of us to quit denying that we're prejudiced. Then we can start rooting out those pockets of prejudice and the specific stereotypes that created them. We can start getting new, valid information, and focus more on the positive aspects of each group. We can deal with people from each group as unique individuals, going beyond the stereotypes to the specific cultural background that provides deeper understanding.

You are probably aware that to be a valuable employee or business associate, you must move beyond the stereotypes and prejudices that exclude whole groups of people. This involves learning how to bridge the divisive walls of prejudice—and help others to do so. Doing so can bring huge rewards: to you, in building success skills and profitable workplace relationships, and to your company, as you work more productively with people from diverse backgrounds. You'll learn why and how we stereotype, prejudge, discriminate against, and exclude people just because they belong to a particular group. You'll learn how moving beyond assumptions and prejudices can boost success for you and your company. Specifically, you'll learn about:

- Why people avoid and exclude others
- Why we stereotype people
- How you can become aware of your own stereotypes and prejudices
- The connection between the authoritarian personality and prejudice
- How and why people become prejudiced
- How people express prejudices
- How prejudice affects people generally and in the workplace
- How people can move beyond stereotyping to valuing people's differences and building relationships that promote profitable collaboration

WHY DO WE EXCLUDE PEOPLE FROM CERTAIN GROUPS?

We may exclude people because we've bought into a stereotyped belief that people from that group are inferior in some way. This means that we prejudge such persons before we ever get to know them. If we don't give them a fair chance on the job, or if our organization is set up in a way that automatically ignores certain groups of people, then we are participating in discrimination against them. The following three terms are often used to describe the separate but related elements of exclusion.

1. *Stereotypes* can be rigid, exaggerated, irrational beliefs, each associated with a mental category, such as a particular group of people. Although stereotypes are not identical to prejudice, rigid stereotypes about people usually lead to prejudice.
2. *Prejudice* is a way of viewing people who are different as somehow deficient, of judging a whole category of people as basically better-than or worse-than others. It means prejudging a person based on a category without giving yourself a chance to get to know the person from a clean slate.
3. *Discrimination* refers to actions towards or practices regarding members of a less-powerful group that result in their being treated differently in ways that disadvantage them.

Stereotyping, prejudice, and discrimination create gaps between people as well as major barriers to tapping the full potential of all the members of a diverse work team or any diverse group. They diminish the potential synergy, innovativeness, and success of such groups.

Discrimination has been built into American institutions and systems. No one is completely immune to its impact, although people from historically disadvantaged groups tend to suffer the worst effects. Civil rights laws have reduced its pervasiveness and intensity, and activist groups are working against it. But groups are made up of individuals, and change begins within one person and expands person by person. The role you play is important.

If you're like most people, you're improving the quality of your beliefs and attitudes toward people who have traditionally been devalued in our culture—and you want to do better at bridging the gaps and connecting in a positive way with people from diverse backgrounds. You want information about how to build rewarding relationships, whether it's with postal employees, politicians, Italian Americans, African Americans, or others you deal with in your day-to-day activities. You want to link, bond, connect, and ally with people in ways that will build strong relationships. This offers many rewards: it can make you a more effective team member if you belong to a diverse work team, help you give better service to all your customers and associates, and in turn boost your company's profits and success. Clearly, the bottom line reward for moving beyond stereotypes to collaborating with people is the boost to your own career success. A very real bonus is the probability that you'll get more enjoyment from working with people and you'll feel better about yourself.

Vignette: How We Stereotype People

The following remarks were overhead at various places:

At a restaurant: "Sorry I'm late—had to wait in line over 10 minutes at the post office. Most of the clerks seemed to be on a break. Well, what can you expect? Postal employees!"

"Yeah, really. But they don't bother me—as long as they don't go 'postal' when I'm around!"

In the office: "I'm not voting for any of them. They're all a bunch of corrupt crooks."

"You're right—and you can't believe any of their promises."

At a party: "Oh, sure, he's good looking and a great dancer, but I probably won't get involved with him. I hear they're all pretty macho when you really get to know them."

"Uh huh, and most of them have some kind of Mafia connection."

WHY DO WE STEREOTYPE PEOPLE?

The process of stereotyping allows us to manage complex realities by using categories to store new information, to quickly identify things, to handle multisensory experiences, and to make sense of things. We may attach strong emotion to these stereotypes, even when they're false, and we often use stereotypes to justify our dislike of someone.

Rigid, limiting stereotypes create barriers to really getting to know people, but you can break free. The first step is understanding how this process of stereotyping works in your everyday life.

Making Complex Reality Manageable

When we stereotype, we form large classes and clusters for guiding our daily adjustments. We must deal with too much complexity in our environment to be completely open-minded. We don't have time to learn all about every new person or situation we encounter. Of necessity, we associate them with old categories in our mind in order to make some sense of the world.

Short-Cutting with Categories

We tend to place as much as we can into each class and cluster. Our minds tend to categorize events in the grossest manner compatible with the need for action. We like to solve problems as easily as possible, so we try to fit them rapidly into a satisfactory category and use this category as a means of prejudging the solution.

Quickly Identifying Things

A stereotype enables us to readily identify a related object. Stereotypes have a close and immediate tie with what we see, how we judge, and what actions we take. In fact, their whole purpose is to help us make responses and adjustments to life in a speedy, smooth, and consistent manner.

Incorporating Multisensory Experiences

For each of our mental categories, we have a thinking and feeling tone or flavor. Everything in that category takes on that flavor. For example, we not only know what the term Southern belle means, we also have a feeling tone of favor or disfavor that goes along with that concept. When we meet someone that we decide is a Southern belle, that feeling tone determines whether we like her more or less than we would if we got to know her on her own merits.

Being Rational—Or Not

Stereotypes may be more or less rational. A rational stereotype starts to grow from a kernel of truth and enlarges and solidifies with each new relevant experience. A rational stereotype gives us information that can help us to predict how someone will behave or what might happen in a situation. An irrational stereotype is one we've formed without adequate evidence.

Adding the Emotional Whammy

Our minds are able to form irrational stereotypes as easily as rational ones, and to link intense emotions to them. An irrational idea that is engulfed by an overpowering emotion is more likely to conform to the emotion than to objective evidence. Therefore, once we develop an irrational stereotype that we feel strongly about, it's difficult for us to change that stereotype based on facts alone. We must deal with the emotion and its ties to our deepest fears.

Justifying Dislike

Sometimes we form a stereotype linked to an emotion related to fear—such as hostility, suspicion, dislike, or disgust—and set up the framework for prejudice toward an entire group of people based on our experience with one or a few. When people become prejudiced toward a group, they need to justify their dislike, and any justification that fits the immediate conversational situation will do.

So, stereotyping is part of the human need to categorize the massive amounts of information we encounter every day. Categorizing and labeling are ways of making sense of the world and managing what we must do. Stereotyping, when used in this technical sense, is a rational thing to do. The problems arise when we make our categories too fixed and our labels too permanent. What most people call stereotyping refers to this fixed, permanent aspect. Rigid stereotyping of groups of people often leads to prejudice and discrimination.

Self-Awareness Opportunity 1—Being Tolerated and Being Appreciated

Purpose: To experience the difference between tolerance and appreciation.

Step 1. Being Tolerated
   a. Think of a time when you felt tolerated. Write a few words about it.
   b. How did it feel to be merely tolerated? Write a few words about your feelings.
   c. How did feeling tolerated affect your relationship with the tolerant person(s)?

Step 2. Being Appreciated
   a. Think of a time when you felt appreciated. Write a few words about it.
   b. How did it feel to be truly appreciated? Did you feel respected? Write a few words about your feelings.
   c. How did feeling appreciated affect your relationship with the appreciative person(s)?

HOW CAN WE PINPOINT OUR PREJUDICES?

Virtually everyone harbors some rigid stereotypes and prejudices. Some prejudice is a matter of blind conformity to prevailing cultural beliefs and customs. However, in most cases prejudice seems to fulfill a specific irrational function for people, such as making them feel superior to others, or using others as scapegoats for the prejudiced persons' own resentment or guilt. Prejudice usually is tied to a person's deepest fears, although the connection is normally subconscious and therefore hidden from awareness. Researchers such as G. W. Allport, M. H. Ijzendoorn, and Joseph Ponteretto have uncovered some interesting facts about prejudice:

- Prejudice is found in all types of people and in every ethnic group.
- Prejudice occurs in the mind but can be acted out in ways that exclude others.
- Prejudiced acts can be performed by nonprejudiced as well as prejudiced people.
- The best way to decide if an action is prejudiced is how it affects another person. You can't prove someone is prejudiced, but you may prove that their acts exclude and disadvantage another person.

Key Aspects of Discrimination

You can discriminate by merely being part of an organization that itself unintentionally discriminates through its traditional business practices. This is because of the power-privilege imbalance that automatically favors a dominant majority and disfavors minorities—unless actions are taken to offset the imbalance.

A *Power Imbalance* is a key aspect of discrimination. Power is a force that is absolutely essential to perpetuate discrimination. For example, an African American clerk may dislike a Euro-American executive and never try to get to know him as a person. Her actions are not called "discrimination" because she does not have the power to take actions that exclude him in ways that disadvantage his career. On the other hand, the executive does have the power to discriminate against her, and that type of power differential is not unusual. Euro-American men still hold nearly all the top-level economic and political power in the United States, as mentioned in Chapter 1. They hold 92 percent of the top-level positions in mid- to large-sized businesses and about 80 percent of the seats in Congress, even though they comprise only about 39 percent of the workforce and 35 percent of the population, according to the U.S. Census Bureau and the U.S. Glass Ceiling Commission. Civil rights measures are based on the fact of power imbalance and represent attempts to break the cycle of centuries of discrimination.

A *Privilege Imbalance* goes hand in hand with a power imbalance, meaning there is a powerful group with distinct privileges that other groups don't have. Most Euro-American men and boys are unaware of the hundreds of privileges they enjoy as members of their group, according to research by Peggy McIntosh; for example:

- When they leave their family or local community in the morning and go out into the world, they can choose to ignore ethnicity, skin color, and other people's differences. People from other groups never have that luxury if they want to succeed in the corporate workplace.
- When they set their goals and plans for social, professional, or political achievement, they don't ask whether a person from their ethnic group or gender would be accepted in the situation.
- When they take a job, coworkers assume they got the job because they're qualified, not because they're a diverse employee.
- They don't have to struggle to be visible, valuable, and important. Educational materials consistently testify to the existence of Euro-American men and their contributions to the United States.
- Wherever they go in the United States, they don't worry about being rejected—just because they're Euro-American men—when they try to join a club, rent an apartment, buy a house, or get a loan. Of course, most rejections are evasive and subtle, but for ethnic minorities they are real.

To better understand the connections between privilege, power, and discrimination, complete the following Self-Awareness Opportunity.

Self Awareness Opportunity 2—How Privileged Are You?

1. What are some privileges that you enjoy in life? List a few.
2. How do the privileges affect your life? Do they affect your personal power? Your ability to achieve your goals? Your success?
3. Which of these (or other) privileges are unavailable to some people because of the group they belong to? Beside each unavailable privilege, write the name of the group.
4. What are some privileges that are unavailable to you that people from certain other groups enjoy? List each privilege and, beside it, the group or groups that have access to it.
5. How does this lack of privilege affect your life? Your personal power? Your ability to achieve your goals? Your success?

Some Types of Prejudice

We talk about prejudice in terms of workplace prejudice, sexism, racism, ethnic prejudice, and other "isms." Workplace prejudice is still active in our culture. Surveys, such as those done by the National Opinion Research Center, indicate that stereotypes are still prevalent and that most of the Euro-American men who run the workplace believe that other ethnic groups are less intelligent, less hard-working, less likely to be self-supporting, more violence-prone, and less patriotic than they are. Such organizations as the U.S. Glass Ceiling Commission and Catalyst have stated in their research reports that prejudice is the biggest advancement barrier that diverse employees face today.

Sexism

Sexism is prejudice based on gender and is said by some to be the root of all prejudice and discrimination. As children we literally begin learning this form of inequality in the cradle. It doesn't involve a majority and minority, since men and women are relatively equal in number. However, women in all countries are a minority in economic and political arenas and have fewer rights and privileges than men.

Racism

Racism is typically a problem in societies such as the United States, where there is a predominant majority group and one or more cultural subgroups. People often use the term racism in discussions of prejudice, which raises the question, "How do I know when I'm dealing with someone of another race, and how can I be sure what race they represent?"

Race as a meaningful criterion within the biological sciences has long been recognized as a fiction and has little meaning in anthropology. This is primarily because of intermarriage among groups, which means that some experts would say there are three races, while others might say 300. Anthropologist Ashley Montagu discusses this issue at length in his book *Man's Most Dangerous Myth*. Yet much of the discrimination in society takes place in the name of race.

Ethnic Prejudice

People who try to distinguish between race and ethnicity typically say that racial traits are inborn, inherited, and given by nature, while ethnic traits are learned, cultural, and acquired through nurture. Since most of the characteristics that vary from culture to culture are learned and are not permanently fixed in our genes, they can theoretically be changed. "Ethnicity" is much more flexible and changeable than "race."

An ethnic subculture is a segment of a larger culture or society. Members of the subculture participate in shared activities in which the common origin and culture are significant ingredients. A subculture is unique because of its particular beliefs, values, and customs, its heroes and heroines, its myths and stories, and its social networks. Ethnic discrimination against minority subcultures occurs when "minority" status carries with it the exclusion from full participation in the society and the largest subculture holds an undue share of power, influence, and wealth in society.

Other Isms

Other isms include ageism, classism or class snobbery, and homophobia, or antigay prejudice. Besides ethnic minorities and women, groups that experience discrimination in the workplace include persons with disabilities, gay persons, older employees, and obese persons. To a lesser extent, persons from lower socioeconomic groups may be targets of prejudice, as symbolized by such derogatory terms as "trailer trash" and "poor White trash." Prejudices know no boundaries, however, and some people believe that all post office employees are deadbeat bureaucrats, all administrators are corrupt political sharks, and on and on.

Self-Awareness Opportunity 3—Examine Your Viewpoints

Instructions: Mark each item True or False. For an interpretation of your responses, see the feedback at the end of this chapter.

1. I have little or no difficulty deciding what's right and what's wrong.
2. I thrive on variety and change.
3. I like my routines.
4. I often enjoy being with people that some would call strange or weird.
5. I know how I feel about most situations and don't need to keep thinking about them.
6. I often ask myself why I did certain things, or why I think or feel as I do.
7. I need to know exactly where I'm going and when.
8. I don't always agree with people from other groups, but I usually understand why they might think and feel as they do.
9. I hate it when people change our plans.
10. Few actions are totally right or wrong; most actions stem from complex situations and have varying effects.
11. There is only one right way to do most things.
12. I can feel comfortable with most situations, even if I'm not sure about what's going on.

13. I prefer to focus on a few simple things rather than a wide variety.
14. People basically create the life they have, and the sooner they take responsibility for it, the better it will be.
15. Most actions can be classified as either proper or improper.
16. I think I know my own strengths and shortcomings pretty well.
17. I don't start a job until I know exactly how to do it.
18. People have different ideas about what's proper and improper; that's fine with me.
19. I need to know what's going on and what to expect at all times.
20. I'm comfortable feeling my way through a task, if necessary.

WHAT IS A PREJUDICE-PRONE PERSONALITY?

While everyone is prejudiced to some extent, the degree of prejudice varies greatly, and a large body of psychological investigation explains why. The original work on the authoritarian personality was done in 1950 by Harvard professor G. W. Allport. Since then more than 1,200 well-accepted scientific studies have been conducted on this topic—far more than for any other personality aspect. Many of these studies, such as those by Dutch researcher M. H. Ijzendoorn, indicate that people who score high on an authoritarianism scale also show a consistently high degree of prejudice against all other cultural groups.

The Highly-Prejudiced Personality

People who are rigid and authoritarian in their beliefs have thinking processes and personality traits that are linked to prejudice. They tend to be more prejudiced than people who are open and flexible. As you begin to understand these key personality traits, you can better understand your own tendencies. You can also see why some people in your organization are more prejudiced than others. You may be able to help them overcome some of the fears that intensify their prejudiced attitudes.

Thinking Processes

The thinking processes of highly prejudiced people are in general different from those of less-prejudiced people. Their prejudice is not likely to be merely a specific attitude toward a specific group, though they may rationalize it that way. More likely, it's a reflection of their whole way of thinking about the world they live in. They're likely to indulge in either-or thinking, such as the following:

- Whenever they think of nature, of law, of morals, of men and women, they think in terms of good/bad, right/wrong, Black/White, maleness/femaleness, and so on. There are few gray areas in their thinking.
- They tend to be uncomfortable with categories that encompass variety, and are more comfortable if categories are limited to similar things.

- Their habits of thought are rigid, and they don't change their mental set easily, but persist in their "tried-and-true" ways of reasoning.
- They have a real need for things to be definite and don't cope well with uncertainty in their plans.
- They tend to agree with such statements as "there are only two kinds of people" and "there's only one right way to do something."
- They divide the world into proper and improper.
- They need precise, orderly, clear-cut instructions before proceeding with a task.

Typical Traits

In other words, highly-prejudiced people have what's known as an authoritarian personality. The personality profile includes these typical traits:

- rigid beliefs
- intolerant of weakness in themselves and others; power orientation
- highly punishing; aggressive
- suspicious, cynical
- extremely respectful of authority; a strong commitment to conform to the prevailing authority structure
- politically conservative

The Authoritarian Link to Prejudice

This set of characteristics usually produces an adult with a high degree of anger, as well as a habit of repressing the anger because of insecurity and fear about expressing it directly. Anger must go somewhere, and in this instance it takes the form of displaced aggression against powerless groups. Meanwhile, the authoritarian person maintains an outward respect for law and order. Almost invariably, when the parents of such people have been studied, they're also highly prejudiced against other subcultural groups. This child gets a double whammy: the predisposition for developing an authoritarian personality, and role models who specifically teach prejudice. Of course, there are exceptions to this profile. Some persons from authoritarian homes are able to choose an open, flexible approach to life. Others, through personal growth, change their beliefs and attitudes in order to become more open, flexible, and accepting of diversity.

Authoritarian persons tend to be rigid, viewing uncertain situations as threatening, in contrast to flexible persons, who may see them as nonthreatening, even interesting, intriguing, or desirable. Since relationships with people from other cultures are less predictable and understandable, authoritarian persons are likely to view them as uncomfortable and undesirable.

Prejudice is clearly more than an occasional incident for people with rigid, authoritarian personality traits. It is embedded in every facet of their personalities. If and when such persons change their prejudiced viewpoints, it follows that they must change their whole life pattern.

The Less-Prejudiced Personality

Tolerant people have adopted thinking processes that are relatively open and flexible:

- They rarely see things in black-or-white terms but as many shades of gray.
- They're usually comfortable differentiating among the variety within a category.
- They can be comfortable with people and situations they're uncertain about.
- They often empathize with those who are different, and are sensitive to their way of seeing and feeling.
- They're self-aware and assess the quality and meaning of their thoughts, feelings, and actions.
- They tend to take responsibility for what happens to them in life and for the life they create.
- They know their own strengths and shortcomings pretty well.
- They've built a great deal of inner security, have handled threats to their self-esteem with inner strength, and can be at ease with all sorts of people.
- They handle moral conflict pretty well, so they can be fairly flexible and tolerant with the ethical mistakes people make.
- They can tolerate ambiguity or uncertainty.
- They feel safe in saying "I don't know" and in waiting until time brings the information or evidence they need.
- They can feel their way through a task, if necessary

The personality you develop within your family environment is one of the many ways you may become prejudiced. Researchers have failed to discover important relationships between prejudice and such variables as age, gender, or income. People with more education tend to be less prejudiced, but the connection is fairly minimal.

HOW AND WHY DO WE BECOME PREJUDICED?

If you can figure out why you adopted your prejudiced beliefs in the first place, you'll find it easier to move beyond those stereotyped assumptions. Prejudices play into these human tendencies:

- The need to feel superior to someone
- The fear of competition for jobs (or land or money or mates or anything else) from the disparaged group's members
- A general frustration due to having a lower status than we feel we deserve, and the resulting hostility that seeks a target, a scapegoat
- A lack of information or education, leading to a simplistic view of the world
- Difficulty dealing with new, uncertain situations and people
- The need to be approved and included by people from the in-group, most of whom are prejudiced themselves, which leads to going along with others' stereotyped assumptions

- The tendency to conform to dominant beliefs and attitudes: "If most everyone I know believes it, it must be true."

History is riddled with many types of overt and covert prejudice, ranging from ethnic or sexist jokes that belittle whole groups of people, to de facto segregation and exclusion, and even to the virtual caste system of slavery and legal segregation. Most prejudice today is of the subtle or hidden form. Prejudice may be compared to certain viruses that hide out, flare up, and hide out again—causing a disease that afflicts and limits individuals but is communicable, making it also a group disease.

Learning from the Culture

People learn prejudice from their culture—family, the media, school, workplace, government, church, in-groups, and a diverse, rapidly changing society. Prejudice is reinforced when we see the contributions of certain groups being devalued or ignored, and when we hear people use negative adjectives and stereotypes for these groups. Prejudice is kept in place when we don't have valid, relevant information about groups outside our own—and when our contacts with people from other groups are only superficial. A major step in moving beyond prejudiced thinking is to learn more about how and why we become prejudiced.

Family Beliefs and Attitudes

Children learn about the world first from their families. Let's take racism or ethnic stereotyping. Family environments that influence children toward racism include these factors:

- Parents avoid discussing issues of racism and other isms because they're too touchy.
- Friends who visit regularly are all of the same group.
- When people such as friends or media personalities make prejudicial remarks, parents don't confront the issue.
- Children remain in segregated schools and play groups.
- Parents don't bother to point out the strengths and contributions of cultures other than their own, beginning with their self-awareness of their own roots and moving on to other groups around them.

The Media

Rigid stereotypes are reinforced by television and radio programs, newspaper and magazine articles, and books by these practices:

- Showing subcultural group members in limited stereotypical roles.
- Failing to show subcultural group members in visible professional positions, such as news anchor, or in positive, leading roles in books, plays, television series, situation comedies, and other programs.
- Allowing unbalanced coverage of subcultural communities, with more focus on criminal activities and tensions than on positive activities and events.

Schools

School systems and school cultures reinforce stereotyping, prejudice, and discrimination in these ways:

- Allowing an administration, faculty, or student body that's not as culturally diverse as the community at large.
- Promoting a learning environment that focuses on only one culture's value system.
- Building the curriculum around European history and the dominant Euro-American culture, paying little attention to cultures of other Americans.
- Ignoring the need for education about ethnic and gender prejudice and discrimination.

The Workplace

The workplace and its corporate cultures reinforce stereotyping, prejudice, and discrimination in these ways:

- Allowing or imposing a glass ceiling that blocks nearly all diverse employees from top positions.
- Encouraging and rewarding only a middle-class and upper-class Euro-American male-based value system rather than incorporating key aspects of the value systems of all major groups who are part of the population.
- Tolerating subtle or overt discrimination or harassment or exclusion at the workplace.

The Government

Behavior by the American government that reinforces discrimination includes these practices:

- Not passing or not enforcing equal rights legislation that is needed to promote fairness and equality for diverse groups.
- Halting or undermining the enforcement of affirmative action programs even though unfair discrimination still blocks or limits the careers of people from certain groups.
- Ignoring, minimizing, or downplaying harassment charges.

Churches

Research by G. W. Allport and J. M. Ross shows that many people actually equate bigotry with organized religion because religious views have so often been used as the basis for stereotyping and prejudice. Their research also indicates that churchgoers are more likely to be prejudiced.

Of course, not all churchgoers are prejudiced. People who attend church primarily for the social benefit it provides are more likely to express prejudice than people who go primarily as a way of finding deeper meaning in life and guidance for everyday living, according to the research of G. M. Herek and others. For the social type, church provides security, comfort, status, and social support and may be an opportunity to belong to a powerful, superior in-group. For the deeper-meaning type, the church's basic creed of brotherhood leaves no legitimate place for rejection, contempt, or condescension.

Identifying with In-Groups

Part of the process of developing an ethnic identity is forming in-groups. What we're familiar with we tend to value as an indispensable basis of our existence. As early as age five, children develop a fierce sense of loyalty to their in-group. Members of an in-group all use the term "we" with the same essential significance, although, of course, members sometimes squabble and fight among themselves.

Prejudice is a form of in-group/out-group bias. Such bias can be based on nearly any group identity, such as blue eyes or brown eyes, and does not necessarily imply a long history of prejudice. In an experiment with school children, Jane Elliott was able to create the main dimensions of discrimination in a matter of hours on the basis of a group separation that was essentially arbitrary—whether a child had blue eyes or brown eyes.

Research by F. A. Blanchard and F. J. Crosby provides evidence that dominant group members tend to believe that when out-group people succeed, it's because they got help or got lucky, but when in-group members succeed, it's because they deserved it, earned it, and had the right traits and skills. In other words, Euro-American males tend to think that when their own succeed in the workplace, it's because of internal traits, but when others succeed, it's because of external circumstances.

In-group bias creates gaps between groups of people, but you can bridge the gaps through increased awareness and a willingness to move beyond exclusion to a more cosmopolitan inclusion.

Being Part of a Diverse, Rapidly Changing Society

As mentioned earlier, countries such as the United States provide a fertile ground for developing prejudice simply because our current situation would be conducive to prejudice in any society. Those conditions are:

- The society is heterogeneous.
- Upward mobility is allowed and valued.
- Social change is occurring rapidly.
- Communication barriers and ignorance between groups are common.
- One or more subcultural groups is large or increasing.
- The increasing size of these groups represents direct competition and a perceived realistic threat.
- Exploitation of people from these groups sustains important interests.
- Customs regulating aggression are favorable to bigotry.
- Traditional justifications for in-group superiority are available.
- Neither assimilation into one culture nor cultural pluralism is distinctly favored or agreed upon as a solution.

HOW DO PEOPLE EXPRESS PREJUDICES?

When someone holds stereotypes that are prejudiced, how do you know it? People may express prejudice by denying it or rationalizing it, by acting it out in various ways from mild to devastating, by subtly discriminating, or by using outgroup members as scapegoats.

Denying and Rationalizing

Two common ways people handle the inner conflict that arises when they hold prejudiced beliefs are:

1. *Denial*—repressing the conflict by denying the prejudice
2. *Rationalization*—offering defenses for the prejudice and justifying it

People often choose denial because if they admit prejudice, they admit to being both irrational and unethical. No one wants to feel pangs of conscience all the time. So it's not unusual to hear the person we perceive as being quite prejudiced saying, "I'm not prejudiced, but . . ."

The most obvious way for people to defend prejudiced beliefs is to gather evidence in their favor, using these kinds of tactics:

- Seeing only those traits, actions, and events that confirm a decision they've already made and simply failing to notice those that don't. "See that Platian loafing over there? Typical!" Not noticing the Platian who is busy and productive.
- Saying it must be true because other people think this way too. "Everybody thinks those people are sneaky" (or dirty, stupid, rude, etc.), claiming truth by consensus.
- Blaming the targets or shifting the blame back onto those who accuse them of prejudice. "It's their own fault they don't get ahead" (that others shun them, etc.), or "They're just as prejudiced as we are" (so that makes it O.K.).
- Defending their prejudiced thinking or action by saying it's the exception to their usual pattern. "Some of my best friends are Platians, but . . ."

Acting Out

We act out our prejudice toward people from a disfavored group with varying degrees of hostile energy. Talking against such people involves relatively little energy, while actively avoiding them takes more. Moving up the energy level, we may discriminate against them, physically attack them, or in a rare extreme of hostile energy, participate in exterminating them. While some people would never move to a more intense degree of action, for others activity on one level makes it easier to move to a more intense level.

Subtly Discriminating

It is no longer considered acceptable or attractive to express stereotypes and prejudices in many social circles, and it can be illegal in schools and workplaces.

Therefore, most people no longer express prejudice directly and openly. Most prejudice today is of the covert and subtle form, sometimes classified as the avoidance-prejudice of liberals—"I don't like the status quo" ("but I don't have a passion for changing it")—and the symbolic prejudice of the conservatives—"We need to become colorblind instead of giving preferences to minorities; affirmative action is reverse discrimination." People have a strong reason to deny and avoid their support of discriminatory situations. Psychologically, if they hold their prejudiced beliefs out of conscious awareness, they can hold onto their self-concept as a nonprejudiced, egalitarian person. They can swear they're not prejudiced when they define prejudice as an intentional, overt act, the old-fashioned type of blatant prejudice that they don't engage in.

Scapegoating

Most societies seem to encourage, officially or unofficially, the open expression of hostility toward certain groups that serve as scapegoats or safety valves for guilt, anger, and aggression. Scapegoating is a form of group projection that helps groups feel superior by projecting their own shortcomings and failures upon out-groups, blaming them for the in-group's problems. African Americans are frequently the scapegoats in U.S. society, from welfare mothers being blamed for higher taxes to youth gang members being blamed for higher crime rates.

HOW DOES PREJUDICE AFFECT PEOPLE IN GENERAL?

Prejudice affects the personalities of the persons who hold the prejudice as well as those on the receiving end. You can work more effectively with people who are prejudiced if you understand the ways that prejudiced thinking influences their life views and their day-to-day actions. You can relate more constructively to people from groups that have traditionally been disparaged in the mainstream culture when you understand how their life experiences may be influencing their behavior patterns.

Effects of Rejecting Others

When you stereotype and reject others as not good enough, the immediate pay-off is feeling "better-than," but it's a cheap thrill. In a world of "better-than's," you're bound to come out "worse-than" in some of the comparisons. Also, the more time you spend immersed in stereotyped, prejudiced, and discriminatory thoughts, the more time you spend in a critical, blaming, judging state of mind. It follows that you'll spend less time in an appreciative, enthusiastic, or joyous state of mind.

The more prejudiced you are, the more you view life through a negative lens. The more your thoughts focus on distaste, dislike, resentment, revulsion, anger, and similar feelings, the more likely you are to experience the anxiety and fear of being despised by others, because that way of thinking is prominent in your experience. Your world becomes more hierarchical, with everyone becoming categorized as better or worse, and people always judging and comparing. You have less space in your mind and less time for appreciating the beauty of the world's diverse people—and the wonder, the joy, and love that appreciation brings.

Effects of Being Rejected

Feeling ignored, excluded, inferior or otherwise rejected is difficult to deal with. The message that you're inferior cannot be hammered into your head day after day without doing something to your character. It may cause you to examine who you really are, to accept yourself, and to become a stronger person for it. Or it may cause you to develop defensive coping behaviors, as shown in Figure 4.1.

Just which ego defenses people develop is largely an individual matter. At one extreme, you'll find "minorities" who seem to handle their status easily, with little evidence that being an out-group member bothers them. At the other extreme, you'll find people so rebellious that they've developed many ugly defenses, so that seem to continually provoke the very snubs they resent. Most people you meet fall somewhere between these extremes, showing some mixture of acceptance and resistance to their status.

The basic "negative" feeling of members of groups disparaged by the mainstream culture is one of insecurity, which may lead to being on guard and hypersensitive. Members of ethnic subcultures must make many more adjustments to their status than Euro-Americans, who interact mainly with other Euro-Americans and only occasionally with members of other cultural groups. But most African Americans, for example, must deal with Euro-Americans every day and are therefore constantly reminded of their "inferior" status in many ways, according to Joe Feagin's studies. In addition, they're more likely to be in a less-powerful position than any of the Euro-Americans they meet. African Americans may become preoccupied with how to adapt to the dominant culture—always trying to accommodate or to succeed in spite of the odds. This often leads to feeling invisible or disparaged or betrayed. Most African Americans, therefore, usually come to view Euro-Americans with deep suspicion. To a lesser extent, this is also true for Latino Americans, Asian Americans, and others. In all groups, the men are more likely to choose ego defenses that strike outward, while women are likely to turn inward, according to G. W. Allport's research.

HOW DOES DISCRIMINATION AFFECT EMPLOYEES?

Discrimination against diverse employees not only affects their career progress, it also affects their trust, motivation, and productivity—and their relationships with the rest of the workforce. It affects them in every phase and aspect of their work experience. Here are some ways companies exclude diverse groups, according to research by Taylor Cox.

Recruitment Practices

Some companies recruit for higher-level jobs by contacting placement firms, publications, and organizations rarely frequented by "minorities." They use these diverse contacts primarily to recruit people for lower-level jobs. Com-

Figure 4.1 *How Discrimination Affects People*

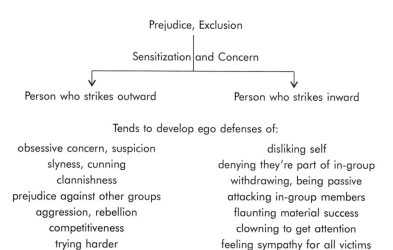

Prejudice, Exclusion

Sensitization and Concern

Person who strikes outward   Person who strikes inward

Tends to develop ego defenses of:

obsessive concern, suspicion	disliking self
slyness, cunning	denying they're part of in-group
clannishness	withdrawing, being passive
prejudice against other groups	attacking in-group members
aggression, rebellion	flaunting material success
competitiveness	clowning to get attention
trying harder	feeling sympathy for all victims

panies who have already selected a Euro-American man for a position may go through the process of recruiting "minorities" merely to meet affirmative action guidelines, with no intention of hiring them.

Screening Practices

Aptitude and intelligence tests may measure the Euro-American way of seeing and doing things but may not be accurate for assessing the aptitude of "minorities" for job success. Also, some firms require diplomas, degrees, and experience that are not really good predictors of job success. Diverse candidates are more likely to lack these credentials, but might have what it takes for job success. Some companies require "minorities" to have experience in areas where they previously had been effectively blocked. And, if companies accept subjective, vague, and arbitrary assessments from previous employers, they may get a distorted view from prejudiced supervisors who are unfair to "minorities."

Terms and Conditions of Employment

On average, women and men from ethnic subgroups earn about 70 percent of Euro-American male salaries, even at the vice-presidential level. Above the worker level, they also receive fewer benefits and perquisites than Euro-American men.

Tracking and Job Segregation

Some companies still have "women's jobs, men's jobs, and minority jobs," even though they're never called that. One example of tracking is the placement of women in clerical work rather than including them in training and development for other, better-paying jobs. To some extent, discrimination in every job phase from recruitment to promotion results in a dual labor market in which diverse employees work disproportionately in occupations and industries with lower prestige, status, and compensation. Within organizations, they typically work in jobs and departments that are less influential and have lower status than those held by Euro-American men, according to the U.S. Glass Ceiling Commission.

Performance Evaluation

Successful performance by women and African American men on tasks traditionally done by Euro-American men tends to be attributed to luck, while Euro-American men's performance is more likely to be attributed to their ability, according to the research of J. H. Greenhaus and S. Parasuraman. Euro-American managers often hold diverse employees to a more limited range of acceptable behavior than the majority group members. Women managers often feel they must walk a tightrope, recognizing that men can show more aggressiveness, ambition, and other traits without being criticized. African American men say they must show less anger and sexuality, to avoid reinforcing stereotypes that cause discomfort. For diverse employees, it amounts to a double standard of acceptable behavior.

Promotion Practices

In many companies, promotion practices are secretive and very difficult for outsiders to understand. Unwritten, informal rules or expectations usually have a much greater impact than written procedures.

Many studies, past and present, indicate that Euro-American male executives and managers continue to harbor stereotyped views of diverse employees, views that shape promotion decisions. A woman is disadvantaged if she's married—"We didn't promote her because she has children and her family responsibilities will interfere." She is disadvantaged if she's single—"We didn't promote her because she's likely to get married, or have children, and quit."

Glass Ceiling Barriers

Several studies, such as those done by two separate U.S. Glass Ceiling Commissions, indicate that the major barrier to promotion up the ladder is the tendency for the men at the top to be more comfortable with their own kind. Here are some reasons.

- They can better predict and understand another person's behavior when that person is like them.
- It's easier to figure out why others in the group do what they do.
- It's easier to establish rapport and build a relationship.
- They're more likely to help others in the group, because people are generally more likely to help in-group members than to help "strangers."

Diverse Standards

Some studies indicate that the reasons given for passing over diverse employees are "lack of initiative" or "not aggressive enough," when the real reason involves a misreading of cultural traits. Latino American and Asian American behavior is often interpreted as "too passive" when managers focus on style, not substance. African Americans' style may be seen as "too aggressive." In fact, some studies, such as those by Ann Morrison, have found that different standards of "getting along with others" have been required for African Americans than for others.

Layoff, Discharge, and Seniority Practices

Many companies use seniority to protect workers who have been there the longest. This usually means that most of those laid off are diverse employees, because they typically have less seniority than Euro-American men. "Minorities" were barred from certain occupations in the past and therefore have been hired only in recent years. If seniority is not used, then older workers may be the most likely to go because they're typically the highest-paid employees.

Career Alternatives

Discrimination can even make it more difficult for diverse employees to choose alternatives to corporate careers that hit the glass ceiling. Most have fewer assets and more difficulty getting business loans than do Euro-American men, which reduces their chances of starting their own businesses or consulting firms. *The Wall Street Journal* has reported government studies of this problem and efforts to alleviate it.

Vignette: "Bid-With" and Job Disaster

Rich was the first African American compensation manager ever hired by Juno Jeans. Because the compensation manager has access to information on salaries and benefits for every person in the company, top management considers it a very sensitive position calling for someone who is discreet, even secretive. Rich seemed to be a mature man with good judgment and the right kind of experience, so they were willing to give him a try.

Juno employees are given the choice of taking lunch at 12:00 or at 1:00, and many play cards or dominoes after lunch. Most of the clerks and hourly people take their lunch at 12:00, and virtually all the management and professional people take theirs at 1:00. Bridge was the game of choice of the 1:00 crowd, while the games of the 12:00 bunch were as varied as their ethnic backgrounds. The African Americans regularly played Bid-With, a game similar to bridge and generally known only in their community. Rich was a wicked Bid-With player but had never mastered bridge. Because of this he usually joined the 12:00 bunch.

The Euro-American executives could not understand why Rich would hobnob with the clerks and maintenance people. To them, it is unwise to become too friendly with people from lower levels, especially when a manager works with sensitive information. It is too easy to relax, forget yourself, and let bits of information slip out. The executives mentioned their concern to Sandra, an African American lawyer in the legal department. She did not agree with their take on the situation. She explained to them that Rich probably just wanted to play Bid-With, and they should not worry about clustering, buddying, blabbing, or similar problems. But the executives' concerns did not go away. Within a few months, they found an excuse to terminate Rich.

Sandra discussed the problem with her husband. "It's too bad, but these guys tend to get paranoid any time they see African American employees bonding—or women professionals talking together, for that matter. They'll make joking comments, such as 'Plotting a revolution?' or 'Ganging up on us?' But beneath the humor, I sense they feel threatened by us. Maybe it's a fear of giving up some power and privilege. Poor Rich, his love of Bid-With did him in. And the company lost a really loyal, talented guy, all because top management has these stereotypes about how managers must act."

HOW DO WE MOVE BEYOND STEREOTYPING TO PROFITABLE COLLABORATION?

You can take a leadership role in helping people in your organization move beyond prejudice by simply being a role model, whether you're the new entry-level employee or the CEO. If you do as the artist Mary Englebreitt suggests and bloom where you're planted, you can begin to experience the power of one. It's contagious. And one plus one plus one can soon become a critical mass for change.

You can start by understanding the negative effects of stereotypes on people's performance and the type of contact that tends to heal prejudice. You can then learn powerful action strategies for moving beyond the stereotypes.

Understand the Effects of Prejudice on Performance

Prejudice and discrimination have a great impact on employee performance. At the deepest level, they undermine employee trust. They also undermine employee motivation and productivity.

Effects on Trust

Prejudice and discrimination sabotage trust. Given the history of intergroup prejudice, trust is more difficult to build across cultural groups than it is within them. "Don't trust Whitey" has long been a motto in African American communities. Diverse employees tend to feel less free to spontaneously express their opinions and ideas in the workplace. This causes many of them to engage in much more internal prescreening or self-censorship in order to fit into the work group.

Effects on Motivation

Many diverse employees have reported that they find it difficult to determine the cause of their events and life experiences, often asking, "Was this event caused by discrimination or by other factors?" This can be a major problem when they attempt to process feedback and to stay motivated: "Is my boss criticizing me because my work is not up to standards or because I'm Latino American?" Expectancy theory holds that the motivation to perform on a job depends on answers to three questions:

1. If I put forth enough effort, will it produce the performance level the boss wants?
2. If I achieve the performance level the boss wants, will I get what I want (praise, raise, promotion, etc.)?
3. Is it worth it to me?

Discrimination can interfere with factors 1 and 2. Even if the boss is not influenced by an employee's group identity when she evaluates performance, if the employee believes she is, then that employee's motivational level will almost certainly drop.

Effects on Productivity

Jane Elliott's experiments with the effects of prejudice on productivity are described in the documentary film *A Class Divided*. Elliott separated students into blue-eyed and brown-eyed groups. On the first day, she told the class that the brown-eyed group was inferior (they wore collars for clear identification of their status). She reinforced this in various ways, such as giving certain privileges to the "superior" group. On the second day, the roles were reversed. On both days the superior group discriminated against the others, calling them names and otherwise excluding them.

The work performance of the "inferior" group declined significantly after just a few hours of discriminatory treatment. The test scores of the students went up on the day they were in the advantaged group and down on the day the same students were in the disadvantaged group. The change in behavior of the teacher and fellow students had an immediate impact on the performance of the students.

The study highlights, among other things, the effect of leader expectations on performance. Leader expectations are communicated to employees in several ways:

- The amount of output the leader wants signals expectations: How challenging and desirable are the goals? To what extent does the leader believe the employee can achieve high goals? How supportive is the leader?
- The overall climate (favorable tone, positive responses, etc.) that leaders set communicates their expectations.
- The amount of input, or the information relevant to getting the job done, that leaders give employees signals their expectations.
- The amount of feedback, or the information about how well the employee is doing, that leaders give communicates or implies their expectations.

You can help set an inclusive tone in your work groups. If the team and the company wants top performance, there must be no out-groups. (See the earlier discussion of in-groups.) Everyone must be a member of the in-group.

Understand the Type of Contact That Heals Prejudice

The types of contact diverse groups typically experience range from superficial contact to true acquaintance, from conflict to collaboration. Only collaboration allows the depth of understanding that heals prejudice and creates inclusion.

Superficial Contact

Where segregation is the custom, contacts tend to be superficial, either because they're very casual or because they're firmly fixed into superior-subordinate relationships. Such contact is more likely to increase prejudice than to decrease it, because we tend to selectively notice behavior that will confirm our stereotypes. Therefore, each contact may serve to prove that our stereotypes are true about such characteristics as group members' physical appearance, ability to communicate, and other traits.

Two of the most visible differences of diverse employees are skin color and sexual characteristics, which often serve as a lightening rod for all kinds of thoughts and feelings about a group. In the case of women, for example, stereotyped traits enable some Euro-American male employees to join together and think of women as one big out-group rather than as individuals.

True Acquaintance

Contacts that go beyond the superficial to truly getting to know a person lead to acceptance of new knowledge. They are likely to lead to valid beliefs about diverse groups and therefore bridge the walls of prejudice.

Conflict

Clashes of interests and values do occur between groups, and these conflicts are not in themselves necessarily an expression of prejudice. Also, some conflicts grow out of economic competition that is not necessarily rooted in prejudice but tends to aggravate any prejudice that exists.

Collaboration

Research by J. G. Ponteretto and P. B. Pedersen indicates that Euro-Americans who live side by side with African Americans of the same general economic class in public housing projects are on the whole more friendly, less fearful, and have less-stereotyped views than those who live in segregated arrangements. Merely living together is not the decisive factor. Whether people are jointly active in community enterprises is what counts. The resulting communication is distinctive and makes all the difference in the relationship that develops.

The conclusion—needing each other to reach a goal—holds true for contact in the workplace. Only the type of contact that leads people to do things together is likely to result in changed beliefs and attitudes. Common goals are all-important. It's the cooperative striving for a goal that engenders solidarity. Equal-status contact is important, but participation and common interests are even more important. Self-managing work teams hold tremendous challenge and opportunity to finally break down prejudiced belief systems and establish the unity companies need. The biggest barrier to effective collaboration may be "not collaborating"—that is, not setting up work teams that must be interdependent in order to achieve crucial common goals. *The key to moving beyond prejudice is working together toward common goals that are highly valued, in situations where people need each other to achieve their goals.*

Vignette: Contact That Counts

A public housing project in Los Angeles was converted to private condominiums, which low-income families were able to purchase. Owners established a homeowners association that met regularly for the purpose of making the neighborhood as livable and vital as possible. During the Los Angeles riots of 1992, homeowners took a united stand against any invasion of their neighborhood, and it was spared from vandalism. Residents who were interviewed by *The Los Angeles Times* credited the friendships built by people from various subcultures for the solidarity they displayed during the crisis.

COLLABORATION SKILL DRILL: SEVEN ACTION STRATEGIES

You have begun the process of moving beyond stereotypes, prejudice, exclusion, and even tolerance, to appreciation, inclusion, and collaboration with "minorities." You are ready to continue the process and to become a role model and coach for others who are willing to move beyond prejudice. Keep these seven strategies in mind.

Strategy #1—Get in Touch with Stereotypes and Prejudices

Our mass media generally supports cultural stereotypes, continually reviving and reinforcing them. Therefore, it's important that intelligent people move beyond shallow, limiting, and harmful stereotypes of diverse groups.

You stand to benefit greatly from moving beyond stereotypes and prejudice, as does your career, your organization, and the planet, for that matter. Staying stuck in prejudice, no matter how hidden or subtle, has great costs. You may have learned from bitter failure in a relationship that your stereotypes were in error, or that your friends or business associates disapproved of your bias, assumption, or exclusionary behavior. You're fortunate if you get such a message to change your ways, for it can help you see clearly that it's in your own interest to change your prejudiced thinking.

Even when you're not confronted by others with your prejudices, and even when you're not consciously aware of them or the effects they have, you probably believe at some level that prejudice conflicts with your deepest beliefs about human value and equality. Most of us, when we catch ourselves in prejudice, don't feel good about it, and if you stop to take a good, hard look at it, you probably don't particularly like yourself when you think and act this way. Except for making you temporarily feel better than someone else, it's not nearly as satisfying to dislike people and look down on them as it is to appreciate them, collaborate with them, and have fun together. Further, prejudice sets in motion a negative cycle of action and reaction that divides, separates, and throws up barriers to building trust. It prevents people from having the productive and harmonious workplace and society that would benefit us all. So how do you break the habit?

The most important step is merely wanting to know about your own stereotypes and prejudices so you can open up to more accurate information. We often hide prejudiced beliefs from ourselves, so uncovering them can be challenging, but it's a challenge worth pursuing. Then you can begin to notice thoughts that occur when you see certain people, judgmental thoughts that lead to feelings of aversion, dislike, suspicion, and similar feelings that prevent good interaction and block collaborative relationships.

Strategy #2—Open Your Mind to Other Viewpoints and Listen

Open up to new ideas so you can replace irrational, rigid stereotypes with some rational, flexible categories, perhaps better defined as background information. Remember, even valid background information you gather and store away about various groups of people is not set in concrete. Think of each category of background information as flexible and open to change. It's there to help you understand where a person might be coming from and to provide clues about what questions to ask. This frees you up so you can get to know people on their own merits, as unique individuals, to empathize with them, and to build honest, trusting relationships.

Accepting

Respect their right to have different beliefs and viewpoints, lifestyles and business images, work styles and job behaviors. You do not need to adopt a belief or custom yourself in order to respect another's right to believe or act as they do. Be willing to listen and learn about diverse people and groups, to examine your own ego needs, beliefs, and viewpoints that block your ability to respect and appreciate others. Be willing to change false beliefs.

Listening

Good listeners are rare. Most of us take turns talking instead of listening to get another's ideas that we might incorporate into our own. Be willing to listen with an open mind to other viewpoints and to new information that might change a biased belief.

Opening

Open-minded persons look beyond labels, categories, and sweeping statements. They insist on knowing the evidence for broad generalizations before accepting them as true. They're open to new evidence that might lead them to modify a category.

Strategy #3—Learn about Other Groups

Educate yourself and others about the key differences among diverse groups. Appreciate those differences—see them as individual, colorful facets of the kaleidoscope of humanity. Once you begin to understand the typical stereotypes, biases, and barriers that members of a particular group must cope with every day, you have a better chance of anticipating how your own actions may be perceived. When you become familiar with a group's values and customs and how they view certain issues, you can better interpret their actions and words. The goal of cultural understanding is to be able to walk in another person's shoes for a while, to see the world as that person sees it, and feel what he or she feels.

Strategy #4—Express Respect and Appreciation

Once you've opened your mind and replaced stereotyped beliefs, the next step is to become comfortable and imaginative in expressing respect and appreciation, primarily through your actions but also through your conversations. Every time you choose to focus on goodwill and trust instead of focusing on fear and mistrust, you automatically move to respecting and appreciating instead of judging and belittling. It can become a healing and profitable habit.

Strategy #5—Open Up to Intuition and Empathy

If you are unable to empathize with "minorities," you may feel forced to be on guard, to put strangers into categories, and to react to them as a group rather than as individuals. If you're unwilling to learn about the background as well as the uniqueness of people you encounter, you're likely to resort to stereotyping. Clearly, the willingness to feel empathy for others—to see the world as they see it and to feel what they're feeling—can help you to move beyond prejudice.

Strategy #6—Build Trust

Building trust can be a difficult challenge given the history of stereotyping, prejudice, and betrayal among diverse groups. You build trust by building authentic relationships, in which you respect and appreciate others and show it through words and actions. When you are consistent, keeping your commitments and showing respect time after time, then people begin to trust you. Where there is a long legacy of mistrust, it may take a long time to build trust. It can be destroyed in a moment of perceived betrayal, and the healing process may be difficult or impossible. The best preventive is to consistently choose an attitude of friendship and trust toward other people, and to act in ways that respect and preserve those relationships. Before you act, ask yourself, "Will this harm or help the relationship?"

Strategy #7—Work with Diverse People toward Common Goals

You have learned that superficial contact alone does not help people to overcome stereotypes and prejudices toward a group. What does work is teaming up with others on projects that help you achieve important common goals.

Go for Creativity and Innovation

Diverse idea pools, like diverse gene pools, provide us with more variety and options. This means more and better innovation, crucial in today's fast-moving, globally competitive companies.

Seek Collaboration

Continually seek opportunities to collaborate one-on-one and in teams in order to bridge cultural gaps. Self-managing work teams can be especially effective because members must take so much responsibility for setting goals, figuring out how to achieve them, and actually doing it. The success of such teams depends on building trust and working closely together. Ask, "How can I create teams of 'minorities' to work toward common goals?" Value unity, which is not uniformity but integration of the goals and efforts of many individuals. See that in unity there can be great diversity. Understand that each part is vital to the success of an emerging whole.

Work toward Synthesis

Share a vision of people gathering together the separate elements that form the whole project and work team. See them bringing the whole into active expression. Envision them acting as one to create a new reality—including new projects, processes, products, relationships, and corporate culture. Understand that synthesis is not the same as melting-pot assimilation.

Go for Synergy

Recognize that extra creative spark, that increment of information, knowledge, friendship, or other benefit that is the by-product of collaboration and synthesis. Use it to carry the team and the organization to new heights of excellence and innovation. Celebrate that added gift, the whole creative package that is more than the sum of what each person brings to the table.

Self-Awareness Opportunity 4—Assessing Your Impact

Harry Palmer, author of *Living Deliberately*, expresses a principle of quantum physics when he says that every time an individual changes his or her belief, the blueprint by which the collective reality unfolds, changes. "Even for the most isolated individual, every moment of happiness, every moment of sadness, every kindness, every critical thought adds its consequence to the blueprint for the events of the world."

1. How are your thoughts and emotions changing the world for the better? Write a few words about this.
2. What kind of beliefs and attitudes are you role-modeling for your coworkers and associates? Write a few words about this.

Skill Builder 1—Opening Up to New Experiences

Purpose: To help you open up to all types of people (especially helpful for people who score above average on the authoritarian personality scale).

Step 1. Examine those motivators and barriers to getting to know people from groups you've been unwilling or unable to relate to. The barriers relate to some type of discomfort and ultimately to some type of fear. Barriers cause us to mentally separate ourselves from others, to contract, withdraw. The motivators relate to an outgoing tendency and ultimately to some type of goodwill. They cause us to mentally reach out, to include, and to expand. They often involve curiosity, courage, and a sense of adventure.

Barriers	Motivators
I don't know what to expect.	It may be fun.
I don't feel comfortable.	It may be interesting.
Maybe they won't like me.	I may learn something.
Maybe I won't like them.	They may like me.
Maybe they won't treat me well.	I may like them.
I may end up looking foolish.	I may end up feeling better about myself.
I don't know what to say.	I may gain experience, perspective,
I don't know how to act.	understanding, empathy, compassion.
Others:	Others:

Step 2. Think of a time when you did not say "yes" to an opportunity to experience a new situation with people you didn't know well. What were some of the barriers that held you back? Check off the barriers that apply in the list shown here. Add others that you experienced.

Step 3. Think of a time when you did say "yes" to such an opportunity. What motivated you? Check off the motivators that apply in the list shown here. Add others that you experienced.

Step 4. In the first situation, what happened after you said "yes"? Was the experience more positive or negative in your opinion? If more negative, what lessons can you draw from this experience?

Step 5. In the second situation, what might have happened if you had said "yes"? What experiences, opportunities, advantages, and lessons might you have missed? What lessons can you learn from this now?

Skill Builder 2—Changing Judgmental Beliefs

Purpose: Finding and changing judgmental beliefs that create conflict.

Step 1. Describe a problem situation. Write a few words about a relationships situation you would like to improve, one that may involve your own stereotyping or prejudice.

Step 2. List your beliefs about the situation. Write a few words about (a) the beliefs you think promote harmony in the situation, and (b) the beliefs you think undermine harmony or promote conflict in the situation.

Step 3. List your beliefs about the other person(s). Write a few words about (a) the beliefs you think support the other person(s) involved in the situation, and (b) the beliefs you think undermine the other person(s).

Step 4. List your beliefs about yourself. Write a few words about (a) the beliefs you think are self-empowering in the situation, and (b) the beliefs that you think undermine you.

Step 5. Examine the beliefs carefully. Focusing on the nonsupportive beliefs, consider the idea that all the things you dislike or despise in others you also dislike or despise in yourself. If you despise cruelty in others, you despise it in yourself, either because you are sometimes cruel with others, or because you are sometimes cruel with yourself, or both. Look for patterns and insights about who you are and how you judge yourself. See if you recognize your self-judgments being reflected in your judgments of others. Write a few words about (a) things you dislike or despise in others, and (b) patterns and insights you see emerging from this self-awareness process.

Step 6. Ask yourself, "Do these beliefs still serve me? Am I ready to change them?"

Step 7. Use the change process: Take responsibility for having created the beliefs that support conflict. Accept and acknowledge that these beliefs are judgmental and that it is perfectly human to have these judgmental beliefs. Embrace them with love and compassion, without judging them. Feel the feelings. Get out of your head and into your body where you sense some feeling, such as the area around the navel. Let feelings of friendship and compassion rise up into your heart area, up through the top of your head. Then let them surround and permeate your entire body with a sense of well-being and serenity.

Step 8. Focus on new, positive beliefs. Ask yourself:

- "What beliefs can I adopt that reflect goodwill and trust to replace the old fear-based ones?" Write a few words about them.
- "What other positive beliefs would facilitate and support harmony in this situation?" Write a few words about them.

Step 9. Embrace these new beliefs. Make them a part of who you are.

Skill Builder 3—Using Your Intuition in Relationships

Be willing to relax into your intuition and listen to its messages as you tune into others, allowing yourself to see things from their viewpoint. When you empathize, you intuit how another person sees and feels a situation, which helps you to understand the person. You therefore have less need to feel apprehensive and insecure. You tend to gain confidence that helps you overcome the need to stereotype or exclude. Accurate perceptions of how others think and feel gives you the ability to avoid friction and to conduct successful relationships.

To be in touch with intuition is similar to listening to your body when your body is speaking to you. Give yourself permission to be intuitive. The more relaxed you are, the better. Relax, ask your inner self for intuitive insight, and allow thoughts and feelings to come to your awareness. If you are sincere, answers will come. However, the moment that you set up expectations about how the event may occur and when, you're immediately limiting your possibilities. Intuition is not linear and rational. Answers may come in unexpected ways and times. They often come as little flashes or glimmers of thought or feeling. Learn to recognize them and to use the power of insight.

How do you know whether the flash is intuition or ego or fantasy? Intuition is never wrong, or else it wouldn't be intuition, so note your flashes of insight and later compare them with actual events. As you practice and get feedback, your intuitive skills will grow.

Skill Builder 4—Picturing Exclusion and Inclusion in Your Firm

Purpose: To use the power of symbols and pictures to help you better understand your thoughts and feelings about prejudice and exclusion.

Step 1. Draw a picture of prejudice and exclusion in your company. Draw anything you like, but do not use words in the picture. Use colors and symbols to express how people relate to one another, which groups have power, how they use power, and similar aspects.

Step 2. Look at your completed picture and respond to the following:

• What immediate feelings do you experience?
• What thoughts come to mind?
• What does your drawing say about exclusion in the organization?

Step 3. Draw a new picture. Show symbolically how people could relate to each other in ways that express respect, appreciation, inclusion, and collaboration. Show how personal power, group power, and organizational power might relate, how it might change, how things would look.

Step 4. Look at your completed picture and respond to the following:

• What immediate feelings do you experience?
• What thoughts come to mind?
• What does your drawing say about how inclusion might change the organization?

Feedback on Self-Awareness Opportunity 3—Examine Your Viewpoints

This self-awareness opportunity is presented before you cover the information on the rigid, authoritarian personality as compared with the open, flexible personality. After you compute your score, go on to the next segment and you will learn what all this means.

Odd-numbered statements represent rigid-authoritarian tendencies, and even-numbered statements represent open-flexible tendencies.

1. Add up the odd-numbered statements you marked as true. That's your rigidity score.
2. Then add up the even-numbered statements you marked as true. That's your openness score.

Since 10 is the maximum score in each category, this gives you a preliminary reading of your tendencies on a scale of 1 to 10. For example, if your rigidity score is 3 and your openness score is 7, your level of openness is about 70 percent and rigidity is about 30 percent. This is only a ballpark figure, of course.

5

Male-Female Bonding

Men make up about 55 percent of the U.S. workplace, while women are 45 percent. Researcher Deborah Tannen has spent much of her career exploring how men and women can communicate better with each other. She concluded that men and women communicate differently because they view the world differently, to such an extent that they actually live in different, parallel worlds. People who have taken the time and effort to learn about these differences—as well as the similarities—say they have boosted their ability to work productively with members of the other gender.

You're about to deepen your understanding of what it's like to be a woman or man in today's society and workplace, and how this experience can affect relationships with the opposite sex in the workplace. You'll learn about the following:

- How myths and stereotypes about men and women compare with reality
- How culture affects male-female traits and status
- How gender roles have evolved and are changing
- How the communication styles of men and women differ
- The differences in the worldviews of men and women
- Women's cultural barriers to workplace success
- Men's responses to new roles and expectations
- How men are responding to new expectations in the workplace
- Understanding sexual harassment
- How to break through male-female barriers and create win-win successes

---

Self-Awareness Opportunity 1—Traits of Men and Women

Purpose: To become aware of your beliefs about gender traits and roles.

1. What are the traits or qualities that you like to see in men, the traits and actions that you admire or feel comfortable with? List them.

2. What are the traits or qualities that you like to see in women, the traits and actions that you admire or feel comfortable with? List them.
3. Keep them in mind and compare them with the traits discussed in this chapter.

What's in a Name? For the purpose of this discussion, I will use *gender* to discuss workplace or social issues that stem from the fact that a person is a man or a woman, and *sex* to discuss situations that stem more directly from one's sexuality.

GENDER MYTHS AND REALITIES

Most of the myths and stereotypes about men and women are either false or distorted, partial truths. In fact, most stem from the patriarchal culture typical of most of the world's societies.

Myth #1—The typical American family consists of a husband with a career and a wife who stays home and takes care of two children.

This myth reflects traditional male/female roles. The woman belongs at home doing housework and raising children, and the man belongs in the workplace earning a living for the family. This pattern was typical from about 1900 to 1960. Now, only about 15 percent of U.S. families fit that description—and even then only temporarily while the children are very young—making these roles more myth than reality.

Myth #2—There are only two types of women: good and bad.

In the past, "good women" were placed on a pedestal, called ladies and treated like little Madonnas or dolls, while "bad women" were called sluts or whores. There was not much of a gray area in between. Women who had reputedly ever had sex outside of marriage were bad and the others were good. This stereotype tends to define women primarily by their sexual relationship to men. It was not until the women's movement of the late 1960s that such stereotypes, along with the resulting double standard for sexual behavior and language such as "ladies," were challenged by a widespread group of people. The myth is now more subtle and less predominant in the United States than in the past, but it's more pronounced in Latino cultures than in the mainstream American culture.

Myth #3—Women's status in society is equal to men's.

The myth is that since women legally earned voting rights, equal opportunity, and affirmative action, they've gained equal status. However, we know that only 5 percent of top managers in the Fortune 1000 and 11 percent of Congress are women. And women at all corporate levels average 30 percent less pay than men. This tells us that although women have come a long way toward economic and political equality, they still have a long way to go. The types of special efforts that have triggered women's progress must continue for women to eventually achieve equal status.

Myth #4—Real men are in control of the situation.

In patriarchal cultures (meaning virtually all the world's modern cultures), being in control has high value. Men have traditionally been given these types of messages by men in authority: "You're letting things get out of control," "Control your wife," "You've got to take charge." This myth implies that men are superior. At home they should be master of the house, and in the workplace they should be the managers. But more and more American women are expecting to have equal relationships at home and in the workplace. Relationship styles and management styles are changing. The trend is that people are expected to control themselves and to take control of their own lives, then come together as equals to collaborate on joint projects. Trying to control others is becoming frustrating and counterproductive for men.

Myth #5—Real men don't cry.

People in our culture typically tell little boys that "Big boys don't cry." Neither are they afraid. They are brave and confident. They may get angry and fight back, but they don't whimper or snivel. In hundreds of ways, men get the message that they should not be emotional nor show their feelings. Most boys learn to hide their feelings. By the time they grow up, many have denied their feelings for so long that they're numb to them and out of touch with them.

Once they're men, it's generally all right to show anger in certain situations, such as to get things done or to defend one's honor. And it's acceptable to show some feelings with one's mate in romantic settings. Otherwise, feelings are to be buttoned up, locked in, and kept contained. And that's the major problem with this myth. Unacknowledged and unexpressed feelings don't go away. They build and fester, contributing to stress and its related illnesses.

Myth #6—Women are too emotional and soft to be real leaders.

The belief that women are too emotional and soft has led to most of the other stereotypes that block women's careers. According to the 1995 Glass Ceiling Commission, these are the ones that create the greatest barriers:

- Women are too emotional.
- Women are too passive, too aggressive, or not aggressive enough.
- Women aren't tough enough to fill some positions.
- Women can't or won't work long or unusual hours—or relocate.
- Women can't or won't make tough decisions.
- Women can't crunch numbers.
- Women don't want to work.
- Women aren't as committed to careers as men.

These traits are primarily learned traits, they are a matter of style rather than substance, and they can be managed and used to advantage in the workplace.

DOES CULTURE DETERMINE MALE-FEMALE TRAITS AND STATUS?

While some traits may have a genetic component, we know that culture plays a large role. In patriarchal cultures, men and women have different status and different roles. Different traits provide a rationale for this and so are emphasized.

Stereotyped Traits

Almost from the moment we're born, we begin learning gender stereotypes and myths. Most of us also begin learning about inequality in relationships from the patriarchal system of family, church, and culture. Although the patriarchal system is beginning to change in the United States, boys and girls are still socialized in very different ways. And boys and girls still grow up in two worlds, overlapping but different.

People generally expect men and women to express different traits, and the traits they admire in men are often traits they don't admire in women and don't expect women to express. Men's traits—such as being aggressive, strong, and independent—are those traditionally expected of business leaders. That's why business women report they must walk a fine line between being considered too feminine and too masculine. The traits they need for business success are not the traits people expect or admire in women, as Figure 5.1 indicates.

This "traits disadvantage" that business women have dealt with is beginning to recede as companies recognize the increasing importance of some of women's typical traits—such as a focus on personal connections, interpersonal relationships, and nurturing leadership—for managing today's participative workplace, which is increasingly peopled by well-educated employees working in self-managing teams. Men who are very aggressive and ambitious may need to develop more sensitivity and patience. All of us can benefit by becoming more well-rounded and balanced, allowing the best of our personalities to emerge from both sides, the feminine and the masculine.

Developing this balance is becoming important for effective modern marriages, too. In the old survival times, men and women needed each other for a balance. Today's power couples, where both partners balance important careers with a fruitful family life, tend to develop themselves as whole persons first, then to form partnerships from preference rather than need.

Traits and Power Differentials

Not only are traits learned, they are affected by the power the culture accords to each group. When we are socialized at home in ways that establish and reinforce a power differential between men and women, male-female interactions in the workplace reflect interactions between the more powerful and the less powerful.

Figure 5.1 *Typical Masculine and Feminine Traits.*

Feminine Traits	Masculine Traits
emotional	aggressive
talkative	strong
sensitive	proud
affectionate	confident
moody	independent
patient	courageous
romantic	disorganized
cautious	ambitious
thrifty	
(Men also said manipulative.	
Women said creative.)	

Adapted from Gallup polls, 1990.

For example, why do some women use tears to influence men, while men tend to use logical arguments to influence both men and women? Yes, through socialization, women have been allowed to express emotions and men have not. But also, men usually have more power in male-female relationships and therefore have the upper hand. It may be that women's logic would be ignored and they feel they must resort to tears in order to have an effect. L. A. Peplau's research study led to two major conclusions about gender and power tactics:

1. *Gender affects power tactics.* Women are more likely to withdraw or express negative emotions, while men are more likely to use bargaining or reasoning. However, in a partnership between gay men, if one partner perceives himself as less powerful, he is likely to use withdrawal or expressions of negative emotions, and the more powerful partner is likely to use bargaining or reasoning. The same dynamics were found between two women in a lesbian partnership.
2. *Power, not gender, is the issue.* Regardless of gender or sexual orientation, people who see themselves as relatively more powerful in a relationship tend to use persuasion and bargaining, while those who feel they are lower in power tend to use withdrawal and emotion.

As Rosabeth Kanter found in her studies of men and women in organizations, behaviors believed to be typical of women are actually behaviors that are typical of the powerless. Regardless of sexual orientation, a partner with relatively less power tends to use "weak" strategies, such as manipulation and pleading. Those in more powerful positions are more likely to use autocratic and bullying tactics. Signs of conversational dominance, such as interrupting, were linked also to the balance of power. Interruption is not so much a male behavior as a tactic of the powerful.

Gender Differences as a Prototype of Group Differences

All cultures differentiate between male and female behavior, and usually when a given behavior pattern becomes associated with one sex, it will be dropped by the other, according to G. P. Murdock's work. Recently, many sociologists and anthropologists have begun to see gender differences primarily as cultural differences and have started applying crosscultural techniques to solving gender problems. Some researchers, such as Richard Brislin and Tomoko Yoshida, say that gender is not just one of many cultural differences, but the most important cultural difference, the root paradigm of difference, just as the inequality of patriarchy is the paradigm of all inequality among groups.

Instead of seeing women's culture as a subculture within each ethnic culture, they declare that the two most basic cultural groups are women and men. Between these two groups we find the prototypical cultural distinctions, after which all other cultural distinctions are modeled. If organizations can learn to accept and deal with gender differences, all other differences can be handled in due course. On the other hand, a great deal of diversity work remains superficial when gender issues are not first recognized and managed. This is because beliefs about gender influence us in the most fundamental ways about how to be with others and make choices in life.

HOW HAVE GENDER ROLES EVOLVED AND CHANGED?

Women in Western cultures have traditionally been viewed as a wholly different species from men, invariably an inferior species. The primary and secondary sex differences that exist are greatly exaggerated and are inflated into imaginary distinctions that justify discrimination. In the past, most men felt an in-group solidarity with half the humans on earth, other men, and with the other half, an irreconcilable conflict, according to G. W. Allport, Harvard psychologist. Allport reports that in the eighteenth century, Lord Chesterfield described the way women were traditionally viewed by men:

> [Women are] children grown large, with little reasoning ability. They are to be trifled with, played with, humored, and flattered, as with a sprightly, forward child. Few men ever consult them or trust them with serious matters, though they often make women believe that they do both, which is the source of women's greatest pride. They are mainly concerned with matters of vanity and of love. (Allport 1954)

The Patriarchal System

Patriarchy refers to the rule of a family or tribe by men, and a social system in which descent and succession are traced through the male line. It began by brute force and muscle power. Once established, men's superiority and advantage were institutionalized into every sphere of life. It is now being undermined because brain power and relationship power are becoming true power. As men's superiority is undermined, some are resorting to extreme measures to hold onto it, even to physical abuse and rape, according to Robert Bly, Sam Keen, and other men's movement leaders.

Men's movement author, Walter Farrell, defines patriarchy as the male areas of dominance, responsibility, and subservience in a culture, reinforced by both genders for the purpose of serving the survival needs of both genders. Patriarchy has given men the authority, privileges, and responsibility that come with being in charge. Women's privileges involved being provided for and protected, if they picked the right man and all went well. Both men and women have been rewarded with "identity" when they followed the rules, and have been punished with invisibility when they failed—or sometimes even death if they rebelled against them. Leaders were picked from the men who best followed the rules.

Feminist Movements

Women's rights groups have arisen from time to time to protest the limitations and unfairness to women and to men that patriarchy imposes. The most recent feminist movement began in the 1960s and has made significantly more progress than any previous movement. Perhaps gender equality is an ideal whose time has come. Feminists come in many political shades and stripes, but most agree with Gloria Steinem's simple definition: A feminist is someone who believes in equal rights for women.

Most feminists believe that the inequality inherent in patriarchy does not serve women's best interest, and that equality in the workplace will lead to equality in the family. They focus on eliminating all discriminatory barriers to women's moving up in the work world as the key to the overall liberation of women. They believe that changes in labor market conditions that women face will force changes in family dynamics. Economic power is a prerequisite to a balance of power in family relationships.

From Patriarchy to Equality

As we've moved from an agricultural economy through an industrial to a postindustrial economy, cultural values have shifted dramatically. The women's movement is a reflection of that basic shift. Marriage relationships are the most influential in a society, because children learn about life and relationships by observing their parents. Leaders of both the men's and women's movements propose that we move beyond patriarchy or matriarchy—beyond hierarchy—to a system that relies on leadership that arises spontaneously from those who are willing and able to lead in particular situations (see Figure 5.2).

Megatrends That Opened Doors

Beginning in the 1960s, a series of megatrends combined to accelerate the pace at which women moved into managerial, professional, technical, and leadership roles that had been almost exclusively Euro-American male territory.

Figure 5.2 *Traditional and New Male-Female Relationships*

	Traditional Marriage Relationships	New Relationships
Major goal	Survival	Fulfillment
Relationship focus	Role mates, to create a whole	Soul mates, whole persons, to create synergy
Effect on roles	Segregated roles	Common roles
Family obligations	Must have children. Woman raises children, man makes money. Woman risks life in childbirth; man risks life in war.	Children are a choice. Both raise children and both make money. Childbirth relatively risk-free; ideally no more war.
Partner choice	Parental influence primary; women try to marry "up."	Parental influence secondary; both marry for love.
The contract	Lifetime; no divorce	As long as both parties want to stay together
Status of parties	Neither party can end contract.	Either party can end contract.
	Woman is property of man; man is expected to provide and protect.	Each is equally responsible for self and other.
Emotional expectations	Both are subservient to needs of family.	Both balance needs of family with needs of self.
	Love emerges from mutual dependence.	Love is based on choice.
	I'll stay no matter what.	I'll stay unless you abuse me or we grow in different directions.

Social Change

The 1960s brought major social upheavals. Those that most affected gender issues were greater acceptance of divorce, greater sexual freedom, and greater acceptance of equal opportunity for women and minorities. Such social changes allowed women more freedom of choice. During the 1970s women began moving into many fields of study and occupations formerly closed to them.

Economic Change

As blue collar jobs moved offshore, a growing number of husbands no longer earned an income that would support a family, and their wives went to work. As divorce became more economically feasible for women, an increasing percentage of women became heads of households. For all these reasons, middle-class working mothers, once a sign of liberation, became an economic necessity during the 1980s. As the average worker's take-home pay went down, family income grew an average of less than 1 percent per year, even with many wives working. Buying a home became more expensive and took a larger share of family income, and renters found it more difficult to save up a down payment. An ever-greater proportion of women will continue to enter the workforce and stay there, even when they have small children. This means that working mothers will be the largest potential source of qualified workers for the next decade.

Emphasis on Ethical Values

The excesses of the 1980s—from the spending of a Donald Trump to the grand larceny of Wall Street dealers and savings and loan officers—brought a new respect for ethical principles. Also, biotechnology is poised to solve many of our health and poverty problems, although people are realizing a corresponding need to define ethical values to regulate this new industry. Several recent surveys indicate that people believe women can bring special talents to dealing with and cleaning up ethical issues, and that people tend to trust women's ethical standards and level of honesty. This applies to both the business and political worlds. Women represent a "fresh face" without the back-room connections and long years of deal making.

Management Style Change

The underlying theme of all the megatrends is the individual. While people are working together in more dynamic ways than ever, the trend is for power in work groups to stem from the power of individuals within the groups. Leaders who know how to empower others have an edge. John Naisbett and his coresearcher Patricia Aburdene note that this megatrend makes the natural management style of most women a plus because:

- Women are usually socialized to win commitment from people rather than to give orders and apply controls.
- Women tend to adapt more naturally to the role of teacher/facilitator/coach than they do to the role of director/overseer.
- Women have historically been trained to focus on helping others achieve success, usually husbands and children.

Current Socioeconomic Profile

Some of the most dramatic changes in gender dynamics center around new roles for women, higher educational achievement, women as heads of households, and a continuing but slowly shrinking pay gap.

Occupations

Women make up 52 percent of the U.S. population and 46 percent of the workforce, but only 40 percent of all managers and less than 5 percent of top managers. While most managers, precision production workers, machine operators, and laborers are men, most clerical and service workers are women. Professionals, which include teachers and nurses as well as doctors, lawyers, and accountants, are nearly half and half, as are technical and sales workers.

Euro-American men are 35 percent of the population and 39 percent of the workforce, yet they are:

- 92 percent of senior managers in mid- to large-sized corporations (5 percent are women; 3 percent are men of all other ethnic groups)
- 82.5 percent of the Forbes 400 persons worth at least 265 million dollars
- 80 percent of Congress (91 percent of the Senate, 78 percent of the House; women made up 12 percent and male "minorities" 8 percent of Congress in 1998)
- 92 percent of state governors
- 70 percent of tenured college faculty
- 90 percent of daily newspaper editors
- 77 percent of TV news directors

According to the 1995 Glass Ceiling Commission, they "dominate just about everything but NOW and the NAACP." It is clear that they hold the most powerful positions in the economic and political arenas.

Nearly 60 percent of wives are in the workforce, raising family income by one-third on average. Women with dependent children are more likely to work than women with adult children. And women are increasingly likely to delay marriage and children in order to finish college and establish themselves in a career.

Education

Although there has traditionally been a male-female education gap, with more men getting degrees, the gap had closed for 1990 graduates, with women slightly outnumbering men. The fields in which women graduates increased the most dramatically are business (taking 47 percent of the degrees in 1990, compared to 9 percent in 1970) and science (taking 51 percent compared to 13 percent in earlier years).

The Pay Gap

In 1990, women's median weekly earnings were 70 percent of men's. The pay gap was more or less 60 to 65 percent from the 1950s to 1980. The 5 percent improvement since 1980 probably reflects men's lower pay, women's higher educational achievement, their choice of formerly male-dominated fields that pay more, and the tendency to delay having children and to take fewer years off from careers once children arrive. The pay gap is especially tough for single mothers. And more families than ever were headed by single women—16.5 percent in 1990, compared to 11 percent in 1970. Among "minority" households, the proportion of single mothers is even higher: for African Americans the figure is now 44 percent and for Latino Americans 22 percent, versus 12 percent for Asian American and Euro-American households.

On average, these women had to survive on about one-third the median income of married-couple families. Therefore, they were nearly six times as likely to live in poverty. In fact, at all ages, more women than men live in poverty. For example, women over 65 are twice as likely as older men to live in poverty. And they live longer—by about seven years on average.

MEN AND WOMEN: GROWING UP IN TWO DIFFERENT WORLDS

Women and men are much more alike than not. Most differences are probably more cultural than physical, and individual men and women vary greatly as to their degree of typically masculine or feminine traits. Still, even though girls and boys grow up side by side, they increasingly live in two different worlds. Because we as a culture and as individuals treat boys and girls, men and women, so differently, their experiences and worldviews are dramatically different.

Cultural Socialization of Girls and Boys

We raise boys and girls differently in our culture. They play differently as children. They have different values and experiences as teenagers. Since we are a patriarchal culture, boys gain more respect as they grow into men. As girls grow into women, they have more difficulty being perceived as competent leaders.

Some differences in the ways boys and girls are socialized in the American culture are shown in Table 5.1. (Note: Read the table one column at a time from the top down, since each column represents various socialization processes for each gender, not a comparison of types of experiences.)

Teenage Differences

Many of the old stereotypes and socialization patterns are still in place for teenagers of the 1990s. Peggy Orenstein's research indicates that girls routinely report feeling:

- resignation about the greater power that society grants boys
- resignation about society's acceptance of boys' greater assertiveness and power to disrupt
- pressure to emphasize appearance and minimize brains to win favor
- pressure to acquiesce in second-rate status
- fear of failure in science and math

Boys and Men: More Respect

As boys grow into men, their time and activities gain respect and tend to be viewed as important, while girls' time and activities are seen as less important. This tendency is tied to the fact that beginning with the Industrial Revolution, men went off to work they got paid for, while women stayed home and did not get paid. In our society, income is seen as an indicator of a person's importance

Table 5.1 *Process of Growing Up, by Gender*

Note: Read each column separately

Girls and Women	Boys and Men
Girls experience a less active childhood than boys.	Boys lead a more active childhood, controlling their world with physical actions.
Girls are taught to be reactive more often than proactive.	Boys are taught to be self-sufficient, autonomous, a closed system.
Girls learn to experience lines of power going from women to men; power is gained through men.	Boys learn to ignore their needs to be dependent.
Girls learn to think ahead about how people might respond, to "psych out" situations, to be "schemers."	Eventually, males begin to deny they even have dependency needs.
Girls are encouraged to believe that a man's approval is more valuable than a woman's.	Males lose touch with the feelings that accompany dependency needs, then with other feelings.
Teenage girls begin competing with each other for male attention.	Boys and men become task-oriented, compartmentalized, mechanical, and highly rational.
Girls and women learn they're expected to be selfless helpers, not have needs for great space, territorial or psychological.	As a result men become quite dependent on women as the emotional, nurturant "translators" or bridges between men and family members, men and others.
Women learn to live for and through others, to define themselves in terms of their relationships with others.	

and value. Women are expected to be respectful of men's more important responsibilities. As little boys become adults, they take on the parent role with women, serving as their protectors. Men are thus seen as competent and tend to indulge women. On the other hand, as little girls become women, they retain much of the child role, needing to be protected and indulged, and thus they are seen as less competent than men.

Girls and Women: Lower Status

Many studies, such as those by Alice Sargent and Rosalind Loring, have shown that males are considered more competent than females, at least outside the home. In one study, people were asked to evaluate an article, some copies with a woman's byline and identical copies with a man's byline. The article with the male byline was rated as better by 98 percent of the evaluators.

In another study of mixed-group conversations, 97 percent of interruptions were made by men. There were fewer interruptions when women were speaking with women or when men were speaking with men. In mixed-group studies of who does most of the talking, men talk from 58 percent to 92 percent of the time. Most women are unaware of this type of domination, perceiving that they did a fair share of the talking in 75 percent of the situations.

Men are allowed to take the lead and dominate in many subtle ways, as Deborah Tannen's research confirmed. For example, both men and women tend to regard topics introduced by women as tentative, whereas topics introduced by men are treated as material to be pursued. Men use humor to take the lead. They tend to remember and repeat jokes, using the opportunity to take center stage and gain control. Most women tend to forget jokes, rarely try to repeat them, and serve as a supportive audience, laughing at the jokes men tell.

MALE-FEMALE COMMUNICATION STYLES: HOW THEY DIFFER

As a result of their different socialization patterns, men and women interpret and relate to their environments differently. Men tend to take more initiative, which results in their being more self-protective and assertive. They tend to be more focused, future-oriented, and objective, with a greater urge to master. Other major differences in viewpoint and focus, according to Deborah Tannen's ground-breaking research, are:

Women's Focus	*Men's Focus*
• Connection	• Status
• Establish rapport	• Report information
• Cooperate	• Compete
• Play down my expertise	• Display my expertise

An awareness of these tendencies can help us to understand why men and women often see things so differently. Awareness also helps us to foresee possible misunderstandings and communication breakdowns, and in turn helps us to improve male-female relationships and to communicate more effectively. Let's explore Tannen's findings in more detail.

Connection or Status?

Women live in a world of intimacy and men in a world of status concerns. Women, in their world, focus on connecting with others via networks of supportive friends. Much of their communication is aimed at minimizing differences and building on commonalties and agreements. The ultimate goal is to attain maximum consensus and to function in relationships where people are interdependent. Men certainly have their old boy networks, but their world of status places higher priority on independence, where the purpose of much communication is on giving or taking orders. The ultimate goal is to attain more personal freedom.

Rapport Talk or Report Talk?

Women like "rapport talk" because it establishes or maintains connections with others. The focus is on feelings and includes personal thoughts, reactions to the day's events, and the details of her life. Men prefer "report talk," because it provides factual information that the listener needs to know and what's going on in the world. Women's major aim in listening is to communicate interest and caring; men's major interest is to get information. Women will frequently reveal their weaknesses, especially when the other person is feeling discouraged. The rationale: Sharing such personal information will make the other feel equal, and thus closer. Men nearly always feel that revealing a weakness would just lower their status in the other person's eyes.

Cooperative or Competitive?

Women's words and actions often revolve around giving understanding, while men's are more likely to revolve around giving advice. These tendencies are probably based on the different ways men and women measure power. Women view helping, nurturing, and supporting as measures of their power. The activities they engage in include giving praise, speaking one-on-one, and private conversations. The main arenas for these activities are the telephone, social situations, and the home. Men perceive different measures of their power, such as having information, expertise, and skills. The activities they engage in include giving information, speaking more and longer, and speaking to groups. The main arenas for these activities are the workplace and public places.

In the work arena, women tend to approach decision making in a participative way: "I cannot and should not act alone when it comes to important decisions." Men tend to feel they must act alone and must find their way without help. Women focus on mastering their jobs and increasing their skills, consulting and involving others in the process, and developing positive relationships with their peers. Men tend to focus on competition and power, hierarchy and status. Women may not stand up for their rights because they want to avoid conflict. Men are less likely to be afraid of conflict and more willing to confront issues in order to clear the air. Men are more likely to be intimidating to others, while women are more often perceived as approachable.

Women are more likely to be uncomfortable in taking the initiative. Because women tend to be more accommodating and self-sacrificing, they are also more likely to allow frustration to build. To overcome problems arising from these tendencies, women can develop assertiveness skills and habits. Men need clear facts in the communication process. They experience more difficulty in coping with unclear situations and expressing mixed feelings. To overcome these difficulties, they can get in touch with their emotions and intuitive side.

Expertise: Play It Up or Down?

A major source of power for managers, professionals, and other leaders is their expertise. Women tend to downplay their expertise, act as if they know less than they really do, and operate as one of the group or audience. Men are more apt to display their expertise and act as if they know more about their area than others in the group know. They're more likely to be comfortable taking center stage.

The male expert's main goal is to persuade, and he often firmly states his opinions as facts. In contrast, when female experts speak with males, their approach tends to be assenting, supporting, agreeing, listening, and going along. They want to emphasize similarities between themselves and listeners and to avoid showing off. Their concerns: "Have I been helpful? Do you like me?" The male experts' approach tends to be dominating, talking more, interrupting, and controlling the topic, whether they are speaking with males or females. They want to emphasize their superiority and display their expertise. Their concerns: "Have I won? Do you respect me?"

The typical female response to male experts' communication is to either agree or disagree. On the other hand, male listeners usually don't understand that the female expert's main concern is to not offend, so the males often conclude that she is either indecisive, incompetent, insecure, or all of the above. They respond by offering their own opinions and information and by setting the agenda themselves; that is, they incorrectly perceive a power vacuum and try to take over.

Support by Agreeing or Disagreeing?

Women tend to show support by agreeing with others, while men help out by disagreeing to reveal problems and provide alternatives. Women's feedback style tends to be more positive and plentiful. They keep a running feedback loop going with such responses as "mmmm, uh huh, yes, yeah." They ask questions, take turns, and give and want full attention. They usually agree, and they laugh at humorous comments. They focus on the meta-message even more than the literal message. Men give fewer listener responses. They are more silent and listen less. They are more likely to challenge statements and to focus on the literal message.

Because women listen so attentively, they may think a man's silence implies concentration on their meta-message, when in fact he may not be listening. Later she says, "But I told you all about that yesterday!" Most men challenge any statement they disagree with, so a man tends to interpret a woman's silence as consent or agreement. Later, when her actions are incompatible with her "agreement," he concludes that she is insincere or changeable: "Women!" As we begin to understand the different worlds that men and women live in, we can begin to find ways to bridge such communication gaps.

Communication Style: Tentative or Assertive?

With their focus on rapport, connection, intimacy, and playing down their expertise, women's communication styles tend to be more tentative than men's. Because the business world is accustomed to an assertive male approach to communication, women's credibility is undermined by a tentative, overly polite, uncertain, or indecisive approach. Several studies indicate that women perpetuate the lower-credibility stereotype with the following types of behavior:

- Women ask more questions, about three times as many as men on average.
- Women make more statements in a questioning tone, with a rising inflection at the end of a statement.
- Women use more tag questions; that is, brief questions added at the end of a sentence: ". . . don't you think?" ". . . okay?" " . . . you know?"
- Women lead off with a question more frequently. "You know what?" "Would you believe this?"
- Women use more qualifiers and intensifiers. Qualifiers or "hedges" include "kind of, sort of, a little bit, maybe, could be, if." Such qualifiers soften an assertive statement, but also undermine its assertiveness. Intensifiers include *really, very, incredible, fantastic, amazing,* especially when those words are emphasized. The meta-message is: "Because what I say, by itself, is not likely to convince you, I must use double force to make sure you see what I mean."

Researchers Alice H. Eagly and Chris Evatt have noted striking similarities between the conversations of women with men and the conversations of children with adults. They conclude that women tend to express their thoughts more tentatively and work harder to get someone's attention, which may in turn reflect basic power differences.

On the other hand, it's not unusual for men to carry assertiveness too far and to be perceived as overbearing or authoritarian. The most effective conversational approach for leaders is usually one that conveys both their sensitivity as well as commitment to their beliefs and statements. Both women and men become more effective when they communicate assertively, expressing their thoughts and feelings clearly but with respect for the thoughts, feelings, and rights of others.

CULTURAL BARRIERS TO WOMEN'S CAREER SUCCESS

Most career women must overcome both internal barriers and external barriers to workplace success that are rooted in the American culture. Internal barriers include self-limiting beliefs about women's abilities and roles. External barriers include the glass ceiling, inflexible work arrangements, and pay disparity.

Self-Limiting Beliefs

Traditions from the past affect today's career woman in two basic ways: (1) how she pictures herself and, therefore, the roles and behaviors she's comfortable with; and (2) what others expect of her—their preconceived notions of her abilities, traits, strengths, and weaknesses, and their resulting beliefs about proper roles and behaviors. These traditional beliefs and expectations often lead to problems with self-limiting and conflicting beliefs. Leaders who understand how such beliefs create internal barriers are in a better position to help women overcome them. Self-limiting beliefs many women still hold include:

- I should not be ambitious.
- I should wait to be asked.

- I should never parade my achievements and expertise, nor "toot my own horn."
- Women aren't supposed to be good in math, finance, computer, mechanical, technical, engineering, decision-making, and other male fields.
- I should stay out of office politics.
- I don't need to nose around in the inner workings of the company (the hierarchy, chain of command, sources of power, career paths).
- It's best to just let others have their way rather than cause a scene.
- I need to steer clear of risky ventures.
- Criticism of my work or ideas is a criticism of me.
- All I need to get ahead is to improve myself and work hard.
- If I do good work, my boss will notice and promote me.

Some women have beliefs that cause them to personalize events, criticism, and messages of others, to react emotionally, and to act out such emotions. These are beliefs typical of the powerless, regardless of gender, and usually are picked up from the women in the family and community.

Some women have difficulty understanding how upward mobility works. If they've rarely worked on teams, they may have beliefs about self-development that prevent them from recognizing the necessity of networking and teamwork. They may neglect developing a power base, and they may not see how they can meet personal goals through helping the team achieve organizational goals.

Conflicting Beliefs

Certain conflicting beliefs that can lead to fear of success tend to be unique to women and may include:

- I want a successful career, BUT Men don't want relationships with strong, achieving career women.
- I want a successful career, BUT Prince Charming may come along, sweep me off my feet, and carry me away to live happily ever after.
- I want a successful career, BUT Good wives and mothers stay home and take care of the home and kids.

The beliefs that limit women and cause conflict all stem from cultural beliefs, values, and stereotypes about women. Therefore, even when women move beyond such beliefs, they must daily cope with people who still hold similar beliefs. Building a network of supportive friends and coworkers can help career women retain a sense of balance and self-confidence as they juggle career demands with home demands. An understanding, supportive manager can make all the difference. Sometimes the manager can take the lead in helping a woman employee recognize the beliefs that may be holding her back.

Pay Inequity

Information in the current profile section of this chapter indicates that although the United States leads the world in proportion of women managers, we are not as advanced in providing pay equity. Median income for full-time women workers was only 70 percent of male workers' income in 1990, with little change since. Some argue that women generally have less training, experience, and job commitment than men, and that this accounts for the pay gap. However, the 70 percent figure represents every management level.

Women vice presidents earn only 70 percent of male vice presidents' income. It's highly unlikely that women who have made it to the vice-presidential level have less training, experience, and job commitment than their male peers. In fact, some studies indicate that most women who make it this far must have higher qualifications than their male peers.

Some analysts believe that in general women are less committed to careers than men because women take primary responsibility for raising children, which requires them to interrupt their careers. A U.S. Census Bureau study indicates that the earnings were the same for women with no work interruption as those who had at least one work interruption of six months or more since age twenty-one. The Census Bureau concludes that structural factors and discrimination, rather than discontinuous employment, explain the earnings gap. And much of the female "gain" reported in some studies actually reflects declining median male wages during the 1980s.

The Glass Ceiling

Fortune magazine's recent survey found only 19 women among 4,012 directors and highest-paid executives, or 0.5 percent, not much better than in 1978 (0.16 percent). Although the United States leads the world in percentage of women managers, the 40 percent figure can be very deceptive for the following reasons:

- 33 percent of managers were women in the 38,059 companies reporting to the EEOC in 1992.
- 25 percent of managers were women in the 200 largest companies.
- 5 percent of vice presidents are women.
- 7.5 percent of all women employees work as managers, compared to 15 percent of all male employees.
- Women managers tend to be clustered in the lower paying, entry levels of management, such as working supervisor and first-line supervisor.
- Women managers' pay lags behind men's at every level, averaging about 70 percent.
- When women move into an occupation in significant numbers, the occupation goes down in status and pay and men tend to move out of it. Conversely, if an occupation loses status and pay for other reasons, women are more likely to be hired into it.
- Women are likely to hit a glass ceiling to top-level, and even middle-level, positions. Therefore, few women are making it beyond lower-level management, and may have little hope of doing so in the near future. The women who make up the "5 percent of top managers" include women who started their own firms.

My recent survey of women managers revealed that 90 percent think the glass ceiling is the most important issue facing women managers. Virtually all who did not head their companies (80 percent) said women were underrepresented at the top in their firms. The major reason given was the reluctance of the men at the top to include women. The following barriers to the top were considered the most important ones to overcome, in the order listed:

- Top management harbors stereotypes about women, especially regarding ability to gain acceptance in a top role, level of career commitment, and decision-making ability.
- Women are often excluded from key informal gatherings where information and opinions are exchanged, deals made, and so on.
- Women's contributions and abilities are not taken as seriously as men's.
- Women have more difficulty finding mentors.
- Women don't get equal opportunities to serve on important committees and project teams.

Leaders who want to attract and retain the best-qualified women must eliminate the stereotypes, attitudes, and practices that create a glass ceiling. Even those women who don't aspire to the top prefer to stay in companies that have opened all the doors to qualified women and have helped them move up.

Two recent surveys of male and female managers of large American companies found that although women expressed a much higher probability of leaving their current employer than men, and had higher actual turnover rates, their major reason for leaving was lack of career growth opportunity or dissatisfaction with rates of progress. Effective leaders are sensitive to career women's needs and are open to helping them meet those needs.

Inflexible Working Arrangements

Women become frustrated when the demands of work and blind corporate loyalty conflict with other valuable parts of their lives and prevent their full participation in the organization. Some corporate systems and practices are designed for men whose wives handle most family responsibilities. Some are designed by men who are workaholics and expect others to be. Such expectations are unreasonable for women who can't ignore family responsibilities but are committed career professionals.

Good employees can be retained through the child-bearing years if leaders are flexible, accepting, and supportive of family needs. Asking for flexible alternatives or family benefits should not be the kiss of death to career ambitions, but it is in many companies. For example, women who take maternity leave are ten times more likely to lose their jobs than employees on other kinds of medical leave. In addition pregnant women are often transferred, demoted, harassed, or fired. "Mommy-track" and part-time work are usually the boring, low-level grunt work that blocks chances of gaining the skills required to advance professionally. These practices and attitudes must be changed if a firm wants to attract and retain career women who also become mothers.

If women are to have uninterrupted careers, rather than just jobs, they need:

- adequate maternity and family medical leave, usually much more than the three months required by law;
- help in obtaining affordable, quality child care and elder care; and
- flexible job structures and benefits, such as flextime, job sharing, part-time arrangements, contract work, and home offices.

Rather than lose competent women who go through a phase of needing more time for their small children, some companies are giving them whatever they need to do part or all of their work in a home office—fax machines, computers, car phones. Some can pack the work into three or four days instead of five. Some need to come into the office once or twice a week for meetings. Some women hire a sitter to help out while they work at home. The major advantages: They're near their children, they can handle crises and illnesses themselves, and they don't spend time and energy commuting every day.

MEN'S RESPONSES TO NEW ROLES AND EXPECTATIONS

Surveys by David Gates and Robert Speer give insight into men's reactions to new gender roles and expectations. About half of Euro-American men think they're losing influence and job advantage, while only a third of other respondents think that.

Losing Power: Personal versus Collective

Recent surveys indicate that the major dilemma men are wrestling with is the power problem—the profound difference between personal and collective power. Most men do not feel very powerful; they report that they are:

- having a harder time making a living than their fathers did;
- dealing with a boss telling them what to do; and
- trying to figure out how to be what women want: sensitive as well as strong, soft and cuddly as well as firm and "manly."

As a result, many men feel they've failed in their gender role. Men's movement leaders say the women's movement has triggered changes for men in every life area, and most haven't adjusted to it yet. Men look around them and see that they're in danger, because men are 83 percent of the homeless, 90 percent of AIDS deaths, and 94 percent of prison inmates. They're three times as likely as women to be murdered, likely to live seven years less than women, and much more likely to die of alcoholism, heart attack, or suicide.

In fact, men live in a more violent world than women. The more violent the crime, the more likely the victim is a man. Yet men aren't allowed to see themselves as victims. After all, collectively they hold the power in the United States. And if a man is Euro-American, his complicity in maintaining the patriarchy is even greater, for the simple reason that Euro-American men continue to dominate in business, government, and the professions.

Yet, because so many men feel personally powerless, some are threatened by feminism and resist changes designed to give women more collective power. Men also live with the knowledge that women are afraid of men. Decent, protective men still know that it's men who make it dangerous for women to walk city streets alone at night, men who rape and assault and beat them so that they are forever frightened. These are some of the contradictions that men must live with; there are many others.

Feeling Pressure to Perform and Pressure to Change

When men were asked, "What are the biggest pressures on men today?" answers indicated that men are feeling much pressure these days, and it's coming at them from all directions. Traditional pressures remain: to succeed in careers, to provide for families, to be strong and courageous and protective. Men also seem to feel a great deal of pressure from women to change their ways, their very natures, and they don't fully understand what's expected of them. Many don't know how to be sensitive or vulnerable and still be the strong protector, the man in control. Adding to these pressures is their sense that it's becoming harder to make a good living, the planet is being destroyed, and politics is a mess.

When males were asked, "Have men been helped or hurt by feminism?" the researchers got emphatic responses from both sides. The majority felt that feminism has generally helped both sexes by allowing us to see beyond traditional roles and stereotypes. About 25 percent were vehemently anti-feminist, blaming the movement for promoting anti-male and anti-family attitudes. Still others held that change is always a double-edged sword, and the full impact of feminism is yet to be felt.

When the researchers asked men, "What are the best and worst things about women?" replies focused on empathy, support, warmth, and nice bodies. But many revealed a deep hurt and resentment for the changing roles women have assumed. And for some, women's emotionalism is a drawback.

Unemployed men commit suicide at twice the rate of employed men. Among women, suicide has no correlation to employment status. Men's self-worth is more tied to their jobs. They often feel humiliated, violated, helpless, angry, and guilty over job loss. At all ages, men's higher suicide rates are likely to be tied to lack of emotional support systems. Men often bond by giving each other criticism, women by giving each other support.

Being Groomed for Violence

Men are more likely to be subjected to violence throughout their lives. In fact, they're trained from childhood to endure and aspire to situations that include violence. Men's advocates suggest some ways in which we subject men to violence and reward them for being violent:

- unnecessary circumcision (without anesthesia) of baby boys
- violent sports (for school boys), such as football, hockey, and boxing
- approval by girls and parents when boys excel at violent sports

- government money to schools to support violent sports and military ROTC
- the draft of young men into military service
- entertainment dollars to adult males for violent activities such as rodeos, car racing, football, boxing, ice hockey, and violent films and television programs
- media glorification of men who use guns and easy access to guns in society

Historically, the "killer male" was essential to survival, marriage, and the family. In the future, the communicative male will be essential. Men's movement author, Walter Farrell, says, "For the first time in human history, what it takes to survive as a species is compatible with what it takes to love." Some men's movement leaders say it's time for us to ask, How do we want our future to be and how do we adapt? All of us have the potential for killer-protector and for nurturer-connector. What will encourage males to develop the nurturer-connector within them? A good start is for each of us to notice when men and boys express nurturing-connecting attitudes, to openly appreciate men and boys who act in nurturing-connecting ways, and to reward them appropriately.

Experiencing Barren Father-Son Relationships

More and more men are becoming aware that the way they were raised affects their leadership style and therefore their careers, as well as every other aspect of their lives. For example, some men are beginning to talk about the lack of loving, touching, even liking in their experiences with their fathers.

Some express a very deep sadness and quite a bit of anger that their fathers had never told them that they loved them, were rarely around, and never hugged or kissed them, even when they were little kids. Along with feelings of emptiness and inadequacy because fathers didn't think their sons were "good enough" to justify their love, there was also a loss of role models: "These men just didn't know what men do. Sometimes they learned the most exaggerated male tendencies, such as adopting strict macho behavior. But they certainly didn't learn about father-child tenderness and love," says men's movement leader, Bernie Zilbergeld. The upside? These men want to avoid the same mistakes with their sons. They are trying to learn comfortable ways to express love to their own children. And they're becoming more appreciative of women's styles of relating to others and its empowering aspects.

Not Asking for Emotional Support

Father-son arm's-length relationships are just one aspect of the lack of emotional support men typically give and get from one another. Most lack the powerful tool that most women use to heal women friends—emotional support for one another. For men, stress often builds, sometimes leading to depression and even suicide.

From adolescence to old age, men are more likely than women to commit suicide. During adolescence, boys' suicide rates go from slightly less than girls' to four times as great. Psychologists speculate that during puberty, boys begin to feel intense pressure to perform, pursue, and pay—to be daring and take risks.

Boys also sense it isn't acceptable to discuss fears, anxieties, and self-doubt. In 1970, young men aged 25 to 34 committed suicide at twice the rate of young women. In 1990, it was four times the rate. Young men's suicide rate increased 26 percent, while women's decreased 33 percent.

Men older than 65 are 14.5 times more likely to commit suicide directly. They're also more likely to skip needed medication and to get inadequate nutrition and thus die through self-neglect. A husband whose wife dies is about ten times more likely to commit suicide than a wife whose husband dies. Men tend to have fewer intimate friends and family than women, so for men, the loss of love is more devastating.

An Emerging Men's Movement

Many men are confused about what's expected of them now, where the boundary lines are drawn, and how they want to be in this new era. Strong women won't put up with a dominating, dictatorial, or brutal man—but they don't want a weak man either. Men's movement leaders are filling the void with ideas about what men need and with meetings to explore the meaning of being a man today. Most participants are heterosexual, middle-class, mid-life Euro-American men.

Robert Bly, a founder of the men's movement, says the women's movement has been wonderful because it speaks of the pain women feel. Men feel a different kind of pain that the men's movement speaks to. Bly doesn't want to bring back the patriarchy, but prefers a new society, where male-female status is more equitable, rather than the "ruling father, subservient mother" hierarchy.

Long before the industrial revolution, fathers nurtured sons and taught them intimacy and emotional resilience through a community of tribal elders. When men began leaving home every day for the workplace, their sons lost this bonding. The price men have paid for running the country is to "stop feeling, stop talking, and continue swallowing our pain and our hurt and keep dying younger than we need to," according to Bly. He focuses on men's need for a father figure, especially during puberty. He speaks of the importance of male initiation rites, the warrior aspect of the male personality, and the "wild man" inside. Men must get in touch with their emotions, with how to express caring and nurturing, and with how to ask for it. Some methods of doing that include group processes, retreats, chanting, drumming, body work, and storytelling.

The men's movement is helping some men move into equitable male-female relationships by giving them permission to be vulnerable and intimate. Men who never learned to share their fear are allowed to do so. Talking about feelings is healing, and when the talk is heard compassionately, even more healing takes place. When men have their men's movement weekends to get in touch with the wild man and warrior parts of themselves, they acknowledge the past with its structure, discipline, and ritual that helped men overcome obstacles, protected women, and sustained human survival. The men's movement also helps men move on to the modern age. It encourages men to give themselves permission to ask, "Who do I really want to become? How do I want to get there?" By doing this, they can reach a deeper level of personal power.

MEN'S RESPONSES TO CHANGES IN THE WORKPLACE

In the past it was extremely unlikely that a man would ever work under a woman manager or be expected to take equal responsibility with his wife for housework or child care—as many do today. On the other hand, men say they were and are expected to do the most dangerous jobs of the society.

Dealing with Women Managers

Recent surveys have asked men what they thought of women managers. Here are some typical comments:

- They obsess on getting one small thing right, and it's blown out of proportion.
- Some are detail-oriented, not conceptual—no sense of corporate mission, the big picture.
- They're too sensitive, take things too personally.
- Some don't get down to business fast enough. First you have to spend time with them on a personal level.
- They're harder on other women. There's more pettiness or jealousy.
- When two women are at each other's throats, it ruins team spirit.
- When women bond together against men, it's demoralizing.
- Unmarried women bosses can make men nervous, especially if their work is their life, and they can work 14-hour days because they have no home life.
- They don't conceal anger or bitterness as well as men.
- We'd rather work for men. Getting a performance review from a woman is like being lectured by mother; it's very castrating.

Studies indicate that men in predominantly male workplaces are more loyal to their companies than men who work with lots of women. It's largely a matter of comfort. Men think they can be themselves around other men, so it's easier to bond. It's also a matter of status, because men attach less prestige to professions that attract a large number of women. Men in traditionally male work environments, such as manufacturing plants, are more upset at the prospect of women invading their turf than are men in hospitals, where women have long been a presence.

Meeting Career Demands

A major source of male frustration, and for some resentment and envy, is that they are trapped in the provider role. A married woman with an employed husband has some choice about work—when, whether, and how much to work. If she has children, the family may need or want the money she can earn, but her decision to stay home with the children or to work part-time will normally be admired by friends and neighbors. It will almost never be considered lazy, selfish, or inappropriate. Men say they don't have that luxury.

When men are asked if they would like to take a six-month paternity leave to be with their newborn child, nearly 80 percent say yes, if it wouldn't hurt the family economically and if their wife approved.

Men are more likely than women workers to agree to relocate to undesirable locations and to work less desirable hours. Full-time working men work 9 hours per week more in the workplace than full-time working women, but the women work about 17 hours per week more in the home. Therefore, women typically work 8 hours more per week than men.

Doing the "Worst" Jobs

Of the 25 jobs rated worst in *The American Almanac of Jobs and Salaries,* 24 are 95 to 100 percent male-occupied. Ratings are based on a combination of salary, stress, work environment, outlook, security, and physical demands. Worst jobs include truck driver, sheet-metal worker, roofer, boilermaker, lumberjack, carpenter, construction worker, football player, welder, coal miner, and ironworker. Men are expected to brave the hazards and do the dangerous, tough jobs.

- Ninety-four percent of workers who die on the job are men.
- We have one job safety inspector for every six fish and game inspectors.
- Every workday hour a construction worker in the United States loses his life.
- Only men are subject to military draft and combat requirements.

Holding the "Protector" Jobs

Men protect the innocent and helpless, the women and children, and the ability to protect generates respect. But men must cope with the dark side of the world in order to protect, and the price is a loss of innocence.

Men suffer the price of war more than women. The aftermath of war is devastating. After World War I, it was called shell shock; after Vietnam, post-traumatic stress disorder. There's also chemical warfare aftermath, such as Agent Orange and the Gulf War Syndrome. Other results cited by men's movement author, Walter Farrell, are:

- More Vietnam veterans have committed suicide since the war ended than were killed in the Vietnam War itself.
- About 20 percent of all Vietnam veterans, and 60 percent of combat veterans, were psychiatric casualties.
- In 1978, more than 400,000 Vietnam veterans were either in prison, on parole, on probation, or awaiting trial.
- In 1990, more than 20,000 Vietnam veterans were homeless in Los Angeles alone.

In cultures where men must be protectors, weakness is ridiculed. Young boys search out those with weaknesses, taunting and picking on them. Valuing men as protectors gives us police brutality, the military mentality, and gangs.

Men are expected to repress their feelings. The most widely respected cancer research cited by the National Cancer Society finds that cancer is six times more likely to occur among people who repress their feelings than among cigarette smokers.

Needing Career-Family Balance

Most men feel a rising pressure to share housework and spend time with their children, since most mothers work outside the home. In 1998, nearly two-thirds of men surveyed said they want the freedom to join women in balancing work-family conflicts during the child-raising years. Men who were surveyed in 1990 reported twice as many work-family conflicts as in 1985. Conflicts include inability to find child care during overtime hours. But few men felt they could be honest with bosses about family demands and often made up excuses such as "other meetings to attend." The message such men want: that they won't be taken off the fast track or considered marginal just because they express work-family concerns and accept family-oriented benefits.

Men need flexibility about relocating, just as women do. The days may be over when companies can insist that moving up the ladder means moving around the country. In 1994, surveyed companies reported that 45 percent of employees turned down requests to relocate, citing family ties or spouse's employment as key reasons, up from 30 percent in 1986. Companies who are retaining good employees are adapting to their needs.

SEXUAL HARASSMENT: UNDERSTAND IT AND PREVENT IT

Wherever men and women work, there is a certain amount of sexual interaction on the job. When does it become harassment? When the behavior is unwanted, unsolicited, and nonreciprocal; when it asserts a person's sex role over her or his function as a worker; or when it creates an environment that seems hostile to the employee. Sexual harassment can be about anyone of any gender or sexual orientation harassing an employee. Sexual harassment is about misuse of power, not attraction and flattery.

The Equal Employment Opportunities Commission has identified two types of sexual harassment:

1. *quid pro quo*—"I'll give you job favors for sexual favors," or "I'll take away job favors unless you give me sexual favors."
2. *hostile environment*—sexuality is discussed, displayed, or used in a way that poisons the workplace for you—this can include workplace porn or a boss who has consensual sex with your coworker, causing an unfair situation for you.

During the1990s, about 75 percent of court cases on sexual harassment were based on the hostile environment form alone, with only about 6 percent based on quid pro quo alone, and 19 percent based on both forms. Examples of sexual harassment from court cases include:

- Physical contact such as patting, stroking, hugging, kissing
- Comments on a woman's clothing, body, or appearance
- Swearing, or "dirty" jokes, pinups, pictures, graffiti, and other visual depictions that are embarrassing or degrading to most women

- Indirect harassment caused by being subjected to an environment where sexual harassment occurs even though you are not a target
- Favoritism that constitutes a hostile environment; for example, when one employee submits to sexual favors and is rewarded while others who refuse are denied promotions or benefits.

Courts have ruled that the standards of a reasonable woman (instead of the traditional "reasonable man") must be used to determine sexually offensive conduct in organizations, when the plaintiff is a woman. The Civil Rights Act of 1991 gives employees the right to jury trials and to limited punitive damages for sexual harassment—in addition to the reinstatement and back pay formerly provided. About 90 percent of sexual harassment complaints are filed by women, and in most cases the male harasser has power over the female harassee.

What Do We Need to Know about Sexual Harassment?

Sexual harassment is pervasive in the workplace. Most surveys indicate that more than half of women employees have experienced it. Sexual harassment is more about power, domination, and hostility than flirting or sexual attraction. A person who is attracted to you in a positive, respectful sense does not harass you.

Men and women view harassment differently. Men have traditionally thought that women who complain of men's sexual advances have somehow asked for it. They have attempted to label such a woman as a seductress, troublemaker, bimbo, fantasizer, frustrated wallflower, voluntary martyr, or nut case. Most women have some sense of the wide disparity between how men and women view sexual harassment and the stereotyped labels that may be pinned on them if they file a complaint. Understandably, most women have refused to file claims, believing that doing so would only make a bad situation worse.

Why Does Sexual Harassment Occur?

The most common causes of sexual harassment stem from people who:

- abuse power in trying to obtain sexual favors
- try to use sex to gain power
- use power to decrease the power of a victim by reference to her or his sexuality and gender identity
- are reacting to a personal crisis
- won't accept that an affair is over
- have a psychological or substance abuse disorder
- are confused about dealing with new gender roles in the workplace

How Do Men Feel about Sexual Harassment?

Most men feel confusion and concern over sexual harassment. They also object when they think women get away with flirting and men get punished for responding.

Confusion and Concern

Most men are confused about just where the behavioral boundaries are drawn now. At a deeper level, there is an anxiety about changing norms. Some men's movement leaders say the workplace is an easy extension of male adolescence, where boys win attention and other rewards for performing and pursuing. Many are confused by the sudden switch in rules, and some are concerned about the possibility of a woman with some ulterior motive falsely accusing them of sexual harassment.

Many men don't understand how their "girlie" calendars and pinups in the office constitute harassment. Some assume they merely make women feel inferior by comparison, and that's why they object to them. Women's advocates disagree, saying that pinups signal that sexiness is what counts in the workplace and everywhere else. Such symbols imply that women coworkers are viewed primarily as sex objects rather than fellow human beings and professionals.

The major concern men have is that women can now threaten men with a sexual harassment charge, and they could theoretically victimize men with false accusations of harassment. Companies can certainly set up procedures for investigating and handling sexual harassment complaints that would make it very difficult for men to be victimized and yet provide protection and fairness for women. Conservatives advocate throwing out sexual harassment laws. Liberals say that would be throwing out the baby (women's legitimate problems with men's sexual dominance) with the bath water (women's potential misuse of the laws).

Objections

Men's specific objections to sexual harassment policies include:

- Women still play their old sexual games, without being penalized.
- Women still buy the romance formula of the man pursuing and persisting, the women attracting and resisting, until the man overcomes her resistance.
- Women still send mixed messages, saying "no, no" when they mean "yes, yes" or "maybe."
- Women still dress and behave seductively in the office. Miniskirts, slit skirts, thin blouses, plunging necklines, heavy perfume, and flirting are all provocative. These traditional indirect female initiatives are signals to most men to take direct initiative.
- Sexual harassment laws often create a hostile environment for men, where the females are like children who must be protected by law.

Some men say that if women would communicate honestly and directly, there wouldn't be a problem. One said, "If a woman tells a man directly, with no mixed messages, that she thinks he's sexually harassing her, at least 99 percent of men will stop in that case." Actually, this is difficult for many women because they consider it direct confrontation, which they take great pains to avoid.

Men's advocates say that sexual harassment education needs to focus on the fact that for men to pursue and persist has been functional throughout history. Today, when we are struggling toward equality, it's no longer functional, at least in the workplace. Women need to understand that to attract and resist is natural because it's also been functional throughout history, but it is no longer functional in the workplace.

What Can Men Do to Avoid Problems?

Let's assume men are the ones who worry about being the harasser, although in a small percentage of cases women are the harassers. If you're a man, you can avoid being accused of sexual harassment by using these strategies:

- *Raise your awareness.* Sexual harassment is a rather complex issue, but you can learn enough to stay out of trouble.
- *Respect the word "No."* When you're at work, it's best to forget the old idea that a woman's "no" may not really mean "no," or that it merely makes the conquest more challenging and exciting.
- *Align your attitude.* Are you still harboring the belief that women are inferior? That men should be in control? If so, work on shifting your beliefs to align with current reality.
- *Support clear policies and training.* These can spell out what harassment is and how the organization will handle it. If you understand sexual harassment, and your company has clear policies about its definition and consequences, you can relax and be yourself (assuming your attitude is in line).
- *Be a role model.* Now that you're savvy about sexual harassment, help other men get it by treating coworkers with respect. For example, refer to women as women, not as "girls," "chicks," "ladies," or similar names. Don't participate in story-telling and jokes that demean women as a group. Let others know you don't want to hear or see women being referred to as sex objects.

What Can Women Do to Avoid Problems?

Women can help ease the situation by becoming aware of men's confusion and complaints and, through a greater awareness, sending clear, straight messages. Some specific recommendations for women are:

- *Avoid the sexual stereotype trap.* Women don't need to automatically and unthinkingly fall into others' expectations about their role. Sex object is one of the age-old stereotypes that women can avoid by dressing and acting in a businesslike, professional way. Check flirtatious or femme fatale tendencies at the office door.
- *Avoid sexual liaisons at work.* The objective of the office sex game is to increase the man's status with other men. This is one of the ways a man becomes "one of the boys" who make decisions about promotions and salaries. A woman may therefore increase the status of any man she has sex with and at the same time decrease her own status.
- *Say no tactfully but clearly.* Women can let men know if they don't like being called "honey," "babe," and similar names. Women can send I-messages when they say no to requests for a drink, lunch, dinner, or date: "I like you,

but I don't go out socially with business friends"; "I like you, but I never go out with married men"; "I value our relationship, but my husband would be hurt if he couldn't share the occasion"; "I like you, but I'm not comfortable with going beyond a business relationship." The underlying message is you're not interested in sexual involvement and will always say no to such overtures.

What Can Organizations and Leaders Do?

As a leader, you can use your influence to ask that the organization's policies be designed to prevent most sexual harassment and effectively handle cases that do occur. Leaders must be sure that cases are handled professionally, so that everyone's rights are protected. Preventive actions include:

- Management establishes and publicizes a strong policy that specifically describes the kinds of actions that constitute sexual harassment and sets out the consequences for offenders.
- Management suggests that if a manager-subordinate relationship becomes "serious," one party should change jobs, out of fairness to other subordinates.
- Management regularly signals that it is committed to fighting harassment.
- The firm provides training seminars designed to sensitize employees to the issue.
- The firm sets up complaint procedures and mechanisms that encourage private complaints of harassment and that bypass immediate supervisors, who are often the source of the problem.

A 1998 survey of 900 companies indicated that complaints have dropped significantly in companies that take these actions.

What Should a Harassed Employee Do?

Let's pretend the recipient of the harassment is a woman, since that's the typical pattern. A woman in business cannot afford to allow any man to persist in actions that constitute sexual harassment. To do so would signal to other men that such behavior may be condoned and would set a poor example for the entire work team. A woman need not accept such a victim role. Here are some specific steps to take.

- *Be clear.* Say no to overtures, tactfully but clearly. Mean it; give no mixed messages. Object to sexually inappropriate behavior, communication, or symbolism—again tactfully but clearly and directly.
- *Confront.* If objectionable behavior continues, tell your harasser that this behavior must stop immediately. Follow up with a memo documenting what you said and hand it to him in the presence of a witness.
- *Document.* Keep notes of what happened, when, and where. Note who, if anyone, witnessed it. Discuss the incident with any witnesses, to nail it down in their minds. Ask them to make a note about it, with a date.

- *Confide.* If you wish to keep the matter officially confidential while you try to put a stop to the behavior, tell only trusted work associates. Ask them to keep brief notes. These people can later testify on your behalf.
- *Look for a pattern.* Chances are very good that he has harassed other women. Seek out women who have worked with him. Engage in discreet, probing conversations to learn if they have been harassed. If you can establish that he has a pattern of harassment, your case is greatly strengthened.
- *Report.* If the harassment continues, find out who you should report it to, often someone in the human resources department. If you need further emotional support and advice, look for a local women's organization that provides such services.
- *Consider alternative steps.* If you don't like the way your organization handles your complaint, you can carry it further—to the EEOC or to court. Consider consulting an attorney who specializes in such cases. Local women's organizations and bar associations may recommend someone. Some courts have recently allowed class action suits where sexual harassment is common in an organization. Carefully weigh the pros and cons.
- *Be timely.* Determine the statute of limitations for reporting sexual harassment in your state. In most states you must file a claim within six months of the last occurrence.

How Should Complaints Be Resolved?

Guidelines for resolving sexual harassment complaints include:

- Take sexual harassment complaints as seriously as other grievances; investigate them as thoroughly.
- Keep such matters entirely confidential.
- Find out what the complainant wants and try to accommodate her.
- Carefully investigate. Appoint an investigative team: one man, one woman, preferably objective outsiders. Look for documentation, witnesses, confidantes, observers.

If the team cannot substantiate that sexual harassment has occurred (she says it did; he says it didn't), tell the complainant why the firm cannot take definitive action, and to report any further occurrences or any instances of retaliation. Tell the accused: the organization had a duty to investigate; he is cleared; but if another complaint is filed, it will have more serious implications.

If the team substantiates that sexual harassment has occurred, use disciplinary procedures that are similar to those used in cases of nonperformance of job duties. Normally, the first offense calls for a warning and some sensitivity training. The second offense calls for some form of punishment: no bonus, no promotion, a demotion, docked pay, temporary suspension. The third offense calls for dismissal.

Insure that no one retaliates against the complainant, no matter what the outcome.

BREAKING THROUGH GENDER BARRIERS TO CREATE WIN-WIN SUCCESSES

Barriers to career success that are often related to gender issues include lack of career planning, pay inequity, glass ceiling issues, lack of proper training, communication blocks, unequal relationships, gender stereotyping, sexual harassment, and career-family conflicts. You can personally help to overcome these barriers by being aware, becoming a role model, and helping coworkers become aware. In the process, you and your coworkers will be changing the corporate culture.

Do Career Planning

Support women and men in developing and implementing their career plans by treating all as valued individuals. Don't assume women are not as career committed as men. Encourage people to answer these questions:

- What do you want from your career?
- What goals do you want to set?
- What contributions do you want to make?
- What events might limit your career efforts in the foreseeable future?
- What sort of work life/personal life balance do you want?
- What can the company do to help?

Career planning may be blocked by self-limiting beliefs. Encourage people, especially women, to overcome self-limiting cultural beliefs. Suggest alternative self-empowering beliefs.

End Pay Inequity

Pay inequity is endemic in our workforce, a huge problem that no leader could solve alone. However, you can become aware of the ways women have been discriminated against when it comes to pay. You can analyze the compensation packages of all the employees under your influence. And you can use your influence to eliminate inequities and to make sure that women and men receive fair compensation.

Break the Glass Ceiling

Do your share to end or overcome all the ways—including those many small, hidden, or subtle ways—that the company discriminates against women.

Give Training

Women need training geared to their particular needs. They may need encouragement to acquire math, computer, technological, and other typically male skills the firm needs. Some women need some all-women classes. Studies indicate that women achieve higher levels of mastery when they take such classes without men around. Women often don't get equal opportunities to attend higher-level management training programs that prepare managers for promotion.

Communicate

Recognize the different ways women and men view the world and communicate about it. Use your knowledge to bridge the gaps. Recognize when a misunderstanding or a miscommunication is rooted in an assertiveness problem. Help to understand and resolve such problems. Relate to others in an assertive manner yourself and teach this approach to others.

Value Equal Relationships

As a role model and coach you can help men understand the dramatic shifts in male-female relationships at work and at home. Help them to see the advantages of equality in relationships; for example:

- Shared responsibility results in less stress for men because they now have help in making the decisions, earning the family income, and other responsibilities that can become burdensome and stressful.
- More authentic communication is a natural result of equality in relationships, as Madelyn Burley-Allen's research on assertiveness training indicates.
- Better relationships with women can be built as aggressive tactics are replaced with assertive ones, since women are less likely to resort to passive-aggressive responses.
- More freedom to develop and express all facets of the self grows from going beyond the limited confines of stereotyped gender traits and roles

End Gender Stereotypes

Many men feel a loss of power, are concerned about reverse discrimination, and express difficulties in accepting a woman as their manager. Help men and women drop the old role stereotypes about men's place and women's place. Take the lead in raising awareness of how such stereotypes limit men and unfairly block women. Speak up when you see people acting out the old myths and assumptions about men's and women's traits, their "place," and their limitations.

Stop Sexual Harassment

Support clear, effective company policies regarding sexual harassment. Make sure that everyone on your team understands the issues and the policies. Be a role model in the way you treat people. If complaints occur, resolve them fairly, and firmly.

Resolve Conflicts in Career and Family Demands

The core gender issues, both social and professional, can only be addressed when women and men explore and create a partnership where professional and social relationships are managed out of respect for individual talents and needs and aligned with a common vision that includes more than profit-making. Such a partnership balances caretaking and breadwinning, and views social, emotional, and spiritual needs on a par with economic responsibility. Key areas that we can bring into balance in organizations include:

- men and women having the freedom to strike a balance between work and home;
- an ability to move beyond woman as sex object and man as success object;
- a balance of men and women taking paternity leaves and maternity leaves without the company stigmatizing them; and
- organizations that provide more flexible systems and benefits for both men and women, without stigmatizing those who take advantage of them.

Most companies must make significant changes to provide the type of flexibility dual career families need. For example, in 1990 only 10 percent of firms with ten or more employees provided such direct benefits as day care or financial assistance with child care.

Promote Gender Equity in the Corporate Culture

The differences in worldviews of men and women suggest some possible difficulties for women in most organizations. They are likely to feel pressured to change their work style and leadership style, and to experience conflict between leadership and gender roles. If they do become more directive, they are more likely than men to receive negative reactions. Actually, a variety of styles can be effective if the corporate culture values and embraces gender differences.

You can recognize ways in which the corporate culture fails to reflect women's values as well as men's. Help to resolve conflicts and disadvantages this poses for women and to start changing the culture accordingly.

Value Gender Differences

For many years women minimized their differences from men and stressed equality, in order to show that they could work as effectively as men and deserve equal treatment and rewards. The men who supported them tried not to notice this most noticeable of differences. Admitting one's differences in the American workplace has traditionally meant accepting inferiority. That's because we tend to jump to the conclusion that differences are either good or bad, rather than a source of interesting possibilities. Those who are different are commonly relegated to the edge of a work group. They may be devalued personally and their contributions ignored.

Value Diverse Traits and Skills

Today's organizations, and those of the future, need a different mix of values, not only because women are present in larger numbers, but because of the ways work itself is changing in the age of the smart machine. Jobs require less muscle and motor skills and more information and people skills. While women continue to acquire many traditional male workplace skills, men must also now master things women have been taught to do well. What these are becomes clearer when we look at organizations run largely by women.

Value Diverse Beliefs and Customs

When women create their own corporate cultures by starting their own companies, researcher J. B. Rosener found that the style that emerges is more democratic and less hierarchical, reflecting these beliefs and customs:

- the basic belief that allowing everyone to contribute and to feel powerful and important is good for employees and the organization
- the tendency to share power and information
- more emphasis on collaborative decision-making
- more democratic, participative, consultative management
- more decentralization of decision-making and responsibility
- greater concern with process and fairness
- more concern with quality of outcomes, while retaining a pragmatic concern for quantitative outcomes
- less autocratic, domineering, ego-involved management
- less concern with titles and formal authority, more concern with responsibility and responsiveness
- less concern for empire building, power, and domination, and less consciousness about one's turf

Value Diverse Leadership Styles

Typical male leadership styles have stressed tasks and achievements first. Women's leadership style focuses on people first, tasks second, and so is more indirect. Rosener's studies show women leaders achieve higher quality and productivity through these strategies:

- a greater responsiveness and concern for individual feelings, ideas, opinions, ambitions, and on- and off-the-job satisfactions
- skill at enhancing other people's self-worth
- desire to get others excited about their work
- more emphasis on skills as a listener and conversationalist
- high value placed on loyalty, longevity, and interpersonal skills

This represents a balance of masculine and feminine strengths, which would work well in today's workplace.

The Bottom Line: Women and men need to work in holistic, balanced organizations that reflect the values and customs of both genders. Such organizations allow and encourage people to develop more of their talents and potentials and to use those talents to achieve personal and team goals.

Skill Builder 1—The Case of New Mother Jessica

Jessica is the mother of an 18-month-old child. She is a loan officer with Trust Bank. Jessica had resigned from her previous job because the maternity leave was inadequate for her to make the adjustment to a new baby. When she went to work for Trust Bank, it was with the understanding that it would not be a high-pressure position—no expectation that she would work overtime or make business trips. However, Jessica is beginning to feel pressure to do just that.

Jessica approaches you, her manager, to tell you that she has decided she must resign in order to find a part-time job, about three days a week. She says, "My son needs more of my time and attention just now. I need to work, and I want to work, but I have decided to give his needs top priority for the next year or two."

As Jessica's manager, what should you do?

1. Respect Jessica's wishes to leave?
2. Tell Jessica that you will lighten her workload?
3. Tell Jessica that there will be no more pressure to work overtime or travel?
4. Ask Jessica how you can help her meet her family needs and still retain her job?

Skill Builder 2—Minicases: Is This Sexual Harassment?

Do you think these actions constitute sexual harassment?

1. **A male supervisor** occasionally compliments his young assistant with remarks such as, "You ought to wear short skirts more often," and "Sit and talk to me a little longer; I'm enjoying the view."
2. **A female doctor** is discharged from a medical residency program. She tries to understand what went wrong. She remembers that she did not react favorably to a supervising professor's invitation to go out for drinks, compliments about her hair and legs, questions about her romantic life. He made comments that seemed to imply that he'd like to help her get through the program, but she sensed that going out with him would be part of the relationship. At first she tried to smile her way through these incidents. Later she gave disapproving looks or turned away. When he kept on, she finally told him one day that she was busy and abruptly walked away.
3. **A male journalist** willingly enters into a love affair with his female supervising editor. She has always rated his work performance as excellent. After a few months, he breaks off the affair. At his next performance review, the journalist receives a less-than-satisfactory rating from her.
4. **Rosita,** an advertising copywriter, has been passed over for promotion. A colleague, Hazel, got the job. Rosita is sure Hazel is having an affair with the boss. Several times in the past year, the boss has gone on business trips that called for a copywriter to go along. Each time he took Hazel instead of Rosita, even though in at least one instance Rosita was the one who had done most of the work on the account he was calling on. Rosita has heard talk from other employees. Rumor has it this is not the first affair the boss has had, nor the first time he has promoted a girlfriend.

Feedback on Skill Builder 1—The Case of New Mother Jessica

1. If Jessica is a valuable employee, this option means giving up.
2. Good, but you will probably need to do more than this.
3. Good, but you will probably need to do more than this.
4. Yes, this is the best answer. Try to find out what Jessica really needs and work with her to help her through this phase of her family obligations.

What actually happened: Jessica's manager, a career woman herself, knows that Jessica is highly effective in bringing in new customers and keeping them satisfied. She also knows that Jessica only occasionally needs to meet face-to-face with customers.

The plan they devised is for Jessica to work three to four days a week, most of those days in a home office. One day a week Jessica comes into the bank for staff meetings. The bank provides a personal computer, fax, and mobile phone for Jessica. In turn, Jessica pays a sitter to watch her child while she's working at home. This arrangement frees her up to do her work, and allows her to be available when her child needs her. It eliminates most of the costly commute time, and the mobile phone allows her to be available to customers throughout the business day, even when she's doing household errands. Five years later Jessica is still with the company, and each year she's one of the top producers. In fact, last year she won an award for being her company's top-producing loan officer nationwide.

Feedback on Skill Builder 2—Minicases: Is This Sexual Harassment?

1. *Yes.* If these comments create discomfort for the assistant, they could be viewed as creating a hostile environment for her. If the assistant cannot bring herself to confront her supervisor about the issue, she should talk with a mediator, such as a human resource representative. The supervisor should be informed about the effects of his behavior and told to stop.
2. *Yes.* What actually happened: The female doctor filed sexual harassment charges, and a highly publicized and controversial court case ensued. While the university did not admit that a hostile environment for women existed, they readmitted the female doctor and made other concessions in a settlement. Insiders speculated that the supervising professor was informally reprimanded and sexual harassment training was given to all persons involved in the residency program.
3. *Yes.* When a supervisor enters into a sexual relationship with an employee, a hostile environment is created for all the employee's coworkers. In this case, the male journalist had an unfair advantage over his coworkers. Because humans are emotional beings, it's quite possible that the performance review was not as objective as it should have been. Since the sexual relationship was entered into willingly by the male journalist, he cannot claim sexual harassment. He can claim that the performance review was not objective, but his involvement in the affair puts him in a weak position. One of them should have changed jobs.
4. *Yes.* If the boss is having an affair with one of his employees, he's creating a hostile environment for the other employees. Rosita may be able to make a case of discrimination based on sexual harassment. The boss is in a weak position if it can be shown that he is having an affair with Hazel. His position is even weaker if it can be shown that he's had affairs with other employees and has shown favoritism toward them. One of them should change jobs.

6

African American Alliances

About 12 percent of the people in the American workplace are African Americans, which accounts for about one in eight employees. People who have taken the time and effort to learn about the African American community and its values and customs say they've boosted their ability to work productively with African Americans. Those who belong to the African American culture say that studying it has helped them to better understand their heritage and their strengths.

It's important in today's workplace to develop the level of understanding needed to build good relationships when associates are from another culture—whether you are a new entry-level employee or a top executive. A major key is to learn about an associate's culture and get a feel for his or her background. The more skilled you become at interpreting an individual's actions against the backdrop of his or her culture, the greater success both of you can achieve through working together.

The African American community is made up of many elements, and, of course, no one person expresses all the values and customs discussed here. You may be tempted to use this cultural information to form new rigid categories. To be fair, stay open and flexible as you interact with individual African Americans. Deal with the unique individual, bringing into play your understanding of his or her cultural background.

You're about to get a little taste of what it's like to be an African American in the American society and workplace, and how this experience can affect interactions in the workplace. Specifically, you'll learn about these issues:

- How typical myths and stereotypes about African Americans compare with reality
- How the current situation is connected to certain historical events
- Key cultural values and customs that are important to people in this community
- Barriers to career success for African Americans and how to break through these barriers
- Assets African Americans may bring to your company and how to use those assets to create win-win successes

MYTHS AND REALITIES

Most of the myths and stereotypes about African Americans are either false or distorted, partial truths. In fact, most stem from the legacy of slavery and segregation that is unique to this American subgroup. In order to justify slavery, a practice that is quite incompatible with the American ideals of human freedom and equality, some Euro-Americans created degrading stereotypes of Africans. Such beliefs are passed along from generation to generation and die hard.

Although the proportion of Euro-Americans who hold the more extreme stereotypes is continually declining, responses to a recent survey indicate the following beliefs are still held:

1. Are Blacks more violent than Whites? Yes, 63 percent
2. Are they less intelligent? Yes, 53 percent
3. Are they more likely to prefer to live off welfare? Yes, 78 percent
4. Do they blame everyone but themselves for their problems? Yes, 57 percent
5. Do they tend to be resentful troublemakers? Yes, 51 percent

Bottom line: We have some work to do on changing these beliefs and attitudes.

Remember, myths are sayings or stories used to bind together the thoughts of a group and promote coordinated social action. Some myths are based on manipulative, hurtful lies, others on harmless little white lies, and some on powerful truths. Stereotypes are rigid, exaggerated, irrational beliefs, each associated with a mental category, such as a particular group of people. Although stereotypes aren't identical to prejudice, rigid stereotypes about people usually lead to prejudice. For example, in the past, perhaps a Euro-American observed an abused slave whose rage finally consumed him and who lashed out violently. The Euro-American began saying to others, "African American men are violent." This became a convenient stereotype, a good excuse for keeping African American men under tight rein. Euro-Americans who accepted the violent stereotype didn't notice that most African American men were not violent, even when degraded and abused. But they noted every time one was violent, and each incident confirmed their belief. This is how stereotyping works.

To get to know what it's like to be an African American, you must understand the stereotypes they deal with every time they leave the family or community circle, or turn on the television, for that matter. To bridge the divisive walls these stereotypes hold in place, you must know what they are, know other realities that balance or refute them, and move beyond myths to a more realistic view of the African American community. The goal here is to appreciate each cultural group's unique value and to strengthen our unity as one culture.

Myth #1—African Americans are more violent than others.

A cultural custom that may perpetuate this myth is African Americans' preference for using direct confrontation to resolve a conflict. Most Euro-Americans, Asian Americans, and Latino Americans prefer more indirect methods. African

American behavior is therefore often seen as hostile and militant when it's not. This is reinforced by—and reinforces—the stereotype of African Americans as prone to violence, according to the research of E. T. Hall.

The reality is that certain behavior that is considered assertive and truthful by African Americans is often interpreted by others as anger or rage about to erupt into violence. What feeds this interpretation is:

- cultural differences about how to express concerns and emotions; and
- the "violent" stereotype itself; we see what we expect to see and ignore actions that don't fit our stereotypes.

While we can prove that African American men have higher criminal arrest and conviction rates, we cannot prove that they are more violent. For one thing, violence is a subjective term. For another, many studies indicate that African American men are more likely than others to be arrested and convicted for the same type of activity, according to Marc Mauer's research.

Mauer also concluded that the United States is one of the more violent cultures of the world. More productive than using African Americans as the scapegoats for creating violence in society would be addressing violence in the media and society at large.

Myth #2—African Americans are less intelligent than others.

In the workplace and elsewhere, Euro-Americans tend to assume that even highly intelligent African Americans are less competent. Some studies indicate that when it comes to Euro-American men helping each other, the other man's ability is the determining factor, not the fact that the man is Euro-American. But when it comes to helping African American men, their ethnicity, not their ability, is the major determining factor, according to studies by F. A. Blanchard and F. J. Crosby.

The reality is that school grades and grades on the SAT exam depend more on socioeconomic status than on any other factor, including ethnicity, according to a metastudy done by the American Association of University Women (AAUW). Children from low-income households, often with no father around, and whose parents have low educational achievement, tend to make lower grades. As socioeconomic status goes up, so do grades—for African Americans, Euro-Americans, boys, girls, and all others.

Many people assume that African Americans value education less than Euro-Americans, since fewer complete high school and college. However, D. G. Solorzano's study indicates that African American high school students, and their parents, have significantly higher aspirations to achieve a college degree than Euro-Americans at the same socioeconomic level. In both groups, the higher the socioeconomic level, the higher the educational aspirations tend to be. Educational progress is improving, according to U.S. Census Bureau figures, but more work must be done in this area:

- Sixty-three percent completed high school in 1990, compared to 51 percent in 1980.
- College enrollment increased 150 percent from about 4½ percent to 11 percent, but was only about half the Euro-American rate of 21 percent.
- Educational attainment is about the same for males and females.

Myth #3—African Americans are lazy and irresponsible.

As a matter of fact, about the same proportion of African Americans as Euro-Americans hold jobs, but African American men receive only about 70 percent the pay of Euro-American men. African American women receive 62 percent as much. In spite of this wage gap, African Americans are industrious and responsible enough to get and keep jobs in down-sized mean-and-lean corporations that must be globally competitive and productive. Historically, they have done much of the hard labor that helped establish the U.S. economy. This myth goes back to the time when most slaves were treated as subhuman children, denied an education, expected to do exactly as the overseer ordered, and offered little or no reward for working harder and smarter. When some didn't act eager and committed, all were branded lazy and irresponsible.

For well-educated African Americans in corporate America, "lazy" and "incompetent" are two of the most frustrating stereotypes. Many who respond to surveys say they're permitted a much narrower range of behavioral styles to achieve their goals than their Euro-American peers, according to research by *The Wall Street Journal*. They also become quite frustrated when they perceive they must work twice as hard and must stay in a position longer than necessary—just to prove they're not lazy and incompetent and that they can handle the next assignment. This stereotype extends to the assumption by Euro-American colleagues that nearly all African Americans are incompetent to handle higher-level responsibilities. Another result: African American professionals are often assumed to be sales clerks, waiters, or other entry-level or menial workers. Social interactions that they enjoy with their colleagues at work may disappear outside the office, where coworkers often literally don't recognize them on the street when they're not in "corporate uniform."

Myth #4—They blame everyone else for their problems.

African Americans have been struggling for hundreds of years to rise up from the massive burdens of the past, including 200 years of slavery, and another 100 years of legal segregation that included barriers to well-paying corporate or government jobs. They understand that this history is still affecting their chances to build a successful career and life. While virtually all community leaders focus on self-help programs, most believe the government should help the inner-city underclass to break out of this prison that was not of their own making. This has led to the stereotype of blaming others and expecting "government handouts."

The reality is that African American progress since the civil rights laws of the 1960s has taken two distinct directions: about one-third have made fairly good progress and are part of the hardworking, tax-paying, responsible middle class. These African Americans are not stuck in a victim mentality that blames others for their difficulties. Not all have been so fortunate, however. About one-third are actually worse-off, if anything—mired down in inner-city, underclass poverty and crime—and in dire need of help. The other third are hovering somewhere between underclass and middle-class status, most of them struggling to make it on their own. Most community leaders credit the progress that has been made to the people's own bootstrap efforts in combination with civil rights laws and certain successful government programs.

The Growing Middle Class

This one-third has been moving up and out to the suburbs, earning more, sending their children to college, and living better. Findings from the 1990 census:

- By 1990, about 30 percent of all African American households had incomes of at least $35,000 (compared with 70 percent of all Euro-American households)
- 27 percent lived in the suburbs, compared to 13 percent in 1967
- 43 percent owned their homes, compared with 68 percent of Euro-Americans (the proportion has remained fairly stable for the past 20 years)
- Median home value was $50,700, compared with $80,200 for Euro-Americans

Cultural values and community support played a role in this progress. Andrew Billingsley's studies identified the following qualities typical of middle class African Americans:

- They have a reverence for learning second only to their reverence for the spiritual.
- Their origins are in the working class, generally in the previous generation— they are first-generation middle class.
- They are more dependent than independent, more employees of others than owners and managers, and have relatively little accumulated wealth.
- Their progress is a major achievement, usually based upon education, two earners, extended families, religion, and service to others.

The Growing Underclass

Back in the inner city, at the other end of the scale, is another one-third (and growing) who are still trapped in abject poverty. Their profile, according to the U.S. Census Bureau, includes these facts:

- African American median incomes have decreased 10 percent since 1970, reflecting the downward spiral of the underclass. African American families overall make only 56 percent the income that Euro-American families make.
- The poverty rate of 26 percent for all African American families has remained about the same since 1980. This compares to 10 percent for all Euro-American families.

- Fifty-seven percent of African Americans live in inner cities, and 40 percent of them are poor (double the 1960 rate), compared to 12 percent of Euro-Americans.
- About 50 percent of all African American children under age six live in poverty, most without fathers. Single mothers and older African Americans are more likely to get caught in the poverty trap than are married couples.

Virtually all African American leaders call for African Americans to work hard to improve their lot. Many self-help programs are offered by local churches. Most community leaders believe further help is needed in the form of civil rights laws and the continuation of successful government-supported programs designed to help young women avoid teenage pregnancies, help babies and young children get a good start in life, give teenagers opportunities to participate in positive skill-building activities, and teach people the job skills most needed in the workplace.

Myth #5—Many African Americans are resentful troublemakers.

This stereotype is related to the violent and blaming stereotypes. It is connected to cultural differences in confronting issues and expressing concerns, and to a history of trying to break out of imprisoning discrimination. It is also connected to inner city underclass crime.

The reality is that most people in the African American community believe in speaking up assertively, especially about perceived injustices, now that they have more political freedom to do so. The point is that expressions interpreted as resentful or troublemaking by persons outside the community may not be meant that way nor seen that way by African Americans—or there may be quite valid reasons for speaking up about unfairness.

CONNECTIONS TO THE PAST

A unique legacy of slavery and legal segregation laid the groundwork for these diehard myths and stereotypes. Of all the ethnic groups in the United States, African Americans have traditionally faced the greatest obstacles, which are built on this foundation of entrenched prejudice and discrimination, usually called racism.

Slavery

During and just after America's colonial years, about 4 million Africans were brought over and made slaves. For 250 years most Africans in this country were slaves; for 150 years they have been free. Slavery had a deep and lasting effect that is clearly present today. Slavery was the culture of our African American neighbors' great grandparents, a culture that affected every aspect of their family life, their beliefs about self and world, their hopes and expectations.

The culture of slavery also affected everyone else in the United States at the time. How could a Euro-American majority that formed a new country committed to equal human rights and freedom condone slavery? Many justified it by denying the humanity of African Americans, viewing them as subhuman and therefore not "persons who are created equal." Many viewed them as advanced apes, among the creatures that God gave man dominion over. Most Euro-American's great-grandparents inevitably handed down the interconnecting beliefs about privilege, inequality, and prejudice—by their attitudes and actions, if not by their verbal teachings. Slavery laid the foundation for the prejudice and discrimination that African Americans must cope with today—and for the resulting social problems their leaders are working to overcome.

After Slavery: Free but Segregated

Soon after the Civil War, African Americans' life in the South resembled their cousins' life in the North. The major difference was that segregation was de facto in the North and legal in the South. By the 1890s, laws provided for the "Negro's place" in neighborhoods, parks, schools, hotels, hospitals, restaurants, streetcars, theaters, and hospitals. In 1896 the Supreme Court said that such "separate but equal" segregation was constitutional. But African Americans knew that separate was never equal for them. When laws didn't keep African Americans in their "place," vigilantes did. Every year hundreds of African Americans who "stepped out of line" in some way were lynched. In 1909 the National Association for Colored People (NAACP) became the first African American organization with the ability to fight for justice in American courts, but its power was very limited.

Vignette: A Slave Family's Ordeal

Sarah was a young slave woman who worked in the cotton fields on a plantation in Georgia. She was well aware that her masters and any of his plantation bosses could force her to have sex with them. How could she refuse and still survive? She had somehow escaped this fate until recently when Mr. Jones caught her alone in the barn. Soon after, she realized she was pregnant. Her husband Jake knew something was wrong. When Sarah broke down and told him the story, he felt completely humiliated and completely powerless in this situation. Sarah gave birth to a boy, Shane. Everyone noticed what light skin and European-like features he had. Mr. Jones frowned when he heard talk about the baby. The last thing he wanted was his wife noticing a slave child that looked suspiciously like her husband. Soon Sarah and Shane were taken to the slave market to be sold. She was torn apart from her husband, parents, and all the people she knew. She never saw them again.

In this case Shane was classified as a Negro, as were all children who were determined to have "even a drop of Negro blood." Before the 1960s it was illegal for persons from "different races" to marry, yet various types of sexual union occurred. These rapes and illegal sexual unions explain why by 1930 anthropologists estimated that 75 percent of African Americans were part Euro-American.

Self-Awareness Opportunity 1—How It Feels to Be Trapped

Purpose: To find common ground with the people who have the experience of being trapped.

1. You've learned a little about the experience of African slaves in the United States. They lived constantly with at least two major dilemmas: entrapment and degradation. They were trapped in situations that provided no real personal freedom and almost no alternatives. They were told in many ways that they were inferior. Can you think of a situation in which you felt similarly trapped or degraded—physically, emotionally, or psychologically?
2. Go back to that time place. Relive the situation. What did you feel at the time? What were some of your thoughts?
3. Find common ground with the slaves of the past. Can you imagine what feelings and thoughts you might have had if you were a slave living on a southern plantation around 1800? What comes to mind? Can you imagine how all this might affect the way you would raise your children? How even your grandchildren might be affected?

When we examine the institution of slavery and its power to diminish its victims, we can understand what a powerful impact it had on all Americans. What most people don't realize is the impact that slavery and, later, legal segregation still have on today's culture and workplace. Marie Davis, an officer of the NAACP, makes the point when she speaks of her grandfather and her granddaughter. Her grandfather was born into slavery and freed at the end of the Civil War, when he was still a toddler. Slavery and the prejudice around it caused most "White people" to accept the myth that African Americans are inferior, almost another species. Marie is reminded of this when her granddaughter comes to her, crying because someone treated her cruelly—just because she's part of the African American community.

THE AFRICAN AMERICAN COMMUNITY: KEY VALUES

Seven typical core values affect how African Americans view themselves, the world, and others, as discerned from the work of several researchers, including Andrew Billingsley, M. L. Hecht, Thomas Kochman, and J. L. White. Some are rooted in African tribal values, others are rooted in the need to bond together and to find inner strength and savvy in order to survive the circumstances of slavery and segregation.

Value #1—Sharing and Interrelating

Interconnectedness, interrelatedness, sharing, and interdependence are seen as central and unifying values in the African American community. This is a prominent theme in African American life and language with respect to:

- interactive dynamics between speaker and listener,
- the power of words to control,
- ways of thinking,
- timing, and
- communication skill.

Sharing knowledge and endorsing the group are related to collectivism, which means putting family and community relationships above one's own aspirations. It's acted out in the sharing of self and material possessions within the family. It's also expressed in the call-response pattern found in meetings of church members ("Amen! Praise God!") and other groups ("Right on, Brother!").

Value #2—Expressing Personal Style and Uniqueness

Personal style is important in the way African Americans talk, walk, dress, work—in every aspect of life. This uniqueness in personal style and expression celebrates the individual. But the response of family, friends, and community is crucial to the expression. It's meaningless unless done in sync with others. For example, they may develop their own style of dancing, singing, or strutting by using both some known forms and their own improvisations. But all this is done with others. Jazz improvisation began with this custom. Musicians play a tune together, but one by one the individual musicians take the spotlight and improvise on the theme in their own way.

In contrast, American individualism refers to a more autonomous expression through personal achievement and self-reliance. It does not rely on the group in the immediate way that African American "personal style" expression does.

Value #3—Being Real and Genuine

At church and at home, African Americans are taught to face up to their circumstances, admit who they really are, and deal with life as it is. Being real and genuine is rooted in a core belief about life: The natural facts, eternal truths, wisdom of the ages, and basic precepts of survival emerge from the experiences of life. Some related common teachings, discussed in L. F. Rose's work, are:

- You can't escape nothing. You got to pay your dues. If you've been through tragedy, it must be you needed it (for personal growth).
- You cannot lie to life.
- You might as well be who you really are, and tell it like it is.
- You learn the truth through direct experience.

Older people, because of their accumulated experiences, are the reservoirs of wisdom. Authenticity and genuineness are tied to the values of personal style, assertiveness, and open emotional expression. It means African Americans tend to confront problems they care about in a direct, loud, and passionate way. This is respected when it conveys sincerity and conviction.

Value #4—Being Assertive

African Americans value standing up for personal rights and trying to achieve them without harming others. Assertiveness is a key symbol of standing up for yourself in the face of oppression and of taking charge of your own life. Coping with prejudice and discrimination often results in an assertive, determined, confrontational style.

Assertiveness is often expressed in a style that is intense, outspoken, challenging, and forward. It may be done with a loud strong voice, angry verbal arguments, threats, insults, a certain way of dressing, or the use of slang. It can range from calm debates to persuasion to intense expressions of anger.

Actions based on this value often cause misunderstandings outside the community. Others often misinterpret mere assertiveness as a form of violence, blaming, or troublemaking, linking it to those stereotypes. This assertiveness value is related to genuineness and "tellin' it like it is," but others may see it as being over-aggressive, coming on too strong, being too argumentative, or stirring up trouble. The most disturbing interpretation is, "Uh-oh, he's about to get violent."

Value #5—Expressing Feelings

African American style is more self-conspicuous, expressive, expansive, colorful, intense, assertive, aggressive, and focused on the individual than the style of most other cultures. Studies indicate that African Americans use more:

- expressive communications patterns,
- direct questions,
- public debate and argument,
- active nonverbal expression,
- emotional intensity, and
- self-presentations through boasting and bragging.

They tend to negotiate more loudly and intensely than others. When African Americans engage in public debate of any kind, their style is often high-key. They see their style as natural and sincere expressions of their thoughts and feelings, and accept others' passionate style in the spirit in which it's intended: honest engagement, participation, and expression that helps people know each other and ultimately contributes to unity. In general, African American culture allows members great freedom to express their feelings.

Value #6—Bouncing Back

Resilience and revitalization are admired and have been a key to survival. Older members are respected because they have

- been through the experiences that can only come with age.
- been "down the line," seen the comings and goings of life.
- survived the cycles of oppression, struggle, survival, backlash, and renewed struggle.

- stood the test of time and adversity, paid their dues, and transcended tragedy.
- most important, learned to "keep on keepin' on."

A lively sense of humor and spiritual beliefs support the bouncing back value.

Value #7—Not Trusting the Establishment

History has taught African Americans to distrust the establishment, to keep their own counsel, and to use caution when communicating outside the community. One result was the use of "code talk" among themselves. For example, "a bad nigger" in African American semantics has traditionally referred to a hero, someone they look up to for his or her courage and guts to stand up to "white folks."

Today, the trust gap still shows up in work relationships when African Americans use protective hesitation before they speak up or take action around Euro-Americans. They take time to think about how their words or actions might reinforce negative stereotypes or how they might make themselves vulnerable to betrayal or attack. Where they have a choice, they may avoid working with Euro-Americans. Trust can be built, but it may be a relatively slow and difficult process. One action perceived as betrayal can break the delicate new structure.

Vignette: Seeing Anew through Informed Eyes

People who have studied the African American culture learn to look for accurate interpretations of behavior. Bill tells about his experience. "I overheard an African American having a telephone conversation the other day. He got so loud and vehement that I became very uncomfortable, even though I wasn't involved. Then I remembered what I had learned about the African American culture. I looked and listened more closely. I saw that he was smiling part of the time and his body was fairly relaxed. Then I shifted my perception, opening up the possibility that he wasn't really angry and about to explode. I began to hear a very different conversation, one in which the guy was just being real and genuine, asserting his thoughts and feelings, and tellin' it like it is."

THE AFRICAN AMERICAN COMMUNITY: TYPICAL CUSTOMS

The core values of the African American community are reflected in typical customs in three major life areas: community life, family life, and personal relationships.

Customs in Community Life

The church took on a major role in advocating social change throughout the twentieth century, with ministers becoming leaders in the Civil Rights movement. The church still plays a central role in virtually every aspect of African American life, including major efforts to help the underclass break out of the shackles that keep them in poverty. Most offer an array of self-help programs.

Customs in Family Life

The sharing value is expressed in the practice of seeing relatives and close friends as an extended family, while the distrust factor results in "tough" child-rearing practices.

Extended Families

Among African Americans, the term "parents" often refers to natural parents, grandparents, and others who assume parental roles and responsibilities from time to time. Relationships with key people who are not blood relatives are considered essential to the maintenance of the family. This custom is rooted both in the African American tribal heritage and in the need to withstand the stress spawned by the slavery system and the survival struggles that are still prevalent.

Child-Rearing Practices

The strict, no-nonsense discipline used by many African American parents, sometimes seen as harsh or rigid to some Euro-Americans, is actually functional and appropriate discipline by caring parents. They see it as preparation for survival in a hostile environment, one that is prejudiced and discriminatory.

Customs in Personal Relationships

The sharing value means that most African Americans place an especially high value on trusting and helping one another. Most have one style for relating to acquaintances and a somewhat different style for relating to friends. And they may appear indifferent or uninvolved in their interactions with persons outside the community.

African American Style with Acquaintances

African Americans are guided in their communication with other African American acquaintances, such as coworkers and casual friends, by the following four types of guidelines:

1. *Follow role prescriptions.* African Americans generally pay more attention to this than Euro-Americans. Still, they place even more emphasis on individual roles that express each person's style than on conventional roles. This reflects their value for expressing personal uniqueness but within group settings for the purpose of group appreciation.
2. *Be polite.* Politeness is viewed as more an individual than societal trait, and deciding your own rules for politeness is more important to African Americans than it is to other American subcultures.
3. *Watch your words.* African Americans tend to be much more cautious about what they say to people outside the community.
4. *Support "brothers and sisters."* African Americans especially value conversations within the community that are supportive, relevant, and assertive, reflecting the cultural values of sharing and being positive.

African American Style with Friends

African Americans are likely to develop closer, more intimate friendships than do Euro-Americans. They're likely to be more intimate in discussions of school, work, religion, interests, hobbies, and physical condition. On the other hand, Euro-Americans are likely to be more revealing and intimate in discussions of love, dating, sex, and feelings about these issues. African American stress on intimacy may fall into these four types of action:

1. *Acknowledge the individual.* Allow others to express themselves through assertiveness and individual style and accomplishment. Appreciate their uniqueness and their individual expressions of who they are.

2. *Develop intimacy.* The value of sharing is achieved through talking about family and other personal topics. It includes these kinds of actions:

- giving and receiving friendly advice, leading to positive feelings
- taking specific actions to establish trust as the most crucial element of relationships
- expressing sensitivity, support, affirmation, honesty, and brotherhood or sisterhood
- accepting criticisms and requests without compromising the friendship

3. *Be supportive.* Do such things as:

- offer solutions for problems or advice on personal issues
- seek mutual understanding
- express individuality
- affirm the other person or the culture
- establish trust and intimacy

4. *Appreciate the culture.* Focus on the similarities in our beliefs, attitudes, and interests. Express pride in our common roots and the cultural background itself.

Male-Female Relationships

African American culture presumes that all women have a general sexual interest in men and are sexually assertive, so they aren't considered less respectable or more available when they express these traits. African American men are more direct in their expression of sexual interest, and the women aren't insulted by this but generally feel confident about how to reject or accept such overtures. The men are normally not offended by a rejection if it's done in good humor, only by being ignored or rejected in a degrading way.

INTEGRATING AFRICAN VALUES: THE NEW URBAN VILLAGE

A growing movement is afoot in the African American community, a movement that emphasizes African heritage and values and integrates them with American values and the American dream. A comparison of the Eurocentric and Afrocentric views, as developed by community leaders, is shown in Table 6.1 to help explain the idea. Compare the two by entire viewpoint, not belief by belief.

Regarding the ultimate goal of a Eurocentric view, many African Americans say the ultimate illusion of the American Dream is that anyone who is focused, educated, and persistent can fight his or her way to the top and enjoy the distinction of being Number One. If being Number One means others are Number Two, and so forth, then obviously everyone cannot make it.

The Urban Village Concept

This is a recent African American approach. It's grounded in the Afrocentric view but also recognizes that the Eurocentric view sets the rules of the American marketplace. A key principle of the urban village is:

It takes a village to raise a child.

The keys to success, from this urban village viewpoint, include networking, mentoring, and cooperative economics. The motto is economic empowerment. Virtually every African American church and community organization now operates some sort of economic program, from economic literacy and job training classes to community loan funds. Weekend mentoring programs focus on bringing together urban youth and business persons and other role models.

The urban village concept incorporates Afrocentric rites of passage, especially important for inner city youth, as well as the principles of Kwanzaa.

Kwanzaa

This is a way of life that honors the African heritage for the purpose of encouraging a greater sense of unity, identity, and purpose among African Americans. The seven Kwanzaa principles focus on unity, self-determination, collective work and responsibility, cooperative economics, purpose, creativity, and faith. Many of its symbols and terms come from African tradition, but it's a creation of African Americans that goes back to 1966. The Kwanzaa annual celebration takes place around the Christmas holidays.

Kwanzaa and the urban village model are approaches that recognize the realities of African American life in the American society. They are seen by many African Americans as positive, empowering, practical approaches that are grounded in the interdependence and spirituality of an Afrocentric worldview.

ISSUES IMPORTANT TO THE AFRICAN AMERICAN COMMUNITY

Here is a summary of some of the issues that are most important to the African American community.

1. Suspicions of people in other groups that most African Americans are underclass criminal types—the reality and paradox of a community with an upwardly mobile middle class but also a downwardly mobile underclass.

Table 6.1 *Comparison of Eurocentric and Afrocentric Viewpoints*

Eurocentric Viewpoint	Afrocentric Viewpoint
Survival of the fittest is a central theme.	Humans are one with nature.
Competition is a major theme in interactions with other humans and nature.	All entities experience cyclical, periodic, and inevitable changes.
Humans devise the battlefields where life is played out.	In humans, these changes are seen as life crises, which are disruptive but can be eased by group rituals of passages from one life phase to the next.
Those who accumulate the most of what costs the most are the winners, the best.	The death-rebirth cycle reflects the law of regeneration and applies to all of nature: systems become spent and must be regenerated. When one life phase ends, a new one begins.
War is the ultimate form of competition: Cold War, Star Wars, war on crime, war on drugs.	
Ultimate goal: to be #1, the symbol of achievement and worth.	Rites of passage reflect nature's cycle: separation from the old, transition to the new, and integration of old and new.

(Based on the work of George Frasier.)

2. The needs of the underclass—the desperate straits of young African American men who are into gangs, drugs, crime.
3. The stereotypes—how African Americans are assumed to be violent, criminal, less intelligent, lazy, irresponsible, incompetent, blame-shifting, resentful troublemakers.
4. Inequality in the legal system, from police harassment and brutality to greater probability of arrest, indictment, and conviction.
5. The lack of a level playing field in all life areas—poverty traps, poor schools, greater difficulty in getting loans for houses and businesses, barriers to getting and keeping good jobs, the pay gap regardless of occupation, inadequate political power.
6. The necessity of constantly dealing with the power and privilege of the Euro-American majority and being pegged at the lowest rung of the societal ladder.
7. The glass ceiling to better jobs in corporate America.
8. The need to act almost White in order to be successful in corporate America; the related need for welcoming, inclusive corporate cultures that respect all persons' ethnicity, value their differences, and appreciate their contributions.
9. Learning barriers—rooted in beliefs about inferior intelligence and resulting in lower expectations, poor schools, lower socioeconomic status, and other educational problems.

BREAKING THROUGH THE BARRIERS TO SUCCESS

You can play a role in helping African American associates overcome the "less-intelligent" stereotype that leads to lowered expectations for their skill development, promotability, and corporate success. You can also play a role in helping them break through the glass ceiling to better jobs. And, by understanding the typical career phases African Americans experience, you can learn how to support them in overcoming typical personal barriers and corporate-culture barriers at each phase.

Barrier #1—Breaking Out of Lowered Expectations: Success Cycles

A real barrier for many African Americans is the stereotype that they are less intelligent. Many have internalized this belief. All must deal with Euro-Americans in the workplace who hold this stereotype and therefore expect African Americans to be less competent learners and achievers.

You've learned that the higher the socioeconomic status of a family, the higher the grades and SAT scores of their children. Once an African American family is able to break the cycle of poverty and get good jobs, the cycle tends to stay broken for that family. The children do well in school and are therefore likely to get good jobs and earn good incomes when they grow up, which in turn increases the likelihood that their children will do well in school. Some predominantly African American schools have identified differences in the failure and success cycles. They've adopted success cycle teaching and learning strategies to help children boost their academic achievement. Some corporations have adopted these same strategies to help all employees, including African Americans, break out of failure cycles and establish success cycles.

What You Expect Is What You Get

Failure and success cycles are affected by what people expect. Here's what expectancy theory is all about: You, in your manager role, communicate in words and actions your beliefs and expectations about what a worker can achieve. If that worker values your opinion, then your expectations have a powerful impact on that person's skill development and performance. If you believe the coworker will do well, she's more likely to believe she'll do well, she's more likely to actually do well, and she's more likely to credit her success to her own ability. Belief leads to performance.

If a worker thinks you're an important person, that you have knowledge or you can make a difference, then what you expect can affect the following aspects of her performance:

- how fully she believes she can succeed
- how hard she tries
- how intensely she concentrates
- how willing she is to take reasonable risks, which is a key factor in developing self-confidence and new skills
- how she interprets her success or failure

Failure Cycle

Here's how the failure cycle works. When you believe a worker has inferior abilities and therefore you have lower expectations for him than for others, you set up a failure cycle as follows:

- You assume that he is intellectually inferior, which leads to
- His internalized belief that he is intellectually inferior, which leads to
- Low self-confidence about succeeding at intellectual tasks, which leads to
- Poor performance on intellectual tasks, which leads to
- Avoidance of intellectual tasks

We can therefore conclude that avoidance of intellectual challenge is affected by fears and self-doubt, which are rooted in a history of strong negative stereotypes that Euro-Americans hold about African American's intellectual capabilities.

When a worker expects to fail, or assumes he can't succeed, or believes "I don't have what it takes," here's what's likely to occur:

- He takes a dim view of trying again.
- He loses his motivation and often gives up trying to learn.
- He blames the failure on his own lack of ability (or aptitude and potential) rather than on inadequate or erroneous effort, which is correctable.
- By this process he, in effect, internalizes the low opinion originally held by you (or others).

What makes African Americans unique in this regard is that they are singled out for the stigma of genetic intellectual inferiority. This negative stereotype suggests to African Americans that they should understand any failure in intellectual activity as confirmation of genetic inferiority. No wonder many African Americans shy away from any situation where the rumor of inferiority might be proved true.

Success Cycle

African Americans tend to experience greater success when they engage in sports, socializing, and entertaining others because of assumptions and stereotypes that they are "innately" gifted in these areas. Many of them have established success cycles in these areas. But suppose you are an important person in an African American worker's life. Here's how you would set up a success cycle.

- You assume that she can master a job task, which leads to
- her internalized belief that she can master the job task, which leads to
- self-confidence in her ability to master the job task, which leads to
- willingness to put forth effort on the job task, which leads to
- development of job skills

If she has a failure during this process, her self-confidence allows her to see it as merely an error, not a sign of incompetence. Failure is just an opportunity to find out what doesn't work and correct it, a lesson for how to succeed next time.

Your positive beliefs and resulting expectations for her success helps her to build self-confidence. She becomes inspired and willing to put forth the effort necessary to achieve specific job goals, which leads to learning, achievement, and growth in that job area. This achievement becomes the foundation for increased self-confidence in the next cycle. The success cycle is a process in which success increases self-confidence and effort, leading to even more success, over and over in the upward spiral. It's circular and feeds back on itself, moving upward in a geometrically expanding spiral, as shown in Figure 6.1, Skill Development Cycle.

What You Can Do

Here's how you can encourage a success cycle during the various learning phases:

1. During the confidence phase. Begin with your own stereotyped beliefs, assumptions, and expectations. Get them straight. When you're sure you have a "you can" attitude, you'll know your verbal and nonverbal messages are likely to convey positive expectations.
2. During the effort phase. Take a positive attitude toward performance evaluation. Encourage African Americans to attribute their successes to ability, boosting their confidence level. Help them to see their failures as either a lack of effort or some correctable error—as a learning tool for creating success the next time around. The key question is, How can I do it differently next time?
3. During the skills development phase. Help African American employees to assume responsibility for their own performance and development, and let them know you are there as a resource person. Pay special attention to training and development, bringing in appropriate new opportunities as skills are built. Keep the cycle going.

Barrier #2—Breaking through the Glass Ceiling

Corporate America cannot yet claim a diverse workplace that looks like America as a whole. African Americans have moved into better-paying occupations but most still hit a glass ceiling at middle management levels or even below, according to government reports.

Barriers to Better Paying Occupations

Looking at the American workforce as a whole, only about 5 percent of all managers and professional persons are African American, though they are 12 percent of the population. This includes government jobs, where they have made the greatest progress, so corporate rates are even lower. Still, this is an overall increase of 52 percent since 1978.

The unemployment rate for African American men aged 20 to 24 remained higher than 20 percent well into the 1990s, more than double the rates for Euro-American men. The most common occupation for African American men is laborer, and for women, clerical. Since the 1960s, women have made better prog-

Figure 6.1   *Skill Development Cycle*

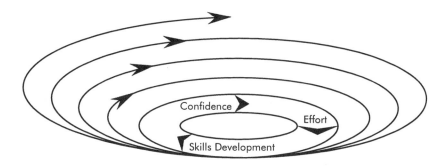

ress than men, most moving from jobs as agricultural or domestic worker to office worker. However, African American women still tend to be:

- placed into training programs for traditionally female occupations
- discouraged from attempting innovative careers
- dependent upon the public sector for employment
- kept out of better private-sector jobs by rigid ethnic barriers

External and Internal Attitudes

In American society, traditional prejudice and discrimination toward diverse groups results in a package of feelings and experiences that most members of these groups bring to the workplace. As a leader, you need to be aware of these factors that affect African Americans in a wide range of ways. Some have managed to ignore or rise above most of them. Others may have a problem in one area and none in the others. Knowing what to look for can help you give the right kind of support.

Whether your role is that of manager, team leader, or responsible coworker, you can identify ways to support African Americans in leaving stereotypes behind and focusing on developing themselves for the next job promotion. The focus may be on increasing their flexibility, networking ability, bottom-line influence, computer literacy, skill in highlighting their own strengths, and other areas relevant to their career plan.

The barriers that most African Americans face in the workplace consist of a mixture of the burdens society has imposed upon them and how that has affected them personally. Most African Americans come to the workplace with some combination of the following factors:

- a history of oppression and exclusion from the mainstream activities of society
- a sense that they're seen as different (in a negative way) from Euro-Americans

- being positioned in a one-down status
- being barred or discouraged from seeking a better position in society—or in life
- lack of equal opportunities
- as a result: lower self-concept, self-esteem, and self-confidence

These problems, and sometimes their solution attempts, have led to other problems, mentioned in surveys of African Americans who have chosen to leave their corporations:

- Hitting the glass ceiling and lack of opportunity and upward mobility.
- Feeling pressured to "act White" and to repress their ethnic identity in order to fit in, make others feel comfortable, and succeed.
- Feeling misplaced in a corporate culture where work life and social life focus only on Euro-American customs.
- Having to prove themselves, over and over again, due to being African American.
- Dealing with the assumption, and resulting stigma, that they are an "affirmative action hire."
- Coping with ethnic stereotypes.

To succeed in most corporate cultures, African Americans must learn to:

- Pay as much attention to monitoring and developing their career strategies as they do to achieving specific job goals.
- Market themselves within the company and outside of it.
- Network and establish relationships with other people in other divisions.
- Tap into the grapevine and keep up with what's going on.

Your opportunity as a leader is to encourage and support them in doing all this.

Barrier #3—Breaking through Blocks at Each Career Phase

You can help African Americans break through career blocks by understanding the career phases typical for African Americans and by giving support at each phase. African Americans who enter the corporate world typically move through several phases that might be described as:

- Entry-level phase—dealing with organizational and personal prejudice
- Adjustment and frustration phase—dealing with their own anger and frustration
- Career development phase—developing skills in conflict management and management of prejudice
- Mastery phase—refining protective hesitation and integrating core skills

Entry-Level and Adjustment Phases

Many African American applicants come to the organization with a positive but naive attitude. They usually encounter personal as well as organizational prejudice and may become angry, hostile, and culturally paranoid. If they decide to stay, they then adjust and plan their growth rather than allow anger and resentment to stifle it. They find ways to recapture their earlier positive attitude, so that negative attitudes cease to be a barrier to learning. Successful African American employees somehow retain a positive attitude even in the midst of prejudiced behaviors.

In the early phases, most African Americans have great difficulty seeing themselves in a leadership position because they've been taught that Euro-American men lead, African Americans follow. They often apologize in various ways for taking leadership or initiative or for being put in even a temporary leadership position. They may have difficulty directing Euro-American males and therefore not be as self-confident as the norm because of discomfort with empowerment. Before they become comfortable with having and using power, their walk may be less assured, their voice tone may lack authority, and their attitude may be more "May I?" than "This is what we can do." Keep in mind that typically, African Americans are required to demonstrate competence at the next level before they are promoted, whereas Euro-American males are typically promoted on the basis of their potential. Ask yourself periodically:

- Am I doing my share to see that people are treated equally?
- That everyone gets a fair chance at plum assignments and promotions?

Even when African Americans achieve the desired results, they typically must devote extra energy to ensure that the results are properly seen by the right people. This is because decision-makers often harbor negative stereotypes that prevent them from seeing such achievements.

- Are you open to seeing everyone's achievements and potential?
- Are you helping others to see clearly?

Career Development Phase

Overcoming African American mistrust of the input from Euro-Americans is still an issue for most African American employees, even at the career development stage. They may establish a one-to-one relationship with their manager, but they rarely expand this to a generalized attitude toward all Euro-Americans. During this phase, African American employees usually keep their misgivings to themselves, choosing instead to behave in a manner of trust. They need to identify and access one or more mentors.

These employees must develop and use a network of supporters, whether the members are prejudiced or not. A commitment to succeed becomes the prime goal of successful employees. By now they should understand that waiting to be adopted by a Euro-American mentor is risky, so they may need to take the initiative to locate potential people in the organization and find a mentor.

- Are you willing to be a supporter or mentor?
- Are you encouraging others to support African American colleagues?

In this phase, two of the most important job skills to be acquired are conflict management and the management of prejudice.

If African Americans can't deal with conflict constructively, they're likely to be blamed as a cause of any conflict they become embroiled in. African Americans tend as a group to be more open and straightforward in their interactions than do Euro-Americans. They typically want to confront conflict directly and solve the problem quickly. In many organizations, however, the norm is conflict avoidance. If so, the African American style will be seen as inappropriate. African Americans are more likely to confront the other person as soon as they're aware of a conflict situation. If that's inappropriate, they'll do it later in private. Euro-Americans in many corporate cultures will discuss the situation with the other person's boss, and may talk about it with others, before they'll openly confront the person involved in the conflict.

- Are you willing to accept an open, direct style of conflict resolution?

Management of prejudice involves a range of skills most African Americans must develop in order to counteract and neutralize Euro-Americans' demeaning, prejudicial actions. For example, protective hesitation is a common African American strategy for dealing with prejudice and the hostile situations it engenders. It's based on the value of distrust of the establishment. The strategy consists of deliberately hesitating before interacting or preparing to interact with Euro-Americans, in order to think about how to protect oneself from possible psychological assault or to avoid reinforcing negative stereotypes about African Americans. Such preventive hesitation involves using caution and preplanning. This behavior has been handed down from parents to children through generations and so comes naturally to many African Americans by the time they're adults. It can be especially helpful at the career development phase when the employee is being assessed for promotion potential.

- Are you willing to understand protective hesitation and to discover the underlying dynamics of prejudice and defense?

The Mastery Phase: Mutual Support

One of the key insights successful African Americans say they used in the mastery phase is that making mistakes or failing is not an option for African American managers. When they fail, they fail for the entire group of African American employees. Most have made protective hesitation a way of life in the corporation. The key to their style is preplanning, careful thought, and caution in relying on Euro-Americans as resources. Through trial and error, they take their rage and use its energy to help them achieve productive results.

- Are you willing to build trusting relationships by consistently being honest, direct, and supportive?

BUILDING ON AFRICAN AMERICAN STRENGTHS

As a leader, you need to recognize the strengths that each of your team members brings to the organization and to build on those strengths. African Americans bring many assets to the workplace that can be used in numerous ways. They can contribute to team processes, to the development of networks and business relationships that are especially valuable for the organization, and to connections with the African American marketplace.

Planning, Creating, Problem Solving

Work teams must deal with fast-paced change—by recognizing niches, developing profitable products and services, moving in on the right opportunities at the right time, solving problems, and optimizing total quality. The best work teams develop a high level of skill in generating ideas, planning, and problem solving—and they do this through synergy, creativity, and innovation as well as by discipline and application.

You can help team leaders and members recognize the value of African American strengths such as expressing personal style for the appreciation of the group, being assertive in expressing feelings and ideas, and not giving up. These traits can add to the team's strengths. Some of these traits may seem foreign to those accustomed to typical business traits and approaches.

- You can help your team realize that a different approach can sometimes score winning points, that "differentness" can be an asset.

Building Relationships

Relationships are the name of the game in the marketplace. Business is built upon networks of relationships among team members, customers, suppliers, other departments, the community, professional organizations, regulating agencies, and others. African Americans have a special advantage when they apply their tendencies toward the following: a people focus, sharing, nonverbal communication skills, and expression of feelings, as detailed in the earlier discussion of values.

For example, in team relationships, African American members can set a tone that could help the team avoid game playing and hidden agendas through focusing on the values of directness, emotional expressiveness, and sense of justice. To be most effective, expression of these values may need to be stepped down to an intensity that other team members can accept.

- You can help African Americans members develop appropriate expressions of their strengths.
- You can also provide guidance about expressing the justice and distrust values in ways that avoid the stereotype of the resentful African American or the troublemaker.

Connecting with the African American Marketplace

African Americans obviously have an inside edge in understanding other African Americans, the community, and the marketplace. They can contribute great strength to the organization in gaining African American market share. African Americans now represent over $300 billion a year in spending power, and the market is growing. These customers and business persons like to do business with companies that "look like America" and therefore include African Americans. South Africa and other African nations also represent growth market opportunities for many organizations, and African American team members provide an obvious advantage in those markets.

- You can recognize these connections and the related opportunities to apply African American employees' understanding of their own cultures and related cultures.
- You can make others aware of these connections and opportunities and use your influence to help African Americans make valuable contributions to the success of your team and your organization.

Skill Builder 1—The Case of Karla, African American Salesperson

Karla is a salesperson at Ellison's Furniture, the only African American on the small sales force of twenty people. She has been very successful in selling furniture, and she makes a good salary plus commission. During the year she has been at Ellison's she has made top salesperson of the month three times. Karla enjoys her work but feels isolated from most of her coworkers. Most of them are Euro-American men, and five are Euro-American women. The manager **Daniel** is Euro-American and has been very supportive of Karla's training, development, and sales work. He often praises her work and encourages her to "keep it up."

    Rachel is the only salesperson who has seemed willing to spend much time with Karla during coffee breaks or at lunch. While Karla doesn't think of Rachel as a close personal friend, she does view her as more than just a business colleague. She's also a friend.

    From time to time Karla has overheard comments of her coworkers about the good times they've had together at various parties and outings that they plan. She can't help thinking about the fact that she is never included. Last week, as Karla approached the employees' lounge, she heard someone saying, ". . . at Rachel's party last Saturday. . . ." Karla stopped dead in her tracks. She felt as if someone had punched her in the stomach. What a blow to discover that even her friend, her only "real work friend," had thrown a party and had excluded her.

    Daniel has noticed that during the past week Karla has seemed quieter and more withdrawn than usual. He is concerned because he believes that Karla's success as a salesperson is largely due to her outgoing, cheerful personality. When he gets a chance to talk privately with Karla, he says, "Is everything okay, Karla? You've been awfully quiet the past few days."

    Karla's best response at this point is probably to:

1. Tell all to Daniel, then continue to do excellent work, being friendly and good-natured with everyone.

2. Confront Rachel with her betrayal.
3. Resign.
4. Deny there's a problem in response to Daniel, then continue to do excellent work, being friendly and good-natured with everyone.

Daniel's best response at this point is probably to:

1. Plan some office social events that include everyone.
2. Institute a team approach to selling.
3. Hold some training seminars that focus on diversity, inclusiveness, and similar issues.
4. All of the above.

Skill Builder 2—The Case of Assistant Manager Doug

Doug is assistant manager of the Nashville branch of Angelo Shipping Company. He's been an employee there for twelve years, since he was twenty-three, and he was promoted to assistant manager a year ago. Last month Doug learned of an upcoming opening in the Atlanta headquarters and applied for it. He believes he has all the necessary qualifications for the position as well as an exemplary performance record. Although there are many African American men working as manual laborers for the company, none are full managers or executives.

John, an executive in the headquarters office, is interviewing applicants for the management position and will make a recommendation to the executive team. Of the four qualified applicants, all but Doug are Euro-American men. John, also a Euro-American, has never worked with an African American manager.

When Doug arrives for his interview with John, he's left waiting in the lobby for an hour. Then a secretary comes in and tells him that John is still interviewing another candidate and will be with him in a while. About 45 minutes later, John appears in the lobby with **Mike** of the Memphis branch. John is talking warmly with Mike, then thanks him and shakes his hand before turning to welcome Doug. They walk to John's office, where John waves toward a chair across from his desk, and Doug seats himself. John and Doug talk for about 10 to 15 minutes, mainly about how Doug feels about his current job and the company. The phone rings. John takes the call, puts his hand over the receiver, and says to Doug, "Thank you for coming in. Could you show yourself out? I must take this call." Doug was shocked, but he found his way out.

A few days later, Doug receives a telephone call from John, who tells him the executive team has selected Mike for the job. He says the executive team felt the position called for someone with Mike's experience. Later, Doug says to his friend Jan, "I know I've been with the company at least as long as Mike, and I've been employee-of-the-month here eight different times. I heard Mike has only won it twice. I don't understand how his experience could be any better than mine. What would make it better?"

Doug's best response at this point is probably to:

1. Ask for a meeting with John to discuss the decision and to clarify what he must do to earn a promotion.
2. Ask for a meeting with the executive team to discuss the decision and to clarify what he must do to earn a promotion.
3. File a complaint with the company Human Resource department.
4. Look for another job.

Skill Builder 3—The Case of Sales Rep Evelyn

Evelyn has been one of the outstanding sales representatives for McCord Foods' West Coast region for the past three years. Her immediate supervisor **Rosalie** is in a quandary about what to do. The Houston office needs a sales supervisor with just the kind of experience and qualities that Evelyn has. However, the last time an African American was transferred into a management position at the Houston office, he faced many problems. The major issue was that key customers didn't accept him and he lost a number of accounts. These accounts were with large, traditional food processing and manufacturing firms.

McCord sells spices, flavorings, and other additives to the food industry. The field is very competitive, and accounts are often won and lost on the basis of the personal relationships between sales manager, sales rep, and purchasing agent. The sales manager periodically travels with sales reps to call on major accounts and potential accounts. The sales manager also enters the picture when thorny customer problems arise.

Louis, who is head of the Houston office, was enthusiastic about Evelyn's resume until he heard that she was African American. He called Rosalie and talked over the touchy situation with her. "Maybe it wouldn't be fair to Evelyn to ask her to move all the way down here and then be faced with a no-win situation," he said.

Now Rosalie must make a decision. She knows that two other well-qualified candidates are being recommended for the position, but actually Evelyn is better suited to the job than the others. Shall she recommend Evelyn for the position? Evelyn has a child in the fourth grade, who would have to adapt to a new school and the Houston environment. If it didn't work out, Rosalie would feel responsible.

The best response for Rosalie at this point is probably to:

1. Recommend Evelyn for the position.
2. Not recommend Evelyn for the position.
3. Tell Evelyn everything and ask if she wants a chance at the position.
4. Recommend that Evelyn be given the position on a temporary, probationary basis.

Feedback on Skill Builder 1—The Case of Karla, African American Salesperson

Karla's Response: Response #1 is the best initial response. Daniel has been supportive and may be able to improve the situation. Doing excellent work and being friendly is always a productive response, though other measures are often needed. It's always wise to generate other job options, for many reasons. In this case, Rachel needs other options for locating a fair and equitable job situation. Response #2 is problematic, since Rachel is under no obligation to socialize with Karla. Friendships and personal "chemistry" cannot be forced.

Daniel's Response: Response #4 is a multi-pronged approach that will probably work best in this type of situation. Of course, Daniel may face some constraints—budgetary, top management acceptance, employee acceptance—but the more workable strategies he can implement, the better his chances of bringing about positive change.

Feedback on Skill Builder 2—The Case of Assistant Manager Doug

Response #1 is not ideal, because John has already shown that he is neither open nor fair.

Response #2 is probably the best action at this point. Doug should try to get an agreement from the executive team that if he achieves certain measurable goals and standards, he will receive a promotion within a certain time frame. It's probably a good idea to report the incident to a Human Resource person in order to get it on record—and to postpone actually filing a complaint with the department until he gives the company another chance to treat him fairly. While it is always wise to generate other job options, it's probably best to explore possibilities with the present company before actually changing jobs.

Feedback on Skill Builder 3—The Case of Sales Rep Evelyn

Response #3 is probably the best option. Instead of "playing God" with employees' lives, managers should treat them as intelligent adults. Most likely, Evelyn can handle stereotypes, prejudices, and discrimination and has been doing so her entire life. Give her the opportunity to assess the advantages and disadvantages of the situation and make her own decision. Evelyn may or may not want this position under any circumstances. Suppose, however, that Evelyn is given full information about the job situation and wants to be recommended. One of the options could be a trial run that would allow her to retain her current home and school situation until she's ready to make a more permanent decision.

7

Asian American Associates

You're likely to have many Asian American colleagues if you live on the East or West Coast or certain urban areas of the country. Only 3.5 percent of Americans are Asian American, but they're clustered in certain cities and regions. People who have taken the time and effort to learn something about Asian Americans, their values and issues, say they've boosted their ability to work productively with these associates.

To help you better understand what it's like to be an Asian American, and therefore to build more empathic relationships, you'll learn in this chapter:

- How typical myths and stereotypes about Asian Americans compare with current reality
- How the current situation has evolved from past history
- The major Asian American communities and the key cultural values, customs, and issues that are important to them
- How you can help Asian American employees overcome barriers to career success
- How you can help your organization build upon Asian American strengths

The best use of this information about Asian American cultural patterns is (1) to help you understand how they might view situations or what their actions might mean, (2) to figure out what questions you might ask in getting to know them better, (3) to avoid forming rigid ideas and new stereotypes based on this information, and (4) to be open and flexible as you interact with individual Asian Americans.

MYTHS AND REALITIES

Most of the myths and stereotypes about Asian Americans are either false or distorted, partial truths. In fact, most stem from the belief that Asian Americans are too "foreign" to really understand. The following myths are based upon the research of Ronald Takaki and others.

Myth #1—Asian Americans tend to retain their foreign ways, so it's difficult for them to fit in.

Asian Americans have traditionally coped with the exotic, perpetual foreigner myth because Euro-Americans have seen them as

- immigrants who represent a small segment of the American population.
- people of color who bear distinct physical differences.
- people from a culture and lifestyle that is just too different for comfort.
- people who can never be completely absorbed into American society and politics.

Discriminatory laws and practices have reinforced this separateness. In fact, one-fourth to one-half of the members of most Asian American groups were born in this country. Many are even third- or fourth-generation Americans. Further, those bilingual Asian Americans who have recently learned English and still have heavy accents can usually be understood by people who are willing to listen for the rhythm and pattern of their speech. Asian cultures can offer much ancient wisdom to those who are open to different ways of viewing situations. Incorporating different ideas can lead to discovery of new business opportunities and problem solutions.

Myth #2—Asian Americans are unemotional and inscrutable.

Euro-Americans often complain that they can't tell what Asian Americans are thinking or feeling, so they're labeled as unemotional and inscrutable. In fact, Asian Americans experience the same emotions as other people. Their cultural values call for self-discipline in expressing emotions and for indirectness in communicating.

Myth #3—Asian Americans are too passive and polite to be good managers.

This is a career-bashing myth with hardly a kernel of truth. One implication is that they're polite and therefore lack the conviction and backbone to stand up to the heat a supervisor must take. Another implication is that they're compliant, therefore passive, which means they don't have the ambition it takes to move up the competitive corporate ladder. The behavior of Asian Americans is often misread by people who don't understand their cultural values and training.

In their own countries, Asians are obviously the business and political leaders. In the United States, Asian American small business owners have established an impressive success record, overcoming great odds. Even women who work on assembly lines can be surprisingly assertive and persistent beneath their "mask" of compliance and cooperation, according to recent studies.

Myth #4—Asian Americans have learned how to make it in American society by working hard and being thrifty.

This model minority myth is true, as far as it goes. On the up side, it makes Asian Americans more acceptable in business and in society in general. But it ignores the complexities and difficulties of their situation, according to Karen Hossfeld's research. The downside is:

- The "hard worker" image sets up unrealistic expectations that they'll gladly make major sacrifices for their work, work for less than Euro-Americans, work harder, and work longer hours.
- It's easy to assume that such a model minority group has no pressing social or political issues that we must address.
- It causes undue resentment from other minorities.

The reality is that Asian Americans pay a high price for "making it." As a family unit, they work harder and longer for less pay than Euro-Americans, and they get less help from society.

Myth #5—Asian Americans can't seem to master English grammar and pronunciation—they have communication problems.

Asian languages are about as different from English as languages can be. Therefore, becoming fluent and proficient is a long, arduous process for Asian American immigrants. Most work diligently and continually to improve their communication skills. In general, they believe in mastering English, and nearly all believe that English should be the only official U.S. language. The reality is that virtually all Asian Americans who here born in the United States are fluent in English and in fact may not be fluent in their ancestral Asian language.

Myth #6—Asian Americans are good in technical occupations, but they don't have creative or leadership potential.

This myth is a faulty distortion that creates a huge barrier to career mobility. It's related to the idea that Asian Americans are technical "coolies," computer nerds, or memorization whizzes, great at crunching numbers but short on people skills and creativity. It stems from the tendency of immigrant students with some language deficiencies to focus on what they can do well, which often includes mastering quantitative tasks and usually includes diligently studying, practicing, and memorizing. As a group, Asian Americans do score better than any other group on math tests. But as a matter of fact, Asian American students demonstrate a broad range of aptitudes and talents. Those who were born in the United States do not have the language problem and are likely to gravitate to a wider range of career areas.

Myth #7—Asian Americans know about all things Asian.

Some Euro-American business persons tend to look upon the company's "token" Asian Americans as the resident experts on all things Asian American—and

Asian, for that matter. This assumes they know everything about the country their parents or grandparents immigrated from, its culture, the adaptation of its people to the American culture, and which local restaurants are the best source of its cuisine. For some Asian Americans, this stereotype has become a pet peeve. The reality is that many of them were born in the United States, are more American than Asian, and may be no more of an expert on "things Asian" than the average American.

CONNECTIONS TO THE PAST

Americans have always valued the ideals of equal opportunity and fairness, but reality has not always matched that ideal. From the beginning, Asian immigrants have faced many obstacles to acceptance in America. Recent generations are more Americanized and face fewer barriers to success.

The Chinese: Gold, Railroads, and Exclusion

The first group of Asian Americans were men from China who came during the 1850s California gold rush. Instead of gold, most found work building railroads and doing laundry. There was overt prejudice against them from the beginning:

- The 1882 Chinese Exclusion Act prohibited further immigration until the 1900s.
- Alien Land Acts and restrictive deeds barred them from owning land.
- They were legally classified as "nonwhite," catching them in the legal segregation net cast around African Americans.
- State laws prohibited intermarriage.
- School segregation was practiced in districts that had significant numbers of Asians.
- Public theaters, pools, and beaches were often off-limits to them.

The Japanese: Migration, War, and Concentration Camps

The Japanese painfully discovered that their achievements in America did not lead to acceptance when, during World War II, they were placed in concentration camps as "potential spies." They lost everything except what they carried with them, and of course they could not earn income during the two or three years they were imprisoned. To Japanese Americans, this wartime exile and incarceration was and still is the central event of their history, making it unique among Asian Americans. In 1988, the U.S. government formally apologized to these families and began paying reparations.

Civil Rights Laws of the 1960s

Most of the discriminatory laws were in force until the 1960s. The new Civil Rights laws had a great impact on Asian Americans' options. Higher education opened up to them, and streams of second-generation students poured in. Most still choose "safe" majors in the professions, such as accounting, education, dentistry, or pharmacy, because employment patterns tend to be less discriminatory in professions in which credentials open doors, and because private practice can be lucrative, especially within one's minority community.

Generation Gaps

To understand significant differences among the Asian Americans you meet, you must understand the different experiences and attitudes of various generations:

First Generation

Those who immigrated from China or Japan in the early years of this century were isolated in their ethnic communities and retain their old cultural ways.

Second Generation

Those born in the 1940s to 1960s are more Americanized but still strongly affected by their Asian cultural heritage. Now mature and aging adults, they're primarily a low-profile group.

Third and Fourth Generation

Those born during or after the 1970s are even more Americanized than their parents and grandparents, but they're still distinctly Asian in some ways. Most are definitely more American than Asian. Some are entering occupations and fields once considered closed to them, such as advertising, the performing arts, journalism, and broadcasting.

WHO ARE THE ASIAN AMERICANS?

The seven major groups of Asian Americans have many common cultural threads. Many of their values and customs are similar, although each culture has its unique aspects. Each group came to the United States under somewhat different circumstances and therefore each has faced different situations. Here are the countries of origin of this 3.5 percent of the U.S. population:

China	24%
Philippines	20%
Southeast Asia	16%
Japan	12%
India	12%
Korea	12%
Other country of origin	4%

The following facts from the U.S. Census Bureau provide a general demographic picture of Asian Americans:

- *They doubled in number* between 1980 and 1990, due primarily to immigration.
- *Over half live in the West* (54 percent).

- *Many are foreign born* (66 percent), with Southeast Asian Americans having the highest percentage and Japanese Americans the lowest.
- *Some are recent immigrants.* 38 percent entered the United States during the 1980s, mostly as refugees; most live in the West, especially in California.
- *They live longer than Euro-Americans,* whose mean life expectancy is 76, compared to 80 for Japanese Americans and Chinese Americans.
- *They have less crime.* FBI reports indicate that arrest rates of Asian Americans for serious crimes between 1980 and 1985 were well below their proportion in the population. Since the 1930s, Asian Americans in California have had lower rates of crime and delinquency than the general population.
- *They're relatively young.* 30 is the median age, compared with the national median of 33.
- *Most groups have larger families,* an average of 3.8 persons compared to 3.2 for all U.S. families.
- *Most speak another language.* 65 percent speak another language at home, 56 percent don't speak English well, and 35 percent are linguistically isolated (virtually cannot communicate in English).

Education: Higher Achievement Than Most

The Asian American devotion to education results in high educational achievement.

Asian Americans Have High Education Levels

They have more high school graduates then average Americans: 78 percent, compared to 75 percent nationally. Averages range from 88 percent for Japanese Americans to 31 percent for Hmong. They also have more college degrees: 38 percent, compared with 20 percent for all Americans.

Asian Indian Americans Are the Best Educated

Americans from India, or of Indian ancestry, are the most highly educated group in the U.S. Over 65 percent of the men and half the women have degrees, compared to 23 and 18 percent for all Americans. Nearly all speak English, and few have language barriers, which is related to India's history as a British colony. More than 72 percent of them have jobs, compared with 65 percent of all Americans. Nearly half of all foreign-born Asian Indian workers are managers and professionals. This is twice the proportion for all Americans, which is 24 percent. They have the highest per capita income among all Americans, $18,000, after Japanese Americans. Many are part of an Indian "brain drain" that occurred during the 1980s and was caused when India trained more professionals than its businesses could profitably employ.

Pay Doesn't Match Educational Levels

- *Asian Americans have more workers:* 67 percent, compared with 65 percent for all Americans. Groups with an employment rate higher than 70 percent are the Filipino Americans, Asian Indian Americans, and Thai Americans. Twenty percent of Asian American families contain three or more workers, compared with 13 percent nationally.

- *Asian Americans hold more high-status jobs:* 31 percent are managers and professionals, compared to 26 percent nationally, due primarily to higher education levels and the tendency to start their own business or practice.
- *Asian American pay is below average:* $13,806 per capita (mean income per person) compared to $14,143 for all Americans. Because more of their family members work, the median income of Asian American families is $41,583, compared to $35,225 nationally. Still they make only 70 cents for every dollar Euro-American men make, on average.
- *Their poverty rate is slightly higher:* 14 percent, compared to 13 percent nationally. Southeast Asian poverty rates ranged from 35 to 64 percent, with Chinese American and Korean American rates at 14 percent, and rates for Filipino Americans, Japanese Americans, and Asian Indian Americans under 10 percent.
- *Japanese Americans are the most affluent:* By 1990 Japanese Americans were the most successful of any Asian American group by most standards. Their educational attainment runs a close second to the top U.S. achievers, Asian Indian Americans. They have the highest per capita income of any Asian American group, at $19,400, well above the national median of $14,100. The poverty rate of 7 percent is near the lowest.

A Unique Group: The Hmong

The Hmong Hill Tribes from Laos have the greatest challenges. As an aftermath of the Vietnam War, the United States has accepted many war refugees from Vietnam, Cambodia, and Laos. About 60,000 belonged to the Hmong hill tribes of Laos, who lived as semi-nomadic farmers, clearing jungle areas to plant crops. They have a strong family and clan system and their families are traditionally large, so they average 6.6 children, the highest birth rate of any U.S. group. They had no experience with a written language until 1960 when missionaries came to Laos. Most speak little or no English and have the lowest educational achievement of any U.S. group. Adapting to a high-tech workplace that's based upon quite sophisticated uses of written information is a major challenge. Only 29 percent of Hmong Americans had jobs in 1990, their average income was $2,600, and most depended on public assistance to survive.

ASIAN AMERICAN CULTURES: COMMON THREADS AND CORE VALUES

Asian cultures have many common threads in the tapestries of their societies, according to such researchers as Esther Chow, Lorraine Dong, Karen Hossfeld, Philip Harris, Robert Moran, Ronald Takaki, and William Wei. For example, Asians generally put group concerns above their own desires and put family and group harmony above all else. Asians tend to accept status differences within a social hierarchy, and they revere education for its own sake. They can communicate without being explicit because they live in tight-knit cultures where people are on the same wavelength, and they often communicate indirectly in an effort to maintain harmony.

Chinese, Japanese, and Koreans are physically and culturally very similar, with many of their cultural similarities stemming from Confucianist focus on putting family, community, and patriotic duties above personal desires. Beliefs of other major Asian religions, such as Buddhism and Hinduism, tend to foster similar group values. The Vietnamese culture has been strongly influenced by the Chinese culture. India has its own culture, with major influences from the Hindu, Buddhist, and Islamic religions and the former rule of the British. The Philippine culture was influenced by the 300-year rule of Spain with its Catholicism. Even so, both India and the Philippines reflect many common Asian values and cultural patterns.

Value #1—Putting Group Concerns before Individual Desires

All Asian cultures are collective, depending a great deal upon each other within close-knit families, extended families, and community groups. Members are expected to honor the group by:

- Seeing the group as the most important part of society
- Focusing on a group of people who are working toward a goal as more important than focusing on each one as individuals
- Valuing group recognition and group reward above individual reward
- Emphasizing a sense of belonging to the group and security within the group
- Extending tight, strong family ties to other relatives and close friends
- Placing central emphasis on a strong network of social relationships
- Making public service a moral responsibility
- Viewing personal saving and resource conservation as more important than consumption
- Placing fairness with the group and community above gaining wealth

Value #2—Promoting Group Harmony

Putting the group first naturally leads to the value of putting group harmony first. Customary ways of achieving this goal include the following beliefs and actions.

Disciplined Emotional Expression

Most Asians are taught that harsh words, scolding, temper flares, and similar emotional expressions will cause the other person to lose face and also to lose respect for the speaker. For example, to show your anger is seen as:

- the same as admitting loss of control
- a lapse in training and self-discipline
- a loss of face for you

As a result, in face-to-face relations, Asian Americans tend to maintain the amenities and cordialities, no matter how they are feeling. All this is true unless things have gone too far—and it's almost impossible for people outside the culture to estimate when things are about to go too far. Only insiders are likely to recognize these subtle signals.

Avoidance of Open Conflict

This includes avoiding personal confrontations, as well as not saying no, not giving others unpleasant messages, or doing so in a very indirect way.

Modesty

Everyone, especially females, is expected to show modesty by:

- Avoiding statements that can be perceived as boasting or self-congratulatory, as in the overuse of the words "I," "me," and "mine."
- Being reticent to talk about themselves or their own accomplishments.
- Not drawing attention to themselves.
- Responding to compliments by belittling their abilities.

Self-Effacement

It's often appropriate for persons to act as if they are of lower status in order to show selfless humility and give honor to others. Highly respected people often assume an attitude of self-effacement in social and business contacts. Putting yourself forward is usually viewed as proud arrogance and invites scorn. To make a joke at someone else's expense and to cause embarrassment is highly resented in business. Also, "good" businesspersons place a higher value on allowing others in the group or community to save face and therefore preserve harmony than on achieving higher sales and profits.

Focusing on Others

The individual is expected to be extremely sensitivity to others' feelings and wishes, giving second place to his or her own feelings and wishes.

Conforming

When persons are flexible, defer to others, or comply with the wishes of others in order to maintain harmony, they show maturity and self-discipline. Asian cultures expect people to conform to the wishes of those of higher status. This maintains harmony even when there is internal conflict between what persons want and what they think they should do. The key thing to remember: When an Asian American gives in to another person, it's not necessarily a passive or weak gesture, but is often a sign of tolerance, self-control, flexibility, and maturity.

Giving Back

Mature persons are sensitive to the need to give to others who have given to them, to pay back devotion, generosity, and favors.

Value #3—Accepting Status Difference: The Hierarchy

Protocol, rank, and status are important parts of all Asian cultures, ranging from the extremes of the Hindu caste system to the Confucian system, which states:

- Everyone is expected to honor certain binding obligations to immediate family, relatives, clan, province, and state.
- Society should be structured to minimize deviations from these obligations.
- Women are subordinate to men, sons to fathers, younger brothers to older brothers, wives to husbands, and everyone to the state.
- Elders are especially respected, even revered, pampered, and appeased. Their every wish and desire is catered to whenever possible. Every home, no matter how poor, provides the best room for the honored grandparent

Across all religions and cultures, the Asian belief in hierarchy includes:

- Valuing a sense of order, propriety, and appropriate behavior between persons of varying status.
- Basing status on occupational position, education, wealth, and family background.

Typical Customs or Behaviors

Typical customs that reflect the status value include:

- When Asians meet someone, they quickly establish whether that person has higher status. If so, they show proper deference.
- They address people by their title and first name in all but informal or family situations.
- They respect seniority and the elderly.
- Parents prefer sons to daughters. Daughters go to their husband's family and so lose the value they could bring to their own parents. As children are growing up, parents must protect daughters and can give sons more social freedom.
- Parents must arrange marriages for their children, aiming for partners with as high status as possible.

Respect for the Manager's Status

In the United States, it's appropriate at certain times for managers to roll up their sleeves and work alongside others to get things done. Pitching in when there's an emergency is a sign you're a good sport, one of the guys. Many Asian Americans, especially the immigrants, would interpret it this way:

- This is an insult to me as a worker.
- You're implying that I can't get the work done the way I should.
- Such work is below your station as a manager.
- I can't have the same respect for you now.
- If you do this again, or do it insensitively, I'll really lose face. I may have to resign.

Value #4—Revering Education

Education is revered in Asian cultures, especially where there's a strong Confucian influence. Being educated is a high moral virtue and is a rigid prerequisite for moving up from lower to higher political and social standing. Scholars are given the greatest respect, have the highest rank, and are often among the most powerful and wealthy in society. Asian Americans therefore

- value education as a moral virtue;
- value position in society, and see education as the best way to achieve a good position and some financial security; and
- consider education an investment in family status.

Value #5—Communicating Vaguely, Indirectly, and Silently

Asian Americans may sometimes seem vague, indirect, or strangely silent.

Being Vague

In close-knit cultures, such as Japan, where everyone grew up in the same homogeneous society, people can speak a sort of "shorthand" and be understood. In fact, being direct and making specific references may be seen as insulting. Being vague, indirect, or ambiguous is valued. As a result, people will often leave their sentences unfinished so listeners may mentally form the conclusion for themselves. After all, they know what the speaker is getting at—to "go on and on" might insult the listeners' intelligence. When these cultural styles carry over into the U.S. workplace, coworkers can become quite confused.

Being Indirect

You've learned that being indirect is an Asian way of avoiding open conflict and preserving harmony. Pay special attention to situations in which an Asian American associate may need to say no, confront an issue, or deliver some other unpleasant message. Remember that even when that person is trying to be direct in the Asian way, you may still consider it indirect. And their indirect message may be so subtle that you don't get it.

Saying No

To say no is an insult, could damage feelings and disrupt harmony, and is therefore bad manners. Asian Americans may say yes, meaning "I heard you," and then go about doing the opposite with little sense of breaking an agreement. When an Asian American man, for example, disagrees with you, says no, or conveys unwelcome information, he may do it so indirectly and subtly that you won't know it's been done. Later, if his actions reflect a lack of agreement, you may conclude that he was not only unemotional and inscrutable, but perhaps evasive, sneaky, dishonest, or even corrupt. Probably, he was merely being polite.

- You can help by understanding these vague or indirect communication patterns and asking your Asian American associates to fill in the blanks.

Not Interrupting

If you were listening to a friend and didn't understand something she said, would you wait, expressionless, until she had finished a long explanation, expecting her to take responsibility for your understanding? Probably not. But if all the people you know believe that's the way to listen, then such behavior would be normal. For many Asian Americans, not interrupting is basic courtesy that is essential for conversations to proceed.

- You can help by encouraging Asian American associates to interrupt you in order to ask questions if they don't understand you

Keeping Longer Silences

When you finish speaking, how do you react when your listener is silent for a minute or more? Most Americans view such long silences as extremely uncomfortable and feel compelled to fill them in with comments or questions. For many Asian Americans, such as Japanese Americans, a few moments of quiet contemplation after listening may be essential, and comments are distracting.

- You can help by becoming comfortable with such silences and refraining from filling such moments with talk.

Other Customs

Other behavioral customs include:

- It's okay to call for someone to come to you by holding out your arm with your palm down, using a scratching movement. To turn your palm up and use the fingers to motion, which is typical in the United States, is considered rude.
- Meals are often more ritualistic, communal, and time consuming than in the United States. The talk is considered more important than the food.
- Colors and numbers often have different meanings than they have in the United States. For example, white may be used for mourning.

The Filipino Culture: Asian with a Latino Flavor

The Filipino culture is primarily an Asian culture with a strong Latino flavor. Many Filipinos have Spanish surnames and most are Catholic because the Spanish ruled the Philippines for 300 years. American rule for the next 50 years established English as a major language. Since their independence in 1950, a unique Filipino culture has been developing. In addition to the typical Asian values, these Latino-type values are also important:

- Importance of saving face, avoiding shame, and maintaining face, honor, and self-esteem—all have a special Latino flavor.
- Personalistic view of the universe and fatalistic view of the future, as explained in the Latino American chapter.

- Very flexible sense of time in social situations, which may begin an hour or more after the appointed time.

The Korean Culture: Some Unique Viewpoints

Korean Americans hold most of the same values as other Asian Americans. Two distinct concepts in the Korean culture that you should know about are *kibun* and nonpersons.

Kibun

Kibun refers to inner feelings. The closest English translation of *kibun* may be "mood." When your *kibun* is good, you function smoothly and easily and feel great. If your *kibun* is upset or bad, you may bring transactions to an abrupt stop and feel depressed, awful. Part of the intention of business people is to enhance the *kibun* of all parties. To damage the *kibun* could end the relationship and even create enemies. Class or status is also involved, with those of lower status doing more nurturing of the *kibun* of the higher status.

Nonpersons

Koreans who fail to follow the basic rules of social interaction are viewed as nonpersons. Foreigners, in a certain sense and to a certain extent, are considered nonpersons. Koreans show very little concern for nonpersons' feelings, their comfort, or whether they live or die. Nonpersons are simply not worthy of much consideration. Korean Americans obviously must modify this attitude in order to function effectively in a diverse society; however, some variation of it probably survives and affects relationships.

KEY ISSUES IMPORTANT TO ASIAN AMERICANS

Some of the key issues you should know about because they're important to many Asian Americans include (1) complications of the Model Minority stereotype, (2) changing male-female dynamics and differences, and (3) educational concerns.

Issue #1—Model Minority: A Mixed Blessing

In the 1960s, reporters began writing about the high education attainment, high median family income, low crime rates, and absence of juvenile delinquency and mental health problems among Asian Americans. Proponents of this model minority stereotype often ask, "Why can't African Americans succeed like this? (and not bother us)." This stereotype has been a mixed blessing for Asian Americans: it carries with it advantages and disadvantages.

Model Minority Advantages

The main advantages to Asian Americans of the Model Minority stereotype are that it showcases their cultural strengths, especially strengths connected with their success in running small family businesses.

Cultural Strengths

The Model Minority image eventually increased job opportunities for Asian Americans. Business managers say they favor hiring Asian Americans because they:

- work hard and are productive
- invest in higher education, even at the cost of financial hardship
- are willing to work unusually long hours
- maintain a frugal lifestyle
- persevere in their goals and their work projects
- identify with the American Dream of hard work leading to a better life
- save small amounts of money until they can invest in a small business
- use frugal strategies to keep their businesses going

Small Business Ownership

A key aspect of the Model Minority image is Asian Americans' ability to start and hang onto small family businesses. Community credit associations and small family enterprises have traditionally been common in Asian countries. Immigrants who can't find work may use these strategies:

- Join mutual aid associations in the ethnic community that provide needed financing and support, and in which members agree not to compete. Associations may loan capital, fix business locations and prices, locate employees, and help members in distress.
- Start businesses that are nonthreatening to the Euro-American majority because they're small and they specialize in limited areas.
- Work long hours for a certain minimum income.
- Give jobs first to family, then to extended family, neighborhood, and ethnic group members, in that order.
- Give employees as much job security as possible, with layoffs a last resort.
- Provide job flexibility to free employees to go to school or work at second jobs.
- Make the primary goal a long range one: to sustain the business over the long term.

Factors that limit growth and expansion include:

- Owners' inadequate English skills
- Dependence on ethnic customers whose per capita wealth is lower
- Reluctance to go outside the Asian American community to get money that would be needed for business expansion

How Small Business Ownership Has Helped Create a Model Minority

Asian American families who have managed to build and hold onto at least a minimal level of business success have achieved the following advantages:

Protection from Discrimination   For most of this century about half the Asian American male population worked for such small businesses, effectively shielding themselves from the open labor market with its discriminatory practices.

Higher Educational Attainment   Owners were able to accumulate money to send their children to college. Between 1940 and 1960 there was a dramatic increase in the percentage of Asian Americans who completed high school and went to college.

More Opportunities   Small business success and higher educational attainment enhanced Euro-Americans' perception of Asian Americans as productive workers.

Disadvantages: Model Minority Costs

Several disadvantages offset the Asian American success story.

- They get less return on their educational investment than do Euro-Americans. Even though about twice as many have degrees, they average only 70 percent of Euro-American men's income.
- They are disadvantaged in getting the better-paying jobs
- Most have a lower living standard than their income implies because 90 percent live in high-cost areas, such as San Francisco.
- More of the family members work than in Euro-American families and they work more hours on average.
- Underemployment is more common. Rather than be unemployed, most will accept low-paying, part-time, or seasonal jobs.
- The Asian American success story overlooks the fact that some recent immigrants, such as Hmong Americans, have major problems.

Issue #2—Male-Female Dynamics and Differences

Most Asian cultures are extremely patriarchal, and women are significantly more subjugated in these cultures than in the American culture.

Family Culture Clash

A culture clash often affects husband-and-wife dynamics, especially in families that have immigrated since the 1960s. That's when women's pay and work status began improving and traditional male jobs in manufacturing plants began deteriorating. Problems often arise over these events:

- The wife finds a better-paying job than the husband, upsetting the male status in a hierarchical family structure.
- The wife must learn to be assertive, decisive, and efficient on the job, which conflicts with her role as a shy, patient, and resilient wife and mother.

- Children at school learn they must speak up, express opinions, and ask why in order to succeed, but are expected to keep quiet and do as they're told at home.
- Girls must also speak up at school, but at home they're supposed to be even more reserved and compliant than boys.

Stereotypes of Asian Women Workers

Women who don't have the educational credentials to land better-paying jobs often take manufacturing assembly line jobs. They typically encounter myths, stereotypes, and other barriers to promotion, such as:

- Immigrant women are more likely to be content with such jobs. In fact, most want to advance.
- They're unqualified for better-paying jobs. In fact, they're trainable.
- They have husbands who earn more than they do. In fact, about 80 percent are the main income earners in their families.
- Their patience and superior coordination better suits them to assembly line production involving tiny, intricate circuitry.
- Their small size makes it easier for them to sit quietly for long periods, doing small detail work.
- Their strong task orientation, high achievement motivation, and hard work qualify them as reliable production workers.
- They're childlike, obedient, and submissive, good qualities for assembly-line work but not for managerial roles.
- Most U.S. citizens would not be content for long with such boring, low-paying jobs, but Asian American women are.

Reality: Beneath the Passive Surface, Active Achievement

Most Asian American women on assembly lines are actually active, goal-oriented doers, according to several studies. They're disadvantaged in at least three aspects of the social structure: being an ethnic minority, a woman, and within a lower socioeconomic class.

The problems they experience with their supervisors (nearly all Euro-American) stem primarily from the following:

- supervisors' perception of their inabilities
- disrespect for Asian women
- unreasonable work assignments
- unfair performance evaluation
- accusation of job errors
- inappropriate decisions regarding promotion
- intolerance of language accents
- apparent discrimination

How do Asian American women handle the problems resulting from these stereotypes? Here are some facts from Esther Chow's research.

- About half have no difficulty challenging their supervisor about problems.
- Well over half have difficulty in expressing anger and in demanding their fair share from supervisors.
- Those of higher occupational status have more to lose and more difficulty demanding their fair share.
- Almost all attempt to establish congenial working relationships with people at all levels of the organization.
- Two-thirds have little difficulty in protesting unfair treatment by their Euro-American coworkers (as distinguished from their supervisors).
- Most had more difficulty protesting to Euro-American women than to the men, since they tend to consider the women as natural allies and hesitate to break that feeling of camaraderie.
- Only 6 percent said they choose to say nothing to offensive coworkers or to ignore incidents they think are unfair

Typical styles for dealing with workplace situations are avoidance or indirect, affiliative, assertive, and confrontational. The style a woman uses depends primarily on how extreme or important the work problem is to her.

Adaptation and Indirectness   Adapting and being indirect seem to fit the passive stereotype. Silence is sometimes a temporary reaction in the process of coping. It may be part of a defensive stand in which they protect themselves from the hurt by pushing their tolerance to the limit. Variations of the approach include avoiding problem situations as much as possible, doing little about them, or hoping a problem will go away. They might write to a supervisor, talk to a supervisor about an offensive coworker, or make an impersonal telephone call to a coworker, all in hopes of finding a solution to the problem. Most don't carry this style to the extreme of quitting, which they would see as defeatist. A frequent pattern is to begin by adapting and later to shift to a more active strategy.

Congeniality   Being congenial is a style sometimes used to show willingness to cooperate in solving workplace problems. It involves personal consideration, friendliness, and candidness to achieve some kind of equity with coworkers. Women using this style may emphasize commonalties, such as being women or being Asian Americans, in order to establish rapport, to dispel issues of inequity, and to neutralize feelings of injustice. They are more apt to use this style with Euro-American women than with men.

Assertiveness   Asserting themselves is a direct style for claiming certain work rights and independence. It includes negotiating their time, effort, intellect, commitment, and personal involvement with other workers. About half the women use this style, and they're more likely to do so when they deal with Euro-American male workers than with females. It includes expressing their viewpoints and judgment of a situation, demanding explanations from offensive workers, and focusing their efforts on problem solving. This approach is active, goal-oriented, and a way of taking charge of their own lives. Women using this approach expect to negotiate a solution to a problem. For example, they may want some agreement about work hours that doesn't interfere with their family obligations.

Confrontation Confronting the persons involved in the situation is a somewhat aggressive style of fighting prejudice and discrimination at work. The women directly protest against those coworkers they view as insensitive and threatening to their survival. They fight back in the face of apparently overwhelming odds in order to protect their work rights and to show they won't compromise themselves to what they see as others' unreasonable demands. Some even go as far as quitting their job rather than be pushed around, the ultimate form of resistance. They see it as affirming self-respect and human dignity, even above job security.

Issue #3—University Education

Educational issues important to many Asian Americans include getting into top universities and establishing Asian American studies programs.

Getting into Top Universities

Many Asian American high school graduates with straight-As have been unable to get into the nation's top public and private universities. The admission rate of Asian American applicants to these universities was lower than that for any other ethnic group during the 1980s. No university has admitted any discriminatory intent, but officials at several have acknowledged that their affirmative action policies and practices may have had an unintentional adverse impact on Asian Americans.

Asian Americans have organized to ensure that their educational rights are not violated, because access to quality higher education, perhaps more than any other issue, is something they feel very strongly about. Many Asians immigrate to the United States precisely to allow their children to receive such education. While most see the value and necessity for affirmative action, in order to level the playing field for all ethnic groups, the community is somewhat divided on affirmative action in university admissions.

Establishing Asian American Studies Programs

Many Asian American university students are asking for a more "relevant" education, meaning a multiethnic curriculum that includes the history of discrimination in the United States and an accurate portrayal of the contributions and struggles of people of color. This interest reflects a new cultural awakening among Asian American students, along with a rising political consciousness. Instead of choosing between their Asian heritage and the American culture, some young Asian Americans are forging a new culture of their own, one that goes beyond a simple blending of East and West. This culture directly reflects the historical experience and current life circumstances of Asians in America. In university courses about Asian Americans, they may get a glimpse of this emerging culture and even be encouraged to help create it.

OVERCOMING BARRIERS TO CAREER SUCCESS

As a leader, you have many opportunities and challenges in working effectively with Asian Americans, in supporting their ability to contribute to work teams, and in building mutual respect and trust. You can help by providing support in overcoming barriers, avoiding typical assumptions and stereotypes, and helping people get to know Asian American coworkers.

Provide Support in Overcoming Barriers

Some typical barriers to job success faced by Asian Americans include:

- Being typecast as technologists (technical "coolies") and therefore not being considered for higher level positions.
- Being discriminated against because Euro-Americans are uncomfortable with their cultural style, which is considered too "foreign and strange."
- Communicating and verbalizing, problems especially crucial with first-generation immigrants.
- Being misunderstood because of their values and behaviors, such as humility and passivity. Such behavior is not necessarily an indicator that they are not qualified for leadership roles.

Avoid Typical Assumptions and Stereotypes

You've learned about the most typical myths, stereotypes, and assumptions that can hamper good working relationships. Here are a few reminders.

Remember, Asian Americans are Americans, not foreigners. Non-Asian Americans have a tendency to look upon Asian Americans as foreigners because of their Asian appearance. Most Asian-appearing workers you'll encounter will be Asian Americans. They're Americanized in varying degrees and possess varying language skill levels. Keep in mind that they aren't foreigners.

Avoid assumptions about language ability. Some leaders assume Asian Americans are fluent in an Asian language and have problems with English. When Euro-Americans make such comments as "You speak very good English" or "Where did you learn to speak English so well?" Asian Americans who were born and raised in the United States may be understandably taken aback. It's one more reminder that even though they consider themselves as American as anyone else, others tend to see them as foreigners.

Asian Americans are often embarrassed or frustrated when others expect them to be bilingual. For example, a worker who is third-generation Chinese may speak little or no Chinese. Let multiple language skills emerge and be used as an asset after you establish the facts. Most important, when discussing an

Asian American employee's skills, qualifications, and career goals, you can help to identify any communication skills or problems that he or she has and try to get remedial training.

Don't assume Asian Americans are cultural ambassadors. Don't try to make an Asian American worker your token Asian expert. Asian Americans appreciate people who don't assume they're experts in their ancestors' culture, just as they appreciate those who don't assume they're bilingual. For example, Japanese Americans who were born and raised in the United States are not necessarily experts in Japanese cuisine, culture, or politics. They do not necessarily agree with economic or political developments in Japan. Again, it's better to ask about special bicultural expertise than to make assumptions.

Avoid such labels as "Oriental." For many Asian Americans the term Oriental, meaning Easterner, conjures up old Hollywood stereotypes (such as Charlie Chan and Tokyo Rose) depicting mysterious, unknowable, exotic Asians. It brings up unpleasant memories for many. Also, some consider it Eurocentric, since it describes Asia as east of Europe. A case could be made that it's west of the Americas, and that the Americas are the East to Asians.

People with Spanish surnames may be Filipinos. Many types of people may have Spanish-sounding names. For example, many Filipinos took Spanish surnames during the era of Spanish colonialism. They are not Latinos, although their values and practices probably reflect a Spanish influence.

Determine Generational Status

There tend to be significant differences between first-generation immigrants and second-, third-, and fourth-generation Americans. By open, direct, but tactful conversations, you can share information about your background and learn about each associate's background. Be sure that your tone or manner is not in any way condescending or patronizing. Getting information can help you to understand the associates' values, viewpoints, and actions. Keep in mind that information you've absorbed about such groups as third-generation Japanese Americans or recently arrived Hmong Americans can only provide general guidelines. Keep an open mind, get to know each individual, and avoid the tendency to use such information to form rigid stereotypes about others.

Ascertain Citizenship Status

For workers who are not American citizens or permanent residents, find out about their status, which can help you better understand their background. For example, some initially come as foreign students, then get work visas. Their values and actions therefore tend to stem from Asian values and practices, and they are less Americanized. Companies must sign papers for Asians to keep their work visas, which frequently makes such workers feel dependent on the company. Such workers may be more submissive, obedient, and compliant, a situation some companies prefer and capitalize upon.

Constantly Question Your Assumptions about Behaviors

Always question your assumptions about why an Asian American acts a certain way. For example, in the American business culture "silence is consent," and if someone doesn't speak up about a decision being made during a meeting, we assume he or she has no objections. But in Asian cultures "silence is golden," and "maintaining harmony is virtuous." Check your assumptions, and then ask. Above all, you can look beyond surface behaviors and get to know Asian American team members personally in order to help them develop their talents and make appropriate career plans.

Help People Get to Know Asian American Coworkers

You can take a leadership role and influence others in the workplace by providing information about Asian American myths and realities, their cultural patterns and strengths, and guidelines for building productive relationships with them. Occasionally review the Asian American values and practices you have just learned. Do further research on your own.

You can help others get to know Asian American associates by including them on team projects. This can provide for in-depth contact with other employees and increased comfort levels.

BUILDING UPON ASIAN AMERICAN STRENGTHS

You can learn to recognize Asian Americans' potential contributions and respond by building on typical Asian American cultural traits, recognizing Asian American values as strengths, applying some leadership strategies, and helping Asian Americans make marketplace connections.

Build on Asian American Cultural Characteristics

Some Asian American characteristics that are especially important in business are that they generally:

1. have an interest in long-range benefits
2. are steadfast, once they decide upon who and what is the best choice
3. stick to their word
4. are punctual

What can you do to build on these cultural characteristics?

- You can identify situations in which these traits are an especially good fit.
- You can point out the good fit to Asian American associates and to others.
- You can help them verbalize to team members the value of developing these characteristics.

Recognize Asian American Values as Strengths

Nearly all values and behavior patterns represent a two-sided coin in the workplace. One side is the advantages these values can bring to the career achievement and organizational contribution of the employee. The other side is the barriers they could erect. You can learn to recognize the cultural and individual values and behaviors of team members. You can figure out ways to enhance them and bring them into the work situation in constructive ways. Here are some ideas.

Obligation to Family

Work with the value of strong obligation to family. In most American corporate cultures, workaholics are rewarded and people who do not consistently put the company first are viewed as lacking commitment. While most Asian Americans place high value on hard work and perseverance, when family members need them, family obligations must come first.

- You can understand and respect Asian American priorities regarding family and work. By doing so, you're likely to win the respect and loyalty of your employees.

Hard Work and Cooperation

Respect their values regarding hard work and cooperation. Some managers take advantage of the Asian American tendency to value hard work and cooperation by piling on the work. Asian Americans are patient, but not stupid. Eventually such exploitation will backfire.

Most Asian Americans emphasize trust and mutual connections, a major aspect of building cooperative business relationships.

- You can help them put their value for trust and mutual connections to good use for the team, the organization, and for their own careers.

Modesty and Humility

Understand their values of modesty and humility. By American corporate culture standards, many Asian Americans may appear to be too passive and too lacking in self-confidence and ambition to be given tough assignments that call for traditional leadership skills. In Asia, such qualities are seen as positive, and the American standards are likely to be seen as egocentric and arrogant, as imposing oneself on others. First- and second-generation Asian Americans tend to value modesty and humility more highly than later generations.

Properly used, such values can be quite appropriate for facilitative team leaders. Further, such values do not mean that the worker lacks self-confidence, ambition, or assertiveness, qualities that vary among Asian Americans, just as they do among Euro-Americans. Asian Americans merely tend to express them in a more low-key, indirect manner. Similarly, we usually reward employees who tactfully question the status quo, speak up, take initiative, or find a better way of doing things. Asian Americans do not necessarily behave in this manner.

- You can help find ways to reward and motivate Asian American employees who are not as verbal or assertive as Euro-Americans.
- You can help show them when and how to be assertive.

Indirectness and Respect

Understand the values of indirectness and respect. Instead of assuming that that Asian Americans are devious, uncommunicative, or dishonest, get to know them as individuals so you can reach a deeper understanding of the values of indirectness and respect in their communication patterns. Another aspect of respect involves the use of space and touching. Asian cultures prefer more space between people when communicating and are comfortable with less touching than is typical in the United States.

- Upon meeting, a slight bow or brief handshake is appropriate.
- Follow their lead about how far apart to stand or sit from each other.

Emotional Expression

Understand how they express emotions. You have learned that Asian Americans are less likely to express emotions than are people from other cultures. To maintain harmony they avoid openly expressing such emotions as anger, resentment, and jealousy. In addition, they may hide their emotions when they sense they're in a "hostile foreign environment" that causes them to feel vulnerable, intimidated, or threatened. People from all cultures are likely to show less emotion, as a protective device, when they feel like a foreigner or minority. You can help by:

- seeing them first as Americans and as a part of the group you're working with; and
- helping them to explore and express feelings that need to come out and be dealt with in order to build honest, trusting, work relationships.

Apply Leadership Strategies

Here are some strategies that may be especially appropriate for Asian American workers.

Enhance Boss-Worker Relations

Explain deviations from traditional boss-worker practices. Asian cultures tend to be more hierarchical and status-oriented than current American corporate cultures. Most corporations have moved beyond the old authoritarian boss-obedient employee model that still fits the pattern of many Asian cultures.

If you're a supervisor, have a conversation with Asian American employees in which you share your ideas of the leader-worker relationship. Once you understand their expectations, you can help them to understand your own deviations from that expectation. For example:

- If they expect the boss to make all decisions, you can explain why workers in this company participate in decision-making.
- If they would be personally humiliated if you pitched in to help complete a task, you can explain how this is viewed in the corporate culture and what it means.

Use a Team Approach

Good teamwork integrates cultural differences. One way to bridge the gap between the Euro-American emphasis on individual initiative and the Asian American emphasis on obedience to authority is to structure tasks so they can be performed by teams. Gradually introduce independent decision-making by doing it as a group. Working in teams can also help Asian Americans and coworkers get to know each other at deeper levels, which breaks down walls of prejudice. It can also take advantage of Asian Americans' group-oriented values and skills.

- You can suggest opportunities for working together in teams.
- You can encourage Asian Americans to contribute their group-oriented values and traits to help the team become more close-knit and productive.

Uncover Relationship Problems

Help bring problems to the surface. Harmony and compliance are two Asian American values that have upsides and downsides. A downside can be an unwillingness to confront relationship problems. Most Asian Americans are taught that in troublesome situations, they should act as though nothing has happened. If they acknowledge a relationship problem, then they must take action, and action may be extremely serious. As a result, they tend to be long-suffering and patient, but resentment may build. In team situations it's usually important to bring problems and troublesome feelings to the surface and to deal with them—if they're important enough to an individual to eventually create communication and relationship barriers.

- You can work with Asian Americans in developing such team-related skills.

Provide Assertiveness Training

You have learned that even minimally educated Asian American women can be assertive on the job when they believe it's necessary or desirable. But because Asian cultures focus on humility and subordinating personal desires for group interests, Asian American employees often need some training about the role of assertiveness in the American workplace. For more than 20 years, Euro-American women have benefited from such training. Asian American employees also respond well to assertiveness training and can reap similar benefits.

- Help provide assertiveness training by your own examples and explanations.
- Encourage your organization to provide formal training sessions.
- Encourage Asian American associates to attend such training. If the situation is touchy, you may want to go yourself and ask them to come with you.

Build Trust

Our history of prejudice and discrimination may have created some trust barriers in intercultural relationships. When Asian Americans perceive that a Euro-American is trying to "buddy up" to them, they may respond internally with some distrust and suspicion. If you're a Euro-American, you must find ways to overcome this barrier.

- Begin by raising your awareness of the ways in which messages can be misunderstood or misinterpreted, and give special attention to clear communication.
- Then, be very consistent in your messages and positions, and always follow through on agreements. Trust is built through the experience of another person as honest, fair, consistent, and reliable. Letting someone down, even once, can shatter newly-built trust.

Show Concern

Express sincere personal concern. Cooperative relationships are normally personal ones. Get to know Asian American workers as people in order to understand their goals and needs, which are usually tied to family status and needs. In this way you show that you understand the value of cooperation and want to establish a cooperative relationship.

- Establish personal relationships with Asian American associates.
- Find out what's most important to them and make their priorities a major part of your discussions and of the relationship.

Communicate Clearly

Cultural differences often cause misperceptions and misunderstandings. Therefore, you must find ways to send clear, unmixed messages that involve requests, assignments, expectations, or explanations. Then you must check for understanding in ways that uncover misperceptions.

- If in doubt, be very specific and factual in making requests and giving instructions. Don't say, "You might want to think about doing *xyz*." Ask, "Can you do *xyz* before you leave today? How does that fit your schedule?"
- Check for understanding. Don't ask questions that can be answered yes or no; for example, "Is that clear?" Ask questions that clearly establish whether the person understands, such as "How do you plan to go about doing that?"

Select Motivators and Rewards

Consider each employee's values when you choose the motivators and rewards you use. Rewards such as individual recognition may not be as effective for motivating Asian American employees as they are with Euro-Americans. The same is true for perks and benefits.

- You can talk with Asian Americans about their values, goals, and expectations.
- Together you can develop rewards that they value and that serve as effective motivators for them.

Help Asian Americans Make Marketplace Connections

Many companies are realizing the potential of the growing Asian American market, and nearly all U.S. companies are doing more and more business with Asian countries in the global marketplace. Asian American employees tend to have a special touch with such clients due to cultural similarities and also are an invaluable resource in developing strategies and action plans for doing business in such markets. Most Asian Americans welcome such opportunities to improve their job prospects.

Help Them Connect with the Asian American Marketplace

Asian Americans have greater buying power than their share of the total population. Companies such as Coca-Cola and AT&T have established Asian American marketing departments and have tried to reach Asian American communities with donations and advertisements. Companies are targeting the rapidly increasing Asian American clientele. They are putting more Asian American models in their television commercials and advertisements. Some are looking to Asian American culture—art, music, dance, clothing designs, movies, and food—for inspiration and to make connections with the Asian American markets.

- You may be able to help your organization to recognize and use Asian American employees as a valuable resource and connection in such efforts.

Help Them Connect with Asian Countries

Virtually all economists expect Asian countries to play a more important role as American economic partners in the twenty-first century. Some locations that are emerging as economic tigers are Singapore, Taiwan, Hong Kong, and South Korea. New trade relations with China are opening up a market of over a billion people.

- You may be able to help your organization see that Asian American employees can provide insights into these global markets and can serve as valuable links.

Skill Builder 1—The Case of Office Whiz Connie

Connie has been working for six years for Crystal Fizz, a manufacturer of drink mixes. She is one of six employees in the plant office, the youngest at age 27, and the only Asian American. Connie has learned how to do most all the major functions in the office and likes her job. However, she's become disillusioned with the work environment. If it weren't for the good pay and benefits, she'd be gone. In fact, she's thinking about looking for a job elsewhere.

Bob, the owner and manager, a year ago hired **Jim,** who performs duties similar to the ones Connie does. Soon Jim was making comments that disturbed Connie, such as "I can't understand what you're saying half the time," and "Why don't you do things the American way—whatever the American way is?" Connie's response has been to ignore and avoid Jim as much as possible. However, Jim was soon being consulted by Bob about various company decisions. Bob sometimes takes Jim with him to important business meetings. Connie is never included in this way, and she recently discovered that Jim makes about 10 percent more than she.

Company employees get four weeks of vacation. Before Jim came, Connie never took all four weeks at one time because of office demands. It was typical for her to come into the office even when she could have taken some time off, simply because there was much important work to be done. Now she finds she doesn't care about that any more. She came back from a four-week vacation last month, and she plans to take all the time off she has coming to her. She feels that she is being treated unfairly and has no real chance of advancement.

- What's the major problem?
- What should Connie do?
- What should Bob do?

Skill Builder 2—The Case of Doug Fong, Manager

Doug Fong is a restaurant manager for Jollytime, a chain of over 250 fast food restaurants. Each restaurant has a day manager and a night manager. Restaurants are categorized as low-level, medium-level, or high-level based on the following criteria: gross sales, annual profit, percentage of increase in sales and in annual profit, and scores assigned by mystery shoppers.

Doug Fong is a first-generation Asian American who has been with Jollytime for ten years and is respected by the other managers. He's a hard worker, often working 12-hour days. Seven years ago he was promoted to manager of a low-level restaurant in a neighborhood that is primarily Euro-American as well as somewhat multicultural. After two years, he was transferred to a medium-level restaurant in Huntville, an African American neighborhood. Restaurant profits increased the next two years, and regional managers were pleased with Doug's ability to handle the challenging Huntville location. They transferred him to Sunset, a "less hectic" restaurant in a multicultural but heavily Euro-American area. Doug told a colleague, "I'm sad to leave Huntville because I've built a trusting relationship with my employees and my customers. There were a few troublemakers around, but I really didn't have any problems."

Doug's been in Sunset for three years. The restaurant was ranked third, then sixth, and then second on the top 50 list of all Jollytime restaurants. Profits increased each year, and customer ratings have been outstanding. Doug has done well in managing employees from many backgrounds. They speak well of him. For example, Kevin, a Euro-American food server, says, "Doug is a great manager; he treats everyone fairly." And Ruben, a Latino American cook says, "I've worked with Doug for nearly three years and he knows how to motivate people."

Doug wants to move up to district manager. He has only a high school diploma, but he's a rapid, eager learner. For example, he's learned to do all the accounting for his restaurant, and the auditors have always approved his work. A district manager oversees 10 to 12 restaurants, overseeing their current operations and improvement plans. The job requires good communication skills and knowledge of accounting principles, including budgeting. Doug has never asked for a promotion. He has operated on the belief that his hard work and excellence speak for themselves, and that he'll be offered a promotion when the time is right. In the past two years, two district manager positions opened up, and the managers who were leaving picked their successors. All the district managers that Doug has met are Euro-American men with college degrees.

Jim Davis was one of the outgoing district managers. His job had been to oversee restaurants in Oakland, which is predominantly African American. Doug decided to overcome his reticence and speak to Jim about the possibility of taking his place. Jim told Doug, "You're an extremely well-qualified manager—no doubt about that. But maybe the Oakland area is not the best place for you." Jim obviously doubted that Doug was assertive enough to handle the employees there. He said, "Let's wait for an opening in an area that's more multicultural. That would be a better fit." A few weeks later **Jordan Jones**, a Euro-American, was named new district manager for the Oakland area.

Now, a year later, the buzz is that Jones has failed miserably in overseeing the Oakland restaurant managers and he'll be replaced soon. **Jack Barnes**, the division manager, will name the replacement.

- What are the key issues or problems?
- If you were Doug Fong, what would you do?
- What should Jack Barnes do?

Skill Builder 3—The Case of Linda Vuong, Asian American Cashier

Linda Vuong has been working for two years as cashier for Computer City, one of a chain of retail electronics stores. It is located in a neighborhood populated primarily by Chinese Americans. In fact, all of the 20 employees, including its managers, are Chinese American, except Linda, who is Vietnamese American. Most of the employees are in their early twenties, attend college, and help support their families. Linda is majoring in business administration and hopes the company will soon promote her to assistant manager. She takes her job seriously, is very customer oriented, and cooperates well with coworkers.

Wallace is one of the store's three assistant managers and is Linda's immediate supervisor. One of the assistant managers is leaving next month, and Wallace is recommending Linda for the job. In his written evaluation that he submits to **Guy**, the manager and co-owner of the franchised store, Wallace includes the following:

- Linda has continuously demonstrated quickness and efficiency in performing job tasks, which include taking customer orders promptly, packaging smaller items properly, and maintaining a clean work environment.

- Linda has good customer skills.
- Customers praise her performance.
- Linda is a team player, helping her coworkers and offering advice on how to improve communications with difficult customers.

Guy seldom interacts with Linda and, in fact, spends minimal time communicating with employees except to exchange greetings. The exception is that he loves to gossip about the local Chinese American community with a few "insider" employees who speak Cantonese. He rarely speaks English to people in the company except to those at an equal or higher level than he. Guy is a concerned employer, paying attention to salaries, work loads, work schedules, and career opportunities within the company, especially for those employees he feels closest to. However, Linda has never had a chance to discuss her career ambitions with Guy.

Linda has not received a pay increase in sixteen months. Guy recently instructed Wallace to delegate more work duties to Linda in order to relieve some of the other employees from job tasks. Not only is Linda expected to do more work without an increase in hours worked, her schedule is often changed to accommodate the requests of other employees who want to attend to personal matters. Linda is hoping all these problems will be solved if she can just get an assistant manager position. This promotion would also allow her to expand her skills and abilities.

Max, one of Linda's coworkers, also wants the assistant manager job. He's definitely in the running, even though Wallace has rarely given him high performance ratings. Wallace has had to talk with Max several times about excessive tardiness. However, Max gets along well with Guy, often chatting and gossiping with him in Cantonese about mutual friends and acquaintances.

Today, Guy calls Wallace to his office and says, "I know you've recommended Linda for the assistant manager position, but I don't think she's quite ready for it. You know, Max has great communication skills, and I think he's better equipped to supervise our employees. Max reads people well, he knows how to get close to people, and that's what we need."

- What are the key issues in this case?
- If you were Guy, what would you do?
- If you were Linda, what would you do?

Feedback on Skill Builder 1—The Case of Office Whiz Connie

The key issues: Unequal opportunity, a hostile working environment, and Connie's lack of assertiveness. The main problem is Bob's differential treatment of Connie and Jim, stemming from what appears to be unconscious bias and subtle discrimination. He is giving Jim more opportunity for advancement by including him in important meetings and decisions. Bob is also paying Jim more for work similar to Connie's, even though Connie, with her longer time in service, should be getting more than Jim. Jim's bias is not so subtle, and he is creating a hostile environment for Connie. Bob, as the employer, is ultimately responsible for the work environment.

Connie needs to speak up about being treated unfairly and with disrespect. She's been patient long enough, and it's getting her nowhere. With Jim, she should be more assertive and tell him when his comments are hurtful and demeaning. With Bob, she should ask for a meeting. Purposes and potential outcomes of this meeting could be to:

- make Bob aware of Jim's behavior toward her
- point out the ways in which she interprets Bob's behavior as preferential toward Jim
- explain to Bob that the hostile environment and discriminatory treatment have discouraged and de-motivated her
- remind Bob of her dedication, high performance, and loyalty over the years
- share with Bob her career goals, long-range and short-range
- reach an agreement with Bob about her future with the company
- get a raise that is commensurate with her service and performance

Bob, in response to the meeting with Connie, should listen with an open mind. Then, if necessary for convincing himself, he should review her performance and her value to the company. He should also realize that if he wants to retain her services, he must change his beliefs, attitudes, and actions toward her and other Asian American women. He is also responsible for setting an inclusive, supportive tone in the workplace, acting as a role model, and seeing that Jim shows respect for Connie.

Feedback on Skill Builder 2—The Case of Doug Fong, Manager

Key issues: Management's stereotypes about Asian Americans' lack of assertiveness. Management has overlooked the fact that Doug has a successful track record in dealing with African American clients and employees. While Doug may lack assertiveness in some areas, it has not affected his ability to manage, even in potentially difficult African American situations. Doug's lack of assertiveness in dealing with management is probably reinforcing the stereotypes they hold.

Doug needs to reassess and adopt some new self-empowering beliefs and attitudes about how to wage a promotion campaign. He should prepare and practice a presentation that stresses his track record and highlights specific achievements and details to back up his claims. He should then request a meeting with Jack.

Jack Barnes should step back and reassess his beliefs and attitudes about Doug and other Asian American employees, as well as review the record. The facts point to the probability that Doug is highly qualified and motivated and that he will do a good job. He has been very patient. If he is bypassed again, he may either become de-motivated or decide to leave.

Feedback on Skill Builder 3—The Case of Linda Vuong, Asian American Cashier

A key issue is ethnic clustering, favoritism, and possibly ethnocentrism on the part of Guy, the manager and co-owner. One aspect of this favoritism is overloading Linda with work and not rewarding her for her dedication and achievement. Linda is in a very difficult situation, since Guy is in charge. If she is aware of the favoritism, it may be worth her while to ask for an appointment with Guy and express her concerns. Her best bet, realistically, may be to find another job where her qualities will be appreciated. Guy needs some training in leadership and diversity management.

8

Latino American Liaisons

About 11 percent of the employees in the workplace are Latino Americans, or more than one in ten people you're likely to work with. Latino American communities include people from many countries. While most of their values and customs are woven from common Latino threads, each country also has its own unique design. For example, you'll find distinct cultural differences among Latino Americans from Mexico as compared to those from Puerto Rico or Cuba or other origins. And, of course, no one person expresses all the values and customs discussed here. This information can give you a deeper, broader understanding of Latino Americans you may meet. However, you already know the necessity of dealing with each person as a unique individual from a particular cultural background.

As you explore the topics of this chapter, try to begin seeing the world as a Latino American might see it—according to information gleaned here from scholars of that community. Specifically you'll learn:

- How typical myths and stereotypes about Latino Americans compare with reality
- How the current situation is connected to certain historical events
- Major Latino American communities, such as Mexican American and Puerto Rican American, their differences and similarities
- Worldviews, beliefs, values, and customs that are important to people in these communities
- Values and customs for conducting personal relationships
- Some key issues that are important to many Latino Americans
- Barriers to career success for Latino Americans and how to overcome them by meeting cultural needs
- How to use Latino American strengths as opportunities to create win-win successes

MYTHS AND REALITIES

Some typical myths about Latino Americans are:

- They're too passive, polite, and lacking in conviction to be good leaders.
- They're too emotional and excitable to fill leadership positions.
- The men are macho and the women easily intimidated.
- They're qualified only for menial jobs.

Most of these myths and stereotypes are either false or they're distorted, partial truths. They often stem from misunderstandings about the ways certain cultural values and customs affect Latino Americans' attitudes and actions. Cultural style, such as passivity or politeness, is often misinterpreted as leadership inadequacy, such as the inability to take initiative and be firm.

Although stereotypes aren't identical to prejudice, rigid stereotypes about people usually lead to prejudice. Latino Americans must deal with these myths and stereotypes every time they leave the family or community circle. Understanding this aspect of their life can help you move beyond stereotypes to bridge the divisive walls such views hold in place. The ultimate goal is to appreciate Latino Americans' unique value to the workplace and to strengthen workplace unity.

Myth #1—Latino Americans are too passive, polite, and lacking in conviction to be good leaders in the workplace.

Reality #1: This myth focuses on style, not substance.

Reality #2: The dozens of Latino nations throughout the world function quite effectively with Latino leaders.

Reality #3: Euro-Americans and others can learn what these behaviors really mean and how they can enhance team relationships and other workplace situations. For example, the values of harmony and positive interpersonal relationships that are so important to Latinos have always been important in the workplace and are increasingly crucial to business success.

Reality #4: Latino Americans do learn to adapt to American corporate cultures and to be appropriately assertive in that arena. Euro-American and other leaders can help them adapt.

Myth #2—Latino Americans are too emotional and excitable to be leaders.

Latino Americans generally hold views about expressing emotions that are different from Euro-American views. More on this later. The resulting behavior is a difference in style, not substance, and the same realities apply here as in the passive/polite stereotype.

Myth #3—Latino American men are macho and the women easily intimidated.

Although Latinos generally are viewed as passive and polite, the men are often stereotyped as being macho with their women—and with each other in bars and similar settings. They're said to have a quick smile and a quick knife and love to fight. The machismo stereotype is that the male is strong, in control, and provides for his family, while the woman is submissive and lacking in power and influence.

Reality #1: This stereotype has not been fully researched, and some studies indicate that male dominance in marital decision-making is not the rule among Latino American couples. Also, machismo style is changing along with changing economic realities and new job opportunities for Latino American women.

Reality #2: Latino cultures have their own brand of patriarchy, as do all the world's cultures. The "quick knife" stereotype is mainly a phenomenon of youth gangs, found in every culture. They're a small minority of the population and rarely affect coworker relationships.

Reality #3: Latino Americans, especially the largest group, Mexican Americans, tend to be one of the most cooperative, accepting groups in the United States, and getting along is one of their highest values. This is true for both the men and the women.

Myth #4—Latino American workers are qualified only for menial jobs.

Related myths are: "They can't speak English well"; "They have only the most menial-level skills"; "They're not productive"; and "They have a mañana attitude."

Reality #1: Latino Americans are a diverse group. Many of them have been in the United States for generations and are highly educated. Members of many groups, such as Cuban Americans, have business qualifications comparable to Euro-Americans. Recent immigrants frequently have language, education, and skill barriers to qualify for better jobs. But companies operating in urban areas with large Latino immigrant populations have found that providing remedial education and job training results in a pool of skilled, loyal workers.

Reality #2: When Latino Americans feel they are part of an in-group, they tend to be extremely loyal. Studies indicate that most identify with the American dream of getting ahead, which means they're willing to learn the skills and approaches it takes—including how to be productive and meet time requirements.

WHO ARE THE LATINO AMERICANS?

The Latino American population consists of three large groups—Mexican American, Puerto Rican, and Cuban American—as well as smaller groups from many countries. Generally, it is relatively young, fast-growing, and concentrated in a few states, mostly in cities. Educational levels and language ability vary by group. Most have lower than average income, higher poverty rates, and face job discrimination, according to U.S. Census Bureau reports.

A Diverse Population of Many Subgroups

You already know that about 11 percent of all Americans are Latino Americans. However, they are most likely to think of themselves in terms of a name that indicates their country of origin, such as Mexican American. Here are major Latino American groups by relative size:

Mexican American	61%
Puerto Rican American	12%
Cuban American	5%
Spanish American	4%
Central and South American groups (total)	11%
Other Latino American	7%

Latino Americans include about a million descendants of Spanish settlers. Many of them have ancestors who lived in the western part of the country before it became part of the United States. Their profile is different because they were never immigrants to the United States.

Fast-Growing and Young: Babies and Immigration

The Latino American population grew by 57 percent between 1970 and 1990, over seven times as fast as the rest of the nation. This growth is expected to continue because of their relative youth and higher birthrate.

- Their average age is 23, compared to 30 for the entire U.S. population.
- They have nearly twice as many children as Euro-Americans, 3.3 compared to 1.8.

Concentrated in Cities in a Few States

The likelihood that you will work with a Latino American depends on where you live. Latino Americans are most likely to live in these states:

State	Proportion of the Latino American population	Proportion of Latino Americans in the state population
California	35%	(one-fourth of the state population)
Texas	20%	(one-fourth of the state population)
New York	10%	(one-tenth of the state population)

Florida	7%	(one-tenth of the state population)
Illinois	4%	
New Jersey	3%	
Arizona	3%	(one-fifth of the state population)
New Mexico	3%	(one-tenth of the state population)
Colorado	2%	(one-tenth of the state population)
Other states	13%	

Most Mexican Americans live in California and Texas, Puerto Ricans in New York, and Cuban Americans in Florida.

The tradition of most Latino immigrants has been that of rural peasant, mostly from Mexico. But by 1980, because of their migration to work in U.S. cities, most were urban dwellers. In America's ten largest cities, an average of one in every four people is of Latino origin: about 60 percent in Miami and San Antonio, 40 percent in Los Angeles, and 24 percent in New York.

Wide-Ranging Educational Levels and Language Barriers

Language ability is related to educational level, which varies by subgroup. English language skills vary. Latino Americans are evenly divided between those who are fluent in English and those who aren't. All speak Spanish. About half still speak Spanish at home, although 75 percent also use English.

Educational levels are low for the Latino American population as a whole:

- 50 percent hold high school diplomas
- 9 percent hold university degrees

The least educated are those from Mexico, Central America, Dominica, and Puerto Rico:

- 45 to 55 percent hold high school diplomas
- 6 to 10 percent hold university degrees

The best educated are Spanish Americans and South Americans, whose levels are almost as high as the national average, closely followed by Cuban Americans. Here is the U.S. national educational average, which is significantly above that of most Latino American groups:

- 77 percent hold high school diplomas
- 21 percent hold university degrees

Education is highly valued by all Latino American groups, even though they have the lowest educational level of any U.S. group. Studies indicate that more Latino American high school students want a college degree than do Euro-American students at the same socioeconomic level. And Latino American parents' aspirations for their children's education is just as high as those of Euro-American parents.

The Cuban American Phenomenon

Cuban Americans have a unique profile that reflects the fact that many came to the United States in the 1960s as business owners and professional persons fleeing communism. As a group, Cuban Americans, compared to other Latino Americans, have:

- High education levels: 67 percent high school grads and 17 percent university grads.
- The largest proportion living in family households (78 percent) and the highest family income ($32,400), near the national median of $35,200
- The lowest poverty rate (11 percent).
- Good language skills: 55 percent speak English very well; none are "linguistically isolated."

Job Discrimination, Lower Income, and Relative Poverty

Here are some key aspects of the Latino American profile:

- Most men are considered minimally-skilled or skilled laborers.
- Most women hold jobs in administrative support, sales, technical, or service fields.
- Twelve percent of men and 17 percent of women hold managerial or professional positions, compared with 27 percent of all U.S. men.
- In U.S. companies of 100 or more employees, Latino Americans hold less than 1 percent of all management jobs at all levels, although they are 11 percent of the U.S. workforce.
- Many Mexican Americans and Puerto Rican Americans remain at a persistent, substantial disadvantage, which is reflected in the overall Latino American earnings patterns. The earnings ratio of Latino Americans to Euro-Americans has been in a decline for several years, with the pay gap increasing by one-half percent per year. Median family income is $25,000, much lower than the national median of $35,200.
- The average poverty rate for all Latino American families is 22 percent, compared to 13 percent for all Americans and 5 percent for Euro-Americans. Causes include fewer job opportunities for the less skilled and educated—and very low wages for those who do have jobs.

LATINO CULTURES: COMMON WORLDVIEW VALUES

Latino American worldviews and values, in a nutshell, revolve around their spiritual values, which include a special closeness to the spirit world and a sense of destiny or fatalism. Based on these worldview values, Latino Americans accept status differences, have their own ways of getting by in the world, are relatively passionate, and express emotions freely. According to various researchers, they use space in a close-up and personal way, and they use time to focus on the present because "who knows what the future may bring?" Most Latino Americans believe in the American Dream but tend to retain certain key Latino values while adopting certain values unique to the American culture. These values, which we'll now explore in greater detail, have been delineated in studies by L. J. Gann, Gerardo Marin, Daniel G. Solorzano, and others.

Worldview Value #1—Closeness to the Spirit World

Most Latino Americans believe that the spirits of family and friends who have passed on are present at certain holiday events, such as the Day of the Dead just after Halloween, and that their spirits in fact move in and out of the physical world all the time. They see nothing to fear from these spirits of relatives and friends. Most think of death as "passing on" and treat death as an old friend or special person. They frequently joke about death and include the theme in games and play activities. This closeness to the spirit world is a basis for other worldview values discussed next.

Worldview Value #2—A Sense of Destiny or Fatalism

Latinos are less likely than Euro-Americans to believe they're in control of their own destiny. This dependence on fate or destiny stems from ancient American Indian mysticism combined with a Latino interpretation of Roman Catholic church teachings. Many believe that outside forces govern their lives, for life follows a preordained course, and human action is determined by the will of God. Those who hold this belief are therefore willing to resign themselves to the "inevitable," bow to fate, and take what comes. This is in direct contrast to the typically Euro-American belief that "God helps those who help themselves," or that people create their own reality to a great extent.

Fatalism can result in an attitude that Americans often interpret as passivity, procrastination, or laziness and that they attribute to a mañana tendency (tomorrow's good enough for me). After all, if it's God's will, if it's written in the stars, why fight it? This belief is tied to the acceptance of unequal status we'll discuss next.

Worldview Value #3—Hierarchy and Status

A sense of hierarchy and status is a strong element in virtually all Latino countries. Basic to what Latino countries have in common is the influence of Spanish culture, which includes an aristocratic hierarchy based on a powerful patron who protects his subjects. They in turn serve him and owe him their loyalty. The patron may be the boss, a politician, a landowner, or a businessman. He makes the decisions, and others don't question him.

Accepting One's Place

Latinos tend to accept their socioeconomic status, even when it's extremely inferior to that of the ruling class. They tend to value the stability that comes with everyone knowing their place and staying in it, living up to societal expectations. Ambition to move outside your socioeconomic group is frowned upon, and people who are seen as "trying to get ahead" are not admired. Such attempts, if successful, are seen as disturbing and disruptive, threatening the relative social position of many people. "Climbing" is seen as crass materialism and greed, and it shows disdain for sensitive human relationships. Partially as a result of accepting a lowly status, most Latinos actually work at very low wages.

Respeto and Power Distance

Where Euro-Americans attempt to minimize differences between persons due to status, age, or gender (sometimes called "power distance"), Latino Americans tend to stress these differences. In Latino countries, those in positions of authority maintain their leadership by their ability to dole out resources to their followers and to help and protect them when they need it. The relationship is reminiscent of a parent-child relationship. The authority figures tend to set clear standards and boundaries for compliance with their policies and rules.

Latino Americans therefore show greater deference and respect (*respeto*) than Euro-Americans toward people who are in power. They place a higher value on conformity and obedience and expect autocratic and authoritarian attitudes from those in charge. They rarely disagree with someone in power, such as the manager, and try to meet his or her expectations.

Worldview Value #4—Expressing Emotions: The Passion Factor

Latino Americans highly value their emotions. The culture encourages them to fully experience their feelings and places fewer restrictions than Euro-American culture on expressing feelings—especially the ones that reflect caring and passion for life. Several studies indicate that this passionate tendency still exists in most Latino Americans. They tend to be passionately for or against a person, idea, or situation, and may see taking a moderate stance as merely a way of hiding your real feelings, which is not a good thing. The longer Latino Americans live in the United States, however, the more they tend to modify the way they express emotion.

Worldview Value #5—Space: Up Close and Personal

In general Latino Americans like to be physically closer to others than do Euro-Americans, so they stand closer together when they converse. This preference is related to their close, mutually dependent relationships, and their frequent expression of warm feelings. They are a contact culture that feels comfortable when physically close to others. Therefore, when they brush close to another, moving into what Americans would consider personal space, there would be no reason to say, "excuse me," as most Americans would. Latino Americans are also more likely to touch each other during a conversation. They may seem pushy as they move towards Euro-Americans, who in turn may seem cold and distant as they back away.

Worldview Value #6—Time: Who Knows What the Future Holds?

Mañana (literally, "tomorrow") doesn't refer to procrastination or laziness, but to the concept that the future is indefinite. In Latin countries it's not unusual for a business person to promise to give you a product or service by the deadline date you want, even though they're unlikely to be able to meet the deadline. The main reason for agreeing is to make you happy in the moment. The present moment is what is most important. The reasoning behind this view is that the future is very uncertain, and some miracle may occur that will enable them to meet the deadline. Therefore, they know they can make you happy now, and they might be able to make you happy then.

Latino Americans typically focus more on the present moment and the past than do Euro-Americans. They therefore spend less time thinking about the future and planning for it, partly because they see the future as too uncertain to do much planning. This view is related to their sense of fate. The typical Euro-American approach is to start with now and project thoughts into the future. The past is past; it doesn't need to get in the way. Latino Americans are more concerned with tradition and more willing to continue with things as they have traditionally been.

The bottom line: Euro-Americans are considered to be generally future-oriented because they stress planning for the future, being able to delay gratification, being on time, and making efficient use of time. Present-oriented Latino Americans put less emphasis on these traits and tend to have a more flexible attitude toward time. They feel they are on time even if they arrive 15 or 20 minutes after the appointed time, even later in nonbusiness social situations. They place greater value on the quality of interpersonal relationships than on the length of time in which they take place. Highly efficient or time-conscious people may be perceived as impolite or insulting.

Worldview Value #7—Adopting the American Dream

Most Latino Americans buy into many aspects of the American Dream. They also express a deep desire to pass on to their children their cultural and religious traditions, especially the Spanish language and commitment to the family. First-generation Latino Americans are naturally less Americanized or acculturated than those of the second- and third-generations, for obvious reasons, but certain aspects of the Latino culture tend to be important across generations. This leads to a merging of the Latino and American cultures.

The Acculturation Process

Immigrants go through a stage of crisis or conflict due to culture shock, followed by finding a way to adapt to American culture, such as

- assimilating completely the American culture
- integrating the American and Latino cultures
- rejecting American cultural patterns

The ability to speak English has become a reliable shorthand measure for evaluating how successfully a Latino American has acculturated, such as:

- assimilating English and speaking it almost exclusively
- integrating the old and the new by becoming bilingual
- rejecting the new and continuing to speak Spanish almost exclusively

The higher the education level, the more successful the acculturation tends to be. Acculturation is important because it affects Latino Americans' mental health status, levels of social support, political and social attitudes, crime rate, and workplace skills. Integration generally works better than assimilation or rejection.

Integration: A Blend of Values

While Latino alienation, anger, and rage exist, most Latino Americans identify themselves with the United States. Only about a third of them identify themselves as Mexicans, Cubans, or Latinos first and Americans second. Most see their heritage as more European than Indian, just as Euro-Americans do. This raises the question: Are most Latinos predominantly Spanish, Indian, or a unique blend? Anthropologists seem to agree that approximately 95 percent are at least part Indian, but the Spanish cultural influence is strong. The cultural mixture of Indian and European elements that occurred in Latin American countries has further blended with the Euro-American in the United States to produce a value system within Latino American communities that is itself a blend.

The American Dream

Despite the prejudice and discrimination that have resulted in segregation and lower socioeconomic status than the mainstream, most Latino Americans believe they're better off in the United States than they would be in their country of origin. Like most Euro-Americans, they are law-abiding citizens. They love their Latino heritage but identify primarily with Euro-Americans and value the American Dream. Most parents work hard to send their children to school. They want them to learn a profession and become solid citizens.

LATINO AMERICAN WAYS: PERSONAL RELATIONSHIPS

Latino Americans place the highest priority on relationships, family, getting along, relating in a personal way, and protecting their honor, while machismo is still a factor in male-female relationships and among male peers. Communication patterns are often indirect and always sensitive to others' feelings. These relationship values, which we'll discuss next, are based on findings by such researchers as H. C. Triandis, R. Cohen, and Leo Grebler.

Relationship Value #1—Familismo

The Latino culture is collective, so family obligations rate higher than individual aspirations. Family and group closeness is their most important priority. Family comes first, and extended family next (extended families are more common). There's a much stronger sense of mutual dependence and undying loyalty than among most Euro-Americans, including greater respect for older members.

Mutual Dependence

Latino Americans typically have high levels of mutual personal dependence that includes these factors:

- relying on relatives for help and support
- feeling obligated to provide material and emotional support to relatives
- being highly sensitive to family relationships
- constantly checking with relatives about the way they see various behaviors and attitudes
- being influenced by relatives' perceptions and feelings
- feeling what family members feel—mutual empathy
- conforming to relatives' beliefs and wishes
- sacrificing for the welfare of the family or in-group members
- trusting the members of the in-group
- expecting that members will ask each other for assistance, and that they'll give it when asked

This value helps to protect each person against physical and emotional stress by providing natural support systems. As a result, Latino Americans place the highest value on building interpersonal relationships in in-groups that are nurturing, loving, intimate, and respectful. While Euro-Americans value such relationships, they also value more confrontational and segmented relationships as an aid to independent growth.

Undying Loyalty

Latino Americans have incredibly strong ties and loyalties to family and friends. If an employee is asked to transfer to another location, many people in an extended family may be involved in the decision. If an employee loses his job or is transferred, the whole family may quit. If one is mistreated on the job, fellow employees who are also relatives will react as if they were personally being mistreated. As a result, disputes can have a more complex quality than Euro-Americans are accustomed to. The net effect may be for Latino Americans to hold back their true thoughts and feelings until they can stand it no longer. Then they may strike out in ways they later regret. Therefore, they may go to great lengths to avoid disputes, or use a third party to intercede or to mediate a dispute.

Relationship Value #2—Simpatico: Getting Along

Getting along involves acquiescing, being simpatico, and being courteous. A potential problem for people from other cultures is figuring out what Latino Americans are really thinking and feeling before resentment builds to the breaking point and the relationship is severed.

Acquiescence

Acquiescence means going along with the wishes of others regardless of your own wishes and agreeing with others regardless of your own opinions and feelings. It may include providing the answer you think another person wants to hear, whether you think it's factual or not. This is a rather extreme type of response frequently used by Latino Americans, especially by less-educated immigrants, men and women alike.

Simpatico

The Latino cultural value of simpatico encourages acquiescence that promotes smooth, pleasant social relations. Simpatico persons

- are polite and respectful.
- don't express criticism, confrontation, or assertiveness.
- show a certain level of conformity and empathy for the feelings of other people.
- try to behave with dignity and respect toward others.
- value working toward harmony in interpersonal relations.

Latino Americans therefore are more likely to give socially desirable responses, avoid face-to-face confrontations at all costs, and view assertiveness quite differently than Euro-Americans do.

Courtesy

Latino Americans place great importance upon courtesy and therefore offer more profuse thanks, praise, and apologies than Euro-Americans are accustomed to. In close-knit Latino cultures a frequent concern is, "What will they say?"

Relationship Value #3—Personalismo: *Relating in a Personal Way*

To relate well to people from a Latino culture usually means relating everything to them on a personal level. Instead of talking in generalities, you would talk in terms of:

- how situations relate to them personally
- their families
- their town
- most of all, their personal pride

Especially for the male, the more the communication is personalized, the more successful it's likely to be. In fact, Latino Americans usually trust only those with whom they have a personal relationship, for only those persons can appreciate their soul. You may have to establish a personal relationship with any Latino American you want to do business with.

Relationship Value #4—Reluctance to Self-Disclose

The value of *personalismo* does not mean that Latino Americans will say what they're really thinking and feeling to people outside their in-group. The value of simpatico and power distance means they're less likely than Euro-Americans to self-disclose. When people reveal personal information, they become vulnerable to how the listener will use that information, and their *amor proprio*, or personal honor, could be damaged. Males are even less likely to self-disclose than females, especially with someone they're likely to interact with in the future, or in culturally unfamiliar situations. When Latino American males do self-disclose, it's usually with Latino American females, who pose the least threat of responding with scorn, rejection, or other blows to self-respect.

Relationship Value #5—Machismo and Gender Roles

Most agree that gender roles are more strictly defined in Latin cultures than in the United States. Men's higher status is more noticeable, they're more dominant, they're allowed more sexual freedom, and there are greater differences in men's and women's socially acceptable activities, attributes, roles, and occupations. The degree and importance of these values varies from one Latino culture to another.

Machismo

The machismo pattern of behavior represents male power and an attitude toward the world, especially toward women. While Latino men generally have a poetic, romantic side, the machismo aspect is aggressive and sometimes insensitive. This image consists of virility, courage, competitiveness, a readiness to fight, and a determination to conquer. Men are expected to be assertive, to be leaders, to be in control, and to earn the respect of other men by their masculinity. Machismo is basically about men impressing each other. In business this means that a man should be forceful, confident, unafraid, and take the lead.

Women's Lot

Women are restricted by traditional views about their sexuality, assertiveness, and work roles. "Madonna or whore, no in-between, that's how we're seen," say liberated Latino women. The Madonna, or good woman, marries as a virgin and martyrs herself to her family. She accepts men as the dominant ones and experiences her lot as saintly suffering. Women are therefore expected to be reserved and modest with men outside the family. Assertive women are generally disliked. Latino Americans are more likely than Euro-Americans to believe that mothers should not have outside jobs. On the other hand, women who do work nearly always have a greater say in family decisions than those who don't.

Relationship Value #6—Communication Patterns

Latino Americans often speak indirectly out of concern for others' feelings and consideration for others' sensitivity to criticism. They may use speech to impress, follow some unique nonverbal patterns, and have clear expectations about how to say hello and good-bye.

Speaking Indirectly

Latino Americans are frequently indirect in their communication with strangers and outsiders. It may appear evasive, but it's intended to be courteous. It may be difficult to determine exactly what they are thinking and feeling. They may use a go-between in order to communicate unpleasant messages or to make requests.

High Concern for Feelings

Latino Americans may tell you what you want to hear, regardless of the "truth," out of great concern for your feelings. This reflects their belief that their own opinion doesn't matter as much as respecting your feelings and giving you the response you'd like to have. This conflicts with the American value of "telling it like it is."

High Sensitivity to Criticism

How Latino Americans take criticism is closely tied to the relative status of the people involved. Usually, if criticism comes from a higher-status person, it's accepted sheepishly; if it comes from an equal, it may be treated with humor; and if it comes from a lower-status person, it may not be tolerated, since this would signal weakness and invite more criticism and even derision.

Saying Hello and Good-Bye

If several people are in a group when you arrive, you're expected to go around and greet everyone, shaking hands, or, if you know them well enough, embracing them. The "Hi, everyone" greeting would be considered rude. Likewise, upon leaving, you're expected to say good-bye to each person individually.

LATINO AMERICAN ISSUES

Many issues are important to Latino Americans, but four issues that will help you better understand your coworkers are: (1) how to overcome segregation and discrimination, (2) how to improve their knowledge and skills, (3) how to improve their workplace status, and (4) how to overcome recent immigration backlash. These issues are discussed in books by such researchers as Clete Daniel, Gregory De Freitas, and Carey McWilliams, as well as in U.S. Government reports.

Issue #1—Overcoming Segregation and Discrimination

The long history of discrimination against Latino Americans, together with the antagonism toward Latino cultures, especially the Mexican and Puerto Rican cultures, expressed by many Euro-Americans, has served to heighten their alienation from the dominant culture. While this discrimination has never been as formally overt as that against African Americans and American Indians, informal discrimination has yielded similar results. Three separate government studies conducted in 1942 found that Latino Americans were probably the most ignored and destitute group in the U.S.—economically, intellectually, and socially.

Occupational Segregation

The huge differences in wage levels and worker expectations between the United States and most Latino countries, especially neighboring Mexico, has always motivated workers to migrate to the United States. The typical practice in the Southwest has been for employers to hire Mexican Americans by the group—as work gangs, crews, or families—to do those menial jobs that are heavily manual, dirty, seasonal, and dead-end. Where unions existed, they usually excluded Latino Americans or established work rules that barred them from opportunities to compete with Euro-Americans. In time, Mexican Americans became stereotyped as being qualified only for menial jobs. Today, they remain disproportionately concentrated in blue-collar occupations and in such industries as manufacturing, mining, and agriculture, where employment opportunities are declining. Overt discrimination has declined, but traditional business practices often result in discrimination that blocks upward mobility.

Residential Segregation

Occupational patterns determine residential patterns. For example, prior to 1950, most jobs available to Mexican Americans were in isolated rural areas of the Southwest. Latino Americans who resided in urban areas could only afford to live in camps or the worst parts of town. Occupational barriers meant they could hardly hope to ever afford much better. As a practical reality, therefore, most were segregated in barrios and barrio schools, just as African Americans were segregated in ghettos and ghetto schools. Since 1950, the Latino American population has rapidly urbanized, but segregation is still common.

The Unnoticed Minority

In 1940, about 90 percent of Mexican Americans lived in five Southwestern states, one of the most intense concentrations of any American subgroup—a pattern that continues in modified form to this day. People in the other forty-three states rarely encountered Mexican Americans and were hardly aware of their existence. Even in the Southwest, they were isolated from the mainstream of American life.

Until 1970, government census records counted Latino Americans as "white," so demographic information about them was virtually nonexistent. Leaders of the "Chicano" (Mexican American) movement won the separate designation battle in 1970 but lost the terminology battle. The government now recognizes Hispanics as a distinct "racial" group for civil rights purposes. The difficulty with this term is its root word "Spain," which brings up painful memories of colonial conquest and domination. Most prefer the term "Latino."

Issue #2—Improving Knowledge and Skills

The language barrier and lower educational achievement of some Latino American workers accounts for a larger share of their earnings differential than is true for other groups. Continuing high dropout rates and low college enrollment indicates that Latino Americans will be the group most damaged by the shift to a better educated, highly skilled workforce. Key barriers are:

- recent immigration
- language barriers and difficulties
- poverty-level family incomes
- higher unemployment in the family
- early marriage and early pregnancy
- immigrants' deficient educational preparation in home country
- poor achievement levels in U.S. segregated schools
- biased treatment in integrated U.S. schools

Inadequate education may also be a hurdle to exercising power in the American political system, the main arena for bringing about needed change. Despite their solidarity and pride of heritage, full participation is impossible as long as many Latino Americans lack adequate education, English literacy, citizenship papers, or clear legal status.

Issue #3—Improving Workplace Status

When we compare the workplace issues of Latino Americans to those of Euro-Americans, several major factors stand out: higher unemployment, lower economic status, problems of new immigrants, educational discrimination, the need for job skills, and employment discrimination.

Employment Barriers: Mexican Americans

Mexican Americans have made impressive progress since the 1950s in educational attainment and occupational mobility. However, many remain at a persistent, substantial disadvantage. Recent immigrants tend to earn the lowest incomes and have the most barriers to upward mobility. Most either don't speak English well or speak almost no English. They tend to be from rural areas and have difficulty adapting to urban life. They rarely have the job skills needed to gain stable employment and make adequate wages. And many lack a high school diploma. Welfare benefits are rarely available to needy Mexican Americans because most of those who need it are either illegal immigrants or noncitizens. Due to male underemployment and unemployment, an increasing percentage of mothers now work.

Employment Discrimination

Workplace discrimination persists because, even if employers do not themselves hold discriminatory attitudes, the practice of using stereotyped beliefs that minorities have lower-than-average productivity will result in employers ranking individual minority group members lower than other job applicants. Inside the company, employer discrimination usually involves the confinement of minorities to less skilled, more unstable job titles and slower promotional tracks, rather than differential treatment of minorities and Euro-Americans in the same jobs.

The Cuban American Success Story

You have learned that the most affluent Latino American people are the Cuban Americans. About 11 percent who came during the 1960s and 1970s were professionals or business owners, compared to 1 percent of Mexicans. Meanwhile, 12 percent of Mexicans were farm workers compared to 2 percent of Cubans. There were many skilled blue-collar workers from both countries. Where Cuban Americans have created their own communities and established a middle-class or upper-class lifestyle, they've experienced little discrimination. However, Black Cuban Americans believe that racial oppression in the United States is more severe than in communist Cuba.

Now Cuban Americans are the large majority of Miami's population, and they have transformed its economy. In 1960, Miami's economy was stagnant, dependent on tourism and retirees. The Cuban Americans used their enterprise and skills to turn Miami into the "new capital city of Latin America." Increasing numbers of Latin American tourists began to fill the city's hotels. Latin American businessmen began investing huge sums in real estate. Miami became "the banking center" for investors from Central and South America. More than 100 multinationals doing business with Latin America have established headquarters in Miami. Now international commerce generates billions of dollars a year in state incomes and thousands of new jobs. Nearly half the Cubans in Miami work for Cuban-owned firms, and about 25 percent are self-employed.

The mass emigration of these professionals became a cultural disaster for Cuba. Most of them are not right-wing conservatives but people of every shade of opinion, including many who had originally supported Castro.

Issue #4—Overcoming Immigration Backlash

Nearly a third of Latino Americans are first-generation immigrants with limited English proficiency that significantly hinders their socioeconomic progress. Controversy rages over the cost to taxpayers of providing social services to these immigrants. People also worry about overpopulation straining the country's resources, and illegal immigrants, who use many social services but don't pay into the income tax and property tax accounts that fund such services. On the other hand, studies indicate that the long-run economic benefits these immigrants generate for the average U.S. taxpayer outweigh any short-run costs. "Immigration backlash" eases whenever the economy improves, but it remains a sensitive issue for many Latino Americans.

OVERCOMING BARRIERS TO CAREER SUCCESS: MEETING CULTURAL NEEDS

Latino American barriers include trying to meet both job and family obligations, a communication style that may conflict with goal achievement and providing accurate information, unwillingness to confront conflict, and promotion anxiety.

Need #1—Meeting Family Obligations

Work is important to most Latino Americans. They want the American Dream. But family comes first. Therefore, when it comes to the following kinds of issues, the Latino American is more likely than the Euro-American worker to put family concerns first, which affects:

- job relocation that requires the family to move
- overtime work that conflicts with family obligations
- the need to be absent in order to deal with family problems, illnesses, or emergencies

Coworkers and managers must put this in perspective in order to understand the true dynamics of the situation.

Latino American workers will generally consult with the family when deciding to take a job, to seek or accept advancement, and whether to leave a job. For you to understand and work with Latino American employees, you must know about and understand their family concerns that impact work decisions and performance.

In Latino cultures people are hired and promoted based primarily on family and personal ties. Latino American employees may expect the company to give their relatives and close friends preferential treatment. Managers may need to explain differences in company policy and in U.S. corporate cultures.

Need #2—Communicating Organizational Needs for Goal Achievement and Accurate Information

Latino cultures tend to value accurate data less highly than the American business culture. Most Latino businesspersons see nothing unusual or harmful in withholding information in order to gain or maintain power. While goals are important, the process of achieving the goals and the symbolic messages implied by various aspects of the process may be more important. In contrast, the success of U.S. corporations often hinges on effective and efficient goal achievement, doing what works, getting accurate data and passing it on to those who need it to do the best job. These values are so pivotal that Latino American employees may benefit from special training sessions on these topics.

Need #3—Turning Conflict Avoidance into Resolution with Sensitivity

The Latino value of simpatico compels most Latino Americans to avoid interpersonal conflict on the job. They try to emphasize positive behaviors in agreeable situations and deemphasize negative behaviors in conflictive circumstances. This affects methods of conflict resolution and needs to be addressed in work team situations. Latino American employees need to understand why conflict is being addressed openly instead of ignored. They need to be reassured about the organization's need for openness, the expectation of openness, and why it is valued. Also, the team needs to respect Latino American members' sensitivities and find ways of resolving conflict that all can accept comfortably. Latino American workers may lead others in finding ways to combine openness with sensitivity and compassion.

Need #4—Dealing Constructively with Promotion Anxiety

Career development has some unique aspects for Latino American employees. For one thing, the employees, especially the men, may see more risk than Euro-Americans in applying for a promotion. If they don't get it, they not only experience a loss but their self-respect will suffer. Also, they may believe they'll be seen as competitive and too ambitious by their peers. Latino Americans tend to view competition as disruptive, leading to imbalance and disharmony. To overcome such barriers, leaders can begin working on career development with employees from the beginning. At periodic one-on-one meetings, career goals and ways of meeting them can be discussed. In this way, each step of development and advancement comes about naturally and the threats are diluted.

OPPORTUNITIES TO BUILD ON LATINO AMERICAN STRENGTHS

You can help Latino Americans use their love of group affiliation to enhance work teams and bring their sense of honor, good name, and idealism to achieve at higher levels by relating to them in ways that show respect for Latino American values and issues. You can also help them make connections with Latino and Latino American marketplaces.

Opportunity #1—Help Latino Americans Enhance Work Team Relationships

Bring into play Latino Americans' cultural values of group loyalty, *personalismo,* and *simpatico.*

Highlight the Group Value

The tradition of small group loyalty among Latino Americans offers a valuable opportunity for leaders to promote group values.

- Latino Americans place a very high value on belonging to a group and on cooperation and harmony within the group. Once they feel they are an accepted part of a work team, they are very comfortable functioning in this structure.
- For best results, Latino Americans need to feel personally close to the people in the group; otherwise, their first loyalty will lie elsewhere.
- Once they're committed to the team, motivational appeals and rewards geared to the team and the employee's contributions to the team can be the most powerful.
- Latino Americans tend to feel extreme loyalty to their in-groups. On the other hand, they may have difficulty adapting to an impersonal culture and to large groups in which personal recognition rarely occurs.

Remember, Latino Americans tend to give higher importance to relationships than to tasks. Keep these points in mind:

- Ask yourself, on a regular basis, How can I make the relationship value an asset?
- Ask, How can I create opportunities for Latino Americans to work on tasks with others or to share projects?
- When delegating, coaching, and giving feedback, speak to Latinos in terms of relationships where possible.

Promote Assertive Expression

Latino Americans' reluctance to self-disclose can pose a problem for optimal team functioning. Use *personalismo* to overcome it. Members often must know what's going on inside each others' heads in order to solve problems and keep operations flowing smoothly. When the corporate culture respects and values Latino Americans, their culture, history, and beliefs, then they are more likely to reveal their thinking and feeling to other team members.

Encourage Decision-Making

In Latino cultures, those in authority make the decisions; subordinates don't pass judgment on leaders' ideas or question their decisions, as this would imply a lack of confidence in their judgment. Sometimes, U.S. managers think they've communicated to Latino American workers that they can make certain decisions, only to find that the decisions are simply not made. In your manager role, you may need to appeal to Latino Americans' wish to be *simpatico*. You can explain in detail the decision-making process. You can reassure Latino American employees about when they can make certain decisions, when the team expects them to participate in making decisions, and when you expect their input, feedback, or questioning of ideas and decisions.

Opportunity #2—Appeal to Honor, Good Name, and Idealism

Coworkers and managers who offer feedback, evaluation, comments, or criticisms of Latino Americans' work would do well to understand and remember the importance of personal dignity, honor, and good name. If this is violated, the employee may feel compelled to leave. It may be futile to try to separate the person from the work or the end result. Latino Americans are likely to take criticism personally no matter how objective you try to be. Therefore, try these tips:

- Make the feedback personal but supportive and offered with great understanding and empathy.
- Always give such feedback in private.
- Always offer it in a supportive, warm, concerned way.
- Always treat Latino Americans as adults.

The idealist aspect of Latino culture can be an advantage when it motivates Latino American employees to support the organizational vision and mission, and to achieve the goals and standards set by the group or the company. Their idealism can inspire and energize other employees.

Opportunity #3—Show Respect for Latino American Values and Issues

Values around hierarchy and status, *personalismo* and simpatico, are important in work relationships. Also, women managers need to understand effective ways of interacting with Latino American men.

The Manager and Respeto

Respect for status and authority runs deep in Latin cultures, but respect for the person, regardless of position, runs even deeper. Latino American employees generally expect that the boss will be demanding. They often expect the boss to tell them what to do and to exercise fairly close direction until it's done. On the other hand, they can be led to use their own initiative if the leader makes it clear what types of initiative are expected and that this does not conflict with the leader's authority. The combination of challenge and support can help them to be productive and feel comfortable on the job. Such an approach is likely to establish an effective working relationship and engage the Latino American's sense of strong loyalty.

Relationships with Personalismo

When a manager is generally warm, friendly, and encouraging with a Latino American employee, a deeper personal respect tends to develop. Otherwise, such employees may assume the manager is displeased with them. On the flip side, when the manager allows the employee to express his or her personality and share personal concerns, a greater rapport develops.

Since almost all relationships are more personalized in Latin America than in the United States, Euro-American leaders may have difficulty understanding the implications of simpatico. In American business cultures, people tend to value the separation of business matters from personal relationships and concerns. However, it's quite possible to balance the Latino Americans' need for their leaders to show personal understanding and warmth and the Euro-American leaders' need for some professional distance. The reverse is also true. Euro-American employees can understand that their Latino American manager's concern for their personal and family matters is not intended as a prying or controlling ploy. It's the leader's way of showing proper concern for each person.

Relationships and Simpatico

A certain charm is seen as crucial for dealing effectively with others, and such simpatico is a quality that increases one's status. In fact, it's the surest form of acceptance in Latino culture. On the other hand, rudeness or insensitivity in a leader is shocking to Latino Americans. To them, courtesy is synonymous with education, and they would wonder how such a rude person could ever be given a responsible position. Latino Americans greatly admire leaders who can get the job done while exercising smooth social skills that boost the employees' self-esteem and honor.

The Woman Manager of Latino American Men

While machismo is often a misunderstood stereotype and is changing, it is still a factor to consider. Latino American men may have more difficulty than Euro-American men in dealing with a female manager. They are likely to react negatively to being corrected or criticized, especially where other men can hear, since this would be seen as a major attack on their honor. The more assertively the woman comes on, the more difficult it is for the employee. Therefore, women managers need to be especially sensitive to these feelings and to search for positive, tactful ways to achieve their purposes.

Occasionally, a Latino American employee will make sexual overtures. It's important for the manager to keep in mind the implications of the Latino good woman-bad woman concept. She can nip such advances in the bud with clear I-messages, such as "I never get romantic with another employee; it wouldn't be fair to the others." She can continue to be warm and friendly, making sure she is also businesslike and professional, sending the clear nonverbal message, "I like you and respect you, and I will not have a romantic or sexual relationship with you."

Opportunity #4—Help Make Connections to Latino Marketplaces

Latino Americans obviously understand Latino cultures better than anyone. They can be of invaluable help in dealing with those markets, customers, suppliers, and other associates. Latino Americans' spending power is at $220 billion and growing. Latino Americans are apt to have key connections in the community. NAFTA and other trade agreements are opening up greater-than-ever trade opportunities in Mexico and other Latin American countries. Corporate representatives who can speak the language and know the customs can provide the company with a valuable edge.

Skill Builder 1—The Case of New Manager Luis

Luis has been manager of the claims department for three months. He's on his way to the office of his immediate supervisor, **Gale**, for their monthly planning and evaluation session. Walking down the hall, his mind is filled with events of the past few months and what he wants to discuss with Gale.

When Luis applied for the management job, he had five years' experience with National Life Insurance. He had taken the screening exam for the new position and did well on both the written and oral portions. One of Luis' coworkers, **Richard**, also took the test and told Luis that he had done great on it.

Richard had come to National about a year before Luis and had trained Luis in some claims department procedures. Luis learned quickly and they soon had a friendly rivalry going. When their boss Gale was recruited from outside the company,

Richard told Luis he heard it was because of pressure to place more women in higher positions. He said the company had recently gone through a government review of its affirmative action program and was found lacking. Richard said, "They brought Gale in mainly because she's a woman." Luis agreed with Richard at the time because he didn't really know the story and he didn't want to argue about it.

Four months ago, Richard told Luis that he really expected to get the claims department manager's job because he had such a good track record with the company and he also had more seniority than the other seven candidates. When Luis got the job, he became Richard's immediate supervisor. Luis felt uncomfortable giving Richard direction. He knew Richard was probably at least as well qualified as he to be boss. He worried about it quite a bit the first month. But he told himself that he must be the most qualified for the job, otherwise he wouldn't have been selected.

During the second month, Luis noticed that Richard and several other employees seemed reluctant to follow his instructions. Luis attempted to meet them halfway by asking why they weren't doing certain things as he had directed, what they felt should be done, and so on. Sometimes it seemed as if these few employees didn't take him seriously. He could see that efficiency and productivity were beginning to be affected by their resistance and balkiness. Time and time again Luis told himself that it would take time for his former coworkers to get used to him as their manager and for him to become adjusted to his new role and responsibilities.

Then just last week, Luis overheard a conversation in the lounge. Richard was talking with a coworker and didn't realize Luis was in the next room:

I don't know about this affirmative action. Why would anyone want to use the past as a reason why they haven't gotten ahead educationally or economically? I think it's time we all stood up for ourselves and accomplish or fail on our own merit, instead of some people falling back on excuses. Why should we American males be discriminated against just because of past history? If people want everyone to be treated equally, then they can't be given an extra advantage at the same time. I know my test scores were higher than some of these people who are being promoted, but they get promoted anyway—just so some job-climbing administrator can brag about his political correctness and make his track record look good. Worst of all, it just amazes me that Luis actually thinks he deserved that promotion.

Luis was stunned at the time. He started thinking about the number of Latino Americans in company management. He could think of only one. Maybe Richard was right. Maybe he really wasn't qualified enough to handle the new job.

- What is the major problem in this situation?
- What should Luis do?
- What should Gale do?

Skill Builder 2—The Case of Evelyn Sanchez, Supervisor

Evelyn Sanchez is a Customer Services Supervisor for Buckman's, a large mail-order house. Her duties include making sure that work is distributed and completed under strict deadlines, approving certain transactions, and reviewing employee's work. She is required to set quarterly goals for herself and to train employees to cross-sell to customers in ways that meet their needs.

Evelyn's team includes ten employees of diverse backgrounds, including African American, Euro-American, Latino American, and Asian American. Most of the employees are bilingual. **Rosita**, a Latina American, is hired as a new member of Evelyn's team. One day, when Evelyn stops by to check on how Rosita is doing, they lapse into speaking their native Spanish. **Ophelia**, an African American team member, is working nearby. She feels uncomfortable because she doesn't know what the two are saying. It's no big thing, and she tries to forget her discomfort. However, Evelyn comes by almost every day and has a brief conversation in Spanish with Rosita. Finally, Ophelia mentions her discomfort to Evelyn. She says, "I feel really left out when you two speak on and on in Spanish—and it keeps happening. I wish we could all speak the same language around here." Evelyn replies, "Lighten up, Ophelia, we're not talking about you, nor are we sharing secrets. We're just chatting, and it's good for our heart and soul to be able to converse in our beautiful Español now and then." Ophelia becomes more disturbed each day as Evelyn and Rosita have their little Spanish conversations. She decides to complain to **Gene**, the general manager.

- What should Evelyn do?
- What should Gene do?

Skill Builder 3—The Case of Gino George, Sales Rep

Gino George is a sales rep for Delcor, a telecommunications company. Five years ago he completed a degree in business administration and went to work in the finance department of Delcor as a junior accountant. He was the only Latino American in his department, and he got along well with his coworkers. He earned good performance reviews and merit increases, and two years ago applied for and got the sales rep job.

Gino likes being a sales rep. He especially likes getting a commission on every sale he makes. Because he's a good salesperson, his salary is significantly higher than it was as an accountant. Gino is proud of the fact that he can help his Euro-American coworkers when they must deal with Spanish-speaking clients. In fact, Spanish-speaking clients have learned to ask for Gino, making him a valuable asset to Delcor. On the other hand, being the only Latino American makes Gino feel somewhat isolated. For example, coworkers frequently "forget" to inform him of meetings or to invite him to group events. Few of them talk with him about anything outside of business matters.

Recently, Gino was going over some files in the office. A couple of sales reps entered the adjacent cubicle and Gino overheard their conversation. **Jeff** said, "I heard that **Dave**'s raising our sales quotas for the spring quarter. Business is always slow in the spring. How are we going to sell more than last year? If we don't meet that quota, we won't get our bonus." **Ralph** replied, "I think it's Gino's fault. He just gives Dave ideas. If he weren't such an eager beaver, Dave wouldn't start thinking that the rest of us should do better." "Yeah," said Jeff, "Any ideas on how we can send Gino back to the accounting department? Let him count beans!" Gino is very upset by the news that his coworkers view his achievements so negatively. He hates being viewed as a troublemaker and difficult person. He decides to pull back on his sales efforts and to be satisfied with barely meeting his quotas.

Today Dave receives the news that he's being promoted and that he should recommend a replacement to take over his job. As Dave goes through the performance evaluations of all his team members, he narrows the choice down to Gino or Jeff.

- Jeff has a high school diploma, experience as a salesperson with one other company, and has been with Delcor for three years as a sales rep. He gets along well with coworkers and is well accepted as "one of the gang."
- Gino is better qualified, with his bachelors degree that includes technical expertise in the telecommunications field. He has been building a better track record as a sales rep than Jeff has, but the coworkers don't seem to be as receptive to him as they are to Jeff.

Dave calls Gino and Jeff into his office. He tells them that they're both in the running for the job and sets up times to interview each of them separately. Gino is concerned. He really wants the promotion, but he's worried about being accepted in the managerial role. On the other hand, if Jeff gets the job, he'll probably offer Gino little or no support and encouragement. He'll probably make it tough for Gino.

- What should Dave do?

Feedback on Skill Builder 1—The Case of New Manager Luis

Key Issue: Prejudice. Richard is verbalizing his prejudice and cynicism and is therefore poisoning the environment. Luis' lack of confidence, assertiveness, and leadership image is also a major problem.

Luis needs to work on developing a vision of himself as an effective leader so that he can become comfortable in the role and build his self-confidence and image. He can do some selective reading and attend some seminars that focus on such issues. Luis needs to discuss the situation with Gale, tell her what he sees as the major problems, offer some solutions, and ask her opinion. Together they may want to discuss Richard's future with the company and his career development. Luis can then meet with Richard to work on a career development plan.

Gale needs to speak with Richard about the situation. She must show full support for Luis, indicate her confidence in him, his qualifications, and his potential. She can point out the reasons Luis was selected for the position and tell Richard that Luis has spoken with her about developing a career development plan with Richard.

Feedback on Skill Builder 2—The Case of Evelyn Sanchez, Supervisor

Key issue: The use of language in the workplace. Most minorities expect that English will be the official language of the workplace and other public places in the United States. In most workplaces, therefore, employees should speak English. It's natural for others to feel left out when they're within hearing distance of a conversation and can't understand what's being said. The tendency is to feel a little suspicious that they're being talked about or that secrets are being shared. Ophelia has made it clear that such conversations bother her. Evelyn, as supervisor, should be a role model of appropriate, sensitive behavior. This would mean confining her conversations in Spanish to private situations outside the hearing of Ophelia and other non-Spanish-speaking employees. Gene should counsel Evelyn about this.

Feedback on Skill Builder 3—The Case of Gino George, Sales Rep

Gino is apparently placing his need to be "simpatico," to get along and not cause trouble, above his need to do well in his job. In some workplace settings, he would be called a "rate buster," an employee who produces so much more than the other workers that the workers hate him and the bosses love him. Dave needs to recognize what may be going on here and work with Gino on this issue. The other sales reps may be exercising subtle prejudice and discrimination by excluding Gino. Certainly, Gino seems to have effective social skills in dealing with customers, making it seem unlikely that his difficulties with coworkers stem from poor social skills. Dave should consider working with the entire group, as well as privately with Gino, regarding diversity training and a show of support for Gino. While Gino deserves the promotion, repair work needs to be done before he takes over the position.

9

Gay and Lesbian Connections

Gay men, lesbians, and bisexuals, sometimes referred to collectively as gay persons, are often called the invisible minority because they don't look different from others in their ethnic group. About one in every 50 persons you work with is a gay person; according to the best estimates of researcher Robert T. Michael and associates, that means 2 percent, or 5 million, Americans. However, if you work in a major metropolitan area, as many as one in every 10 to 20 persons you meet may be gay.

To become comfortable with gay associates, and in turn to build good working relationships, you need to get a feel for their lifestyle, community, and background. The more skilled you become at interpreting individual associates' actions against the backdrop of their background, the greater your chances of working well together. The goal of this chapter is to help you understand what it's like to grow up gay and be a gay person in today's workplace, according to scholars from the gay community. Keep an open mind and try to begin seeing situations as a gay person might view them. Specifically, you'll learn:

- How typical myths about gay persons compare with reality
- How these myths have come about and how they impact people
- What it's like to grow up gay
- Key aspects of the gay community
- Recent findings about why some people are gay
- How people manage a gay identity in the workplace
- Legal rights gay persons do and do not have
- Barriers to career success for gay persons and how to break through those barriers
- Assets gay persons may bring to your organization and how to use those assets to create win-win successes

MYTHS AND REALITIES

Most of the myths and stereotypes about gay persons are either false or distorted, partial truths. In fact, most stem from a belief that gay persons perversely choose an unnatural sexual orientation. The American Psychological Associa-tion has concluded from recent scientific studies that this belief is unfounded. Here are seven myths and stereotypes that gay persons must face.

Myth #1—Gays cluster in certain occupations.

Many people believe that gay men flock to the occupations of hair stylist, de-signer, dancer, and similar creative, "feminine" jobs. Evidence suggests that gays and lesbians do not cluster in a few occupations but are found in a wide range of occupations, as diverse as the general population. A *Fortune* magazine survey of 6,000 gay persons found more gay men and women in science and engineering than in social services; 40 percent more in finance and insurance than in enter-tainment and arts; 10 times (1,000%) more in computers than in fashion. The true part of this myth is that some gay employees feel forced to cluster in certain jobs or departments because they feel safe there and unsafe in other, perhaps more appropriate, areas.

Myth #2—People who associate with gays are probably gay themselves.

This belief is sometimes called "courtesy stigma" or stigma by association. When "straights" associate with gays, only to be suspected of being gay them-selves, they may respond with anger or they may back off. Therefore, stigma by association can create barriers to gays' efforts to establish the support networks and mentor relationships they need for career success. Closet gays (those who hide the fact that they're gay) become even more fearful of associating with other gays and of being "found out."

Myth #3—Gays in sensitive or high-level jobs are security risks.

This stereotype is downright vicious in its impact. No evidence has appeared to support the belief that gay persons represent an increased security risk. But the myth persists in this form: Gay employees try to keep their sexual orientation a secret. Therefore, they're easy blackmail targets for con artists and spies, which in turn makes them a security risk; so they shouldn't be hired or promoted into sensitive or high-level jobs. Even if this were true, the fair solution would be to remove the stigma from gayness and protect gays from discrimination, not to use the "potential blackmail target" rationale to inflict further discrimination. In 1995, President Clinton signed an executive order barring the use of this crite-rion for personnel decisions involving placement of federal employees.

Myth #4—Gay persons don't have normal, lasting relationships.

This myth depicts gay persons as people who are abnormal and promiscuous and who don't have the type of committed, lifelong relationships that represent the marriage ideal in our culture. Studies indicate that most gay persons very much want to have enduring, close relationships, and many do. Over half of all gay men and 75 percent of lesbians are involved in a steady relationship at any one time. Studies of older gay persons find many relationships lasting 20 years or more. When couples are asked the best things and worst things about their relationships, gay and straight couples have basically the same answers.

Another aspect of this myth is that gay persons don't have normal relationships with friends and therefore don't have strong support networks. While they do experience psychological stress from social rejection and stigma, most have made significant progress in overcoming these obstacles and creating rich, satisfying social networks. Overall levels of support received by gay and straight persons is similar, with slightly higher levels reported by gay persons.

Myth #5—Gay men act feminine and lesbians act masculine.

Most straight persons believe that gay persons possess the characteristics of the opposite gender. They also believe the reverse side of the coin, that men who act feminine are likely to be gay and women who act masculine are likely to be lesbian. In fact, gayness in and of itself does not establish which types of sexual roles and behavior people will adopt. The expression of sexuality is diverse and functions along a continuum, rather than in an either/or manner.

A conflicting myth is that gay partners take on clear husband and wife roles, which seems unlikely if both gay male partners act feminine, and likewise if both lesbian partners act masculine. In fact, masculine-feminine roles were often important for gay relationships in the past, but in recent years gender-linked roles have sharply declined. The most common relationship pattern is the friendship model that emphasizes equality, companionship, and sharing.

Myth #6—Gay sex is immoral and gay persons are promiscuous.

This view usually comes from a far-right religious belief and therefore cannot be rationally proved or disproved. Constitutional rights concerning the separation of church and state are supposed to provide some protection in the legal system and in the workplace against discrimination that is based on personal religious beliefs. However, that system has traditionally not worked for gays.

Another view of "promiscuous" sex is that some persons, regardless of sexual orientation, engage in it. The sexual behavior of gay persons who are in the closet, especially married persons, usually stems from their fear of discovery and the resulting need for secrecy and anonymity. This prevents "normal," long-term relationships.

Related to the belief that gay sex is immoral is the belief that AIDS is God's punishment for gay persons. In fact, anyone can contract AIDS; it just happened to gain a foothold in the gay community first. Ignorance about the disease has led to the myth that people who come into contact with gay persons are exposing themselves to AIDS. However, AIDS can only be contracted through sexual intercourse or through the bloodstream. Therefore, casual contact in the workplace is not a threat.

Myth #7—Gay persons are a bad influence on children.

The extreme form of this myth is the belief that gay persons are sexual perverts and therefore tend to be child molesters. Scientific studies have repeatedly disproven this myth. Each year, a few straight and gay persons are convicted of child molestation, and sexual orientation is not a factor. One aspect of this myth is the idea that gay men are looking for very young men and boys as partners. In fact, a majority of young adult gay men prefer a male partner who is older, a majority of those around age 30 prefer a same-age person, and of those over 35 about half prefer a younger partner. About that proportion of straight older men prefer younger women.

Another fear is that gay persons will influence children and youth to become gay. This false fear is the basis for trying to bar gay persons from becoming teachers, counselors, and youth group leaders—and to deny gay parents their child custody rights. The reality is that sexual orientation is almost certainly determined biologically before birth and lasts throughout life. A person might deny their orientation or experiment with another orientation, but not really change. Also, research by G. D. Green and F. Bozett on gay parents and children clearly indicates that their lives are remarkably like those of straight parents and children. There is no evidence that gay parents are more likely to negatively influence their children's development, nor that their children are more likely to become gay.

PAST CONNECTIONS AND CURRENT IMPACTS

During the past fifty years beliefs about gay persons have rapidly evolved from "They're mentally ill sexual deviants whose lifestyle is depraved and illegal," to "They have a right to express their sexual orientation and most are solid citizens." Antigay prejudice is more common among certain segments of the population than others, and it negatively impacts both the holders and receivers of the prejudice.

Milestones in History

Here are some key events in gay history.

- 1952   American Psychological Association (APA) classifies gayness as a mental illness rather than a choice to be "sexually perverted" or "depraved."
- 1969   Stonewall riots and first Gay Power meeting, New York.
- 1970   Gay pride parade in New York attracts 10,000 gay persons.
- 1973   APA announces that homosexuality is no longer considered a mental illness.
- 1990   APA states that gay persons cannot change their sexual orientation. They can choose to suppress it but pay a high price emotionally and psychologically. That choice is virtually always based on self-hate internalized from the culture.
- 1992   President Clinton issues an executive order ending "gay security risk" as a rationale for personnel decisions and proposes removing the military's ban on gay persons.

Stonewall: A Turning Point

Stonewall refers to four days of gay riots that occurred in New York in response to a routine police raid on a Greenwich Village gay bar called Stonewall Inn. Since then, Stonewall has become the symbol of gay resistance to oppression and gay empowerment around the world. To gay persons, it marks the birth of the modern gay political movement, "that moment in time when gays and lesbians recognized all at once their mistreatment and their solidarity," in Martin Duberman's words.

Current Profile

In the past, almost no one would admit to being gay, for obvious reasons, so accurate demographic information was impossible to gather. We know more now about how many gays there are and what their lives are like.

The 2 Percent Estimate

The Kinsey studies of sexuality in the 1950s indicated that gays were perhaps 10 percent of the population, but these statistics are now questioned. A recent extensive and well-respected survey indicates that:

- 2.8 percent of men are gay
- 1.5 percent of women are gay
- 2.15 percent of all persons are gay

This proportion of gay persons holds true for all ethnic groups, economic categories, social classes, age groups, and other demographic categories.

Higher Educational Levels and Jobs

By the 1990s, research by Beverly Green and G. M. Herek indicated that, as a group, out-of-the-closet gays are highly educated and function effectively in responsible, well-paid occupations. They achieve significantly higher educational levels than the population at large. About 60 percent hold college degrees, compared with about 20 percent of the total population. Significantly, more gays hold well-paying professional jobs and jobs that require creativity and innovation.

Lower Pay for Comparable Work

Researcher Lee Badget, in a nationwide poll, found that gay men's wages were 27 percent lower than wages received by straight men of the same race and region who had comparable educational attainment and job positions.

The Nature and Impact of Antigay Prejudice

Antigay prejudice is the key barrier to gay persons being accepted in society. It affects every aspect of their lives. To understand antigay prejudice, you need to know why people prejudge gay persons, which people are likely to be most prejudiced, and the effects it has—on those who prejudge as well as on gay persons.

Why Are People Prejudiced?

Reasons given for prejudice against gay persons include:

- I believe in traditional gender and sex roles and feel threatened by gay couples.
- A man should act like a real man, and a woman should act like a real woman.
- I feel uncomfortable with gay persons. I'm not sure what to say or how to act.
- Maybe they'll come on to me.
- Maybe they'll be jealous if I'm friends with a same-sex person they're attracted to.
- Maybe I'll get AIDS by being around them.
- I have to show disapproval of gays so people will know for sure I'm not one.
- Lesbians believe women don't need men. That really bothers me.

Who Is Likely to Be Prejudiced?

People with antigay attitudes are more likely than others to have the following characteristics:

- male, older, less well educated
- reside in rural areas, the Midwest, or the South
- don't personally know a gay person
- describe themselves as high in assertiveness and low in "feminine" traits
- members of a conservative religious denomination
- strongly religious

G. M. Herek's research indicates that the major predictor of whether a church member will harbor antigay prejudice is whether or not the church has a fundamentalist orientation. A major aspect of fundamentalism is a literal interpretation of the Bible. For example, when discussing beliefs about gay persons, church leaders and members tend to focus on biblical passages that they believe condemn homosexuality. Critics argue that such interpretations ignore other core biblical values, such as "Judge not that you be not judged," "Love your neighbor as you love yourself," and "Do unto others as you would have them do unto you." Others charge that biblical interpretations vary widely, passages can be taken out of context, and almost anything can be proved by quoting the Bible.

What Does Antigay Prejudice Do to People?

The picture of prejudice is not pretty. When gay persons are excluded, ridiculed, or assaulted due to antigay prejudice, the impact on their lives can range from the mild to the devastating, from difficulty adapting to the workplace culture to deep psychological damage. The people who hold onto antigay prejudice are affected, too. They typically experience more guilt, discomfort, and a draining away of joy than do less prejudiced people, according to research by M. D.

Kite and K. Deaux. And they can cause conflict and discomfort for straight co-workers who hold gayness to be normal.

WHAT'S IT LIKE TO GROW UP GAY?

Growing up gay usually involves a process of gradually becoming aware of one's gayness. In virtually all phases, gay persons must deal with the damage to self-esteem caused by rejection and prejudice.

Living through the Phases of Gay Awareness

Virtually all gay persons go through four distinct phases of dealing with their sexual orientation.

Stage #1—Denying

In the past most gay persons denied their gayness because of its devastating consequences. This involves blocking the recognition of same-sex feelings in a variety of ways. Some maintain these defensive strategies indefinitely and hold back their same-sex feelings, consuming huge amounts of psychological energy in the process. Those in denial usually marry and have children, making a valiant effort to fit into a straight world.

Stage #2—Recognizing

Most openly gay persons say they first became aware of same-gender attraction before adolescence. In fact, nearly half of gay men say they were sexually attracted to males before they learned there were such sexual relations in the adult world. Gay adolescents who overcome denial will begin, by stages, to gradually tolerate the fact that they're having significant same-sex feelings.

Stage #3—Experimenting

Next comes a phase of experimenting with same-sex feelings and activities. Some gay persons increasingly feel that same-sex feelings are normal for them. Obviously, parents and society don't socialize children to be gay, and gay youngsters are not prepared to deal with antigay prejudice and the resultant wounding of self-esteem.

Stage #4—Accepting and Coming Out

The coming out process represents a shift in the person's core sexual identity and may trigger intense emotional distress. Denial of same-sex feelings may recur from time to time, but as they begin to accept their same-sex feelings, they develop a sense of identity as gay persons. Ideally, this gay identity is successfully integrated and accepted as a positive aspect of who they are. Those who are able to accept their sexual orientation and "come out" usually join gay support networks and have access to healing acceptance within the gay community. Studies indicate that gay persons who are more open about their sexual orientation have higher levels of self-esteem and psychological well-being.

Dealing with the Damage to Self-Esteem

Most gay persons are socialized in a middle-class environment, yet the adoption of middle-class values traps them in antigay prejudice. Becoming aware of their gayness inevitably means their self-esteem is wounded. All around them, gay teenagers see their straight friends' sexuality being anticipated, embraced, and cultivated, while their own sexuality is not. Dating, becoming engaged, marrying, and having children hold joyous implications for others, but not for them. The result of this devaluation and neglect is often a sense of loss: loss of self-esteem, loss of initiative, and loss of the belief that they're entitled to a full life.

When gay persons use the closet as a long-term survival tool, they lose the spontaneity we all need for authenticity in relationships. The constant pressure to conceal parts of the self and the constant dread of being found out creates stress. Coming out is a great relief for gay persons, but the downside is facing direct antigay prejudice. This can lead to lower self-esteem, self-rejection, and new types of stressors. The major way most gay persons handle this is by joining the gay community and building support networks.

WHAT'S THE GAY COMMUNITY ALL ABOUT?

Gay persons who come out of the closet tend to migrate to gay communities in major metropolitan areas. Gay persons within this community have as wide a variety of lifestyles as the rest of the population. They have close friends in support networks that loosely form a gay community, as well as straight friends and associates outside the community. Singles may frequent a gay bar scene, while couples tend to focus on their relationships and sometimes on parenting roles.

The Gay Community

The gay community consists of many distinctive groups. Friendship binds the members of each group together in strong, ongoing relationships. Couple relationships may be stable and long-lasting. Noncouple members may be linked within the group and between groups by tenuous but repeated sexual contacts or by supportive friendships. As a result of these bonds and their relatively small numbers, gay persons within a city tend to know of each other. They have a number of common interests, values, and customs. Such communities have links to each other across the country and even internationally.

Most openly gay persons function in two cultures—the larger culture and the gay community—and may be considered bicultural. Most spend at least half their leisure time with other gay persons. A common pattern is to have two sets of friends, one straight and the other gay. Ethnic minorities who are gay have even more complexities to deal with.

Support Networks

Forming a community with other gay persons is an important part of self-acceptance. For gay persons, it relieves their sense of being uniquely different and isolated, and allows them to jointly form a set of beliefs about sexuality that counter the negative beliefs of the dominant culture. The main function of a gay community or group is psychological, to provide a social environment of acceptance and support that gay persons cannot find elsewhere.

Gay Couples

A steady couple's relationship is claimed by about half of gay men and three-fourths of lesbians, and many establish lifelong partnerships as they mature. Within the gay community, couple relationships are given a status similar to that of marriage. The two partners are sexually available to each other on a continuing basis, expect that the relationship will be relatively long-lasting, and present themselves as a social couple. Being out of the closet makes this possible. In fact, the gay promiscuity myth stems from the fact that being in the closet means one must indulge in secret sex whenever the opportunity presents itself.

Gay Parents

Many gay persons have married in hopes of overcoming or curing their gayness and having a "normal" life with children. Why would such a gay married person later accept his or her gayness and come out of the closet? The most common reason is falling in love with a same-sex person. Once this happens, the married gay person tends to move from a covert, highly compartmentalized lifestyle, with all the surface appearances of suburban married life, toward openly gay lives. Divorce is a part of this movement, but most retain a commitment to and responsibility for their children, to the extent that the courts will allow.

In some states gay persons may adopt children. Regardless of how they became parents, almost all gay parents report that their children are straight and are typical for kids of their age and gender. Most have positive relationships with their children, try harder to create a stable home life, and are more egalitarian, but otherwise are basically the same as straight parents, according to studies by T. S. Weisner, J. E. Wilson-Mitchell, and others.

Community Issues

Five issues that are especially important to the gay community:

1. How people think of gayness: are you born with it or do you choose it?
2. How to counter the myths and stereotypes that result in antigay prejudice.
3. How to gain equal rights in the legal system—workplace rights, military rights, partnership rights, and parenting rights.
4. How to become accepted in the workplace, to come out of the closet.
5. How to manage a gay identity in the workplace once out of the closet.

ARE PEOPLE BORN GAY OR STRAIGHT?

Whether people are born gay or choose a gay lifestyle is perhaps the most crucial issue in the gay community's political struggle for equal legal rights. The major groups that are attempting to block gay political efforts use the rationale that homosexuality is a perversion and a sin against God and family values. Further, they claim gay persons choose this lifestyle and need counseling to help them become heterosexual or to abstain from sex altogether. The gay community vigorously refutes this viewpoint and sees it as their major barrier to achieving equal rights.

Recent scientific findings indicate that gay persons are born with that sexual orientation, though people can and do choose to experiment. Some persons are basically bisexual, and less is known about that orientation. You can better understand sexual orientation by seeing it as one of the many layers of human sexuality, by seeing each sexual quality in terms of a continuum rather than in either-or terms, and by reviewing some key findings regarding biological causes of sexual orientation—which we'll do next.

Sexual Factors: How Deep and to What Degree?

Sexuality is most realistically viewed as having five layers of depth, the deeper layers being more innate, an unchanging part of us, and the superficial layers being potentially changeable. All sexual factors can be expressed in relative degrees of intensity.

Layer #1—Sexual Identity: Male to Female

The deepest, core layer refers to whether we identify ourselves as male, female, or transsexual. Scientists describe the miniscule proportion of persons who are transsexual as men or women who are physically indistinguishable from average men or women but who believe they're trapped in the body of the wrong sex. Some of them choose to have sex-change operations and do in fact change their sexual identity from male to female or vice versa. On the other hand, for nearly all persons, sexual identity, being male or female, is the least changeable aspect of their sexuality.

All our forms and questionnaires offer only two gender choices: male or female. But we all know some people who seem extremely masculine or feminine and others who seem much less so. On the sexual identity continuum, people who are extremely masculine or feminine would fall at either end, with many people in between and transsexuals at the center. Being male or female, then, is not simply an either-or situation.

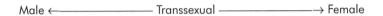
Male ←——————— Transsexual ———————→ Female

Layer #2—Sexual Orientation: Gay to Straight

Wrapped around the core sexual identity layer is sexual orientation, meaning whom we are sexually attracted to—men, women, or both. A very small proportion are described as bisexual. Some bisexuals may be attracted to both men and women; others to either a man or a woman at any one time frame of their life.

We say a person is either gay or straight. But some people are more confirmed in their gayness than others. On the sexual orientation continuum, the large majority of the population is at the straight end. At the gay end, are 2.15 percent who are exclusively gay. In between are bisexuals and people who have had some gay experiences. For example, nearly one-third of all men, and about 10 percent of all women, report they have had overt same-sex experiences, most during their adolescent years.

Straight ←————Some gay experiences————Bisexual————→ Gay

Sexual orientation is somewhat more flexible than sexual identity. Some straights are "less straight" than others and may be able to "choose" a gay orientation, although nearly all gay persons say that in retrospect they have always been gay and it is not a choice. Similarly, some gay persons are "less gay" than others and switch to a straight sexual orientation after they have had one or more gay relationships, although this is relatively rare.

Layer #3—Sexual Preferences—What Turns a Person On

Moving away from the core, we find the types of scenes, fantasies, or body parts that arouse a person. Sexual preferences can and do change more readily than the deeper layers of sexuality. For example, a woman, when she's 20, may be turned on sexually by men with dark hair, but when she's 30, men with red hair may be more attractive to her. A man, when he's 20, may be turned on by dependent women, but he may prefer more independent types when he's 30.

Layer #4—Sexual Roles

Even more superficial are sex roles, those ways of being and doing that are adopted primarily by males and those adopted by females. For example, a woman may shift from her professional career role to the wife and mother role as she returns home from the office each evening. A man may shift from football coach to family cook when he returns home.

Layer #5—Sexual Performance

At the most superficial layer, we find the different ways that people behave when the time seems right for making love. Both men and women may choose from many behaviors that they think will make lovemaking more exciting or satisfying or comforting, for example. People can and do vary these behaviors regularly—from the way they flirt to the way they help their partner reach fulfillment.

The Causes of Sexual Orientation: Genes and Hormones

We return now to the major issue of whether some people are born gay or choose to be gay. To begin with, how can we explain the fact that gays are found in every society even though no known society socializes children as homosexuals? None has ever set up gay role models. For example, American parents, after years of teaching their little boys about male sex-ways and their little girls about female sex-ways, have traditionally been shocked and disappointed upon learning their child is gay.

If persons are not socialized into the role of homosexual, it doesn't seem likely that they choose their sexual orientation. If this is true, then persons who are predominantly gay can no more will themselves to become straight than straight persons can will themselves to become gay.

The idea that gayness is fixed before birth and is biologically based is the prominent belief among scholars today. Some research indicates a genetic basis for homosexuality. Other research points toward hormonal influences before birth.

Genes

Scientists have detected a "gay gene," as reported by Dean Hamer of the National Cancer Institute. They do not claim that it is solely responsible for gayness, nor that any gene can dominate any behavior trait. Instead, they are saying that genes influence behavior through indirect and complex paths that require inputs from the physical body, the environment, and the culture.

Gayness in Twins and Siblings

Studies of the sexual orientation of identical twins point to a genetic basis for gayness, according to J. M. Bailey. Since identical twins occur when the mother's egg divides after conception, twins begin life with identical genetic material. If gayness occurred only because of one or more "gay genes," then theoretically every twin who is gay would have a gay sibling. Actually, about half of those who are gay have a twin who is also gay. This indicates that gayness is not entirely genetic. On the other hand, if genes played no part, we would expect that only 2 percent of gay twins would have a gay sibling because that's the incidence of gay persons in the general population. The fact that about 50 percent of gay twins have a gay sibling makes a strong case for the important role that genes must play in determining sexual orientation.

Hormones

Hormones secreted in the mother's womb during pregnancy affect the hormone balance of the child and whether that child will eventually be sexually attracted to opposite-sex or same-sex persons, according to researcher Martin Seligman.

Bottom line: Human sexuality is complex, and scientists don't know yet how all the factors interact to produce a person's sexual orientation.

MANAGING A GAY IDENTITY IN THE WORKPLACE

A central career focus for gay persons is managing their sexual identity. Gays who are in the closet must deal with the stress of "living a lie," while gays who come out must deal with people's reactions, according to author R. Rich and others.

Gays in the Closet

For those who haven't come out, vigilance is constant. They must devote great energy to pretending they have a lifestyle they don't or avoiding the lifestyle issue altogether. The fear of disclosure is ever present, resulting in anxiety and stress.

Counterfeiting a Straight Identity

How do gay persons manage to stay in the closet without raising suspicion? Many create fictitious spouses or opposite-sex lovers. Some complain about their status as a confirmed single, as someone unlucky in love, as a man with an old war wound, or as a woman with an inconsolable broken heart from an early tragic love affair.

Many corporate cultures make being straight and "coupled" a prerequisite for acceptance and involvement. Invitations to business-related events include mates or dates. If gays accept these invitations, they must make up an excuse for not having a mate, or they must bring an opposite-sex mate to keep up the pretense. If they shun such events to avoid the discomfort, important career opportunities can be lost.

Gay pretenders often complain that their social lives don't reflect their inner reality. Not surprisingly, they feel they're treated as if they are "someone else." They pay the price of enormous wasted energy from the effort needed to keep up the pose and the anxiety over possible discovery. They also must cope with the ethical problems implicit in living a lie. Perhaps most crucial, they must deal with the feelings of isolation and detachment that result from not being "who you really are."

Dodging the Issue

Gay persons who evade the issue of gayness tend to avoid all discussions of sexuality and to insist that others respect their privacy. They withhold the sexual information that people usually exchange in conversations, information about wives and husbands, girlfriends and boyfriends. They try not to answer such personal questions without people realizing they're not answering. Strategies include changing the subject and asking the questioner a question, perhaps softening their evasions with humor.

They have no way of knowing what conclusions others have made about avoidance of personal talk. They wonder, but never know, if others think they are gay. They may have no work-related social contact at all, leaving them feeling alone and separate. Most eventually bump into a glass ceiling imposed by their social isolation. They just don't quite "fit in" with upper management.

Gays Who Come Out

Gays generally carefully calculate the risk before they come out at work. According to such authors as J. D. Woods and J. H. Lucas, when gay persons first come out, they experience great relief but must immediately deal with antigay prejudice. They do find strategies for coping, and virtually all say that coming out is worth it.

Calculating the Risk

Coming out is anxiety filled and liberating at the same time. Gay persons say that when they disclose their sexual orientation, (whether by choice or because someone guessed it or told others, their first response is apprehension and anxiety about their job and the workplace. They don't believe being gay affects their work performance but that prejudice against them does. Most believe their career progression will be slowed or blocked. In fact, about one in three gay persons who have come out say they have experienced some form of job discrimination.

As the awareness and coming-out process unfolds, gay persons' natural tendency is to want to end the deception. They calculate the probable effects of coming out on their job security. Those who are most likely to come out have one or more of the following factors that provide some security. They

- are self-employed;
- have professional credentials;
- work directly with customers, so their dependence is dispersed across many persons outside the company;
- hold jobs that have concrete measures of success; and
- have unique, irreplaceable skills that are needed by the company or within the industry.

Facing the Reactions

The most immediate reactions gay persons face when they come out can include:

- becoming the target of verbal abuse and nonverbal hostility
- increased stress levels stemming from harassment
- a backlash of negative attitudes
- being fired or demoted
- being heaped with effusive sympathy and support

Professionals may find their effectiveness compromised and their authority undercut. Teachers often feel that they must always be on guard. For example, they may think twice before giving a student a hug and saying "Great job," because it could be misinterpreted.

In the long run, they must still spend much energy managing their gay identity, and most of them must also deal with being a token gay in a straight work group. The most important strategy gays adopt is to build a support network, although being gay makes this more of a challenge. Strategies for managing the fact that they're admittedly gay include minimizing their gayness, making it seem "normal" to straights, and offering it as an asset to the firm.

Minimizing Gayness

Some minimize the visibility of their sexuality with the goal of lessening their vulnerability. They fear that if they become too visible, or if gay persons in the organization appear too numerous, they will trigger hostility. They say there's a big difference for most straight persons in knowing about a gay person's sexuality and actually engaging in conversations on the subject, seeing them with a gay partner, and especially seeing them touching, dancing, or embracing. Most straight persons feel safer when gays limit discussions of their gayness to veiled comments and insinuations.

Normalizing Gayness

Gayness is the natural sexual orientation of more than 2 percent of the population, but most straight persons don't think of it as normal. Therefore, many gay persons use a strategy of subtly influencing others to see gayness as normal. They talk about their relationships and lifestyle in terms that highlight similarities to straight life, speaking of family, romance, and civil rights. They speak of many of the same concerns as coworkers, such as making house payments, dealing with "in-laws," or finding a date. Their purpose is to transform the unusual into the commonplace and acceptable and to give coworkers a framework for thinking about gay lifestyles. In doing this, they shift the focus away from what is "different" in their sexual orientation so that others may see the similarities between gay and straight relationships and relate to them as people first. Just like straight persons, gays know that beneath their sexual self is a core self that is more essential and encompassing, a more complete and complex self. They have the strong belief, "Whether I'm gay or not, I'm still me."

Making Gayness an Asset

A few gay persons are able to showcase their gayness as an advantage to the company. For example, they may highlight their multi-faceted connections with the gay community and marketplace and with talented gay professionals who might be recruited as employees, consultants, or suppliers.

Heaving a Sigh of Relief

Despite the hassles of discrimination, virtually all gay males who have come out say they don't regret the decision. The most important result is an overwhelming sense of relief at being finally open, followed by reduced stress, enhanced self-image, and feelings of freedom. Gay persons who come out experience less anxiety and depression, have more positive self-concepts, and feel better able to fully experience their emotions and interests, according to the research of P. J. Schmitt and L. A. Kurdek.

WHAT LEGAL RIGHTS DO GAY PERSONS HAVE?

Gay persons probably make up the largest minority group facing workplace discrimination that is not protected under federal civil rights statutes. Gay persons are not protected from discrimination in employment, housing, parental matters, military service, and other areas. No state law provides for gay employees' partners to have access to the same benefits married partners enjoy. In most states, they must face formidable barriers to parental rights. Many states retain old laws that make gay sex a crime even though most Americans believe that both gay and straight persons have a fundamental right of privacy for adult, consensual sex.

Struggling for Equal Employment Rights

The most crucial issue that affects gay persons' daily lives is employment discrimination. The employment-at-will doctrine holds that employer and employee enter an agreement as legal equals because the employee can quit "at will" and the employer can fire "at will." In most states, this doctrine remains a serious obstacle to worker protection from arbitrary and "at whim" personnel decisions. Congress has repeatedly refused to include sexual orientation in the antidiscrimination legislation of the Civil Rights Act.

Very few gay government employees have specific workplace protection, for example:

- Federal employees who are gay have no protection.
- Some laws actually require discrimination against gay persons; for example, military regulations.
- State government employees who are gay are protected in only nine states.
- A few city and county government employees are protected.

Even fewer gay corporate employees have specific protection, for example:

- Gay persons who work for private employers are protected in only four states and in a few cities.
- Gay union workers are protected in theory, but unions have traditionally been lax about actual protection for gays.

President Clinton has made three major proposals regarding gay rights:

1. An executive order that ended the use of "gays as an automatic security risk" in federal government personnel decisions.
2. A proposal for the acceptance of openly gay persons in the military, which faced much resistance and was modified to the "don't ask, don't tell policy."
3. The proposed Employment Non-Discrimination Act, which extends the civil rights protections given other groups to gay persons and which must be passed by Congress before becoming law.

Pursuing Family Rights

Gay activists are fighting for basic equal rights for gay couples. Currently, as they point out,

- Gay partners cannot file joint income tax returns.
- Gay employees usually cannot include their partners in their health plans.
- When gay persons become seriously ill or die, their partners can't legitimately take time off to attend to the illness or funeral.

- When gays are hospitalized, their partners may be barred from their bedside by hospital staff because they're "not a family member."
- They are often denied custody, or even visitation rights, of their own children and are not allowed to adopt children in most states.

SPECIFIC WORKPLACE BARRIERS

Your gay associates face many barriers in the workplace, most stemming from cultural myths and stereotypes. These barriers use up energy, drain productivity, and block profitable collaboration, so it is important for you to do your part in removing them.

Barrier #1—Prejudice and Discrimination That Drain Corporate Assets

Most gay persons remain in the closet at work. In fact, 81 percent of lesbians and 76 percent of gay men fear they would be the victims of job discrimination if they came out at work. About one in three gay persons who have come out say they have experienced some form of job discrimination.

Talent Drain

Gay persons look for workplaces where it's safe to be themselves. They may move toward a "gay ghetto" within the company where they can socialize with others who are on the edges rather than in the mainstream. Eventually, most look to other companies that meet their needs and offer opportunities for growth. Gay employees are especially likely to leave companies that

- condone antigay prejudice, yet require extensive business-related socializing.
- have vaguely defined managerial roles, but stress social skills that assume everyone is straight.

Many gay employees leave such limiting corporate cultures to expand their careers in:

- smaller companies
- gay-run businesses
- their own business
- corporate cultures that treat gays fairly

This exodus represents an important talent drain.

Energy Drain

Antigay prejudice creates an expensive diversion of human resources. Gay persons must learn to suppress ideas and actions that might invite suspicion, to monitor the way they dress and every word they say. Managing their identity at work consumes enormous amounts of energy, time, and personal resources. In prejudiced corporate cultures, closet gays must disguise their lifestyles or avoid the issue of sexuality altogether. Open gays must deal with various types of prejudice and discrimination. All must cope with high levels of stress that could be eliminated by a supportive work environment. The drain on energy and thus productivity is clear.

Productivity Drain

Prejudice also poisons work relationships and fosters misunderstanding. In its presence, many gay employees feel forced to either deceive, disengage, or resign, taking with them whatever investment the company has made in their development. For straight persons, prejudice sets up limited behavioral boxes that may seem comfortable and safe, but in actuality stifle ways of thinking and behaving that might fall outside the boundaries. What a waste! The bottom-line result of antigay prejudice is to create walls of silence and mistrust, which in turn lowers productivity.

- Antigay prejudice stems primarily from lack of information about gay persons and the gay community. Everyone needs access to training that provides this information. You can help encourage your associates to pursue such training.

Barrier #2—Blocks to Spontaneity: Seeing Gays as Abnormal

Gay persons need to be seen as persons who are just as normal as straight persons. Sexuality is only one dimension of human beings. Although it is certainly a major dimension, time spent in actual sexual activity is very small in the whole scheme of things. Gay persons are as highly individualistic as the population at large, with the same variety of interests, abilities, and traits.

Gay persons' sexual orientation, by itself, is disruptive only when others despise them for it. When gayness is feared and despised, everyone may become fearful about actions that might be viewed as symptoms of gayness. For example, when any type of same-sex affection and closeness may be viewed with suspicion, spontaneous collaboration among employees is inhibited. This is especially true for men, whose standards of "manliness" compel them to remain relatively distant, competitive, and independent. When men's tendencies to express their feelings or to nurture others are devalued, men tend to be suppress them. Masculinity can become a burden when men perceive they must constantly take charge of situations, speak their minds, and view compromise and accommodation as signs of weakness.

- The solution is simple but not always easy to implement: *Accept gayness as a normal expression of human sexuality for some people.* When gay persons are as valued as anyone else, people don't need to worry about appearing gay.

Barrier #3—The Sexual Double Standard

The Myth: The workplace is essentially asexual.

The Reality: Dating, engagements, weddings, mates, spouses, marriages, and children are discussed everywhere in the workplace, always from the straight person's viewpoint.

The Myth of the Asexual Workplace

Most people believe that, ideally, sex or sexual orientation should have nothing to do with the workplace, yet the symbols of straight sexuality are everywhere. In fact, personal and professional roles are not at all separate in most corporate cultures. The interactions there are colored by sexual possibilities, expectations, and constraints. Sexuality is often on display, explicitly or implicitly, in dress and image, jokes and gossip, looks and winks, fantasies and affairs. Sexuality is there in the range of persuasive behaviors we call flirtation or seduction, as well as those coercive behaviors we call sexual harassment.

Actual sexual contact at work is rare. Yet we humans are sexual creatures, even though we're much more than that, and our interactions are always colored by sexual possibilities. We can't help but bring our sexuality to work. It often underlies such intangible assets as rapport, familiarity, charisma, and "chemistry." When we channel it constructively, it can be the source of intense feelings of personal commitment and loyalty to the work team.

The Sexual Double Standard

The myth of the asexual workplace leads to a hidden double standard for expressing sexuality: it's generally okay for straight persons and not okay for gay persons. For example, it's okay for straight persons to discuss their sexual partners, such as husbands, wives, and lovers, and the children produced from such unions, but it is not acceptable for gay persons to do so. This is based on the belief that being straight is normal and desirable, but being gay is not.

Questions about marital status are a matter of course in professional circles, part of getting acquainted. When a man speaks of his wife at work, others interpret this as a statement about his social role as husband, not about his sexual performance as a straight man. People typically inquire about how he met his wife, how long they've been married, and similar facts. His sexual relationship is so socially acceptable, it's treated as asexual. When a gay man speaks of his male partner, the focus tends to be on so-called "unnatural sex."

This double standard compels gay persons to remain silent while others talk about family life. Gay persons must mask and repress their sexuality while others do not. For example, many gay persons won't entertain coworkers at home because it's too risky, especially if they haven't come out. Some say, "I'd love to invite people from work to my home, but I can't because I don't know what their reaction to my partner would be."

One reason gay persons like working in San Francisco or New York is the tendency for people who live there to mind their own business. They simply view what others do outside of work as those persons' private business, which they may choose to discuss or not. Many gay persons say they love the indifference. It's so much better than judgment or pity. Because of their early experiences with censure and worse, their sexuality is always an issue with them, a perpetual threat in the straight world, something to be constantly monitored there.

Any kind of double standard is perceived as unfair by those it discriminates against. Gay employees, to feel as valued and accepted as others, must feel free to discuss their personal lives in the ways that other employees do. Everyone in the company needs information about the sexual double standard and how it affects gay employees.

- You can help set the tone by viewing a gay associate's life at home and in the gay community as normal and positive. Your attitude will come through and will allow the gay person to feel at ease in discussing personal-life events as you and other coworkers do.
- When referring to employees' couple relationships in general, consider using the term "partner," which is inclusive, instead of "husband" or "wife."

Barrier #4—Walls of Silence That Deaden Creativity

Discomfort and avoidance of gay issues are typical in many corporate cultures. One danger is that people will get in the habit of not talking in order to avoid sensitive, sexual topics. This spills over to not talking about business topics. Such walls of silence tend to deaden relationships, which can then deaden the synergy and creativity that can spring forth from lively interactions. They expand the productivity drain.

Like all forms of prejudice, antigay prejudice creates barriers between different groups of people, ensuring that they will have a distorted, insufficient understanding of one another's needs and talents. The bottom-line result is an atmosphere of mistrust. Prejudice denies gay persons and coworkers the kind of trust and rapport that would enable them to discuss problems frankly. The result is a "spillover of silence."

- You can help to cure the prejudice and discrimination that builds these walls by being willing to openly discuss gay issues, by communicating regularly with gay associates, and by focusing on building rapport and trust.

Barrier #5—Treating Gay Persons as Tokens

Over half the gay persons in a recent survey said that a major reason they came out was their desire to educate others about gay lifestyles. Others refuse to come out precisely because they don't want to do "all that explaining." Some who come out find that being a symbol or token of the entire gay community means they can't quite be themselves after all, even though they're "out." They sense that coworkers are probing, testing their attitudes about gayness in general. Some token gays feel they're being dissected and examined, and that they're "on," performing, instead of just being themselves.

Token gays are likely to become lightning rods, targets for coworkers' attitudes toward the entire category of gay persons. Their mere presence may raise related issues beyond their immediate work performance. Whether gay persons are in the closet or out, fear of discrimination, together with impaired self-esteem, can motivate them to work harder and be better. Some suffer from double or triple stigma, such as also being a woman and an African American, and work even harder to compensate. But the pressure takes its toll, and burnout can be a result.

- You can help set a tone of acceptance. Treat gay persons as individuals whose achievements and failures reflect the person, not the gay community. Help educate others about the unfairness of viewing people as tokens.

Barrier #6—Hostile Corporate Cultures and Gay Ghettos

When gay persons perceive the corporate culture to be hostile, they may seek refuge in a safe job or position. They may find a protected niche in a large organization and stay out of the spotlight that goes along with high-visibility assignments, broad decision-making responsibilities, and major promotions. They may gravitate to departments that have a reputation for tolerance or in which other gay persons are clustered, sometimes called gay ghettos.

In ghetto-type jobs, the required skills are likely to be the hands-on type with clear job duties, and performance can be measured more objectively in terms of sales figures or concrete tasks completed. Therefore, these jobs are safer, more secure, and can provide a haven of tolerance in a larger, more biased organization. But comfortable niches nearly always have glass ceilings and walls all around them—in this case "lavender" glass.

- You can help to eliminate gay ghettos by encouraging a corporate culture that values and welcomes gay persons—as well as people from all types of groups.

Barrier #7—The Lavender Glass Ceiling

The "lavender" glass ceiling is what gay persons say blocks them when they reach a certain level of responsibility, so they never go higher. As managers and professionals move toward the top, reputation is everything. Careers are ruined by the perception that people are not "playing on the team" (i.e., that they are gay). Many say that the executives above them feel uncomfortable with bringing gay persons into the inner fold. Some executives rationalize that clients or employees won't accept a gay person at a high level, that relationships are more sensitive at that level, and that the company image might suffer.

Leading-edge companies don't fire people for being gay, but most gay persons are sure that gayness creates a lavender ceiling. And, knowing your job is safe is not the same as having a warm, inclusive environment where people accept you as you are and therefore give you an equal chance.

BUILDING ON GAY PERSONS' STRENGTHS

As a leader, you need to recognize the strengths that each of your team members brings to the organization and to build on those strengths. Gay persons bring many assets to the workplace that can be used in numerous ways. They can contribute to creative team projects, to the development of networks and business relationships that are especially valuable for the organization, and to connections with the gay community and marketplace.

Opportunity #1—Follow the Lead of Savvy Organizations

Do you want to help your organization stem the talent drain? You can provide company leaders with examples of how other leading-edge companies are attracting and keeping talented gay employees.

Microsoft

"When we lose a viable employee, we've probably lost upward of $2 million," said Microsoft's diversity director. The world's largest computer software company set a goal in 1990 of making sure that gay professionals have everything they need to stay productive, and their diversity program is an integral part of that strategy.

Lotus

In the early 1990s, Lotus recognized that many gay employees have the same deeply-committed relationships that married employees have. The company allows gay employees to include their partners in their health plans and similar benefits. It was the first major, publicly-held U.S. company to do so. Since then a number of large companies have made similar changes in their policies.

Levi Strauss

In the early 1990s, Levi Strauss became the largest employer to recognize gay partners for purposes of employee benefits, such as health care and life insurance. A gay employees' association was formed with company encouragement. Each year the members hold a Gay Pride Celebration at the San Francisco headquarters facility, which top management attends.

Such leading companies as Apple Computer, AT&T, Digital, DuPont, Hewlett Packard, Oracle, and Xerox—as well as smaller firms—now have gay employee organizations and nondiscrimination policies. These high-tech companies are painfully aware that their most talented employees can easily switch jobs and go to competitors that provide a more tolerant social atmosphere and better benefits. Competition is the newest reason for companies to offer domestic partner benefits. Top managers also know the high cost of replacing highly trained engineers and other technical workers. Companies that fall behind can expect a talent drain.

Opportunity #2—Recognize That Gay Persons Have High-Value Skills

As a practical matter, nearly all companies must have business reasons for focusing attention on a problem and for spending time or money on solving it. Companies are most likely to combat prejudice when they have economic incentives for doing so.

Gay persons are over-represented in the pool of highly educated, well-qualified employees, possibly representing 5 to 10 percent of such workers, according to Robert T. Michael's survey. This is precisely the type of worker that's getting harder and harder to find and keep. Companies need a reputation for diversity in order to be able to hire and keep high-potential gay employees. So long as prejudice, and double standards block their career paths, the collective creativity, knowledge, and energy of millions will be lost to companies.

Gay employees also have much to offer in business situations where a knowledge of the gay community is needed. They are likely to have an inside track on how to market products to gay customers, how to provide services to them, the implications of AIDS, and other business issues that involve gay persons. In addition, they can energize work teams. Most have experiences and insights that don't come with conventional lives—a cutting-edge sensibility, freedom from marital responsibilities, and a sensitivity and compassion for members of out-groups.

Opportunity #3—Help Gay Employees Build a Corporate Support Network

Gay persons can have the same problems in building support networks as other minorities. People are most comfortable with others like themselves. Therefore, it may be difficult for gay persons to make key connections and to find mentors. This may be especially true in nonaccepting corporate cultures, because other gay employees tend to hide out in order to avoid backlash, and other employees tend to avoid guilt by association. However, in flexible corporate cultures that encourage minority employee groups, gay employee associations tend to spring up. Such groups are providing many of the same benefits provided by support networks within the gay community at large, as well as specific workplace benefits.

Opportunity #4—Encourage Company Benefits for Gay Employees' Partners

To the gay or lesbian who is in a loving, long-term relationship, working for a company that provides benefits to state-recognized spouses but not to same-sex partners creates an atmosphere that devalues their couple relationship. Also, corporate antidiscrimination policies regarding gay and lesbian employees would almost certainly have a positive psychological impact on them. The change would probably trigger some negative backlash among certain straight employees in the short-term. Top management support for an accepting, nonprejudiced environment, however, can produce positive results for all employees in the long run. Clearly, an accepting environment is likely to result in higher productivity for gay workers.

Opportunity #5—Promote Education about Gay Issues

Most employees base their opinion of gay persons on common stereotypes and myths. Leaders can provide educational seminars for all employees to inform them of the facts and to initiate discussions of concerns and of new attitudes. A frequent concern is AIDS anxiety, a key fear many people have regarding gay persons. The antidote is facts and figures. For example, AIDS is no longer a predominantly gay disease; it infects all segments of the population. It's not normally contagious and is spread only through very specific types of activities, almost none of which normally occur in the workplace. Savvy companies are building AIDS awareness into company policy, providing informative training sessions for all employees, and giving them written materials that explain the issue.

Opportunity #6—Help Create a Savvy Corporate Culture

A corporate culture is based on the basic beliefs and values of its founders and leaders that are accepted generally by most employees. These values are expressed in everyday rituals of communication and interaction, the stories that are passed around about the "big wheels," and the people who are allowed into the grapevines and inner circles. Values are also expressed in corporate policies and procedures and the ways they are carried out.

One example of changing the corporate culture, is to change the belief that gayness is abnormal to the belief that it is normal for some persons. As a result, you and others in the company value gay employees as normal, contributing associates. In turn, you accept their family and community activities as normal and become comfortable with discussing their lives with them in the same ways you talk with others about their lives.

Gay persons need to work in a corporate culture that accepts them as valuable persons, one that values nonjudgmental caring of one human being for another. They need to feel as welcome and included as straight persons feel.

Assess the Culture

All organizations benefit by looking squarely at the basic assumptions and beliefs that underlie their goals, values, and boundaries, and questioning their fairness. You can use your influence to encourage such questioning and the adoption of needed changes in the corporate culture.

- You can encourage your associates to analyze the corporate culture to see how it encourages or allows antigay prejudice.
- You can jointly identify barriers gay persons encounter and ways to remove the barriers.
- You can find ways to make the culture safe for gay persons, and to open up new opportunities for profitable collaboration.

Heal Antigay Prejudice

Gay advocates say the workplace issue should not be one of denying sexual orientation but rather respecting all persons' rights to privacy and to a harassment-free environment. You can help your organization face the gay workplace rights issue. If your organization needs to move beyond antigay prejudice, you can help by encouraging specific company actions designed to reduce prejudice and eliminate discrimination.

- You can serve as a role model, setting the example of being as fair as possible in all your dealings with gay persons.
- If you're a supervisor, you can make personnel decisions based on individuals' work performance and potential, not sexual orientation, and encourage others to follow your example.
- Encourage company leaders to establish clear policies that ban antigay discrimination and specific procedures for implementing such policies.

Make It Safe for Gay Applicants

Gay persons need to "come out" at the time of hiring in order to be most productive within an organization. If they feel they must come in as closet gay persons, they may gain respect and credibility as straight persons in the organization, based on their skills, creativity, and competence. This credibility may be decimated if they later come out, because coworkers may think they've been deceived all along and trust is shattered. The leading-edge companies that are attracting talented gay applicants have a reputation for accepting gay employees as normal, valuable contributors. They have created corporate cultures that reflect this belief.

- You can encourage your associates to adopt this belief, which in turn will impact the corporate culture.

Skill Builder 1—The Case of Gay Rumors

You are a supervisor in the computer section of a large bank. One of your best computer technicians, **Diane**, has worked there for three years. She has been an excellent worker up to now. Lately, however, her productivity has fallen off and she has called in sick several times. The other day you noticed a cartoon about lesbians stuck on the wall near Diane's desk. You've also overheard some gossip in the restroom implying that Diane might be a lesbian.

- What should you do?

Skill Builder 2—The Case of Clients' Comfort Zone

Carmen studies the file folder on her desk. As head of the Western Regional office of the Hartford Company, a lending and investment firm, she must decide how to handle a touchy situation. She's thinking about **Jayson**, one of her most productive employees. Jayson has been in the special customer department for two years, dealing with customers who have a net worth of $200,000 to $1 million. He has done an excellent job of handling these customers' needs to invest their available cash and to get loans for business or home-buying purposes.

Don, in the custom portfolio department, is being promoted and transferred, and Carmen has been considering who should take his position. Don deals only with customers who have a net worth of over $1 million. This is a different group, mostly older and more conservative than the customers Jayson has been working with. The only problem Carmen worries about is the fact that Jayson is a gay man. Carmen knows that at least one or two of Don's customers have made antigay comments. She's concerned not only with the possibility of losing some customers, she wonders if it's fair to Jayson to throw him into such a sensitive situation.

- What should Carmen do?

Skill Builder 3—The Case of Frank, a Gay Assistant

Frank is hired in February as an administrative assistant at Graphics Express, a Palo Alto, California, software firm. He considers it an excellent opportunity because the company has made a commitment to provide him with career development opportunities and to give him the backup resources he needs to carry out his projects. The resources include clerical help. Frank and his supervisor **Bradley** hit it off well, and Frank looks forward to a successful, rewarding career at Graphics Express.

Frank makes no secret of the fact that he's a gay man, because he prefers to start off on an honest basis with his coworkers. Soon after he comes to work, however, one of his coworkers, **Jennifer**, begins making derogatory comments about gays to him. Frank tries to ignore these put-downs, but Jennifer escalates them to direct insults about Frank's sexual orientation. The comments upset Frank. He discusses them with his partner, saying, "It hurts to be treated this way in this day and age. I thought that in this city and this company I would be left alone." Frank and his partner agree that the best response is to continue ignoring Jennifer's negative comments and to focus on doing a good job.

The situation takes a turn for the worse, however, when **Katie**, who works closely with Jennifer, brings some disturbing news to Frank. Katie says that Jennifer frequently complains about Frank to others when she's in the employee lounge. Katie says, "Frank, I hate to be the one to tell you, but I think you should know. Jennifer's saying you're unfit to represent the company to customers because you're gay. She says you tarnish the company and all of us with your perverse lifestyle."

This time Frank decides he must take action. It's one thing to put up with remarks directed solely at himself, but mudslinging in the presence of all his coworkers is more than he can take. He schedules a meeting with **Jeff**, the human resources director, and informs him of the situation. Jeff promises to look into it. This meeting takes place in early May.

In late May, Frank's supervisor, Bradley, is promoted. Frank shares Bradley's elation over the promotion, but when he hears who will take Bradley's place, his heart sinks. His nemesis Jennifer will be his new supervisor. Frank decides to try to make the best of it, to ignore Jennifer's hostility, and to do the best job possible.

By the end of June, Frank can see that his goals are becoming more and more difficult to achieve. Jennifer is giving Frank more and more assignments, often menial and tedious ones, and makes it clear that Frank is expected to complete them by deadline without receiving additional clerical help or overtime. The final straw comes in late July when Jennifer tells Frank he can no longer depend on the help of Deborah, the clerk who has worked most closely with him in the past.

Frank immediately goes to Jeff, the human resources director. Frank brings Jeff up to date on the situation, saying:

Jeff, you said you'd look into this problem of Jennifer's hostility toward me. It was difficult enough when she was merely slandering me. Now she's in a position of direct power over me, and she's setting up impossible performance standards for me. The situation has become so stressful that I have great difficulty sleeping, and I've been putting in such long, hard, tension-filled days that I'm beginning to feel drained all the time. What can you do to relieve this situation?

Jeff promises to investigate the situation but makes no further commitment.

Now it's late August, and Frank is trying to decide his next move. He feels exhausted, he's had a respiratory infection for six weeks, and his doctor tells him he must get more rest.

- What should Frank do?
- What should Jeff do?

Skill Builder 4—The Case of Edna, Lesbian Employee

Edna has been working for Whizware, a Silicon Valley software company, for two years. She is 26 years old and for some time refused to believe that she was gay. She married her high school sweetheart, but the marriage ended in divorce after a year or so. Now Edna is living with her lesbian partner **Janice**. The relationship is good, and Edna finally feels comfortable about her sexuality. However, she has not told anyone about her sexual orientation except a few close lesbian friends.

Whizware has many liberal policies, including flextime, three-week vacations, and a relaxed dress code. Most of the employees are under age 40. Recently the company encouraged a gay support group to form. Edna was astonished that out of about 350 employees, 52 attended the first meeting. While this turn of events is heartening to Edna, the response of many coworkers is not. Most of what she hears is pretty nasty and hateful, with few accepting or supportive comments.

Having a divorced status has helped Edna to pass for a heterosexual. She says, "I don't deliberately lie, but when my colleagues talk about child care and how hard it is to find reliable help, I can safely murmur something about being glad I didn't have children when I was married. But at the same time I can be sympathetic to their problems, which of course I am."

The longer Edna is employed by Whizware, the more difficult it is for her to maintain her counterfeit identity. The workers tend to know a great deal about each other's lives outside the office. Edna knows, however, that most people are more interested in talking about themselves than hearing about other's lives, so she staves off friendly curiosity by showing more interest in the details of their lives than she actually feels. She says, "Most of my coworkers respect my privacy and assume I'm mourning my failed marriage."

Edna periodically travels to Vancouver and Dallas as part of her job of training clients in the use of Whizware products. Occasionally, a colleague or executive will travel with her. Recently **David Southam**, Vice President, accompanied her to Vancouver. As Edna says, "He had a little too much to drink and definitely became too friendly. I had a tough time convincing him that 'no' means 'no.'"

Edna has never heard any office gossip about Southam being a womanizer, but she's concerned that he may seek revenge for her rejection of his overtures. If he does, and if her lesbian relationship with Janice becomes known to him, she would be especially vulnerable. Southam made several antigay remarks while under the influence and clearly was against the gay support program recently instituted at Whizware. After thoroughly bashing the program, he said, "*#* faggots, who needs 'em?" He also made several nasty cracks about **Jane Goodman**, one of the founders of the gay support program. Edna is terrified of the prospect of being regarded in the same devastating way by Southam. On the other hand, when Southam is sober and on the job in Silicon Valley, he's well respected. However, Edna wants to avoid traveling with him in the future.

Edna's partner Janice suggests that Edna could file a sexual harassment complaint against Southam, which could solve any future travel problems. This prospect horrifies Edna, who says, "I'm just gonna try to get out of traveling with him." She knows this might not be possible, because one of Whizware's best clients is located in Dallas. The strategy for keeping this client satisfied depends on Edna's technical knowledge combined with Southam's customer relations skills.

- What are the key issues in this situation?
- If you were Edna, what would you do?

Feedback on Skill Builder 1—The Case of Gay Rumors

First, get the cartoon off the wall. At the first opportunity, hold a staff meeting and include a discussion of cartoons, jokes, and attitudes that are appropriate in a multicultural work environment. If possible, arrange for some diversity training for everyone. Meet with Diane and discuss her recent productivity and illness. Be supportive and ask if there is a problem that you might help to remedy. If Diane mentions the cartoon or gossip, be open, nonjudgmental, and supportive. Give Diane the clear message that prejudice and discrimination against gay persons is not acceptable to you and that you will not condone the expression of such prejudice by her coworkers. Let her know that for you, her private life is private and that how much of it she reveals to others is up to her. Discuss possible solutions to any problems that she is experiencing now, letting her take the lead.

Feedback on Skill Builder 2—The Case of Clients' Comfort Zone

Carmen needs to make her decision on the basis of Jayson's performance and potential, not on a couple of customers' antigay comments. She should ask herself, If Jayson were not gay, would he be my obvious choice for this promotion? If the answer is yes, Carmen should discuss the possibility of the promotion with Jayson. She should be open, honest, and tactful with him in discussing possible customer prejudice. Jayson deserves an opportunity to propose how he might approach and handle such problems.

Carmen and Jayson might consider a best-case scenario in which all the clients like and accept Jayson, and he brings in new clients—and how to make that a probability. They can also consider a worst-case scenario in which certain possibly antigay customers take their business elsewhere. What might be the impact on the company, on Jayson, and on Carmen? If Jayson believes he can succeed in the position and meet the company's expectations, Carmen should give him the chance.

Feedback on Skill Builder 3—The Case of Frank, a Gay Assistant

The key issue is blatant harassment and discrimination by Jennifer against Frank because of his sexual orientation.

Jeff, the Human Resources Director, has a responsibility to discuss this with Jennifer and to explain the implications of her behavior. If she doesn't mend her ways, Jeff should take the case to top management. In fact, he should seriously consider informing them of the situation even before he discusses it with Jennifer and possibly getting their backing. This can strengthen the case he makes to Jennifer. She should either stop the harassment and discrimination or be dismissed from the company. Jeff should urge management to transfer Jennifer or Frank at once. Ideally, Jennifer would be transferred if Frank prefers to stay where he is. A basic principle of fairness is that once harassment is established, the harasser should be the one to leave.

Frank's Options: He should get relief from this impossible situation or leave the company. Before leaving, he should consider taking matters into his own hands if Jeff continues to be ineffective. The logical first step is to discuss his concerns with Jennifer. If things do not change for the better very quickly, he should break the chain of command and go to Jennifer's manager.

What actually happened: In August Frank took a six-month leave of absence. In February, when he attempted to return to his job, the company told him they no longer needed his services. Six months later Frank's attorney filed a suit against the company for $1 million, claiming employment discrimination based on the fact that he was harassed on the job and eventually fired because of his sexual orientation. This took place in Palo Alto, California, where no laws specifically protect gay persons working for private enterprise. This is true for most places in the United States. An antidiscrimination law to protect gays was passed by the California legislature in 1994 but was vetoed by Governor Pete Wilson. He claimed that a general protection law regarding discrimination was all that gay persons needed.

Feedback on Skill Builder 4—The Case of Edna, Lesbian Employee

Key issues include:

- Coming out or staying in the closet is probably the most important issue here.
- Sexual harassment of Edna by Southam is an issue.
- Antigay prejudice on the part of Southam and others is a crucial issue.

Edna, for her own mental health, should seriously consider coming out. If discrimination occurs, she could file a complaint. However, most states and cities have no civil rights protection for gay persons, so any complaint would need to be based on unfair employment practices. An alternative is to find a job with a company that is less prejudiced and to start off on the right foot by stating that she's a lesbian.

10

Persons with Disability: Bridging Comfort Gaps

About one in every sixteen persons you're likely to encounter in the workplace is a person with a disability. About 49 million Americans have disabilities that fall under the Americans with Disabilities Act (ADA) definition: "a physical or mental impairment that substantially limits one or more of the major life activities." About 26 million are considered severely disabled. One-third of all persons with disabilities, about 16 million, are employed in the workplace.

Strictly speaking, everyone has some type of impairment, perhaps a missing toe or finger, mild near-sightedness, or difficulty learning advanced mathematics. The people classified as disabled are impaired in a major life function. For some, the difference this makes in their lives is relatively minor; for others, such as quadriplegics, it's enormous.

A major key to building profitable relationships is to learn about a disabled associate's community and get a feel for his or her background. The more skilled you become at interpreting an individual's actions against the backdrop of his or her background, the greater success both of you can achieve through working together. Keep in mind that there are many types disability and each person deals with their disability in a somewhat unique manner. Avoid the temptation to use this lifestyle information to form new rigid categories.

As you explore the following topics, designed to help you understand what it's like to be a person with a disability, try to begin seeing situations as you think a person with a disability would view them. Specifically, you will learn:

- How typical myths about persons with disabilities compare with reality
- Major reasons why people devalue and exclude persons with disabilities
- How the current situation is connected to certain historical events
- What it is like to be a person with a disability
- Key facts about the Independent Living Movement
- What you should know about the Americans with Disabilities Act (ADA)

- Barriers to career success for persons with disability and how to break through these barriers
- Assets that persons with disability bring to your company and how to use those assets to create win-win successes

MYTHS AND REALITIES

To get to know what it's like to be a person with a disability, you must understand the stereotypes they deal with every time they leave the family or community circle, or turn on the television, for that matter. Most of the myths and stereotypes about persons with disabilities are either false or distorted, partial truths. In fact, most stem from people's discomfort with disabilities based on their fear of becoming disabled themselves. Persons with disabilities must cope with a wide range of myths and stereotypes, prejudice and discrimination, from mild to devastating in impact. They form invisible barriers between people, more powerful even than the steep steps and narrow doorways that block persons in wheelchairs.

People usually don't openly express their attitudes of avoidance or discomfort toward persons with disabilities. For example, most people don't voice their pity or distaste, nor avoid all eye contact, conversation, touching, or proximity. Avoidance attitudes are more likely to be expressed indirectly in the form of exclusionary practices, sometimes said to be necessary for the safety or convenience of persons with disabilities, or of people in general. The result is that most people don't have persons with disabilities around them, which relieves them from feeling uncomfortable or distressed. Our goal here is to enable you to understand the barriers and opportunities that persons with disabilities face—and in the process to become comfortable with working with them.

Myth #1—Persons with severe disabilities are childlike, dependent, and in need of charity or pity.

In fact, many persons with severe disabilities have a great deal to contribute and are able to work and to manage their own lives through the Independent Living Movement, which you'll learn about later.

A related myth is that a disability is a constantly frustrating tragedy. In fact, many persons with disabilities say that a disability need only be an inconvenience if it is dealt with as an inconvenience. Developing intelligent accommodations is one way to accomplish this. Although severe disabilities pose huge challenges, even they can be viewed primarily as a challenge to be overcome rather than a hopeless tragedy. For example, world-renowned physicist Stephen Hawking has stated that his disabling condition left him with not much to do but use his mind creatively and productively. Carolyn Vash, who has an impairment, suggests that we view her as being in a different situation, not necessarily a less-fortunate one—in the deeper, eternal sense.

Myth #2—Persons with disabilities are unable to lead normal lives.

Most persons with disabilities can live relatively normal lives and want to do so. Most are impaired in only one functional area. They tend to compensate for their impairment in numerous ways. They're able to do most things as well as anyone and usually can do some things better. Many people with disabilities view their limitations as a fact of life but go to work and participate as actively in society as they can. Persons with disabilities are increasingly well educated, with 75 percent completing high school in 1994, compared with 60 percent in 1986.

Myth #3—Persons with disabilities can only do menial or entry-level jobs, and most don't want to work.

In fact, persons with disabilities are successfully employed at almost all levels in nearly every field. More than 90 percent of net new job openings in the 1990s are in information-intensive and service occupations, and at least 90 percent of persons with disabilities are capable of filling such jobs.

Most people with a disability want to work, regardless of the extent of their impairment, and see work as a major route to self-fulfillment. They want to find work that draws on their skills and talents and helps them live a more abundant life.

Dissatisfaction with life is reported by four times as many adults classified as having disabilities as other adults. This dissatisfaction is related to their desire to work and to live a normal life. About 80 percent of adults with disabilities who do not work say they would rather have a job. Many who are unemployed are younger persons with mental disorders, as shown in Figure 10.1.

Myth #4—Employees with disabilities create safety risks, increase costs, and are less flexible and productive than other workers.

In fact, a review of 90 hands-on studies, described by Taylor Cox, reveals that compared to other employees, persons with disabilities

- have better safety records.
- do not normally cause increased health care costs.
- have equal or better turnover and absentee rates.
- have equal or better job assignment flexibility.
- are productive; more than 90 percent of 1,451 workers at DuPont rated them as average or above average on overall job performance.
- have better than average attendance records compared to those of nondisabled employees.

Myth #5—Employees with disabilities are more difficult to work with.

Two large surveys of managers and coworkers of persons with disabilities indicate the following:

Figure 10.1   *Reasons People Receive Disability Payments*

	All	Younger <50	Older 50-64
Mental disorders	28%	40%	17%
Heart disease	18	7	25
Arthritic disease	19	12	23
Cancer	3	3	4
All other	32	38	31

- Eighty percent of managers say they are no more difficult to supervise than others.
- Fifty percent of managers rate the following qualtities as better than those of other workers: willingness to work hard, reliability, punctuality, and attendance.
- Eighty percent of coworkers say they are just as productive as others.

WHY ARE PERSONS WITH DISABILITIES EXCLUDED?

Most devaluation of others refers to regarding someone as inferior, a lesser being, not very capable, not very useful, possibly burdensome, not beautiful, and generally one down. Devaluation follows close behind outright oppression when it comes to psychologically damaging consequences. It's the most common and devastating attitude facing persons with disabilities. They consistently experience devaluation in the eyes of others, and therefore their own, whether their disability is physical, sensory, or mental in nature.

The form and degree of devaluation is heavily influenced by the surrounding culture. Devaluation can be blatant or subtle. The Nazis blatantly killed disabled people. Most societies are so subtle that their devaluative practices have gone unrecognized as such for many years, until the new breed of disability activists began to call attention to them. In both the East and the West, for example, it has been common to segregate the disabled into their own schools and workplaces.

Personal Beliefs That Affect Devaluation

The prevailing beliefs of the culture have a distinct effect on how people view persons with disabilities, according to disability activists such as Carolyn Vash.

Western Viewpoint

Most Western philosophies hold that we each have only one life to live. Therefore, being disabled has other implications, from "It's just God's will and we can't know why," to "It's God's punishment for something the victim did or something the victim's parents did," to "It's a tragedy because we're here to enjoy life." The American culture puts a high value on standard modes of reasoning, a cultural model of physical beauty, and the physical, material world. These values result in seeing a person as a personality inside a body, so when one or both of those has been damaged "permanently," not much is left. Those who are more spiritually oriented understand that the spirit is not damaged just because the body or personality is damaged.

Eastern Viewpoint

Most Eastern philosophies include the idea of the reincarnation of the soul in multiple lives. Many believe that before coming into a new lifetime, at a spiritual level we choose our parents, our body, and our total life situation. We do this in order to learn certain lessons and have certain experiences that deepen our awareness and understanding and promote our spiritual growth. Disability thus becomes a growth experience. This is not to say that all Asians view disability in this manner, but some persons with disabilities see this viewpoint as more constructive and empowering than the Western view.

Media Influences

In the past, films and television programs often presented persons with disabilities as villains, criminals, monsters, and tragic figures. All these stereotypes express the idea that disability involves the loss of an essential part of the person's humanity. The figures were often portrayed as almost subhuman. Think of Captain Hook, the hunchback of Notre Dame, mentally impaired Lennie in John Steinbeck's *Of Mice and Men*. In these cases, disability implied the loss of moral self-control, often due to the bitterness and isolation that resulted from the fear and bigotry of others.

During the 1970s and 1980s, we saw persons with disabilities in the media who chose suicide as an escape from their "living death" or "vegetable existence," even though they retained many life functions. In many films, disability implied total physical dependency and separation from the community, and the victims were unable to adjust to their disability. Death was presented as the only logical and humane solution to a horrible situation. Other dramas focused on bitter, self-pitying victims whose families eventually got tough in order to help the person with disability adjust and cope. The focus was usually on victims who worked courageously and achieved remarkable feats.

Both types of stories featured the theme of overcoming adversity, based on the concept of disability as primarily a problem that requires the person with the disability to accept the situation and find the emotional resources to cope and overcome. Social stigma and devaluation were not the issue and society was let off the hook.

A few recent productions have directly dealt with the issue of prejudice. Others have presented persons with disabilities as normal persons who happen to have some functional impairment. Deaf and paraplegic persons have been portrayed as attractive and sexual, entering relationships out of the strength of their own identities. Certain activist groups are trying to influence media decision-makers to focus on these more realistic aspects of disability.

Fear of Becoming Disabled

People don't like to think about losing control of their destiny, or that the hand of fate could strike them as well as the person with a disability who they see before them. This fear can lead to extreme discomfort and distress upon even seeing persons with disabilities, much less spending time with them. What people fear, they tend to shun and stigmatize. Fear can also lead to blaming the disabled for their predicament. Some people find comfort in believing that persons with disabilities must have brought it on themselves through sin, carelessness, or self-sabotage. In turn, they can tell themselves that they would never bring such a disaster upon themselves, and this makes them feel safer.

Unfamiliarity and Discomfort with Persons with Disabilities

When people have had little or no experience with persons with a certain type of disability, the unfamiliarity can be disconcerting. People are frequently confused and uncertain about how to act and what to do. Some avoid making eye contact with such persons because they got punished for "staring" when they were children and were told not to ask questions.

Unfamiliarity can cause people to focus on the equipment surrounding some people—braces, crutches, wheelchair—and keep them from really seeing and tuning into the person. It can cause people to look at an interpreter, leaving out the hearing-impaired person, instead of viewing the translator as a mechanism for communication and focusing on the person they're communicating with. In all these cases, the person with the disability gets little or no eye contact and becomes something of a nonperson.

Self-Awareness Opportunity 1—What If You Became Impaired?

Purpose: To increase your awareness of the experiences of persons with disabilities.

Step 1. Various Activities. List some barriers you would face in a typical day if you lost your ability to walk, your vision, or your hearing. Consider how you would manage the activities shown in the column to the left if you had each of the impairments shown on the right. What barriers would you have to overcome in each case?

	Mobility Impaired	Visually Impaired	Hearing Impaired
• getting up in the morning, getting ready			
• getting to work or school			
• doing your work, communicating, etc.			
• having lunch			
• using the restroom			
• other activities? (list)			

Step 2. Getting Dressed. Put on a tight blindfold, or close your eyes and don't peek. Go through the motions of getting dressed or a similar task. What problems do you experience? Which are the most difficult?

Step 3. Sight and Sound. During a television drama, try the following experiments:

- Wear a blindfold for 5 or 10 minutes.
- Mute the sound for 5 or 10 minutes.

What are the key differences between no-sight and no-sound? What insights does this experience suggest to you about visual and hearing impairments? Write a few words about them.

CONNECTIONS TO THE PAST

Cultural attitudes and policies toward persons with disabilities have changed dramatically in this century. Persons with disabilities say that the most serious barriers to living reasonable lives and doing their work are not necessarily their own physical or psychological disabilities. The worst barriers are external: other people's stereotypes and attitudes, and the buildings, vehicles, walks, steps, and restrooms they must negotiate. Some highlights of historical change uncovered by researcher P. K. Longmore include:

Before 1850	Traditional moral attitude: take care of the disabled.
1850s	Provide special schools for the trainable.
1880s	Institutionalize the disabled in large centers.
1880s-1920s	Involuntary confinement and sterilization.
1930s	Rehabilitation for some. Sight-impaired advocates fight for participation in society.
1940s	F. D. Roosevelt, who uses a wheelchair, is U.S. president.
	World War II opens doors to disabled workers because of manpower shortages; March of Dimes, Cerebral Palsy associations are formed.
1950s	Focus on rehabilitating and adapting to the environment.
1960s	Disabled-rights advocates organize to change their environment; Urban Mass Transportation Act and Architectural Barriers Act encourage access.
1970s	Federal law requires access and accommodation from some employers and organizations; some states pass similar laws; Independent Living approved by Congress and some states.
1980s	Independent Living Movement; Air Carriers Access Act.
1990s	Federal ADA requires access and accommodation from most employers and in nearly all public buildings.

A new day dawned for persons with disabilities in the late 1960s, as it did for many groups. Many of them began viewing themselves as part of a minority group that must manage its own brand of stereotypes and discrimination from others, develop and affirm its own values and issues, and take charge of its own destiny. They began to fight in the civil rights mode of other minorities, to formulate their rights, and to demand protection for those rights. They have campaigned for and won new laws ever since, culminating with the Americans with Disabilities Act, which was phased in during the early 1990s. As a result, school administrators began installing ramps and elevators instead of counseling people with disabilities to stop wanting to attend classes held upstairs. Managers began to remove discriminatory hiring practices instead of advising applicants with disabilities to start liking the few jobs they would be allowed to do.

WHAT'S IT LIKE—HAVING A DISABILITY?

Human beings are more alike than different, regardless of variations in their physical bodies, sensory capacities, or intellectual abilities. Being a person with a disability is like being any other person, only with an impairment that prevents you from performing one or more major life functions. This means you learn to make better use of the physical abilities you do have, as well as your inner resources. It means you are constantly struggling to become more independent and to live a "normal" life. Women's experiences are somewhat different from men's, primarily because of cultural beliefs and expectations about what makes a "real" woman and a "real" man. What it's like to have a disability has been explored by authors who themselves have gone through the process, such as Carolyn Vash and P. K. Longmore.

Facing Abnormal Situations

Being a person with a disability means having normal reactions to abnormal situations. Some abnormal situations are biological, such as having multiple sclerosis, which involves progressive nerve deterioration. Some are environmental, such as inaccessible entrances. Other abnormal situations are social, such as having a salesperson ask your companion, not you, what size you wear.

Not being able to get a job is an economic example. Some abnormal situations are obvious, such as a restroom door you can't get through. Others are subtle, such as people using or not using the word "cripple" when you're around. Some may be pleasant, such as being allowed to board the airplane first. Others are unpleasant, such as not being allowed to board at all. Persons with disabilities are continually perceiving and experiencing things that the majority of people around them cannot validate. Unless they are in regular contact with people who are similarly disabled, their sense of isolation and the lack of consensus for their ideas and feelings are added to the list of abnormal situations. Being part of a community of persons with disabilities is important.

Being Male or Female

Being male or female does not imply better or worse reactions for persons with disabilities, only different ones. It's more acceptable for women to be helpless in our culture, to be in touch with their feelings, and to express them more freely. However, women are expected to be more physically perfect specimens than men, beautiful in face and figure. By definition, women with physical disabilities cannot hope to meet this social ideal.

Mastering the Physical Environment

The main issue for mobility-impaired people is accessibility, and safety is the main issue for the visually impaired. Inaccessibility has implications for survival. For example, if wheelchair users cannot get into a building, they can't get a job there. If they can't get over the curbs, up the stairs, or into the restrooms, they literally cannot function even though they have many other abilities. The most typical ways people with disabilities cope with problems of inaccessible or unsafe facilities are by:

- minimizing their own disabilities by developing every possible adaptive skill
- keeping up the good fight to get remaining environmental barriers removed

Some wheelchair users are interested in the development of wheelchairs that climb steps. Most prefer to see ramps and elevators wherever steps are used. What do wheelchair users do if they're working in an upper floor of a skyscraper and fire breaks out, rendering all the elevators unusable? Some feasible plans do exist, but they are rare. When deaf passengers take an unknown bus route, how can they know when they're reached their street destination? These are the crucial emergencies and everyday problems that disabled-rights advocates are trying to resolve.

Dealing with Bureaucracies

The various bureaucracies that persons with disabilities must deal with may include live-in institutions and social service agencies.

Living in an institution has a profound impact on the disabled person's experience and few people prefer this option. By their very nature, institutions restrict residents' freedom and violate their privacy. The staff makes most of the crucial decisions about the patients' lives. Those patients who are most willing to cooperate with the staff, therefore, may eventually be the least prepared to resume effective, assertive autonomy when they return to the outside world. Those who have been in institutions say it's the attendants who make the most difference in their quality of life while there.

The disabled must often interact with agencies that provide vitally important services. These interactions can be supportive, but they can also be stressful. According to disabled advocate Carolyn Vash, when dealing with agencies "in order to receive the benefits they need, disabled people must tell all, hand over the reins, and oftentimes swallow much, possibly for a very long time."

Looking for Technological Support

How well the culture is able to provide the latest in technological tools and therapies makes a great difference in how well the disabled can solve their functional problems. The U.S. culture provides a great deal of independence and convenience through motorized wheelchairs, powered lifts, electronic magnifiers, talking calculators, portable teletypewriters, computers, and similar aids.

Self-Awareness Opportunity 2—Relating to Wheelchair Users

Purpose: To raise your awareness of your reactions and attitudes toward persons who use wheelchairs.

Instructions: Have paper and pen handy. Follow the directions for each step and jot down brief answers to the questions.

Step 1. Person in a Wheelchair.
  Relax by closing your eyes and breathing deeply. Think of a person in a wheelchair and focus on this mental image. Notice the thoughts and feelings that come up. Open your eyes and write a few brief sentences about the thoughts and feelings that came up, as well as your answer to this question:

- What did you see first when you pictured a wheelchair user: A wheelchair? A person within a wheelchair? Or a person?

Step 2. Person in an Easy Chair
  Repeat Step 1, but this time think of a person sitting in an easy chair. When you write about your thoughts and feelings, answer this question:

- What did you see first when you pictured an easy chair user: An easy chair? A person within an easy chair? Or a person?

Step 3. Person in a Wheelchair and Person in an Easy Chair.
  Repeat step 1, but this time think first of a person in a wheelchair and then think of the same person in an easy chair. Shift the mental image back and forth several times. When you write about your thoughts and feelings, answer this question:

- How did shifting the mental image affect your thoughts and feelings about the person? How did it affect the way you position the person within your own mind and therefore how you're likely to relate to such a person?

WHAT IS THE INDEPENDENT LIVING MOVEMENT?

The Independent Living Movement (ILM) consists of community-based programs with significant consumer involvement. These programs provide services needed by persons with severe disabilities in order to increase their self-determination and to minimize their dependence on others, according to authors Nancy Crew and Irving Zola.

Throughout most of our history, people who were so severely disabled as to need an attendant had only two options:

- to be cared for by family or friends
- to live in a maintenance-care institution

The alternative of being provided with funds to live as an independent adult did not yet exist. By 1980, independent living was becoming the standard as a result of laws that recognized the human and monetary needs of the disabled.

People with disabilities are saying that they are uniquely qualified to plan ways of meeting their own needs. They want to predominate in the advisory boards of professionally run agencies. They want to take over the key jobs of providing services to the disabled. The new type of service organization consists of independent living programs operated by and for the disabled.

Independent Living Arrangements

The independent living situation can be as large and formal as an apartment complex of several hundred accessible, fully equipped units that offer extensive personal services and are planned along with adjacent accessible shopping and employment facilities. It can be as modest and informal as one person with a disability living in an ordinary apartment and having an agreement with a neighbor to provide needed morning and evening attendant care. Many in the disabled community believe that the full range of possibilities should be made available to allow for individual choice—which is the keystone of independence. The independent living concept specifically includes the provision of needed assistance from other people that, when given, allows even very severely disabled people to live free from the control or determination of others.

Training for Assertive Communication

Assertiveness training offered by community organizations is becoming common for persons with disabilities. They're learning to speak up for their rights rather than leave the job to professional rehabilitators and other concerned advocates who are not themselves disabled. For example, they learn as patients how to interview physicians who say little or say it in technical jargon. They learn to get necessary information upon which to base their own decisions. They learn as students how to get helpful cooperation from teachers when they are physically unable to fulfill course requirements in the usual ways. As citizens, they learn to get the help that they're entitled to from agencies, without triggering resistance from agency workers. Persons with disabilities often rely on funds and services from public agencies, and failure to get what they need can mean poverty or institutionalization.

Training to Supervise Personal Service Employees

Supervisory training is essential for tactfully and assertively dealing with personal service employees, and community service organizations often provide this training. Many persons with disabilities must hire and supervise attendants, readers, drivers, or interpreters. Abuses are reported regularly, such as mistreatment, unreliability, exploitation, quitting without notice, and subtle cruelties of withholding help. This occurs when disabled employers don't know how to screen out poor risks during the hiring process or how to create a rewarding job for those they do hire. They must make the job intrinsically rewarding, because the public funds provided often don't constitute a living wage. To survive, psychologically as well as physically, people using personal service providers must develop skill in their selection and supervision.

Education for Career Success

During the past few decades, public education for young people with disabilities has progressed from no education at all, to special education in segregated class-rooms, to a concerted effort to integrate students with disabilities into main-stream schools. Major problems resulting from segregating disabled students from the mainstream include:

- Employers cannot imagine that job applicants with disabilities could function in their work settings because they never saw them functioning in school.
- Employees have trouble relating to coworkers with disabilities because they had no opportunities for contact from their earliest years.
- Students with disabilities do not get an equal education.
- Orientation toward college preparation is usually virtually absent.

The ILM recognizes that persons with disabilities must have access to optimal educational experiences in order to become self-sufficient.

Integration into Work and Community Life

The goal of the inner and outer struggles of the disabled is to break out of poverty and restrictive environments that offer nothing to do and no one to do it with. A related goal is to stay out of institutions and back bedrooms and break into the mainstream of everything—school, work, politics, and love affairs. The ultimate goal is to live a more or less normal life in a fairly normal community. Integration into the workforce can be managed in a variety of ways, often in a gradual, step-by-step manner. An emerging trend is for employers to participate in this process by giving on-the-job training to the disabled.

Vignette: Ed Roberts—an Amazing Success Story

In 1962, when Ed Roberts, paralyzed from the neck down, applied for help from the California Department of Rehabilitation, they said no. The counselors argued that it was "infeasible" to think that Ed would ever be able to work. But Ed was persistent; he was accustomed to fighting such battles. At the age of 14 he had polio and heard the doctor tell his mother, "It would be better if Ed died, because he's going to be a vegetable." Right then Ed decided that if he was going to be a vegetable, he'd be an artichoke: prickly on the outside, with a tender heart. His motto was "I'm paralyzed from the neck down, not from the neck up." He used his tough mind and soft heart to fight for disabled persons' rights and to change forever their place in society.

Ed had to persuade his high school principal at Burlingame High to give him his diploma even though he had not completed required classes in physical education and driver's education. He won that battle, and in 1962 he won the battle to get into the University of California at Berkeley, one of the top-ranking U.S. universities. On Ed's first day he was lifted out of his wheelchair and carried up the steps to Room 201 of Cal Hall. A local newspaper headline read, "Helpless Cripple Attends UC Classes."

Later, he organized a group of mobility-impaired students who called themselves the Rolling Quads. They in turn started the Physically Disabled Students' program at UC Berkeley, with the main goal of solving all problems that created barriers to academic achievement. They provided such services as finding attendants, accessible apartments, and 24-hour emergency wheelchair repair service. A broken wheelchair could mean weeks of missed class sessions.

When Ed graduated from UC Berkeley in 1972, he and fellow students founded the Center for Independent Living. It became the model for similar centers across the nation. Ed also founded the Independent Living Movement. In 1975, he became the head of the California Department of Rehabilitation, the very same state agency that had at first opposed helping him go to school. He held that position for seven years, until 1982.

In 1984, Ed Roberts was awarded a MacArthur Foundation "genius" award of $225,000, which he used to establish the World Institute on Disability, an influential policy and research center based in Oakland, California. When he died at age 56 in 1995, colleagues called him "the Gandhi of the disability rights movement."

THE ADA—WHAT YOU NEED TO KNOW

The 1990 federal Americans with Disability Act (ADA) applies to virtually all government and private business operations. Its main provisions are set out in five sections or titles, as shown in Figure 10.2.

The ADA definition of disability is broad and subject to interpretation by the courts. It is directed mainly to those who are hearing impaired, sight impaired, and mobility impaired, all of whom comprise about 1 percent of working-age adults. However, the ADA definition can include people with such chronic conditions as diabetes, heart disease, HIV, AIDS, past (but not present) drug addiction and alcoholism, and mental and emotional illnesses. It could potentially cover 25 percent of all workers.

Most large corporations have set up ADA task forces to ensure that all the provisions are met. Some smaller business owners have formed regional groups by type of business, such as restaurant, clothing store, or grocery store owner associations. Such associations plan their response to the ADA with the help of professionals, such as consultants and attorneys, and take the large-corporation viewpoint in handling the changes. For example, some send newsletters to employees to inform them of the provisions of the act, proper etiquette in dealing with persons with disabilities, hiring techniques, what the business is doing to adhere to the act, and other helpful information.

Keystone: Equal Opportunity and Reasonable Accommodation

The major stated goal of the ADA is for organizations to manage their affairs in a manner that includes all groups of applicants and workers with disabilities, where reasonable accommodation can make inclusion possible. The major factor that determines if an accommodation is reasonable is whether it imposes an undue hardship on the employer. Another ADA goal is to increase the employ-

Figure 10.2   *The Americans with Disabilities Act*

Section	Purpose
Title I. Employment	Prohibits employment discrimination.
Title II. State and Local Governments	Requires accessibility and prohibits employment discrimination, similar to the 1973 law.
Title III. Public Accommodations	Requires accessibility to restaurants, theaters, stores, etc.
Title IV. Telecommunications	Requires accommodations, such as telephone relays for the deaf.
Title V: Miscellaneous	Catchall section with a variety of technical provisions.

ment rate of persons with disabilities in order to reduce the cost of government subsidies to them and to enable them to enjoy a more productive, satisfying lifestyle. The major provisions of the ADA are:

1. to require employers to clearly state bona fide job requirements;
2. to provide equal opportunities for qualified persons with disabilities who can meet the job requirements; and
3. to provide reasonable accommodations that will allow otherwise qualified persons with disabilities to do the job, as long as such accommodations don't cause undue hardship for the employer.

Clearly Stating Job Requirements

Job descriptions are a key factor in preventing unnecessary discrimination against the disabled. Essential job functions must be clearly spelled out. If physical ability is essential, the exact activities must be specified; for example, "lift a 5-pound packet 5 to 10 times a day." Requirements that are not truly necessary to do the job must be eliminated.

Providing Equal Opportunity

The ADA states that a job candidate may not be discriminated against on the basis of disability, history of disability, or perception of disability. In the past, most employers would not consider hiring candidates who have been in mental institutions, have a history of epileptic seizures, have attended classes or schools for the mentally retarded, or have similar indications of disability. The tendency was to see only the potential problems and ignore the positive contributions such persons can make. The law also protects family members from discrimination, such as an employer's assumption that caring for a disabled relative will be a job distraction.

The ADA bars discrimination in all aspects of employment, including hiring, compensation, training, and promotion. Employers also must give disabled employees equal access to employee benefits, including medical insurance.

Providing Reasonable Accommodation

Title I of the ADA focuses on "reasonable accommodation" by employers for disabled workers, where such reasonable accommodation will allow them to do the work. All employees must be given reasonable accommodation, whether they're new employees, have been with the company for some time, or became impaired after being hired.

Reasonable accommodation can occur during the recruiting and hiring phase and includes accommodation in job descriptions, medical tests, employment tests, job interviews, and all other preemployment activities.

Human resource professionals must determine ways to make testing and interviewing procedures realistic and fair for all persons. Persons with disabilities who are fully competent to meet the demands of a job may have difficulties in completing the normal job-screening process successfully. Be sure that testing procedures actually measure those performance capabilities that are required by the target job and that tests are required for bona fide job requirements only.

Medical Screening

Companies cannot perform medical screening prior to hiring a person. That means they cannot require applicants to provide a medical history, nor can they require them to pass any sort of medical test. After hiring, medical screening and other types of screening are permitted only if all workers are included. Those who are thought to be disabled cannot be singled out.

Employment Tests

Reasonable accommodation must be provided for persons with disabilities. For example, reasonable accommodation for visually impaired persons might include reading the test to them or providing the test in large print or Braille. Tests must truly measure whether or not candidates have the ability or potential to be successful on the job.

Job Interviews

Interviewing procedures must protect persons with disabilities from discrimination. For example, interviewers cannot legally ask job applicants about such matters as physical or mental impairments, medical history, drinking habits, or phobias. What if an applicant voluntarily discloses a disability? The interviewer is not legally allowed to follow up with questions about the disability. It is not all right to ask directly about a disability, but it is all right to ask persons with disabilities whether they can and would do a particular type of work or job and how they would manage the job. There is a fine line between legal and illegal questions here, for the interviewer cannot ask what kind of accommodation the applicant might need to perform the job until a conditional job offer is made. After this point, applicants can be asked to demonstrate or describe how they would do the job. If applicants indicate the need for an accommodation, the employer must either provide reasonable accommodation for the demonstration or allow the applicants to merely describe how they would perform this function.

On-the-Job Accommodations

The key questions for employers are

- What are the one or two things I must do as an employer in order to give this person an opportunity to succeed?
- How can I level the playing field for this person?

Reasonable accommodation for some jobs, especially professional or technical positions, might be as easy as providing an amplified telephone receiver or larger computer screen. It is frequently an action as simple as providing flexible scheduling for work arrival and departure. It might include providing an interpreter for a hearing-impaired worker to attend a training session or reassigning job functions so that a wheelchair user handles telephone calls while another employee stores and retrieves folders in file cabinets.

Protection from Undue Hardship

The ADA states that employers are not required to make accommodations that would cause them undue hardship. This exemption applies when the measures necessary to allow a disabled person to do a job are unduly expensive or interfere with a business necessity. The major test is how the accommodation would affect the entire budget of the organization. Most cases of undue hardship occur in small businesses. Some don't have the profit margin, cash flow, or capital cushion to take such measures as remodeling a building or providing readers or interpreters. What constitutes undue hardship is decided on a case-by-case basis, since the range of disabilities and types of jobs are so vast that no set of legal formulas could begin to cover them. Some guidelines may eventually be worked out through precedents set in court cases.

The Cost: Mostly None or Small

Most accommodations cost nothing at all, and the great majority are easily made by even the smallest businesses. Often it's as simple as allowing more flexible times to arrive and depart from work or rearranging a work area. Studies of costs, reported by Joseph Shapiro, indicate the following:

- Fifty-one percent of all accommodations cost nothing.
- For the other 49 percent, the average cost of an accommodation was $300.
- Less than 1 percent of accommodations cost $5,000 or more.

Many companies are discovering that just by being flexible and opening up their attitudes toward persons with disabilities, they gain workers who are highly committed, productive, and loyal.

OVERCOMING BARRIERS TO CAREER SUCCESS

Persons with disabilities report that major barriers to their career success include making coworkers comfortable with their disability, finding adequate transportation to and from work, getting the technological support they need, and getting on-the-job training as well as the ongoing training and development that builds the skills they need.

Barrier #1—Making Coworkers Comfortable

The sensitivity and socializing issues are related to corporate culture and to the level of employee awareness. Companies that have taken a leadership role in disability issues are providing training sessions for all employees in order to raise their awareness and provide skills for working effectively with this group. Influencing corporate culture change can open up many opportunities to utilize the talents of persons with disabilities—as well as other groups that are disadvantaged in the workplace.

Barrier #2—Finding Adequate Transportation

Transportation barriers are probably the simplest to overcome. Major cities now must modify their public transportation systems to provide lifts and ramps for persons with mobility impairments. Also, managers can work with these employees to solve transportation problems.

Barrier #3—Getting Technological Support

You know that technology can substitute for sensory and motor capacities, which opens up occupational options previously considered unavailable to those with certain disabilities. They are therefore able to engage in higher-level and more demanding kinds of work. With computer modems, fax machines, and similar technology, many computer-based types of work can be done at home, which eliminates the transportation barrier.

Barrier #4—Getting On-the-Job Training

Taking a broad view of how to integrate persons with disabilities in the mainstream workplace, leaders have identified five levels on an ascending scale of increasing integration:

1. Home-based or homebound employment, which is being upgraded with the advent of computer and telecommunications technology
2. Sheltered workshops that predominantly hire workers with disabilities
3. Semi-integrated units in mainstream industry that offer some disability-related accommodations and some shelter
4. Fully integrated employment in mainstream industry with some disability-related accommodation
5. Competitive employment with no disability-related accommodation

Sheltered workshops and semi-integrated work units can be provided by companies that need committed workers. The growing trend in such work preparation programs is to use mainstream industry as the setting for work training, evaluation, and adjustment, instead of using rehabilitation facilities. The trainees get acclimated to actual business situations, and employers and employees get to know the trainees through the relatively nonthreatening training process. Actual job performance sampling is also the best predictor of job success and the best way to identify problem areas and needs for further training.

These types of programs are used by the *crews* programs (Community Rehabilitative Employment Work Sites). This type of training program provides a gradual shift from rehabilitation training, to on-the-job training, to regular employment. About 70 percent of trainees in *crews* programs have mental disabilities, such as learning problems or retardation. They work in groups at workshops located in centers for persons with mental impairments. They are trained and supervised by trainers familiar with the skills needed by particular industries, such as assembling and packaging skills. Once trainees become productive, they are paid by the center to perform work for affiliated private businesses, who in turn pay the center.

Barrier #5—Getting Ongoing Training and Development

Some studies, such as those by S. Stace, indicate that most organizations are less likely to provide training and development opportunities to employees with disabilities than to other employees. This reinforces a tendency for persons with disabilities to define their viable career options rather narrowly. Leaders can encourage broader definitions of career goals, help persons with disabilities to develop career plans, and provide appropriate training and development opportunities. Reasonable accommodation in the training function can pay off handsomely.

BUILDING UPON THE STRENGTHS OF PERSONS WITH DISABILITIES

It makes good business sense to accommodate persons with disabilities, for they usually make excellent employees who enrich the company talent pool. Highly qualified persons with disabilities are most likely to apply to companies that have corporate environments that are friendly to them. They're most likely to be productive in such companies and to stay with them. Corporate cultures are likely to change when leaders recognize the many benefits that employees with disabilities bring to the organization, from skills and commitment, to connection with a multibillion-dollar marketplace.

A step in changing the culture is for employees to attend training sessions that provide information about persons with disabilities. Such training should set the stage for adopting positive attitudes toward persons with disabilities and using positive language when referring to them. You and your company can follow the lead of successful companies in changing the culture and help persons with disabilities to make marketplace connections.

Strategy #1—Provide Diversity Training for All Employees

Employee training should include exploring the beliefs, myths, and stereotypes that lead to devaluation of the disabled; giving accurate information about current facts, trends, issues, and profiles; and developing approaches that help coworkers appreciate all persons with disabilities and work effectively with them. Training should include positive attitudes and language as well as specific information on how to relate to and assist people with various specific disabilities.

As coworkers become better able to see beyond a person's abilities or disabilities and to form relationships with the "normal" core person within, the quality of work life is further enhanced. Training should include some guidelines for personal interactions with the disabled. For example, helpers should not rush in and take over when they think a person with disability needs help, such as finding the way or getting through a door. They should ask whether and what type of help is needed. The FAQs at the end of this chapter give some suggestions for assisting persons with various types of impairment.

Strategy #2—Adopt Positive Attitudes toward Employees with Disabilities

The following are some constructive attitudes that business leaders can adopt for working with the disabled, attitudes that leaders can encourage among all employees.

Realize That People with Disabilities Are Not All Alike

They have some common experiences and they are also highly diverse. On the one hand, many ask to be considered in the same vein as an ethnic minority. Most belong, in varying degrees, to a disabled community, with distinct cultural values, vocabulary, in-jokes, mutual support, and common issues. On the other hand, they ask that we also think in terms of diversity, for their disabilities and abilities range widely. Each person has his or her individual strengths, weaknesses, and peculiarities.

Focus on What People Can Do

The traditional tendency is to focus on the impairment. Cooperate with these employees in taking a can-do attitude. Focus also on what people, disabled and nondisabled, can do together. See persons with disabilities as basically normal people who happen to have lost some function. Recognize that this does not define their character. They are people first, and their disability is only something they must cope with; it's not who they are.

Move through Fear of Disablement

Be aware of the fear of many people, and perhaps your own unconscious fear, of being around persons with disabilities. Others typically do not want to be reminded, "There but for the grace of God go I. This could happen to me." Almost everyone has fear regarding the issues of body image and brain power.

Accept Persons with Disabilities as Normal Persons

Don't think of them as sick, as patients, as victims, or as abnormal. Remember that we all have some disability; it's just a matter of degree. Most persons with disabilities can marry, have sex, have children, and live many aspects of a "normal" life. The key is that they must work in order to have a full life. Their resources must be used in order for them to gain the sense of purpose, meaning, and achievement that all people want.

Explore Possibilities for Persons with Mental Retardation

Even the mentally retarded can usually do some sort of meaningful work. Some are classified as "high functioning mentally retarded" or "high functioning Down's syndrome."

Never Treat Persons with Disabilities as if They're Childlike or Childish

Some persons with disabilities, especially the mentally impaired, may appear childlike to some people because of certain mannerisms that go along with their impairment. Respect for them as adults is essential. So are realistic assessments of their capabilities and the tailoring of assignments, expectations, and guidance to fit their level of ability.

Focus on the Benefits

Research reported by Taylor Cox indicates that employees with disabilities tend to be:

- very enthusiastic—because they're happy to have real employment
- eager to succeed—they're adaptable and cooperative
- absent and tardy less
- a terrific resource—one that has been wasted in the past

This adds up to highly committed, loyal employees.

Strategy #3—Use Positive Language

Certain language habits tend to focus on a person's disability rather than on the person, and to support stereotypes. Such labels can hurt, especially when their effect is to isolate people from the rest of society. The terms we use to refer to persons with disabilities can be loaded with unintended meanings. Most activists prefer terms that are descriptive rather than euphemistic, emotionally neutral rather than charged, and words that don't elicit negative stereotypes.

The term "persons with disabilities" is preferred when referring to the group as a whole because it focuses on persons first, rather than the disability. In most contexts, the term "the disabled" doesn't acknowledge the person at all and focuses only on the disabilities. The term "disabled persons" at least acknowledges that persons are being discussed, but "persons with disabilities" is

Figure 10.3 *Terms that Are Realistic but Positive*

Preferred Terms	Terms to Avoid
Persons with Disabilities	Differently Abled
The disabled (as a protected class)	Physically Challenged
Sight Impaired, Blind	Handicapped
Mobility Impaired	Crippled, Lame, Gimpy
Hearing Impaired, Deaf	Deaf and Dumb
Emotionally Impaired	Insane, Crazy
Neurologically Impaired	Moron
Mentally Impaired	Retard

even better because it puts persons first. The use of the term "the disabled" is acceptable when referring to persons with disabilities as a protected class.

Such terms as "differently abled" and "physically challenged" are not descriptive and attempt to avoid the issue. They're politically correct in the worst sense. "Handicapped" was considered acceptable for a time, but the word stems from the phrase "cap in hand" and carries the connotation of begging. Now most persons with disabilities avoid it.

Such terms as "hearing impaired" or "sight impaired" are specific and descriptive. They're often more accurate than "deaf" or "blind" because they refer to those with varying degrees of impairment, as well as those with total loss of an ability. The worst terms carry emotionally devastating stereotypes and tend to focus on the negative: "deaf and dumb," "crippled," "limp," "lame," "gimpy."

Avoid such phrases as "John is a diabetic," and use instead "John has diabetes." When you say that someone is an alcoholic, arthritic, drug addict, or mental retardate, the implication is that he or she is nothing more than that. More realistic language is "Sue has a drinking problem," or "Jan has a learning impairment."

Prefer the active to the passive, such as "person who uses a wheelchair" instead of "person confined to a wheelchair," or "He is a wheelchair user" instead of "He is wheelchair bound." Use tact in dealing with disabilities. In some cases, persons with disabilities do not want to deal with their disability. They don't want to talk about it or be reminded of it. This presents the greatest challenge for the manager.

Strategy #4—Follow the Lead of Successful Companies

Hewlett Packard is on the top-ten list of corporations that actively recruit from a pool of disabled workers. Their leaders say that the "HP Way" is to treat persons with disabilities with dignity and respect. It was among the first large corporations to set policies for a disability-sensitive workplace. This includes holding seminars to inform all employees about various types of disabilities, developing a mentorship program, and supporting an employee network for employees with disabilities. You can encourage people in your company to take similar actions.

Strategy #5—Make Marketplace Connections

Employees with disabilities are a valuable resource for understanding this market of nearly 50 million consumers. They can help the company create communication bridges for marketing to persons with disabilities. In 1997, disabled persons' incomes came to over $800 billion. Yet many companies have made no efforts to target this huge market. Those who do are likely to find some profitable niches.

Companies that design products and services for disability markets often find an even larger general market for the same or similar products and services. This principle is sometimes called universal design. Designs that work for persons with disabilities are also frequently more workable for the rest of the population. Examples include big-button telephones, voice-recognition and voice-output computers, safer bathtubs, easier-to-open boxes, and easy-to-grip tools. Special service designs can also apply to larger markets. For example, personal services targeted at disability markets, such as grocery shopping and home meal delivery, can also fill a need for working parents and others.

Skill Builder 1—The Case of Judy, Severely Disabled

Judy was paralyzed from the neck down. She must have help getting out of bed, getting dressed, and getting into a motorized wheelchair. Judy says that she still has the greatest ability of all: her mind, which is as sound as ever. She says if she can find a way to attend the university, she will get a degree in public administration, the field in which she wants to have a career. She has come to you, a vocational counselor at the state Department of Rehabilitation, as the first step in getting the state funding she needs in order to pursue this educational and career goal. Your responsibilities are:

- Regarding education: to predict the possibility and probability that an applicant will actually complete the educational program he or she enters.
- Regarding occupation: to predict the possibility and probability that an applicant will actually get and retain a job in the proposed field.
- Regarding funds: to allocate scarce state funds for rehabilitation in a manner that produces the best results for persons with disabilities and for society.

Considering Judy's situation and your responsibilities,

- What should your decision be?

Skill Builder 2—The Case of Paul, Who Becomes Disabled

Paul works for the San Francisco AIDS Foundation as a developmental system associate. He's been there for nearly three years and his work has become an asset to the foundation. He is solely responsible for overseeing the database system, which he helped create. His responsibilities include tracking donations and generating the foundation's budget reports and income statements. Paul's performance evaluations have always been excellent.

A little over a year ago, Paul was diagnosed with Aggressive Liver Disease. This disease eventually results in liver failure. Paul is waiting for a liver transplant and hopes a donor will make one available within the next three to five years. Last year Paul took a four-month medical leave of absence to get his disease under control. Since his return, he has managed to keep his performance up to par, even though he must miss work for his doctor's appointment each week. The main physical problems that Paul is currently experiencing are fatigue and the nausea caused by the drugs he must take.

Paul knows he cannot continue working forty-hour weeks, and the commute to and from work is an energy drain he'd like to avoid. Paul starts thinking that he could do most of his work at home. He would need a computer, modem, and dedicated telephone line. He researches this idea and determines that this would require an initial investment of $2,500 plus about $20 per month in telephone charges. Paul is thinking about asking for a meeting with his manager **Claudia** and requesting that the foundation provide him with the equipment for a home office. As far as he knows, no other employee has ever asked to do most of their work from a home office. However, Paul is concerned that if he doesn't make better use of his failing energy, he'll be required to go on disability leave until his liver transplant comes through.

- What is the key issue?
- What should Paul do?

Skill Builder 3—The Case of Jill, Visually Impaired Manager

Jill Dovetsky is the Human Resource Manager of Spirit Clothing Co. She has been visually impaired since a very young age and is almost totally blind. In spite of this, Jill earned a degree in business administration and worked her way up to Human Resource Manager within five years of joining Spirit.

Jill has had a positive influence on the company's policies toward persons with disabilities, and Spirit's workforce includes one of the highest proportions of employees with disabilities in the industry. Last month, on November 15, the Accounting Department Manager announced his retirement plans. Jill has met with the Spirit executive team and determined that they want a manager who will bring in "new blood," someone fairly young with recent university training but also a good track record in the field. They want someone with new ideas, new energy, and hopefully someone who will stay with the company for many years.

Jill has interviewed many applicants for this job and is leaning toward **Amy** as the probable best fit. She's now in the process of interviewing three finalists for the position and would like to make the selection before the Christmas holidays. She schedules a 5:30 p.m. meeting with Amy. The interview goes well. Amy seems to have most of the right answers to Jill's questions and responds satisfactorily to the few concerns that Jill has about Amy's qualifications.

They've been chatting for well over an hour when **Rick**, Jill's assistant knocks on the door and enters the room. Rick says, "Hey, why are you two sitting here in the dark?" As Rick turns on the lights, Amy lets out a sigh of relief, and it seems to Jill that a heavy weight is lifted from Amy's shoulders. Jill responds, "Well, you know me, Rick, lights or not, it's all the same to me. Amy, I must apologize for forgetting the time of day. But surely you know it's okay to remind me?" Amy seems quite flustered and stammers, "Oh, that's okay, it's . . . it doesn't matter."

Later, when Jill discusses the incident with Rick, he said, "Amy seemed very nervous and uncomfortable when I came in. I saw a definite sense of relief when I turned on the lights." Jill said, "Mmmm, too bad. We have several persons with disabilities in the Accounting Department—and in fact many throughout the company. The person we hire for this management job must know how to deal with disability situations and issues."

- What are the key issues in this case?
- If your were Amy, what would you have done?
- If you were Jill, what would you do now?

Feedback on Skill Builder 1—The Case of Judy, Severely Disabled

This case is modeled after the actual case of Ed Roberts, featured in the showcase vignetter in this chapter. Remember, Ed had to fight for admittance to the University of California at Berkeley. The California Department of Rehabilitation at first turned down his application on the grounds that he would probably not be able to complete his education nor use it in the work world. Ed not only graduated, he was a campus leader. He went on to found the Independent Living Movement and to become head of the state agency that had opposed helping him go to school. He headed that agency for seven years, won a MacArthur Foundation "genius" award, and established the World Institute on Disability. His colleagues called him "the Gandhi of the disability rights movement." Whatever you say to Judy, you should keep in mind that when disabled persons are fully committed to achieving their goals, they've been known to accomplish miracles.

Feedback on Skill Builder 2—The Case of Paul, Who Becomes Disabled

Key issues: Reasonable accommodation for Paul's disability, and the concept of telecommuting and the virtual office. Paul should ask Claudia to provide him with equipment for a home office—as a reasonable accommodation for his current disability. Paul can focus on her desire to maintain work quality and productivity. He can be flexible in meeting Claudia's organizational needs, such as coming in for weekly staff meetings. Claudia should seriously consider retaining Paul as a valuable employee, since his performance evaluations have always been excellent. It makes sense to work with him through this difficult time period. Such support is likely to deepen his loyalty and commitment to the organization.

Feedback on Skill Builder 3—The Case of Jill, Visually Impaired Manager

The key issues are:

- Knowledge of working with persons with disabilities and comfort level in applying that knowledge
- Realistic standards and expectations for candidates regarding diversity skills

Amy surely is aware of her discomfort in the interview and her lack of information on how to handle such situations. She can contact Jill and discuss the issue and what she plans to do to overcome this gap, such as finding books and seminars on the subject. She can ask Jill's advice regarding this learning process.

Jill can schedule another meeting with Amy, since she's the leading candidate in every other way. In this meeting, Jill can determine Amy's openness and willingness to learn more about persons with disabilities and to gain comfort and skill in working with them. If she decides Amy could quickly come up to speed in this area, she can hire her with the condition that she will undergo training.

FREQUENTLY ASKED QUESTIONS (FAQS) ABOUT PERSONS WITH DISABILITIES

FAQs about persons with disabilities reflect the need to understand the specifics of working effectively with such persons, according to disability advocates Chalda Maloff and Susan Macduff. Here you'll find answers to FAQs about persons with (1) mobility impairments, (2) visual impairments, and (3) hearing or speaking impairments.

FAQs about Persons with Mobility Impairments

Q: How do I offer help to a person with disability? Or should I?

- Offer help; it's never the wrong thing to do. It can always be declined if not wanted, but always *ask first* if the person wants you to help and take *no* for an answer.
- If help is wanted, ask specifically what you can do and how to do it, or suggest something and get agreement.
- If you assist another helper, remember the person with the disability is in charge.
- Handle the helping situation as unobtrusively as possible; avoid a "circus."

Q: How do I help persons using wheelchairs, crutches, and so forth?

- Never grab their appliances except in cases of obvious immediate physical danger.
- After helping, stay a moment and make sure matters are in hand before leaving. Let the person know you are leaving.

Q: Should I open doors for persons with mobility impairments?

- Everyone can use help with doors at times.
- Hold the door itself, rather than their arm or wheelchair—until the person is completely inside.

Q: How can I be considerate of people who use wheelchairs?

- Avoid blocking aisles and other spaces that a wheelchair user needs to access—don't block them with briefcases, wastebaskets, and so on.; push chairs under tables or desks; be aware.
- When having a conversation with a wheelchair user, try to seat yourself in front of the person, so you can talk eye-to-eye. If you must stand, step back so the person isn't required to look up to you.
- Reaching elevator buttons may be impossible for a wheelchair user; offer to help.

- Users of nonmotorized wheelchairs may need help getting up inclines or around barriers, but never begin pushing a wheelchair without asking permission.
- Never release the chair without warning, so the wheelchair user is always in control.
- Be sure you know exactly where the person wants to go.
- Begin pushing a wheelchair cautiously if you are not familiar with it. Go slowly at first; wheelchairs can gain surprising momentum.
- Note the size and protrusions of the chair, such as protruding foot plates. Pay attention to the terrain, such as step-downs, and watch where you're going.
- When entering a crosswalk in a street, remember the wheelchair user's feet may be further out than you think and may be dangerously close to passing traffic.
- Going up steps, lean the chair back to raise the front wheels and push the chair up frontwards.
- Going down steps, ask if the person prefers going down frontwards or backwards. Either way, raise the front wheels and keep them up until the entire chair is down the step. The occupant should always be tilted toward the back against the backrest instead of toward the front where there is no support.

Q: How do I show consideration for persons who walk with difficulty?

- When approaching steps, walk alongside them and offer your arm, which they can grasp, giving them control and support. Grabbing their arm can upset their balance.
- If more help is needed, put your arm around their waist.
- Any time a person falls, ask how you can assist, or offer your arm for the fallen person to take if he or she needs it. Don't grab the person.

Q: What should I consider when I'm planning activities that require mobility-impaired persons to go to unfamiliar places?

- Mobility-impaired persons need to know in advance whether they will encounter a difficult barrier—such as inadequate parking places, ramps, and restrooms.
- Find out what kinds of parking arrangements they need.
- Wheelchair users need access to restrooms with hallways and doors wide enough for the chair, enough space inside the stall, and perhaps a handle bar by the commode.
- Never insist on simply carrying a disabled person over, around, and through obstacles. They may find it demeaning, unpleasant, or even scary—and it could be dangerous for both of you. All of us prefer to be independent and self-possessed.
- When in doubt, ask the disabled person for some tips on places that are accessible and comfortable.

FAQs about Persons with Visual Impairments

Q: What should I consider when giving directions to visually impaired coworkers?

- The single most useful thing you may be able to do is to furnish relevant information about the immediate surroundings. Often just a few words will do.
- Furnish simple information without hesitation, any time it seems appropriate.
- When giving directions, be sure you really know where the target location is.
- Find out what types of directions are most helpful; this will depend on what the person can see or not see. Use numbers, where possible. Ask yourself, How many blocks down the street? How many doors down the hall?
- Give directions that are as specific as possible. Describe turns or curves as *left, right, clockwise,* and so on. Terms such as *north* or *south* will probably be irrelevant.
- Describe anything out of the ordinary along the way, such as possible safety hazards.
- Tell persons with some vision about large, noticeable landmarks.
- Be as complete as necessary without overloading the person with information.
- If you think the place is simply too hard to find, offer to take them there.

Q: What should I do when I'm walking with a visually impaired person?

- City streets pose one of the biggest hazards for visually impaired persons. Offer your arm, but do not clutch the person's arm. Be sure you understand which street the person wants to cross.
- Don't leave the person until she or he is safely up the opposite curb.
- If the person does not take your arm, walk closely enough for her or him to reach over and touch you. Avoid getting separated in crowds.
- If the person takes your arm, walk slightly ahead to guide the way and proceed normally. Never push the person ahead of you.
- Avoid sudden turns or jerky movements.
- Tell the person when it's time to step up, step down, or step around some obstacle.
- Watch for overhead obstacles, especially with a taller companion.
- When approaching steps, elevators, or other possible barriers, pause and briefly describe what's ahead.

Q: What should I know about helping persons who use canes?

- If a person touches your foot with a cane, step aside and let her or him pass.
- Don't touch a cane without permission.
- When walking with a person who uses a cane, offer your arm.

Q: What should I know about helping persons with guide dogs?

- Guide dogs and service dogs are used by a minority of visually impaired persons to help them get around and by mobility impaired persons to perform certain tasks.

- A guide dog is on duty any time it's wearing a harness.
- Take care to do nothing that will interfere with the dog's performance. Have faith in the dog and do not interfere unless there is a genuine emergency.
- Don't disrupt the routine and training by touching, feeding, petting, playing with, speaking to or commanding the dog unless you're encouraged to do so.
- If you have a dog, keep it away from the guide dog.
- When walking with someone who is using a dog, offer your arm.

Q: *What should I consider when I'm communicating with visually impaired persons?*

- Be aware that they rely on sound and touch to know what's going on.
- When you first meet a visually impaired person, feel free to shake hands. You might say, "May I shake your hand?" to cue them that you're extending your hand.
- When you meet the person thereafter, identify yourself, and any others you are with.
- When you would normally hand a business associate a business card, brochure, or other written material, give the visually impaired person the option to accept. You might offer to stay a moment and help interpret the material.
- When you enter the presence of visually impaired persons, speak to them and let them know you're there. Otherwise they may be unduly jolted when they hear you make some noise. Also, let them know when you're leaving.
- When leaving in a public place, say how long you'll be gone. Consider whether you need to offer to guide the person to a place where he or she can wait comfortably.
- When visually impaired persons hear your voice, they may be unsure whether you are talking to them or to someone else. They may remain silent rather than respond to comments they think might be meant for someone else.
- Address them by name when you're in a group or in public. If you don't know their name, stand directly in front of them and begin speaking. You may also gently touch their arm or repeat yourself to be sure they understand.
- Don't yell.
- Offer to describe visual sights.
- Speak up tactfully when some aspect of their grooming seems unpremeditated.

Q: *When making plans that include visually-impaired persons, what should I keep in mind?*

- If you're planning to meet outside the office, the key issue is likely to be transportation. Give some advance notice so they can arrange for a ride.
- If you're not sure whether a visually impaired person would be able to attend an event, ask. Invite them and allow them to make the decision; then respect their wishes.
- At restaurants, remember to offer help in reading the menu and calling the server.

FAQs about Persons with Hearing or Speaking Impairments

Q: What do I need to know generally about working with persons with hearing or speaking impairments?

- Most people with speaking impairments have normal hearing, and many hearing-impaired persons have excellent speech skills, particularly those whose hearing impairment is not of long standing or is not severe.
- When you initiate a direct conversation with communication-impaired persons, begin by asking, orally or in writing, how best to communicate.
- When introducing communication-impaired persons to others, make every effort to introduce only one or two persons at a time. Try to find a quiet spot and pronounce names slowly and distinctly.
- If you're asked to make a telephone call for a communication-impaired person, get the key information first, perhaps asking the person write it down for you.
- Before you hang up, check to be sure the message is complete, and after you hang up, give a complete report.

Q: What do I need to remember about lip-reading?

- When talking to persons who use lip-reading, position yourself about three or four feet directly in front of them with adequate light on your face so they can see your lips.
- Face them squarely without looking down or turning your head.
- Keep your hands away from your mouth and avoid eating, smoking, or chewing gum.
- Be aware that lip-reading is tiring, so avoid long monologues. Use a give-and-take format. Take a break during longer conversations.

Q: What do I need to remember about communicating nonverbally?

- Your eyes are especially expressive, so remove dark glasses, hats, and so on. Maintain a natural and relaxed manner without straining to exaggerate.
- If nonverbal communication is inadequate, find other methods.
- When both speaking and using gestures, be sure the gestures correlate with the speech. Random motions throw the listener off balance, trying to sift them from the real clues.

Q: How about writing out messages?

- Writing out messages is slow but is sometimes used. Be creative when you communicate in writing. Often a simple diagram, picture, or map is most effective.
- Watch the person's face as he or she reads your message, just as you would do if you were speaking, so you can gauge the understanding and reaction.
- When persons begin writing to you, don't talk or otherwise distract them until they finish. Allow them to finish writing before you try to read the message, and read the entire message before you begin to answer.
- In a group, offer to read the person's written message aloud to others.

Q: How should I communicate when a professional interpreter is used?

- Professional interpreters who use sign language may be used by people with severe impairments. When you speak through an interpreter, your key goal should be to respect the dignity and autonomy of the impaired person who is the "listener." The interpreter is merely a device in this situation, a tool.
- Face the hearing-impaired person and speak as though no interpreter were present.
- Direct all your comments to the listener, the person with whom you have business, saying, for example, "Your project is being reviewed." The interpreter will relay these exact words to the person.
- Never direct comments intended for the listener to the interpreter, saying "His project is being reviewed." This has the effect of excluding the listener, implying that he is a helpless bystander.
- Remember to look at the listener, not the translator, and to speak to her or him in direct address, using *you*, not *he* or *she*.
- Avoid engaging an interpreter in side conversations that exclude the other person.
- Remember that any translation process is difficult. Choose simple, specific words to be as clear and direct as possible, avoiding slang.

Q: How about communicating by telephone?

- A telecommunication device for the deaf (TDD) is used by many people with speaking or hearing impairments for communicating by telephone. If you don't have a TDD, you can still communicate through the device by going through a voice exchange system, available in most cities.
- Regular telephone communication with a hearing-impaired person is often possible without translator equipment, if the person has enough hearing ability.
- Organize your message ahead of time so you can convey it in a concise, direct manner.
- Try to quiet the noise at your end.
- Talk clearly and firmly directly into the receiver. Speak moderately slowly and pause at the end of a sentence.
- Be prepared to spell, rephrase, or use more creative ways to get your message across.
- If you have trouble hearing or understanding, ask for clarification as soon as you start getting lost.
- Keep the conversation short unless you are encouraged to extend it.

Q: How do I plan and conduct meetings that include communication-impaired persons?

- Select a room with good acoustics and a minimum of extraneous noise.
- Check ahead of time to determine what devices or services, such as interpreters, are needed.
- Offer the people with impairments preferential seating, where they will have a good view of speakers. Ask what they prefer.

- Ask speakers to stay in one spot rather than pacing the floor, for lip-readers.
- Pay special attention to the use of visual aids, handouts, charts, illustrations, and other communication aids.
- Write down new words or terms as you introduce them; it is almost impossible to lip-read an unknown word.
- Write down important facts.
- Repeat all comments or questions from other people in the room before you respond to them.
- If you sit next to a hearing-impaired person in a meeting, be as quiet as possible. If you must communicate with the person during the meeting, write a brief note.
- Allow the hearing-impaired person to observe any notes you're taking.
- Afterwards, offer to answer questions.
- Make occasional eye contact with speaking-impaired persons, to see if they have anything to contribute to the discussion.
- If they can't speak up quickly, you can create a break in the conversation and encourage them to participate.
- If you sit next to a speaking-impaired person, offer to ask questions for her or him during the meeting.

Q: How do I work effectively with persons with hearing impairments?

- The first step is getting their attention without startling them. Stand in front of them and say their name loudly, but don't shout. If you don't know their name, stand directly in front of them and begin speaking. You may also gently touch their arm or repeat yourself to be sure they understand.
- If they don't respond, tap them lightly on the arm or shoulder. If you're not within touching range, wave your hand and try to make visual contact. You may also get attention by knocking on the desk or rapping on a nearby wall, as many are sensitive to such vibrations. Flipping the light switch will get the attention of everyone in the room, so use this method with greater selectivity.
- Effort and concentration are needed by hearing impaired persons in order to understand the speech of others. Conversing at length while walking down a hall or street may be exhausting or impossible.
- You may be able to help as an interpreter when a hearing-impaired person is trying to understand someone with a foreign accent or a child with a high-pitched voice.
- Giving needed information is one of the most helpful things you can do—especially about any sound that may spell danger, such as honking horns, sirens, and alarms—but also information that comes over public address systems, radio, and other sources where lip-reading is impossible.

11

Older-Younger Persons: Bridging Generation Gaps

Older Americans are the fastest-growing population group. Nearly half of all Americans are older than 40 and so are protected by age discrimination laws. Nearly one-third are older than 50, and baby boomers, as they turn 50, are dramatically increasing the size of this group. Now that it's illegal to force persons to retire, and medical breakthroughs help people stay vital at every age, more people are working into their 70s and 80s. All this means that more and more of your coworkers are likely to be persons older than 40.

Older workers who keep their skills and knowledge up to date are likely to have higher incomes than younger workers. But those who don't are more likely to lose their jobs. If they do, they then face more intense problems than their younger counterparts with unemployment, underemployment, and lowered wages. Those who keep their jobs must deal with ageism, the barriers some managers have to investing in training for older workers, and the resulting lack of new job skills. They must cope with the generation gap that can occur as new generations of younger workers enter the workforce. Older workers must also deal with retirement expectations—their own, their organization's, and the culture's—as well as decisions around retiring, not retiring, partially retiring, or starting a new career.

People who have taken the time and effort to learn some facts about older persons say they have boosted their ability to work productively with such persons. Supervisors say such information helps them understand how to help older employees stay motivated, growing, and contributing to the organization. Coworkers, teams, and organizations gain a leading edge when they learn how to utilize the wealth of experience, knowledge, and talent that many older employees bring to the workplace.

In this chapter you'll explore what it's like to be an older person in the American workplace. Remember, the more open you are to putting yourself in their place and seeing things the way they might see them, the better your ability to feel comfortable with people of all ages and to build productive work relationships. Specifically, you'll learn:

- How typical myths and stereotypes about older persons compare with reality
- How the current situation is connected to certain historical events
- Generation gaps and how to bridge them
- How ageism in the workplace affects older persons and organizations
- What you should know about the Age Discrimination Employment Act
- How skills obsolescence affects the employment and wages of older employees
- When and why people retire, and the need for more options
- How to build on the strengths that older employees bring to the organization

MYTHS AND REALITIES

Betty Friedan and Steven Sandell have surveyed a number of interesting studies of age discrimination. They found that most of the myths and stereotypes about older persons are either false or distorted, partial truths. In fact, most stem from the high value the American culture places on youth and appearance, and the tendency to avoid facing one's own aging and eventual death.

Remember, although stereotypes aren't identical to prejudice, rigid stereotypes about people usually lead to prejudice. For example, you've heard that people lose their mental abilities after a certain age. When older coworker Joe forgets an appointment, you think "Uh-oh, Joe's losing it." But when younger coworker Janet forgets an appointment, you think, "We all forget sometimes. She must be really busy." Each time a "Joe" forgets, your belief is reinforced, and soon you develop a rigid belief that all older persons lose their mental abilities and become forgetful. The ultimate goal in becoming aware of myths and stereotypes is to refute those that are false or rigid, and to move beyond them to appreciating each generation's unique value and contribution to the workplace.

Myth #1—People quit learning when they get old.

One of the most untrue and degrading myths is "You can't teach an old dog new tricks." It's common and career-devastating for management to ignore training for older workers—and for older workers to believe training won't pay off for them. In fact, while the most rapid rate of learning occurs at very young ages, the capacity to learn remains high throughout life. They're not only trainable and retrainable, but also a unique resource.

Intellectual performance remains robust throughout life for healthy people. From age 30 onward there is a slight mental slowdown in reaction time, but older workers compensate by increasing their speed on certain complex repetitive tasks. Other functions, such as vocabulary choice, get better with age, and the brain continues to develop throughout adult life. Some brain cells die each year, but connecting branches between them—pathways for the nerve impulses that create thought, feeling, and memory—keep sprouting and spreading, more than compensating for the loss of cells.

Forgetting names and poor concentration are not connected with normal aging. They're often connected with new priorities, more years of information, more names to sort through, and heavy work loads. Actually, 92 percent of persons older than 65 show no significant mental deterioration. Only about 8 percent have such symptoms as partial memory loss and slowing reaction time.

Research uncovered by author Betty Friedan indicates that age actually brings some positive changes in certain mental abilities. The type of intelligence that involves experience, meaning, knowledge, professional expertise, and wisdom continues to increase even though speed in completing IQ tests may decline. Older workers bring a lifetime of experience to the learning situation. That's why they tend to be better at problem solving, to draw on more information for decision-making, and to be good mediators.

Further, people do not deteriorate in either basic mental competence or intelligence, even in their 80s, if they remain healthy and continue to be physically and mentally active and stimulated. For example, through mental activity, people can continue to develop vital new brain connections until the end of life and even reverse deterioration. Yet the false stereotypes of older persons may keep them from seeking or getting continuing education and the right kind of health care.

Myth #2—Older workers are more rigid and dogmatic.

Evidence indicates that dogmatic behavior is unrelated to age. What is related to age is a tendency to become more caring, accepting, and "mellow." This means that older persons tend to handle crises better than younger workers and to see the humor in life's slings and arrows.

Nurturing and Accepting

People are more likely to mentor others and become more accepting of life as they age. Carol Ryff's studies indicate that men and women tend to change their behavior during middle age to focus more on mentoring younger persons, showing more concern for guiding the next generation and feeling more of a sense of responsibility to younger persons. Beyond middle age, people tend to become more accepting of life, to adapt to the triumphs and disappointments of being human, and to view past events as inevitable, appropriate, and meaningful. While basic character traits tend to be stable, people's experiences and personal development become more varied with age.

Respect

One implication of the myth of rigidity is that older workers resent being told what to do by younger managers. In fact, no one really likes being told what to do, and younger workers are more apt to respond negatively. Older workers do appreciate receiving some respect for their years of experience. When managers get them on their side, they're less likely than younger workers to be vying for the manager's position, to quit, or to be disloyal. Their accumulated wisdom can be very helpful to managers and coworkers.

Creativity

Also implied in the myth of rigidity is that older workers are not very creative. In fact, creativity and intellectual activity is still vital in persons older than 100, according to a Social Security Administration survey of such people. When creativity is encouraged and rewarded, and when the environment is structured to enhance it, older workers bring a greater richness of ideas, stemming from their abundance of life experience.

Myth #3—Older workers are less productive, just coasting to retirement.

In 1998, over 100 leading image consultants were sent pictures of gray-haired men, along with pictures of the same men with darker hair. Their reaction? While they assumed that 49 percent of the dark-haired men would be "very capable," they gave only 27 percent of gray-haired men that rating. Scripps Howard News Service reported that researchers expected gray-haired women to fare even worse, due to gender bias.

Gray-haired persons, and those who otherwise look older, are seen as less capable and less productive than they were when they were younger, but Betty Friedan's research refutes this myth. There is no significant performance decline that's caused by aging in the case of engineers, scientists, blue-collar workers, clerical workers, and production workers. And several studies suggest that older paraprofessionals and clerical workers outperform younger workers. U.S. Department of Labor studies reveal that age has little effect on manual-labor workers through age 50, and the declines in productivity after age 50 never exceed 10 percent, on average. A study of 1,700 managers working in diverse organizations showed that when managerial performance is measured in terms of such bottom-line indicators as return on total capital, growth of stockholders' equity, earnings per share, and sales growth, no significant differences in performance could be related to the age of managers.

For some older persons, but not all, some age-related decline may occur in speed and accuracy of movement, perception, hearing, vision, and certain types of problem-solving skills. However, researchers have concluded that these declines would affect performance in only a few jobs requiring extremely high levels of sensory or cognitive skills. Workers older than 60 are functionally able to excel in nearly all occupations, drawing on years of experience and good judgment. Overwhelming scientific evidence, reported in *Retirement Living*, indicates that older workers:

- enjoy higher morale
- have a greater sense of organization commitment
- are more involved in their jobs
- rate work as more important to their lives
- have the highest job satisfaction of any age group
- rate needs for job security as more important
- are less likely to report an intention to leave the organization
- are much less likely to leave the organization

Age stereotypes depict older people as frail and fragile, as having lost the vitality and energy necessary to make a full commitment to a career. Actually, large differences exist with respect to the health and well-being of persons in every age category. While some people remain very healthy in their 80s, and even in their 90s, others become mentally and physically old at 40. Recently, changes in lifestyles, dietary habits, and exercise patterns, along with better medical interventions, have dramatically changed the health picture for older persons.

In summary, the evidence on the performance of older workers and managers generally indicates that they perform as well as their younger counterparts on almost all criteria. Chronological age is a poor indicator of a person's mental and physical well-being and an inadequate basis for predicting vocational performance. Individual differences within age groups account for much more variation in performance than does age. Managers should carefully assess each employee's capabilities with an eye toward matching them to job requirements.

Myth #4—Older people have higher absenteeism and accident rates.

The accidents myth is totally false. Bureau of Labor Statistics data shows that occupational injuries occur at a lower rate for older workers. In many instances, older workers are better risks than younger workers across a variety of jobs, even when risk exposure is controlled. Some studies indicate that their accident rate is less than half that of younger workers. All managers agree that older workers tend to be more careful.

The absentee myth is essentially untrue. Older employees' overall attendance record is much better than that of younger workers. For one thing, people older than 65 are less likely than those who are younger to suffer from the acute illnesses that require hospitalization and absenteeism. Also, younger workers are more likely to take days off for caring for family members, for dealing with love affairs, for going to the beach, and for other "mental health" reasons. Most older workers have outlived their responsibilities for dependent children and elderly parents and are free to concentrate on their careers.

The kernel of truth in the absentee myth is that older workers are more likely to be absent for unavoidable reasons such as illness. The older we get, the more likely we are to develop chronic diseases and to become disabled, primarily because of heart disease, arthritis, or cancer. However, medical breakthroughs are helping people to avoid and cope with these diseases. And nearly all older persons remain healthy until the last few months of their lives; for example:

- 95 percent of persons older than 65 live independent lives
- 95 percent of persons aged 70 have no serious disabilities
- 80 percent of persons aged 80 have no serious disabilities

The absentee myth is based on an image of age as bringing on inevitable decline and deterioration, which in turn is tied to a dread of aging and of dying. It causes people to deny that old age even exists for them. And the more age is denied, the more terrifying it becomes. Prejudice and discrimination toward the elderly are actually created by the American culture's obsession with and idealization of youth and by our refusal even to look at the reality of age on its own terms. Subconsciously, we think that if we can keep old people out of sight, we can hold on to the illusion of eternal youth and rarely have to face the fact that we all age and die.

Myth #5—Older workers are not as attractive to clients.

This myth contains the kernel of truth implied by our discussion of the American tendency to be obsessed with youth and fearful of old age. However, it overlooks the truth that beauty is in the eye of the beholder—and it's only skin deep.

Gender Differences

Since women's value is more firmly tied to looks than men's, women stand to lose the most as they age. If a man is old, ugly, and wise, he's a sage. If a woman is old, ugly, and wise, she's a hag, a witch, a crone. But in prepatriarchal societies, the elder women were generally considered founts of wisdom, law, healing skills, and moral leadership, according to Betty Friedan's study. Their wrinkles would have been badges of honor, not of shame. By contrast, our society regards elder women as relatively unattractive and useless.

When men are considered to be in their prime, in their 50s and 60s, women are considered to be over the hill. The aging woman is often surprised and hurt by the unexpected hostility she encounters as she slips into old age. The combination of sexism and ageism turns older women into invisible citizens of the modern world. We make them invisible by rarely featuring them in films or television programs, and generally passing them by as social and professional leaders.

Media and Advertising Stereotypes

Older people are generally pictured as "ugly, toothless, sexless, incontinent, senile, confused, and helpless," and old age is so negatively stereotyped that "it has become something to dread and feel threatened by." These were the conclusions of the Gray Panthers' nationwide volunteer force called Media Watch, reported in *Advertising Age*. The sales pitches for products that promise to stop or cover up aging send the message that age is acceptable only if it passes for or acts like youth. A multibillion-dollar beauty industry exploits women's well-founded fear of looking old. Many people proclaimed a real breakthrough in the 1980s when the female stars of the TV series *Dynasty* were considered still attractive and employable at age 50. A 1993 consumer survey, reported in *Advertising Age*, found that most consumers older than 35 now believe that a woman can be beautiful at 40, or 50, and even past 60. This was hailed as great progress—even though it implies that women past sixty-something have no chance.

Yet the U.S. population is about one-third older persons over age 50, one-third youngsters under age 20, and one-third adults in between. Assuming youngsters are not potential customers for many of the products and services that companies sell, people 50 and older represent nearly half the potential customers that most companies should target. Companies who project an image of older persons in a positive way, with attractive, natural older role models, will hit pay dirt, especially with the Me-generation of baby boomers, as discussed later.

Myth #6—One That's True: You're only as old as you feel.

Remember, a myth is a symbolic saying or story whose function is to bind together the thoughts of a group and promote coordinated social action. Some myths are essentially true, and this is one of them. Scientists are discovering that aging is mainly in the mind. The best ways to slow the mental aging process are:

- maintaining a positive attitude
- remaining mentally and physically active

These activities bring us to Myth #7.

Myth #7—One That's Very True: Use it or lose it.

This myth is not only true, it's a key to staying healthy and alert as we grow older. We can retain our vitality and health best by using our minds and bodies. Physical and mental exercise, along with a healthy diet, are the specific keys. Energy levels peak in the early 30s and normally drop about 7 percent per decade, primarily because people tend to become more sedentary. But physical exercise can dramatically slow the energy drop.

Aging decline has in fact been reversed with changes in diet, exercise, lifestyle, and environment. People who reach age 65 in the 1990s are more likely to be healthy, active, and financially self-sufficient than any previous generation. We must learn to view age as continued human development, a continuation of personal growth, not of decline and decay. Staying independent and connected to people in the workplace, community, and family are crucial to vital aging and longevity. The key is to move on to new growth in the last third of life.

PAST AND PRESENT PROFILE

In 1860, people over age 65 were less than 3 percent of the population, but they had great economic and political influence relative to their proportion. They dictated the behavior of younger family members because they owned the farm or family business, and they knew more than anyone about making money from it. New generations adopted the occupations and lifestyles of parents and grandparents, so older people's knowledge and experience were indispensable. They were at the center of economic and social life, from trade and commerce to finance, political organization, and religious training. By the 1930s, most who lived to old age faced poverty, loneliness, and ageism, according to J. C. Hushbeck's studies. What happened in between?

Separation of the Generations

Between 1860 and 1920 we moved from an agricultural to an industrial economy. Mass production led to the "de-skilling" of most workers. The rapid pace of work, the need for stamina, and a rapid wearing-out of laborers led firms to prefer hiring younger applicants. This put older workers at a physical and technological disadvantage. As people moved to cities to get jobs, the nuclear family became the norm, housed in small quarters, and the older generation was separated from the younger.

Fewer and fewer older persons were able to be self-supporting or economically productive. Many were faced with no property, no job, and uncertain family support. Industrial pension plans were usually nonexistent or inadequate when it was time to retire. Social security and improved company pension plans have improved the retirement picture, but most retirees are still socially isolated, ghettoized, and ignored.

Current Profile

Today, people are living longer, so what constitutes "old age" is changing, and the population of older persons is growing larger by the year. Now that childbirth is safer and less frequent, women are outliving men.

How Old Is Old?

For business purposes, we might say it's older than 40, because that's when protection from discrimination kicks in. Other government sources seem to disagree. For example, the Bureau of Labor Statistics says it's 55, but the Census Bureau says it's 65. Gerontologists say that because people live longer and remain healthier, it's now more realistic to use two age categories:

- young-old, currently 65 to 75, soon to be 75 to 85
- old-old, now older than 75, soon to be older than 85

How Many Are Old?

About 13 percent of Americans are currently older than 65, a huge increase during this century, and the trend is expected to accelerate in the coming twenty-five years, as shown in Figure 11.1.

Women—Older and Poorer

About two-thirds of people older than 65 are women, because they live longer. The older they become, the less likely women are to be married because their husbands die before they do. Therefore, older women are more likely to live alone, in contrast to older men, most of whom are married and living with their wives. And women are twice as likely to live in poverty, with 16 percent classified as poor. Nationally, about 10 percent of older persons live in poverty, but in nine southern states, the rate is 20 percent or more.

Figure 11.1 *Proportion of Americans over Age 65*

1900	1990	2015, Projected
4%, 1 in 25	13%, 1 in 8	17%, 1 in 6
3 million	31 million	54 million

AGEISM: HOW IT WORKS AND HOW TO MOVE BEYOND IT

Ageism means that as you progress from being perceived as a middle-aged employee in the prime of life to an older employee, you are likely to be increasingly devalued, avoided, and discriminated against. Such actions are usually subtle but occasionally blatant. We need our older employees. They're the fastest-growing population group at the same time that the U.S. labor pool is shrinking. It's time for everyone in the workplace to reassess negative views of older workers. We all have a stake in how society will treat our future selves.

Impact of Ageism on Careers

The social impact of ageism can deflate your ego, but the career impact can deflate your bank account. Benson Rosen and Thomas Jerdee reported on a study sponsored by *Harvard Business Review (HBR)* and found that younger managers stereotype older workers as being rigid, too old to train, declining in competence, and less creative than younger workers. When the researchers compared the ways younger managers treat 30-year-olds and 60-year-olds, they found that:

- Managers perceive older employees to be relatively inflexible and resistant to change. They therefore make much less effort to give older persons feedback about needed changes in performance.
- Managers provide very limited organization support for the career development and retraining of older employees.
- The promotion opportunities for older people are somewhat restricted, especially when the new positions demand creativity, mental alertness, or the capacity to deal with crisis situations.

How Managers Withhold Feedback and Encouragement

The *HBR* study provided managers with a case involving customer complaints about employee performance. Most of the managers said they would have an encouraging talk with a 30-year-old employee, but they would reassign a 60-year-old. Clearly the managers saw the older employee as more resistant to their influence, even though there was nothing in the case to support such a perception. Reassigning the older employee, rather than encouraging him or her to improve performance, deprives the employee of the opportunity to improve performance. Such actions make the effects of age stereotyping very difficult to overcome. By transferring older employees, managers avoid a direct test of their own assumptions about older workers' rigidity and resistance to change. Such managers cut off the opportunity to learn whether this age stereotype is valid or not.

How the "Too-Old-to-Train" Stereotype Creates Blocks

Employees over age 50 are vulnerable to problems of career obsolescence. Both managers and their older employees need to commit themselves to continuous career development in order to keep older workers' knowledge and skills up to date. One of the cases in the *HBR* study revealed managers' assumptions that older workers are not motivated to improve their job-related skills. These assumptions are reflected in decisions to avoid investments in the continued development of older employees. Assumptions about retirement practices can also influence these decisions. While 74 percent of managers would allocate funds to send a 30-year-old employee to a production seminar, only 53 percent would allocate it for a 60-year-old. Managers may balk at paying for expensive training for older employees, believing they'll soon retire. But younger employees change jobs more frequently, so investment in their training may also be "wasted."

How the "Less-Creative" Stereotype Hinders

Managers are less likely to promote older employees. Managers in the study were asked to decide whether a sales rep should be promoted to a marketing director position that called for fresh solutions to challenging problems. They rated the outlook for successful performance as much less favorable for a 60-year-old candidate than for a 30-year-old, and indicated very little support for promoting the older candidate.

How the "Declining-Competence" Stereotype Discriminates

Managers are more likely to give demanding new jobs to younger workers, reflecting the stereotype that connects age with declining mental alertness and resulting nervousness. The majority of managers viewed a 30-year-old employee as more suitable for a new role calling for poise and mental alertness. The *HBR* study revealed a pattern in which older employees are seen as less able to cope with higher-level positions when role requirements conflict with age stereotypes. Therefore, the probability of a promotion is somewhat lower for an older employee than for an identically qualified younger person.

How to Move Beyond Ageism

Yes, the older you get, the more devaluation and discrimination you are likely to face. That's because we as Americans tend to view old age quite negatively, often equating it with loss of abilities, vitality, and attractiveness, as well as with illness, nursing homes, and death. It's not surprising that many younger people prefer to avoid older people and the depressing thoughts their presence may trigger. But such pictures are increasingly false. To move beyond ageism, we must begin dealing with the new facts of life. We must adopt accurate, life-affirming beliefs.

The Third Age as the Vital Age

We're entering an era when old age will be a full one-third of life for most people:

1. Youth is the first 30 years of life.
2. Middle age is the second 30 years.
3. Old age is the third 30 years, from age 60 to 90.

Many people today are retaining great vitality throughout the Third Age, embarking on a new adventure and finding new wholeness. They have a burning need to be part of an enterprise larger than the self, whether in the workplace or the community at large, to contribute to humanity, and to pass on something to the next generation.

The Need for New Beliefs

What if we reexamine our devastating stereotypes of age as do-nothing retirement, deterioration, and decline, and change our beliefs? What if we begin to value older persons as fountains of wisdom, support, and vitality—a slow-burning, steady energy, now past the flash fires of youth? What if we begin to allow and expect that they will continue to grow, develop, and unfold in the last third of life as they have during the first two-thirds? Won't we have much to gain and little to lose? Wouldn't such new beliefs lay the foundation for bridging the generation gap?

BRIDGING GENERATION GAPS

Older and younger employees often experience a communication gap that is caused primarily by the differences in their experiences and values. Understanding the key themes for each age group can build a base for understanding and can reduce stereotypes, prejudice, and discrimination.

The Generation Gap

The *HBR* study indicates that younger managers are less likely to support older employees' training. But managers in the over-50 age category are more likely to recommend financial support to enable an older employee to attend a technical seminar. In promotion decisions, older managers are much less likely to be influenced by the candidate's age. They are equally likely to promote both a younger and older man, and they would favor the creation of a new supervisory position for both a younger and an older woman. We might conclude that an older employee has a better chance of fair treatment from an older boss. We might also conclude that the older boss has lived long enough to begin seeing that age stereotypes are not necessarily true. We all need to be aware of these kinds of generation gaps. Including older managers on any decision-making panel can provide the balance needed for fair decisions.

Generational Values and Customs

How can you understand what makes each generation tick? Learn about their key values. Each generation internalizes the cultural ethos (essence of the key values) that are typical of the larger culture at the time that generation was coming of age. They incorporate that cultural ethos as they deal with the issues of the day and as they respond to major historical events. Figure 11.2 summarizes research on the ethos of various American generations of this century, based on studies by L. J. Gann, P. J. Duignan, and Susan Jackson.

Matures range in age from fifty-something to seventy, a relatively small group that includes most of our current business and political leaders. They grew up in the 1930s to 1950s. Most share a strong work ethic and place a premium on job and financial security. Some, especially ethnic minorities, are first- or second-generation immigrants who still retain many customs from their home cultures, such as dress, music, principles of family life, respect for authority figures, and patriotism. Most hold to the traditional values that Americans are known for around the world. They tend to ask, Why do young people think the world owes them a living?

Baby Boomers are now mostly in their thirties and forties and some are turning 50. They grew up in the 1950s and 1960s and entered the work force in the 1970s and 1980s. Their large size gives them significant social and economic clout. In their youth they tended to be either quite traditional or radical. Some are former hippies and yippies, and many are now yuppies. Some, such as the hippies, were suspicious of big business and big government. A few, such as the yippies, took to the streets to demonstrate against the Vietnam war. Many have experimented with drugs, and their slogan in the 1960s was "Don't trust anyone over 30."

They grew up in more permissive homes, and they place great value on work that is self-actualizing. Some rejected their parents' focus on upward mobility and dedication to work. They insisted on finding and expressing their own individuality and pursuing a lifestyle that leaves ample time for the pursuit of leisure activities. Their focus on their personal development led to their designation as the "Me Generation" in the 1970s. In the 1980s, however, they encountered economic stagnation and disappointments in the workplace. Many, such as yuppies, found that in order to succeed in careers they had to sacrifice the kind of home life and personal life they desired.

Baby Boomer employees are battling their own midlife crises, and even at midlife are focusing on discovering the meaning of life.

Generation Xers are now in their twenties and early thirties. They are a smaller group than the Boomers. Some are children of hippies and other counterculture types. Because this group is greatly divided between the haves and have-nots, clear statements about who they are have not yet emerged. One thing for sure, they are more diverse, accept diversity, and even insist on it. Most tend to be less materialistic and more idealistic than the their yuppie predecessors. Many are from broken homes and so tend to want marriages that work and that last. Many have adopted their parents' values of personal growth and development.

Figure 11.2 *Generations and Their Cultural Ethos*

Birth Years	Era	Key issues	Cultural Ethos
1930-1945	Matures	Great Depression	Surviving; security; saving
		World War II	Defending freedom; duty
1946-1964	Baby Boomers	Postwar	Rebuilding; demanding
		Civil rights	personal freedoms; individuality
		Me generation	Seeking personal fulfillment
1965-1975	Generation Xers	Information Age	Spanning the global village; cutting edge, fun, diversity

Generation X workers want to avoid stress and burnout; they search for jobs that will let them have a personal life. They want stress-free fun and are attracted to anything they consider leading-edge but also like certain old things in new packages, such as the new Volkswagen Beetle.

Mellowing with Age

Younger people, ages 18 to 25, are more likely to see themselves as emotional, nervous, competitive, uncooperative, and not helpful or supportive of others. Having arguments that lead to physical blows occurs almost exclusively among young men. People younger than 30 are much less likely to vote, to make charitable contributions regardless of income, or to participate in voluntary organizations. Spirituality plays a relatively minor role in the lives of most young people and takes on increasing significance as they age.

Older persons, regardless of generation, tend to grow mellow with age. Studies by Walter Gove of Vanderbilt University suggest that as we age, we become less self-absorbed, more cooperative and attentive to others. We function more effectively, becoming more serene and less emotional. We act in more socially accepted ways, are more community oriented, and are more likely to see others as friendly and considerate. Finally, we become more spiritual, having a stronger interest in spiritual activities and turning to spiritual beliefs that comfort us.

The Impact of Cross-Generational Work Teams

As corporate structures become more flexible and weblike, as layers of hierarchy are removed, previously segregated generations of employees find themselves working together and even rotating jobs among themselves. Another factor throwing the generations together is the entry and reentry into the workforce of middle-aged women, former retirees, and young student interns and apprentices.

Four generations of workers may now find themselves working side by side. This provides rich opportunities for all of them. Younger employees have much to learn from older ones, ranging from alternative philosophies of life to practical tips gained from life experiences. Older workers can gain much from younger ones, ranging from learning about what's new to absorbing a fresh, high-energy outlook.

Strategies for Bridging Generation Gaps

Bridging the generation gap at all levels is becoming more important in the workplace because networking and relationships are more central to job performance. Here are a few bridging strategies to start your thinking. You may come up with others on your own.

Use Diverse Teams

Except at work, many young employees may have few relationships with older persons other than their parents and grandparents. One remedy for this experiential gap is to make assignments to teams and committees so that employees of different ages will work together. Studies discussed in Chapter 4, "Beyond Stereotypes to Profitable Collaboration," indicate that meaningful contact among diverse employees can reduce prejudice. Contact that involves working together toward meaningful goals is most likely to bridge generational differences.

Open Up Communication Lines

Be aware of communication across the generation gap. People tend to communicate within their own age groups rather than between them, because they seek perspectives similar to their own and support for their opinions. Also, younger workers may shun and thus isolate older workers, creating a communication gap. Part of diversity training can be helping younger people find ways to include older workers in communication lines and vice versa.

Use Diversity Training

Training should include information that makes younger workers more aware and sensitive of older workers' needs, strengths, and potential contributions—helping them replace myths and stereotypes with facts.

Training can also include information that makes older workers more aware of their own actions that foster the generation gap and suggest alternate actions. For example, a person's image is a powerful communication tool. An image that promotes rapport usually includes dressing in style, maintaining good grooming, enjoying an active personal life, showing a warm sense of humor, not offering knee-jerk judgmental criticisms of fellow workers or repeating the same old comments, contributing new ideas, and giving credit to coworkers.

Diversity training should also focus on building relationship skills with older employees. Training can focus on utilizing varied generational strengths as well as individual strengths. It can also include information about the desirable traits of older employees, according to studies by Carol Ryff and others that compare older with younger employees. For example, older workers are likely to be:

- more cheerful
- more committed to the organization and involved with their jobs
- more stable, reliable, and careful
- less likely to have accidents, be absent, or quit

Training seminars can start with a frank discussion of differences in generational values and how these differences are reflected in supervisory styles and in expectations about worker loyalty, commitment, and career aspirations. Case studies that present typical, specific problems in the relationships between younger and older workers can be analyzed and solutions explored. For example, problems may occur when a young woman is assigned to supervise a much older man—and in other situations where traditional status relationships are switched. Finally, training participants can develop ways to stress generational unity when working together to achieve common job goals.

THE ADEA: WHAT YOU SHOULD KNOW

Before the Age Discrimination Employment Act (ADEA) was enacted in 1976, many large companies would not hire workers older than 40 and most required retirement at age 65. The act, designed to help overcome the effects of ageism on the careers of older persons, provides guidelines in the areas of recruiting, hiring, selection, promotion, and termination. The act has had a favorable impact on older workers, with minor negative side effects for others.

Major Provisions of the Act

The ADEA is intended to:

- Protect workers over age 40 from discrimination
- Promote employment opportunities for older workers capable of meeting job requirements
- Protect nearly all employees from forced retirement at any age

It covers private employers of twenty or more persons, labor organizations, employment agencies, and all government employees.

Providing for Valid Assessments

The major exception to age requirements occurs when an age requirement is a "bona fide occupation qualification" (BFOQ), reasonably necessary to the normal operations of a business. Also, differential treatment of employees based on reasonable factors other than age, such as physical fitness, is permitted. The ADEA does not preclude the discharge or discipline of an older worker for good cause. For example, an employer might defend a personnel decision on the ground that the older employee could not meet performance standards or that his declining functional abilities represented a potential threat to the public safety. Careful documentation of such actions is critical if an age discrimination suit is filed. The EEOC (Equal Employment Opportunities Commission) is responsible for enforcing the ADEA.

Ending Recruiting Discrimination

An example of recruiting discrimination is the practice of focusing on college graduates. Since age tends to be highly correlated with college graduation, the policy of recruiting future managers only from the ranks of college seniors potentially discriminates against older employees with comparable credentials. A corporation would be especially vulnerable to charges of age discrimination if admission to its executive training programs were limited exclusively to recent college graduates.

Ending Selection Discrimination

Job application forms can no longer require applicants to state their age, nor can interviewers legally inquire about age. The issue is whether an applicant is capable of performing the job. An age limit is a BFOQ only when it can be shown that all, or almost all, persons over that age cannot meet the requirements of a specific job. A construction firm might be able to show that virtually no one over age 70 can meet the physical requirements for carrying 60-pound loads up a ladder. However, a restaurant chain or airline will have a difficult time showing that organization image, or even customer preferences for attractive young hostesses, is sufficient justification for rejecting an otherwise qualified over-40 job applicant.

Age limits are likely to be upheld as a BFOQ in jobs with stringent physical demands that also involve public safety. Accordingly, it is not uncommon to find age limits governing the selection and retirement of airline pilots, air traffic controllers, police officers, and firefighters. These are jobs requiring strenuous physical exertion or work under stressful conditions, where even a slight decline in reaction time could endanger others' lives, and where public safety is involved. Even in these instances, it is wise for companies to have statistical or medical data to back up decisions about physical incapacities associated with aging.

Ending Promotion Discrimination

Organizations most often get in trouble with age discrimination suits concerning promotion when they follow inconsistent promotion policies and then try to justify their decisions after an employee files a complaint. Personnel actions are more defensible when they are based on a systematic, objective, and job-related performance appraisal system.

Ending Termination Discrimination

Decisions to terminate older workers are almost always difficult because motivations for such termination can be subject to many interpretations. Perhaps the best defense against a charge of age bias is the ability to show that the decision was based on the employee's substandard performance or some similar legitimate business reason. Managers must be prepared to demonstrate that the employee's behavior was measured fairly and objectively, and that the employee was given a reasonable opportunity to bring her performance up to standard. Managers should also be prepared to show that they didn't harass the employee in an attempt to "run her off."

The End of Mandatory Retirement

People who opposed the elimination of mandatory retirement pointed to the possibility that retaining older workers would delay the promotion of some younger workers. It could also block the progress of women and minorities who entered promotion pipelines only after affirmative action programs were in place for several years. These workers are often just waiting for employees in higher positions to retire so they can move up and into their jobs. Researcher Benson Rosen found that the end of mandatory retirement has affected only about 4 percent of these workers, so the concerns appear unfounded.

PREVENTING SKILLS OBSOLESCENCE

The most pressing problem for many of today's older workers is occupational obsolescence, which can lead to unemployment, underemployment and lower wages.

Savvy business persons see the benefits of helping older workers move into the twenty-first century, when physical strength and endurance will not be important factors in most jobs. Factory jobs will probably account for less than 10 percent of employment after the year 2000. New jobs are being created in fields devoted to computerization, robotization, and human services, and these jobs require radically new skills.

How Skills Obsolescence Occurs

Several factors make up the job obsolescence picture:

- After age 50, age differences in years since schooling are associated with an appreciable skills disadvantage to older workers.
- Older workers tend to have less schooling than younger employees and are less likely to have degrees in business, computer, and similar high-demand fields.
- As we move from a manufacturing economy to an information and service economy, older workers' skills are too often industry-specific and not readily transferable.
- New jobs in high-tech fields call for specific kinds of education and training.
- Many companies are reluctant to invest in further training for older employees, and employees may be reluctant to invest in their own training.

Many managers hold stereotypes that older workers are harder to train and will soon retire anyway. They don't see older employees as part of a pool from which future leaders can be drawn. This may not be direct discrimination but it has the same effect. Managers assume that training for older workers has a shorter payback period. But let's look at reality:

- Turnover rates are increasingly higher for employees of all ages.
- New technologies become obsolete in ever-shorter time spans.
- More people remain relatively healthy and vital well into their 70s and 80s.
- More older workers are planning to work for many more years—if companies offer a welcoming environment that meets their needs.

These facts suggest that the exclusion of older persons from training programs may be more a habit and a result of stereotyping than strict cost-benefit thinking.

Older workers internalize these stereotypes, and many are less likely to invest in extensive retraining on their own. Rosen Benson's research indicates that younger workers are willing to make greater investments on the assumption that they have more time before expected retirement to pay back the costs and to reap the financial benefits of training. Since the younger ones earn less than the older, their time-out from work in order to attend school costs them less (in terms of wages they would have received if they had continued working).

Results: Unemployment, Underemployment, Lower Wages

Skills obsolescence often leads to unemployment for older persons. During downsizing phases, older workers are more likely to lose their jobs than their younger peers (and their skills are more likely to become obsolete), because they've usually worked up to a relatively high pay scale. And once unemployed, they're likely to experience longer periods of joblessness than their younger counterparts due to obsolete job skills and age discrimination—and they're more likely to take a pay cut. Older women and minority men are likely to be hit the hardest.

How to Prevent Skills Obsolescence

Equal opportunity for older workers calls for companies to design policies that provide affordable and useful training to workers of all ages. Policies need to ensure equal access to this training, as well as to the more secure and better-paying jobs. When older workers find themselves with obsolete skills, in dead-end jobs or career ruts, their motivation and job performance are likely to decline. The potential is still there, but it's underutilized. Leaders can remedy this situation through career planning and appropriate training.

Career Planning

In these times of rapid technological change, the most important goal of career management programs may be to identify job categories where future organizational needs are likely to be low and to help employees in these jobs to plan a new career path. Organizations can prepare employees to move into high-demand career tracks compatible with their interests, skills, and aspirations.

Older employees can be encouraged to do ongoing career planning. This begins with a critical self-analysis of interests, skills, and potential. The employee should then develop short-term and long-term career goals, specific and in writing. Next comes written plans for achieving goals, including how to use strengths and overcome obstacles. Written plans help the employees and their managers to assess progress along the way. Finally, especially important for older employees, is making Plans B and C—backup plans to cover the possibility that their career progress may get seriously sidetracked.

Training to Prevent Skills Obsolescence

Technological change creates new opportunities for employees who are trained in business, technological, and scientific fields. It also leads to the displacement of middle managers and production workers, especially older workers with obsolete skills.

Preliminary evidence suggests that the training approaches most compatible with the cognitive strengths of older employees:

- permit self-paced learning
- focus on experiential learning rather than abstract learning, hands-on activities rather than theory alone

On the other hand, most people probably respond best to this type of training.

Some companies provide a tuition reimbursement plan designed to help retiring workers prepare for second careers. Senior employees begin to draw from their educational fund a few years before retirement and continue to draw from it for a few years after retirement. Employees who acquire skills in the company's "critical needs areas" may be offered post-retirement, part-time, or consulting positions.

RETIREMENT: WHETHER, WHEN, AND HOW?

It's time to overcome the myth that everyone should retire by age 65. Currently, 80 percent of employees have retired by age 70, but the retirement decision is a complex one that should not be decided upon by age alone. In fact, we could say the decision is a life-or-death one, and people should carefully consider the many key factors that affect retirement.

People generally view retirement as a chance to finally be free from onerous responsibility and hard work. Yet retirement means loss for many, so it may in fact lead to decline and deterioration. Typical concerns are:

- loss of the identity that comes from career roles
- loss of power—organizational power, earning power, prestige
- loss of challenge to continue developing abilities and potentials
- loss of inner fulfillment that is tied to work performance and achievement
- loss of the social ties and social status that are career-connected
- loss of involvement in the active mainstream

In our culture, prestige and self-worth are based largely on occupational status and income, especially for men. And women who haven't had careers of their own often bask in the reflected light of the husband's occupational status. For men and their wives, the sense of loss usually sets in a year or so into retirement. On the other hand, career women are less likely than men to be defined by their careers, but retirement can be just as traumatic for them.

Betty Friedan reports that in 1950, nearly half the men older than 65 were in the workforce; by 1976, the proportion had dropped to one-fifth. Laws forbidding mandatory retirement were passed shortly after. A third of retirees would stay with the company and move on to some new type of work or different work pattern—if they could. But the stereotype of older persons being retired persons is so ingrained in our culture that most people don't even question it. In fact, most people don't even know there are laws against forced retirement.

Factors That Affect the Employee's Decision

The factors that have the strongest and most consistent influence on the timing of retirement are health considerations and financial well-being. Gender and educational level also appear to affect retirement intentions. The answers to the following questions will provide insight into the likelihood of an employee choosing to retire. The three most significant questions are:

1. Can the employee afford to retire?
2. Does disability or declining health make retirement desirable?
3. Is the employee male or female?

Women tend to retire earlier than men, which may be related to the fact that women have been concentrated in lower-level jobs. Workers with less formal education tend to retire earlier, perhaps because they are clustered in more physically demanding and less intrinsically motivating jobs. Ethnicity has not been associated with patterns of early retirement. The following are some factors that have a less significant impact on retirement plans.

Men over 65 who continue to work are primarily at the bottom—or the top—of the occupational ladder. Most of those at the bottom are working from financial necessity. Those at the top work for the meaning, enjoyment, and vitality it gives them. They're more likely (than those who retire) to keep up with new developments and transmit and advance them. They also have a greater sense of their own identity and are better able to act contrary to public opinion and others' expectations.

Work = A Longer Life

You may have heard that many men die soon after retirement. Does this mean people must keep working in order to keep living? Betty Friedan's studies indicate that if retirement doesn't lead to new purposes that involve continued work or a new line of work, it often ends in early death, or is experienced as a living death. While satisfying work tends to increase longevity, unsatisfying work tends to reduce it. Depression is a typical symptom of a retirement without satisfying work and often leads to reduced immunity to disease or to suicide. In 1980, when persons 65 and older were 11 percent of the population, they committed 25 percent of reported suicides. The male-to-female suicide rate goes from three-to-one for young men and women, to ten-to-one among those 65 and older. The tendency of men to define themselves by their occupational roles—and the loss of those roles—is considered a major factor in post-retirement depression and suicide.

People who experience growth, change, and "aliveness" after age 60—those who don't complain of boredom, stagnation, or loneliness—have several things in common:

- They're passionately committed to a career or other vital activity that uses their mature qualities of broader perspective and greater wisdom and that motivates them to keep developing a variety of abilities.
- They don't expect their most valued qualities to decline with age—such traits as trust, risk-taking, adaptability, nonconformity, and ability to live in the present moment.
- They don't need to pretend to be young, but they don't think of themselves as old.
- They refuse to conform to traditional old-age stereotypes in their choice of lifestyles and friends, and they have friends of all ages.

BUILDING ON OLDER PERSONS' STRENGTHS

You now know that the older population is ballooning. Baby boomers are entering their 50s, and by 2020 about one in six Americans will be older than 65. Some business leaders are preparing for the changes this implies. Some sociologists are predicting that the boomers won't be as accepting of age stereotyping and discrimination as recent generations have been. Businesses that treat them more positively will have a definite advantage.

To build on their strengths, you can begin by understanding their needs and helping them get what they need to do a good job. You can support strategies for keeping older employees on the payroll by such actions as offering flexible career options, making fair appraisals, and making the corporate culture more welcoming. You can help them make connections with the growing over-50 marketplace.

Opportunity #1—Understand How Educational Level Affects Needs

Current changes in the nature of work can be threatening to older employees with limited skills, but they may be challenging and intriguing to other, better-educated older employees. You can help less-educated workers face their fears and make new plans. On the other hand, you can support better-educated workers in using and expanding their skills.

Recognize Fears of the Less-Educated

As seen by many older employees with limited education and skills, the employment picture includes the following:

- Technological change is a threat.
- Retraining is scary or unacceptable.
- Unions are not much help because they're going along with management to eliminate the old jobs and retrain for the new jobs.
- Government is not much help because its programs are also geared toward retraining.

Help these coworkers face their worst fears and become comfortable with the worst-case scenario. Lead them in understanding that age is not necessarily a barrier to handling change and learning new technological skills. Help them to make career plans for gaining new skills and knowledge and to get support for the training they need.

Support Goals of the Better Educated

Better-educated, more highly skilled older employees tend to be more flexible and to see a brighter job picture:

- They often want a few minor adjustments in their work situation.
- They may desire to work a few hours less per week.
- They often want to be freed from the prison of the 5-day, 40-hour week or the arduous commute to the workplace.
- They may wish to be liberated from the controls on time and place of work implied by traditional employment contracts.
- They may want more flexibility and discretion in their work. Many may want to work at home on a full- or part-time basis, perhaps for more than one employer.

You can help them develop arrangements for time and place of work that will allow them to continue making valuable contributions to the team and the company.

Opportunity #2—Understand Older Employees' Motivational Needs

A vicious cycle of declining motivation can affect older employees. Here are the factors:

- Managers who expect a decline in motivation among older workers might make age-based managerial decisions that in fact lead to decreased motivation for these employees.
- To the extent that an older employee perceives that his or her efforts no longer lead to promotion or other significant rewards, his or her motivation tends to gradually decline.
- Limited opportunities for development and lack of feedback about performance may further reduce the older worker's motivation.

- In today's relatively flat organizational structures, there are shorter ladders to climb and fewer promotions to give. Many ambitious employees reach career plateaus much earlier than in the past. Employees need to become aware of this fact and to be given opportunities for lateral moves to expand their career growth and development.

It's likely that lowered motivation may result, not from aging itself, but from managerial expectations and treatment of older employees. If this is so, then policy changes to eliminate discrimination against older employees represent only a first step. Additional efforts to help managers and coworkers identify age stereotypes and eliminate their effects on everyday decisions need to be made. These efforts must also deal with all the practices that tend to support and perpetuate the stereotypes

Opportunity #3—Adopt Strategies for Meeting Needs

Some simple general strategies for understanding an older employee's concerns include listening with awareness, developing empathy for their situation in life, and helping them to manage the changes they encounter.

Listening

Listen to older workers and be a supportive sounding board. You'll learn a great deal about their strengths and problems that way, gain insights to solutions to problems, and gain from their knowledge and experience. Encourage small group meetings of older workers for the purpose of getting in touch with their interests, desires, talents, and needs and then communicating those to coworkers and management.

Developing Empathy

If you live long enough, you'll be an older person one day, if you're not already. Ask yourself, What will I do when I'm no longer "young and cute"? and then put yourself in the older person's shoes. Look for the individual personality inside the older exterior. Be open to many kinds of beauty. Focus on skills, experience, contribution, and performance rather than narrow ideas about physical appearance. This is a positive strategy for relating to persons of all ages.

Managing Change

Encourage older workers to stay current. Help them to respond positively to change, to develop the new skills and acquire the new information they need in the changing business environment. Many older employees need a little encouragement to help them overcome the limitations imposed by cultural myths.

In organizations where self-managing teams are replacing most of the hierarchy, help people bridge the generation gap. Help older employees to pace themselves and avoid burnout. Stamina may decrease for some, but they can still be productive workers. Learning time may take a little longer but will be mastered.

Opportunity #4—Support Corporate Cultural Changes

If business leaders want to retain productive older workers, they must bring about changes in corporate cultural norms. For example, we know that managers who hold age stereotypes are normally less willing to approve promotions, offer training opportunities, and work out performance problems with older workers. In fact, studies indicate that managers age 40 and over tend to be rated significantly lower than younger managers on readiness for promotion, even when education, performance, and job tenure are comparable. Such age stereotypes contribute to an organizational climate that discourages continued employment opportunities for older employees. But when companies are able to develop supportive organizational norms that encourage older workers to stay on, all middle-aged and younger workers get a clear message: The contributions of senior employees are recognized and welcomed here.

Clearly, the information economy will ease the transition to longer working lives. Working with computers in service-sector occupations such as medical diagnostics or insurance services is much less demanding physically than assembly line, construction, and other manual labor. It's unrealistic for us to expect people to spend almost a third of their lives in retirement. The challenge leaders in traditional organizations now face is how to tap the knowledge of their older workers while keeping promotion opportunities open for younger employees.

Adopt a Variety of Change Strategies

Here are just a few examples of the many specific actions organization leaders could take for the purpose of making the culture more welcoming to older employees:

- The achievements of older workers are recognized and publicized.
- There is a shift away from celebrating retirements and toward celebrating continued contributions.
- Managers and coworkers do not anticipate retirement simply because of an employee's age. After all, people may retire at 50 or 80 or any other age—and may leave for any reason at any age.
- All employees are trained to understand the ADEA and any other legal considerations governing the employment of older workers.
- All employees participate in training to overcome deep-rooted assumptions and expectations about what senior employees can and cannot do.
- Training also raises employees' awareness of the pervasive influence of age stereotypes on day-to-day interactions and decisions, and helps them move beyond myths and stereotypes.
- Training provides all employees with skills to bridge communication gaps between young managers and senior employees.
- Training is designed to explore value differences and similarities between younger and older workers, and to move to appreciation for the diversity of values, as well as the unity that common values provide.
- Expect and encourage creative thinking and innovative results from employees of all ages.

Value Older Employees

If the corporate culture values and supports older workers who delay their retirement, they're likely to stay longer. Your attitude has its impact, just as every employee's attitude counts, so you can influence the value that people generally place on the contributions of older workers and the belief that effective workers should be retained as long as possible. Some organizations actually encourage direct group pressure on people to retire. Other organizations encourage a more subtle expression of norms calling for early retirement. Such pressures do have a strong influence on employees' retirement decisions.

Respect Employees' Retirement Decisions

We know that companies can no longer force employees to retire, but they can and do offer them tempting rewards to retire. Failing that, they can resort to subtle pressure: lower performance evaluations, onerous job assignments, taking away responsibilities or perks, exclusion from desired projects or meetings. Finally, the employee gets fed up, gives up, and retires.

Studies indicate that managers are less likely to pressure employees to retire if they view them as having some of the following traits and life situations: younger, financially troubled, likely to make a poor social adjustment to retirement, supported by the union, engaged in personal activities that are compatible with business interests, and still earning higher performance ratings. Of these reasons, most experts agree that the only rational, valid reason for encouraging one employee to stay over another is higher performance ratings.

This leads us to why and how an organization can hold onto its effective older employees.

Opportunity #5—Support Strategies for Retaining Older Workers

Currently more than half of Americans are out of the workforce before age 63, and 80 percent are out by the time they're 70. The goal of a retention strategy is to retain older workers as long as feasible. Such a strategy can benefit the organization and society as well as older employees.

Benefits to the organization of an effective retention strategy are that it:

- lowers pension costs
- lowers turnover rates and resulting turnover costs
- provides longer and larger paybacks for investments in training
- contributes to high employee morale
- enhances the organization's reputation in the community

Benefits to society of an effective retention strategy are that it:

- lowers social security costs
- adds to U.S. productivity and the tax base
- contributes to the social integration of the older population

Benefits to older employees of an effective retention strategy are that it:

- keeps them physically and mentally active
- maintains or enhances their self-respect
- provides them with income
- satisfies their social needs by keeping them in daily touch with other active people at work

Opportunity #6—Support Flexible Career Options

Most companies are offering senior employees the wide range of employment options they say they want. Those companies who do offer such options normally make workers retire from their current level. Then the companies hire them back at a much lower wage, often on a temporary basis.

Surveys indicate that about one-third of retirees would prefer to stay with the company and move on to a different kind of work or work pattern. They say they would postpone retirement if they were offered the right job modifications and more flexible retirement options. Permitting major job modifications could launch senior employees on something of a second career, while opening career paths for younger employees.

Many companies have only two alternatives for older employees: keep working or fully retire. More suitable options may include

- part-time work
- job changes or restructuring
- job rotation
- job sharing
- tandem staffing
- periodic sabbaticals
- temporary assignments
- flexible scheduling
- various phaseout-to-retirement options
- contract consulting
- other creative career options

Some companies are providing training programs that focus on alternatives to complete retirement and on post-retirement employment options and second-career opportunities.

Some type of part-time work seems the natural way to make the transition from full-time work to retirement, or to deal with certain disabilities on either a temporary or long-term basis. Survey responses indicate that older workers want to retire gradually. Yet, sudden retirement, not part-time work, is typical. Why is retirement usually sudden? Primarily because so few career options are available to older employees. While many say they would prefer modified work and schedules, flexible options are seldom available. When they are, the pay is often so low that workers choose sudden retirement.

What managers personally can do to help is be flexible, choosing from the various strategies others have used or creating new ones that fit the situation.

An example of a phase-out option is to establish a company temporary employee pool. Retirees who wish to work on a part-time basis sign up. Where appropriate, the company provides refresher courses to employees who have been away from the job for some time. Retirees may be called on to fill in during vacation periods or to add their expertise to special projects. At higher levels, they're hired as consultants and work on a project fee basis.

Opportunity #7—Make Fair Assessments and Performance Reviews

Leading-edge companies have clear policies for managers, teams, and coworkers: Leave myths and stereotypes behind and make realistic assessments of older persons' abilities. Be sure you are fair and objective in evaluations.

Realistically Assess Ability and Disability

Managers and coworkers are likely to misinterpret health information on older employees if they hold stereotypes regarding the declining health of older people. Identical health conditions may be perceived as more serious and disabling for older workers than for younger ones. One study indicated that when medical reports emphasize capacities or functions that an employee can successfully perform, managers recommended continued employment. When medical reports emphasized disabilities, managers recommended part-time assignments, phaseouts, and termination—even when the health problems were not likely to interfere with the ability to do the job, in some cases.

Disability laws could come into play in these instances. A systematic and comprehensive approach to health evaluations might include the following:

- Current and complete job descriptions, with emphasis on physical and psychological demands
- Medical reports that emphasize both employee capacities and limitations associated with illness or injury and that focus on job-related implications of medical problems
- Training for managers in interpreting medical reports in order to make better decisions regarding further employability
- Job redesign as one strategy for meeting the needs of senior workers with health problems

Give Fair Performance Evaluations

Good performance appraisal systems provide the accurate, objective information that managers and team coworkers need in order to make important decisions about motivating, rewarding, promoting, training, transferring, and terminating employees. Appraisals should be based only on job-related behaviors and achievements that are related to a job analysis, behavior standards, and agreed-upon measures. A management-by-objectives process is considered the most legally acceptable.

The appraisal system should generate the documentation that would be required to prove that personnel decisions comply with the law. All employees should get periodic feedback that highlights their strengths and weaknesses and explores the implications of their present performance for future career moves. This feedback should help dispel any misconceptions and misunderstandings employees may have and should help them create realistic expectations about their future with the company. Effective two-way communication between employees and their managers can usually prevent costly age discrimination suits.

The bottom line: think of the last third of life as a time of continuing growth and learning, a time when people deserve constructive performance feedback that can help them continue to improve.

Opportunity #8—Help Make Connections to the Over-50 Marketplace

The over-50 marketplace is exploding. People are living longer, older consumers tend to have more spending power than in the past, and the Baby Boom generation is turning 50. Older Americans offer a booming market in financial services, from insurance to estate planning. They are still a relatively untapped market in housing, clothing, travel, and investment services. Just as women professionals have an edge in understanding women's issues and relating to women customers, so older professionals and employees have an edge in understanding elders' issues and relating to older customers. And many older persons appreciate seeing that older employees are valued in the companies they do business with.

It's good business to retain older employees, to seek their views in designing "senior-oriented" products and services, and to position them for customer contact in the over-50 marketplace—but certainly not to limit them to these roles. The contributions people can make to the organization are not limited by age. In fact, the experiences and insights that come with age normally enhance a person's contributions. However, we may need to create a new, true myth about valuing older persons, a myth that moves younger employees to see and appreciate those contributions.

Skill Builder 1—The Case of Wendy, an Older Worker

You're in charge of Bache Investment's college recruiting. You cannot remember a more hectic time in your life. When you were promoted to this job, your boss told you that the job would test your energy and endurance. During the past two months, you visited twenty-four universities and interviewed more than 200 MBA students for entry-level investment advisor positions. The experience has been exhausting. Because of your reading schedule, you have relied heavily on your assistant **Wendy** to handle many duties that you usually attend to personally.

Since returning to the office from your recruiting trips, you have become increasingly aware of Wendy's aloofness. You sense that she is purposely avoiding you. You also noted that she quickly looks away when you question her about a late travel voucher or a missing file. A little investigating reveals that Wendy is behind in her routine responsibilities and is now over a week late with an important EEO/AA report. Wendy's failure to attend a monthly staff meeting was the last straw. You are determined to get Wendy back on track or to find someone else who is capable of managing the workload. You leave a note for Wendy, requesting that she meet you in your office at 8:45 Monday morning.

Now take the role of Wendy. You have been having doubts about your ability to manage the growing workload and about your future at Bache Investments. Returning to full-time work four years ago at age 53 represented quite a change for you. Although you had worked as an executive secretary before your marriage, your previous positions had been much less demanding than this position. At home, your husband has also noticed a recent change in your behavior. He tells you that you seem tense and short-tempered and asks if you're having problems at the office. You confide that you think your boss is subtly pressuring you to quit. You explain that he told you to complete several complex monthly EEO/AA reports without reducing your regular workload. You confess to your husband that the reports require many statistical calculations, some beyond anything you ever encountered. Completing the reports accurately seemed to take forever. You tell him how you have worked through lunch hours two and three times a week. You relate how you skipped staff meetings just to catch up on regular paperwork. You have been feeling overwhelmed and incompetent. With only six more years to go before you plan to retire, you wonder why your boss wants to force you out. Perhaps your future with the company will be resolved at the Monday morning meeting with the boss.

- If you were Wendy's manager, what would you do?
- If you were Wendy, what would you do?

Skill Builder 2—The Case of the Youthful Supervisor

José is 27 years old. From a Latino American family, his parents were strict and taught him that older people deserve great respect and are usually the ones in authority. His father was the undisputed head of the home, and his grandfather was the highly respected patriarch of a large clan. José has been transferred from a field assignment and promoted to team leader of a product promotions group. One of the team members, **Scott**, is in his 50s and has been with the company for nearly ten years. Scott reminds José of his father in some ways.

José must meet with Scott to make suggestions for improvements on his part of a current team project. José senses that Scott is somewhat defensive toward him and a little resistant to taking constructive criticism and suggestions from him.

- José asks you for advice. What would you say to him?

Skill Builder 3—The Case of Stockbroker John

Leigh is Human Resources Director for Goldman Funds, an investment firm. Her job is to hire stockbrokers who have the ability to create wealth for Goldman clients and for the company. Leigh has been in this field for twenty years and spent many of those years as a stockbroker herself, so she knows how demanding the job can be. Most of the stockbrokers are young, unmarried, and devote 60 to 70 hours a week to their jobs. Most of them also spend several hours a week maintaining their physical fitness in order to deal with the stress of the job.

Leigh is interviewing applicants for a stockbroker position that just opened up. The most unusual applicant is **John**, unusual because he's 67 years old while the other applicants are in their 20s or 30s. John had a long career in the insurance industry, with many years as a salesman, a few years as a claims adjuster, and the remaining years as an executive. John retired when he was 62, and within a year, he was extremely bored with retirement activities. He enrolled in the local university and has just completed a master's degree in finance. He earned grades that ranked him in the top 10 percent of his class.

John comes across as very personable in the interview. He tells Leigh, "I've always loved to sell, I've always loved dealing with calculated risks, and it's very important to me to get to know the clients I serve and to make a contribution through my work." Leigh is impressed, but she's concerned about how many years they can reasonably expect John to work. Leigh is also concerned about the high turnover rate that seems to come with the stockbroker position. One of her goals is to lower the employee turnover rate.

- If you were Leigh, what would you do?

Skill Builder 4—A Case of Maggie's Way

Maggie, age 55, has been an office manager with the Pillsbury-Mason law firm chain for the past fifteen years. She is extremely dependable, loyal, and committed to her job and the firm. She has received performance awards and is highly valued and respected in the firm.

Jake was hired a few months ago as an administrative assistant. He just graduated with honors and holds a brand-new degree in business administration with a concentration in management. His goal is to become an office manager very quickly. He knows he has what it takes. However, he had only a few months of actual office experience before taking this job, so he's having a little difficulty adapting to his coworkers and the office environment. Jake's main frustration is that he has many good ideas, and he wants to take action on them. He knows he could run this office in a minute, but he's blocked because "Maggie's Ways" control the entire office.

As the other employees say, "Maggie's Way" is sometimes confusing, but Maggie is very competent and always on top of everything. The problem is that her ways are sometimes unique, so it's difficult for new employees to understand or to find things. Her procedures generally are very simple and to the point, but sometimes they're so simple that others tend to look right over them, especially in a hectic office. On the other hand, when it comes to many procedures, Maggie insists that employees take their time, go through the proper channels, and follow her office manual. In contrast, Jake believes in getting things done efficiently, finding short cuts, avoiding time-consuming overcautiousness, and basically getting on with it.

Jake's experience is that he has difficulty understanding many of Maggie's requests. He frequently sees the best way to handle a procedure or task, but Maggie always wants him to do it her way. When he tries to explain how a procedure could be improved upon, Maggie listens politely, but it always ends up that the procedure is done her way.

Last week, Jake was under a great deal of pressure to complete a project. He took things into his own hands, did it his way, and got it out on time. When Maggie found out, she confronted him. Tempers flared and they exchanged some heated words about each other's management style. **Stan**, one of the law partners, walked by as this exchange was going on. He's concerned. Pillsbury-Mason is known for its quiet, calm, harmonious environment.

- What are the key issues?
- If you were Stan, what would you do?
- If you were Maggie, what would you do?

Feedback on Skill Builder 1—The Case of Wendy, an Older Worker

As the manager, start out on a supportive note in your meeting with Wendy. Let her know how much you value and appreciate the things she does that help you achieve your goals and that make you more effective in your job. Ask her how she views your working relationship and her work in relation to yours. Ask how you can support her. Your goal is to reassure Wendy so that she will volunteer any problems that may be the source of her strange behavior and performance deficiencies. Remember, there are several general causes of performance problems: skill deficiency, environmental deficiency (lack of equipment or other support), and attitude deficiency. Try to pinpoint the sources of the problems by encouraging Wendy to discuss her work and her experiences.

As Wendy, think through what you would like to achieve on the job and what your career goals are for those years you'll probably be working. Ask yourself what you think a reasonable workload should be for your current job. What do you think are the sources of your current problems? What are some different ways they could be solved? When you meet with your manager, be as positive as possible. Be candid with him about the problems you're experiencing. Offer some possible solutions, and ask his advice. Discuss your job goals and career goals and ask him for his input and support in achieving those goals.

Feedback on Skill Builder 2—The Case of the Youthful Supervisor

José can focus on respecting his own position as team leader and at the same time respecting Scott's maturity, experience, and ability. Self-respect and respect for others are very easily maintained simultaneously with a little thought and practice. José can find ways to maintain self-confidence and a vision of himself as a leader of all types of persons—books and seminars are devoted to such topics. As long as José is comfortable and confident in his leadership role, he can freely ask for Scott's ideas and input without undermining his own authority. In fact, this way of treating an older father figure is also a very good way to treat all employees.

Feedback on Skill Builder 3—The Case of Stockbroker John

Key issues: Hiring older persons; dealing with ageism; and assessing the impact on employee turnover of hiring an older person.

Leigh, as a practical matter, must weigh her concern over employee turnover rate with her favorable impression of John as a potential salesperson. Knowing that John is not interested in a do-nothing retirement, and knowing that older employees are much less likely to voluntarily change companies, Leigh can assume that John will be an employee as long as he is physically able to work. As a result, Leigh should be able to approximate the number of years John might be with the firm—say 8 to 10 years. If this compares favorably with the average tenure of the firm's salespersons, it should relieve her concern about turnover in John's case. As a legal and ethical matter, not hiring John because of his age constitutes age discrimination.

Feedback on Skill Builder 4—A Case of Maggie's Way

Key issues: Generation gap; ageism; over-zealousness of a new graduate to apply his textbook knowledge to his current job; tendency of an entrenched employee to protect her turf and the work processes she's developed.

Stan can counsel Jake concerning the issues. Stan's goal should be to encourage and support Jake's enthusiasm while reigning in his tendency to challenge Maggie's authority and invade her territory. Stan can explain that when a newcomer enters any group, he must first become accepted as an insider, as part of the group, before his attempts to change the group are likely to be accepted. One way of becoming an insider is to support and praise those aspects that make the group effective and successful. Jake can look for elements of Maggie's Way that he can sincerely appreciate—and regularly communicate his approval to Maggie and others. Once he's a solid member of the team in Maggie's mind, he can offer suggestions for making "a great process even greater." At that point, Maggie will be likely to accept such proposals. In the meantime, Jake will experience a great lesson in human relations and group dynamics.

Jake is in for ongoing conflict with Maggie if he doesn't take a new approach. Since he's the newcomer, Jake is likely to be the loser in the long run. Jake can seek advice and counsel. He can find some books and attend some seminars on the issues involved in this situation. If Stan offers him advice, Jake would do well to seriously consider it. His goals should be to make allies of Maggie, Stan, and as many others in the office as possible—and to avoid making enemies.

Maggie has the upper hand, so she can continue to ignore Jake's suggestions. She can reprimand him for refusing to follow established procedures; she can downgrade him for this violation in his performance evaluation; and she can take the matter to the partners if Jake persists. On the other hand, Maggie would do well to harness Jake's enthusiasm instead of feeling threatened by him. She can even ask for his suggestions about problem processes and situations. Once she convinces Jake that she's a reasonable person who wants to find the most effective way of achieving job objectives, he's more likely to listen with an open mind to her explanations of why certain procedures have been established and why some of Jake's suggestions may be problematic.

12

Beyond Appearances: Appreciating All Sizes and Shapes

Appearance discrimination is rampant in our society—especially for those who are "overweight." If you gain as few as 20 or 30 pounds over your "ideal" weight, you may suddenly face new career problems and even a lower income, yet about one-third of all Americans have done just that. Weight discrimination affects women more than men, probably because it is related to the Beauty Myth and to appearance discrimination in general. Virtually all the publicized lawsuits have been filed by women, and the appearance discrimination support groups and organizations have been created and joined primarily by women.

One area of contention is the term to use for people who are considered medically and legally "obese." Some activists prefer the term "fat" and don't like "overweight" as a label. But "fat" still offends many people, and "large" is not descriptive, since it can include a tall or muscular man who may in fact have an appearance advantage. I will use the term "obese" since I'll be discussing both medical and legal implications.

Between one and two million people are considered "morbidly obese" according to Marian Burros' research. They weigh at least twice as much as the top of the medically recommended "normal weight range" for persons of their height, build, and age. For adults, this means people at least 100 pounds above the normal weight range.

Such extreme obesity may be related to physical disability. Until 1995, such persons had no legal protection from discrimination; then state courts ruled that they were protected under the Americans with Disabilities Act. Obese persons are on average just as productive as other workers, but some accommodation may need to be made on account of their size. These people have begun organizing to fight one of the few remaining types of discrimination that has gone unchallenged. They see weight discrimination as the final frontier in the civil rights struggle and hope to eventually expand the federal Civil Rights Act to cover obese people.

Whether the issue is weight, height, attractiveness, skin color, or other aspects of appearance, your goal is to learn more about the experiences of various types of people. And the ultimate goal is to move beyond myths and stereotypes to working productively and profitably together.

Get ready to learn what it's like to be an obese person in the workplace. As you do, imagine seeing situations the way an obese person might see them. You'll also learn about other types of appearance issues. Specifically, in this chapter you'll learn:

- How typical myths about obese persons compare with reality
- How fat prejudice affects obese persons
- What the Beauty Myth is and how it affects obese persons and others
- Rights that obese employees want
- Rights that most employers want to retain
- Emerging law concerning obese persons' workplace rights
- How you can help obese employees overcome barriers and contribute their strengths to the organization

MYTHS AND REALITIES

Most of the myths and stereotypes about obese persons are either false or distorted, partial truths. In fact, most stem from people's discomfort with obesity based on their fear of becoming obese themselves.

Myths are sayings or stories used to bind together the thoughts of a group and promote coordinated social action. Some myths are based on manipulative, hurtful lies, others on harmless little white lies, and some on powerful truths. Stereotypes are rigid, exaggerated, irrational beliefs, each associated with a mental category, such as a particular group of people. Although stereotypes aren't identical to prejudice, rigid stereotypes about people usually lead to prejudice.

To get to know what it's like to be an obese person, you must understand the stereotypes they deal with every day. To bridge the divisive walls these stereotypes hold in place, you must know what they are, know other realities that balance or refute them, and move beyond myths to a more realistic view of obese persons. The goal here is to appreciate each person's unique value and to strengthen our unity as one cohesive team, organization, and culture.

Myth #1—People get overweight by eating too much and not exercising enough.

This may be true for most people. However, obese people consume no more calories per day than other people, according to 19 out of 20 studies on this topic. To get down to normal weight range and stay there, an obese person must eat excruciatingly less than a normal-weight person, probably for life. In addition, greatly overweight people have a complex physical situation. Large size probably causes the inactivity of greatly overweight persons, not the other way around. In 1993, a National Institutes of Health (NIH) panel wrote that evidence increasingly indicates that overweight is not a simple disorder of willpower but a complex disorder of energy metabolism. The experts concluded that diets are almost always disasters, with dieters regaining the weight they had lost.

Myth #2—People are overweight because they lack willpower.

This very basic myth says that individuals should be able to control themselves, and there is something morally wrong with them if they keep giving in to fattening foods. It says that being overweight means being "a weak-willed slob." It also ignores the "obesity gene" factor.

Willpower Doesn't Work in the Long Run

Choice and "willpower" are certainly an element in weight gain prevention for the average person. Since we've seen plenty of people who decided to lose weight and then did it within a few weeks, we believe that willpower is the key. What we ignore is the fact that virtually everyone who is significantly overweight gains it all back within a few months or years.

When researcher Martin Seligman reviewed the dieting studies, the best result he could find was one in which 13 percent of the dieters maintained their losses after three years. About 90 percent gain all or almost all their weight back within four or five years, many within a few months. It may be that the 10 percent who succeed over the long term (1) watch every bite they eat, (2) are more or less obsessed with watching their weight, and (3) were close to their natural weight anyway and would weigh only a few pounds more if they had never dieted.

The "Weight Gene" Can Mutate

Scientists at the Rockefeller Institute in New York have discovered a genetic mutation they think is responsible for at least some types of obesity. As a result of this "faulty" gene, the body's fat stores don't tell the brain how big or small they are, so the brain may not be able to properly regulate appetite, food intake, and/or food metabolism in ways that in turn regulate the body's fat stores.

Myth #3—Obese people just need to get on the right diet.

After years of reviewing the scientific literature on dieting and weight loss, Martin Seligman concluded that:

- Dieting may make overweight worse, not better.
- Dieting can have negative side effects, such as repeated failure and hopelessness, depression, fatigue, bulimia, and anorexia.

Myth #4—Being obese poses health risks; being thin does not.

Seligman's review led to less-firm conclusions about the health risks of overweight, but he makes these suggestions:

- Underweight is clearly associated with substantially greater risk of death. Staying 20 percent or more underweight, as virtually all high-fashion models do, can over time greatly reduce stamina, impair the immune system, and lead to other types of health problems.
- Mild to moderate overweight, 10 to 30 percent over so-called ideal weight, may possibly be associated with a marginal increase in mortality, particularly for those at risk for diabetes.
- Substantial obesity of 30 to 100 percent overweight possibly causes health damage and may be associated with somewhat increased mortality.
- Morbid obesity, over 100 percent overweight, may well cause premature death.

Seligman suspects, but is not yet certain, that the weight fluctuation hazard may be larger than the hazard of staying mildly overweight. Gaining weight gradually during adulthood is normal and healthy, but going on diets dramatically increases the risk of heart attacks and strokes later on. Therefore, a new eating disorder might be called "being 20 percent over your so-called ideal weight and ruining your life and health by dieting." An example is the 5'6" medium-frame woman who weighs 165 pounds instead of 135 and repeatedly gains and loses weight through dieting.

Myth #5—People who diet are healthier and live longer.

A study of 466 flight attendants by researcher Lyn Dettmar found that 25 percent of them weighed five pounds or more than the airline's top limit. Within this "overweight" group, half either made themselves vomit or used laxatives to lose weight. Dettmar concludes that such dieting creates more stress than the added weight would create, as well as eating disorders.

What does contribute to health is moderate exercise, wholesome natural foods, minimal fat and alcohol intake, eating only when hungry, and eating slowly and only until satisfied. For example, S. Blair reported on a couple of studies that revealed the importance of exercise. In a study of 13,000 people, the least-fit 20 percent had a much higher death risk than even the next-to-least-fit 20 percent. In another study using a large sample of men, the death rate of sedentary men was 30 percent higher than those who exercised moderately.

Weight is not always an indicator of longevity. Although people in the "normal" weight range of those insurance company weight charts do live longer than heavier ones, on average, how much longer is in great dispute (so is how many people are exceptions to the rule because of bone structure and muscle development). In fact, no study has compared the longevity of people who stay within their so-called ideal weight without dieting to people who maintain it with dieting. Those who constantly diet may in fact shorten their lives.

Myth #6—Obese people are less productive workers.

Most jobs don't require much physical activity, and there's no reason obese persons can't be just as productive as others. Activists concede that obese people are not appropriate for all jobs, such as those performed in tight quarters or those requiring certain physical abilities. Airline attendants and ballet dancers are examples. But for most jobs, obese persons should not be disqualified from applying. They should have a chance to take whatever physical tests are required. If the job requires running down a track every day, let all the applicants show that they can run the track. In addition, employers should consider making reasonable accommodation to obese persons, as they do to persons with disabilities.

Myth #7—Poor persons are more likely to be obese.

The myth that poor persons are more likely to be fat implies that they are less informed and less in control of their lives. In fact, it's more likely that obese persons make less money because they're obese than that being poor leads to a higher incidence of obesity. This is a major workplace issue that we'll discuss in detail later.

HOW DOES FAT PREJUDICE AFFECT PEOPLE?

Perhaps the cruelest aspect of obesity prejudice is that people tend to believe the obese could become slender if they simply summoned adequate willpower and self-discipline, in other words, character. The devaluing of obese persons often has the effect of invading their privacy.

The Message: You're Inferior

Obese women say that little glances and comments they receive are often more damaging than overt discrimination, wearing away at their self-esteem and confidence, reinforcing the message most have heard since childhood: "You're inferior because you're fat." Some typical humiliations obese persons have reported include the following:

- Frances went to see a doctor to get treatment for what appeared to be strep throat. The doctor insisted that she weigh in, then focused more on her overweight than on her illness. He insisted that she must immediately begin to lose 75 pounds.
- Joan's companion was stopped by a policeman for speeding. He gave Joan a ticket for not wearing a seat belt, even though she explained that the belt in her friend's car wouldn't reach around her body.
- Bill was embarrassed at the grocery checkout when the women behind him commented about two items of "fattening foods" that he was buying.
- Stephanie was trying to find a job. Time after time, she would send a resume and cover letter and the phone response was enthusiastic. When she showed up for the interview, however, she often saw shocked faces and heard, "We think you're overqualified," or "We've changed strategies."
- Karen applied for a job as a legal secretary. The attorney was impressed with her skills and told her he would hire her—if she could show a 10-pound-a-month weight loss when he weighed her in his office.

- When Jay walked into the staff meeting, two of the men jokingly grabbed their doughnuts, implying that he might scarf them down.
- Rosita was enjoying lunch at a seafood restaurant with two coworkers. One said, "You know, Rosita, that butter you just put on your bread comes to over 100 calories." The other said, "Yes, and I noticed you ordered a salad with figs, which are loaded with calories."

One activist said, "We're the last safe prejudice. The fat person is the last person employers can safely kick around." When they leave their homes each day, one to two million obese Americans find themselves in a world built for small people, a world in which they're continually reminded they don't fit. Some of the problems they encounter:

- sitting: finding chairs anywhere that will accommodate them
- flying: fitting into tiny airplane seats
- going to a theater: fitting into tiny theater seats
- traveling in cars: fitting into small cars, dealing with seat belts that won't reach

The Assumption: You Are Your Body

The modern culture of dieting is based on the idea that the personality becomes the body. A related belief is, our size does change when we diet, so we must be able to choose it and therefore control it. For many overweight people, the misery is not so much about how they look, but that they feel to blame, that they've been bad to allow their bodies to get fat. Their fat is seen as perverse bad manners, and they can't walk to the corner store without risking insult.

Naturally-thin Sally saw naturally-obese Janice eating a cookie at lunch and commented to Aretha, "How is she going to lose weight that way?" This assumes that Janice should diet all the time, and that she can. It pinpoints a whole category of food that should be denied to Janice. It views Janice's unwillingness to forgo cookies as an act of rebellion. And it assumes that what Janice eats is everyone else's business.

At times, obese persons feel truly reduced to being just a body and nothing more. As damaging as "conventional wisdom" about overweight has been, the more recent psychological viewpoints may be even more damaging:

- Obese people put on weight as a defense mechanism.
- They're trying to hide inside all that fat.
- They're trying to feed their hungry, empty hearts.
- They're seeking release from the loss of mother or father . . . and on and on.

One woman who was obsessed for years with keeping her weight far below its natural point said, "By fussing endlessly over my body, I ceased to live in it." She gave up dieting and entered her body again with a whole heart. She says that by letting go of dieting, she freed up mental and emotional energy and space in her life-space for more productive and joyful thoughts and activities. She will no longer pursue a thin elusive body that others say she should have. She says, "It was a terrible distraction, a sidetracking that might have lasted my whole life. By letting go, I go places."

Devaluation and Rejection

Devaluation and rejection are two of the biggest hurdles obese persons must overcome in achieving self-esteem and claiming a place in the world. To illustrate how extreme our culture is about thinness, consider a comment made in the film *The Money Pit* by reed-slim actress Shelly Long to her estranged husband Tom Hanks: "Well, I haven't been out of the house much lately; you know, I put on a few pounds." The implicit message was that she felt so bad about her appearance, she had been hiding out at home, and certainly had not had any romantic encounters!

Marian Burros asked William Dietz, director of clinical nutrition at a Boston hospital, about obesity stereotypes and myths. He replied that because of these myths, neither the government nor the health industry in this country are committed to obesity as a public health problem. He said, "We've ignored it and blamed it on gluttony and sloth." Many people believe that gluttony is a sin, and most believe it reflects laziness, lack of willpower, food addiction, and lack of self-esteem. But "fat activists" point out that people naturally come in different shapes and sizes and that for most obese people, obesity is a relatively uncontrollable genetic condition.

A Cultural Obsession with Thinness

What does it mean when more than 80 percent of U.S. women say they dislike their bodies? Coincidentally, 85 percent of them weigh more than the average fashion model, who in turn weighs 20 percent less than the average woman. The pressure to be very thin starts quite early for little girls. Their role model since the 1960s has been the most popular American doll of all time, Barbie. It's estimated that about one in a million women would naturally have proportions similar to Barbie's, but little girls start trying at a very young age. In fact, by age 10, about 80 percent of them have been on a diet. Later we'll discuss the tyranny of the Beauty Myth, especially for women, and obese persons' right to challenge it.

Women: The Hardest-Hit

A recent survey reported by Esther Rothblum indicates that 90 percent of employees cite acceptable weight as essential for a successful career, ranking it fourth, ahead of attractiveness and youthfulness. Intelligence, job qualifications, and education were the first three essentials. Since the stereotype of the ideal woman makes her much thinner than that of the ideal man, more women than men are affected by weight discrimination.

Rothblum also found that men must be significantly heavier than women before they experience the same discrimination. As shown in Figure 12.1, employers are slightly more likely to directly urge overweight men than women employees to lose weight. But even moderately overweight women are dramatically more likely than men to experience abuse by coworkers.

Figure 12.1 *Discrimination—Men and Women Employees*

Type of discrimination	Men (%)			Women (%)		
	Average	30-40% overweight	300 lbs or more overweight	Average	30-40% overweight	300 lbs or more overweight
Not being hired	—	—	42	—	31	62
Fired/pressured to resign	—	—	11	—	2	17
Urged to lose weight	15	27	69	11	33	60
Abused by coworkers	15	47	—	23	62	73
Abused by supervisors	3	13	52	2	39	45
Needed to conceal weight	—	—	17	—	10	25

Based on the research of Esther Rothblum, University of Vermont, 1993.

Alternative Beliefs

Our entire society suffers when people are forced to fit into one appearance mold. Filmmaker Frederico Fellini became legendary by filling his films with many colorful characters. Diverse people make films fascinating, and they also make life fascinating and rich for us—once we give up our ego judgments and relax into the diversity. When will we start accepting diversity in size and shape, all sizes and shapes, instead of believing that beauty comes in a very narrow range of acceptable packages?

You could find hundreds of positive beliefs to adopt about obese persons. Author Sally Tisdale shares her own belief: "When I really look at the people on the street, I see a jungle of bodies, growing every which way like lush plants, growing tall and short and slender and round, hairy and hairless, dark and pale and soft and hard and glorious. They are all loved and lovable."

THE BEAUTY MYTH AND ITS IMPACT

The Beauty Myth says that good-looking people, sexually attractive people, all look a certain way. The acceptable range of body sizes and shapes—including the sizes and shapes of key body parts, such as facial features, breasts, hips, and legs—is extremely narrow and limited. And it's becoming slimmer and younger all the time, especially for women. The myth implies that the ideal woman always looks and acts about 25. When they're 15, most girls are trying to look and act 25. When they're 35, 45, and 55, many women are still trying to look and act

25. When they finally give up the impossible task, many feel invisible and ignored.

Naomi Wolf, author of the book *The Beauty Myth*, argues convincingly that people in our culture didn't hate fat until women began to join forces and reject their inferior status. She says that until women got the vote "fat rounded hips and thighs and bellies were perceived as desirable and sensual." Can it be that the more powerful women become, the more pressure we unconsciously place on them to be smaller and to get rid of the curves that make their bodies different from men's?

Author Kim Chernin theorizes that we do this to women as a way of diminishing "mother power"—to wipe out the memory of the "primordial mother who rules over our childhood with her inscrutable power over life and death." Wolf adds, "A man's right to confer judgment on any woman's beauty while remaining himself unjudged . . . is the last unexamined right remaining intact from the old list of masculine privilege."

Anyone has the right to challenge the Beauty Myth by asking such questions as, "Who says so? Who made that rule?" in response to fashion and beauty decrees—and by asserting their human rights to consideration and respect. It's not easy, however.

Cultural Conflicts

To begin with, the weight-loss industry has billions of dollars at stake in Americans' obsession with slimness and dissatisfaction with their bodies. It has on its payrolls some of the most prominent weight-loss scientists, who publish journal articles recommending new, improved diets and warning of the health risks of being overweight. Instead of carefully evaluating their claims, and investigating the credibility of the sources, Americans tend to jump on every new diet bandwagon, shelling out billions each year for the privilege of depriving themselves of the foods they want when they want them.

Our values set up eating conflicts; for example we love fattening foods and hate fat people. Consider these random but related facts:

- Kellogg's spent $32 million per year advertising Frosted Flakes in the early 1990s, while only $34 million per year was spent for all obesity research in the United States.
- Advertising and commercials for calorie-rich junk foods flood the media, consumption of fast foods is increasing, and so are the overweight.
- Fast food is usually junk food—it's seductively available, convenient, cheap, and tasty.
- Americans spent $40 billion a year on diet programs and diet products in the early 1990s, double the amount spent in the early 1980s; adding diet-related foods sold in food stores, the amount was $80 billion.

In magazines, television, the movies, and shopping malls, women are constantly urged to prepare or indulge in fattening foods—by tantalizing recipes for fudge cake, smells wafting from the Mrs. Fields' cookie counter, and such. In the same media, at the same time, they're bombarded with female role models of beauty and talent who are thinner than almost all the actual women in the population.

In 1980, the average Miss America contestant weighed six pounds less than 1960 contestants, and the average *Playboy* centerfold became noticeably thinner. Meanwhile, the average woman weighed six pounds more. These trends continue in the 1990s. As a people, the more obsessed we've become with diets, the more we weigh. Defining overweight as 20 percent or more above the "normal" range, we find the United States leads the industrialized nations in overweight people.

New Self-Affirming Patterns

Recognizing that size acceptance is an issue for all women—not just large women—is a first step toward solving our nationwide eating problems, according to psychotherapists Jane Hirschmann and Carol Munter. After all, it's our cultural intolerance of certain body sizes that sends us to diets in the first place. And diets often turn us into compulsive eaters or into people obsessed with food, calories, weight, and body size. Hirschmann and Munter use the following process to empower the obese women they work with to stand up for their rights:

- Stop hating your body by challenging those thoughts that put your body down. When you think, "My stomach's too big," shift to, "Who says so? Who made that rule?"
- Make friends with your body and become its loving caretaker; give your body unconditional acceptance and love.
- Become aware of concerns and needs that "bad body thoughts" might mask.
- Reclaim your appetite, dump diets, and learn to eat in response to stomach hunger instead of "mouth hunger" triggered by unconscious needs.
- Assert yourself when people insult your body or intrude into your business.

This process of challenging cultural myths includes many strategies and tactics for dealing with the complexity of overweight. The goal is to give people a solid basis for changing the way they think about their bodies, food, and eating, and to establish new, self-affirming patterns.

WHAT RIGHTS DO ACTIVISTS WANT?

Obesity activists say that everyone has a right to be accepted for the person within rather than the exterior physical appearance. In the workplace, people have a right to be valued for their potential and actual performance.

Rights That Affect Many

The right to be protected from weight and appearance discrimination would affect many persons. For example, about one-third of Americans are considered 20 percent or more overweight, and the percentage is increasing. This means

Figure 12.2   *Americans 20 Percent or More above "Normal Weight"*

	1980	1990
All Americans	25%	30%
Euro-American women	24%	33%
African American women	44%	50%
Mexican American women	44%	50%

Adapted from a report by Marian Burros, New York Times.

that 75 million Americans could be the victim of some degree of obesity discrimination. Those who are the targets of extreme discrimination are referred to legally as the morbidly obese, and one to two million Americans fit this description.

The actual proportion of overweight Americans remained at about 25 percent from 1960 to 1980. Then in the following decade, it rose to 30 percent. Obesity is increasing even faster among young people than among adults. Twenty percent overweight means about 25 pounds over for an average 5'4" woman and 30 pounds for an average 5'10" man. Obesity varies by ethnic group but is increasing in every group, as shown in Figure 12.2.

Some Basic Rights

Obese persons are beginning to fight discrimination. The size acceptance movement has been active for about 20 years. An underlying principle is that by accepting yourself just as you are, you develop the strength, self-esteem, and confidence to fend off the insults, attacks, and discrimination the world heaps upon obese persons. Sally Tisdale states, "Rejection can't kill you. With the right attitude, rejection can make you stronger. Don't hide out at home. Go out in the world and risk rejection."

Critics say that social preference for thinness is too ingrained in the culture to be legislated away. Activists reply that these same arguments were used for other forms of discrimination. "It's the same as saying you can't hire black salespersons because the customers won't like it, or that you can't hire women because they can't handle male customers' resistance to buying from women," says Art Stine of Michigan's Department of Civil Rights. His department investigates 10 to 20 cases of weight discrimination each year.

At least three national organizations have emerged in recent years to take up the cause of obese Americans. The activist group that's been most prominent in the media recently is the National Association to Advance Fat Acceptance (NAAFA). With 4,000 members in 75 chapters nationwide, NAAFA's goals include:

- improving the self-esteem of obese people
- ensuring their civil rights
- challenging our fat-rejecting culture through education, legislation, and the courts
- achieving equal access to employment

NAAFA leaders say they like the word "fat." They don't like the word "overweight," asking, "Over whose weight?" They say the word "obesity" suggests a medical disorder. NAAFA has reclaimed the label "fat" much as some African Americans have reclaimed "nigger" and some gays the term "queer"—but these are still very controversial terms. Certainly not all obese persons agree that they want to be called fat, and most people in our culture have been conditioned to avoid calling people fat. For this reason, the most common term is the medical and legal term "obese."

The International Size Acceptance Association (ISAA) is focusing on legal workplace rights by asking people to sign petitions to send to legislators. ISAA has attracted national news media and created some interest in this issue.

Legal Workplace Rights: Money Matters

Until recently, overweight people had no legal rights for protection from employment discrimination based on weight. Those who are starting to fight back against such discrimination have been forced to resort to two related legal rights:

- protection under the ADA, which treats obesity as a disability in the workplace
- protection under the constitutional right to privacy, on the basis that personal eating habits should not affect how an employee is judged at work

Sally Smith, executive director of NAAFA, notes that one person may be 100 pounds over society's ideal, and others may be just 10. Talking to interviewer Jan Wahl, Smith said, "If employers can use it against the greatly overweight person today, what's to keep them from using it against the slightly overweight tomorrow?"

People who weigh more not only find it more difficult to get and keep jobs, they also make less money:

- One study found that businessmen sacrifice $1,000 in salary for every pound they are overweight. Obese women tend to earn less, too.
- Among women who earn more than $50,000, only 13 percent are obese, while among women in the poverty category, 30 percent are obese.
- In a study of women of all weights, Harvard sociologist Steven Gortmaker found that the overweight women, averaging 5'3" and 200 pounds, had household incomes that averaged $6,710 below those of thinner women, and that they were 10 percent more likely to live in poverty. Overweight apparently keeps people from becoming as affluent as they might otherwise become.

- Obese women are more likely than thin ones to lose socioeconomic status over the course of their adolescence and young adulthood, no matter how well they originally do on achievement tests or how affluent their families. The heavier the woman, the greater the job discrimination, according to a seven-year study of 5,000 women.

Even women of average size or only slightly heavy are often encouraged to lose weight and are more likely to be passed over for promotion than thinner women. This phenomenon is much more common for women than men.

To End Appearance Discrimination, Too

The workplace rights problem goes beyond weight discrimination to the Beauty Myth and the broader issue of appearance discrimination. Attractive people tend to earn about 5 percent more than those with average looks. And homely workers make about 7 percent less than those with average looks. That's a 12 percent pay gap between the homely and the attractive. Women considered to be unattractive are less likely to work than other women and tend to marry men with lower levels of education.

Attractive people are widely regarded as being more intelligent, friendly, honest, and confident than others, all traits that could influence employers and customers to discriminate in favor of them. Attractive children are rewarded with more praise from parents and teachers, influencing their self-esteem and confidence, both valued in the marketplace. Certain occupations cater to attractive employees more than others, but favoritism toward good looks and prejudice against homeliness is pervasive in most jobs. Even within any given occupation, good-looking people make more. When the appearance ratings of 700 MBA graduates were correlated with the salaries they were earning ten years after graduation, better-looking men made as much as $10,000 per year more.

WHAT RIGHTS DO EMPLOYERS WANT TO RETAIN?

Employee appearance and size can affect the success of certain businesses. Employers want to retain the right to achieve fair, reasonable business goals. In theory, activists in the fat acceptance movement do not disagree with this principle. In practice, the two groups may disagree about what is fair and reasonable.

Some employers who run airlines, fashion stores, restaurants, beauty salons, and real estate agencies say they have a right to establish an image and hire only employees who fit that image. Civil rights advocates counter that the only criterion should be performance. One employee who lost 40 pounds, said, "I did my job well before, and I do it well now. Weight has nothing to do with it." Another said, "Who are employers to play God, to judge what is acceptable or beautiful? Rubens painted large women who were beautiful. It seems clear to me that hiring and promotion ought to be based on your ability to do the job."

Some employers say that customers won't do business with obese persons and that coworkers won't respect them or work well with them. Activists reject the circular reasoning and the ethics of this argument, noting it was also used to resist equal rights for minorities and women. They say it's morally unacceptable for employers themselves to discriminate against obese persons just because prejudiced customers and coworkers might discriminate against them. Such actions signal that employers accept prejudice and encourage it. Just as it is the employers' responsibility to stop sexual harassment of women and ethnic discrimination toward African Americans, it's also their responsibility to stop harassment and discrimination toward obese persons.

Some employers claim that obese employees cost more in health care and sick time. Health professionals suggest that yo-yo dieting could make both obese and thinner persons less healthy. And some obese persons are reluctant to seek medical care because doctors often don't respect them, are condescending and patronizing about their weight, and harangue them to lose weight. Others don't have health care coverage. Nevertheless, there are no respectable studies showing that obese persons cost more because of health problems.

WHAT LAWS PROTECT OBESE WORKERS?

Persons who suffer weight discrimination by employers have only recently gained some legal protection. Laws take two forms:

1. *Legislation.* The most powerful and direct are laws specifically prohibiting discrimination based on weight, height, or other aspects of physical appearance. They follow in the tradition of civil rights laws prohibiting discrimination on the basis of race, creed, color, gender, and similar characteristics.
2. *Court Rulings.* Less direct are court rulings that equate obesity with disability and require employers to make reasonable accommodation for obese employees.

Most activists agree that the best protection is to add weight discrimination to the other types of discrimination prohibited by the federal and state civil rights acts.

Legislation: Civil Rights

In the late 1990s, Michigan was the only state in the country with a law that specifically protects the employment rights of overweight people. Weight and height were added to its civil rights statutes. The cities of Santa Cruz, California, and Washington, D.C. are among the few local governments that have added such clauses to their civil rights laws.

Massachusetts and New York began considering legislation in 1994 that would add height and weight to civil rights statutes covering employment and housing. A similar bill failed in Texas. California's civil rights laws, while not specifically covering weight, were the basis for a million dollar court award to a 400-pound man. He had sued the automotive parts firm that had fired him after 10 years' employment. In September 1995, after a six-week trial, he was awarded back pay and reparation for emotional distress.

Right to Privacy Law

Another legal avenue is the right to privacy, based on the principle that one's personal eating or exercise habits should not affect how one is judged in the workplace. The American Civil Liberties Union has launched a national project to fight an employer trend to meddle in employees' private lives, such as their eating, drinking, and smoking habits.

Court Rulings: Disability

New Jersey law regards obesity as a disability that automatically triggers discrimination protection regardless of the cause of the obesity. In most of the states where obese employees have won their lawsuits, their cases were based on the ADA. Their attorneys claimed that obesity should be viewed as a physical disability. This is risky at best, since some experts still claim that obese people could lose their excess weight if they really wanted to.

The disability argument did prevail in a federal appeals court in 1993. A woman sued the Rhode Island Department of Mental Health after she was denied a state job because at 5'2" she weighed 320 pounds. Lawyers for the state agency said the law should not be interpreted to cover obesity, because obesity "is caused by voluntary conduct and is not immutable." They argued that the plaintiff could lose weight and rid herself of any disability arising from her obesity at any time.

But the judge and jury ruled that there was credible evidence that the metabolic dysfunction causing weight gain in the morbidly obese lingers even after weight loss. Their decision was upheld in a federal appeals court, which said that discrimination against the obese could constitute a violation of the ADA. The court further stated that: "In a society that all too often confuses 'slim' with 'beautiful' or 'good,' morbid obesity can present formidable barriers to employment."

The court briefs and opinions don't indicate that obesity in itself is necessarily a disability. Instead, the reasoning is that when persons are discriminated against, either because their obesity limits their activities or because employers perceive obesity as a disability that limits their activities, then such persons can be protected under disability law.

EEOC Support for the Disability Approach

The Equal Employment Opportunities Commission (EEOC) filed a brief in federal appeals court in the Rhode Island case. EEOC lawyers urged the court to consider obesity just as it would view many other conditions not specifically mentioned in the ADA, based on how long the person has been affected by the condition and how difficult it would be to change. Noting that obesity isn't a "traditional" disability, the EEOC said that "although it's possible for an obese individual to lose weight, obesity is a chronic, lifelong condition." It further stated that a condition does not have to be involuntary or immutable to be covered. The EEOC did not indicate that a person must be "morbidly obese" in order to be protected from discrimination, and the ruling probably opens the door for claims from more moderately obese employees. Discrimination claims under the ADA must be filed first with the EEOC.

The idea behind the ruling is that the way persons look shouldn't affect their ability to get and keep a job. NAAFA activists say being fat doesn't necessarily mean poor health, and it's too bad that in most states their only recourse in fighting discrimination is through laws meant to protect the disabled. Several overweight persons interviewed by Jan Wahl said the predicament was offensive because most of them are not disabled and are in fact very healthy people.

OVERCOMING BARRIERS AND BUILDING ON STRENGTHS

You have an opportunity to enlighten the corporate culture and to influence employees to move beyond the Beauty Myth to an appreciation of people for their inner qualities and contributions to the organization.

Help Meet the Needs of Obese Employees

Here's a summary of the basic needs of obese employees:

- protection from discrimination and harassment by managers and employees
- respect for their privacy
- acceptance of them as they are
- appreciation of their value as human beings and of their contributions
- accommodation that will help them do their job
- fair and equal compensation

Look Below the Surface

You can move away from a focus on the superficial aspects of corporate employee image, such as size, shape, facial features, and other aspects of the Beauty Myth. An in-depth corporate image focuses on such inner strengths as being honest, respecting others, keeping agreements, honoring commitments, delivering the goods on time, providing top-quality service, being positive, focusing on others' strengths and contributions, seeing the humor, the love of life, the summoning of courage, and on and on. These qualities seem old-fashioned in a way. Yet aren't they really the raw materials that leaders can skillfully draw on to create a highly motivated and committed world-class workforce?

Help Develop Policies on Obesity Harassment and Discrimination

Employers and managers have a responsibility to stop the harassment of obese employees and to stop discriminatory actions against them. The first step is to develop policies and procedures designed to provide equal opportunity and fair treatment of obese persons. Affirmative action programs and equal opportunity policies already in place for minorities and women can be used for guidance in remedying discrimination. Company policies and procedures designed to prevent sexual harassment and to handle such cases can serve as a pattern for preventing and handling cases of obesity harassment.

Make Reasonable Accommodation

Although obese persons are not necessarily disabled, those who are greatly overweight usually need some type of accommodation. The best way to find out is to ask tactfully what can be done to help them to be as productive and successful as possible on the job. Comfortable, sturdy seating arrangements are nearly always needed and appreciated, not only at a work station or executive desk but also in meeting rooms, lounges, dining facilities, and any other place the employee frequents in the course of the job. If a company car or other transportation is provided, arrange for adequate size in seats and seat belts.

A few obese persons have difficulty getting around. The same provisions that are made for other mobility-impaired employees can be made for these employees—such as electric carts, ramps, elevators, and convenient parking.

Enlighten the Corporate Culture

You can encourage change in those company practices and habits that degrade and discriminate against obese persons through your own example, through appropriate storytelling, through making them heroines and heroes when they excel, through visibly supporting them in other ways, and through providing information and training for all employees about obesity issues. Corporate diversity training programs can include a segment on obese persons. Every employee needs to complete such a segment.

You can focus on the contributions of obese employees and on their positive qualities. You can unfailingly respect their dignity and refuse to countenance disrespect in the form of wisecracks, jokes, put-downs, unsought advice, and similar behavior.

Consider New Marketing Opportunities

Some leaders are breaking the mold and giving talented obese persons job opportunities in such high-profile jobs as television news reporter, talk show hostess, and situation comedy star. Some say that such media personalities seem approachable, like a "next-door neighbor," and people feel comfortable with them. Business leaders need to examine this opportunity to relate to new types of customers and perhaps open up new markets.

Skill Builder 1—The Case of Chris, a Job Applicant

Chris is 35 years old, has two years of college, and weighs 350 pounds. In response to a newspaper ad, Chris applied and interviewed for a job at Worman's Hardware Store. He didn't get the job, but when he learned of another opening, he called the chain store's personnel coordinator, **Georgia**. Georgia told Chris the store wanted more experienced people. She also told him, "There is some concern about your weight and whether you can physically handle hauling heavy items of hardware and supplies." Chris has ten years' experience in retail selling, although he has never worked in a hardware store.

- If you were Chris, what would you do?
- If you were a top manager at Worman's, how would you view this situation?

Skill Builder 2—The Case of Laura, Public Relations Manager

Laura was 40 years old and had successfully held several managerial positions in public relations. When she applied for a job at a major East Coast medical center, she was wearing a slenderizing dark suit and had been on a strict diet for two months. She got the job but didn't report for work until a month or so later. In the meantime, Laura relaxed her diet regime. As usual after such diets, she was starved and tired and quickly went back up to her usual 230 pounds. When she arrived for her first day on the new job, **Murray**, the director of public relations blurted out, "My God, you've put on a lot of weight since we interviewed you. I'm not sure this is the image we want for the hospital."

From that day on, Laura was constantly pressured to diet and watched to see if she was slimming down. Laura felt demeaned, set apart from the others, and was subjected to humiliating comments. She had an expensive professional wardrobe, but **Jan**, her boss, told her to wear only black or navy. Laura knew that meant "camouflage your size." She says, "Every time I walked into the office, I got a quick once-over to see what I was wearing and whether I had lost weight." At a staff meeting, Jan asked Laura to tell everyone about the liquid diet she was starting.

For the next year, Laura was successful in her job. She got national publicity for the hospital, raised large sums of money, and developed award-winning programs. Nevertheless, she was called into Jan's office one Friday afternoon and fired. Jan didn't mention her weight directly, but said, "Things that should have changed didn't change."

- What is your opinion of the way Murray and Jan handled Laura's case?
- Do you think Laura should have done anything differently?
- What do you think she should do now?

Skill Builder 3—Louis' Career Goals

Louis has been working for Manko's, a privately-owned printing firm, for about five years. The firm specializes in designing and printing forms used by automobile dealers. Louis' duties include taking phone orders and arranging for the shipping of the merchandise to clients. The shipping aspect requires lifting boxes of forms. His job calls for good customer relations skills, and over the years he has helped the firm develop and retain a loyal clientele.

Louis' doctor tells him that he's about 150 pounds over his ideal weight. This has been the case for nearly all his adult life, at least since his early 20s. Louis has dieted and lost weight several times in the past years, once even losing 125 pounds. As he says, "I've tried every dieting gimmick in the book, and I always end up at about the same weight in the long run." Louis has always been somewhat self-conscious about his weight, for he was a little "pudgy" even as a child. His mother frequently cautioned him about his eating patterns, saying, "Louis, you don't need to eat seconds; you've had enough to eat." Or, "No, Louis, you don't need to eat cookies; try an apple or an orange for a snack."

Louis' weight has not been a problem at the print shop. He gets along well with the employees, as well as the customers he relates to by phone. There are four employees: a printer, two outside salespersons, and Louis, who handles everything in the office. The owner, **Bill Manko**, relies on him to keep the office running, and the salespersons rely on him to do favors for their customers, such as shipping forms ASAP, providing information about the proper type of form a customer needs, and explaining to customers how to use certain forms.

Bill tells Louis that the firm has grown enough to need another outside salesperson. He's looking for a good person. Louis realizes that the job would be a good opportunity for him to expand his career, and he decides to apply. When Louis approaches Bill about the job, Bill seems quite surprised and says, "Well, let me think about it, Louis." A few days later, Bill says to Louis, "I think you're a better asset to the company in your present job. You don't quite fit the sales rep image, and we need your know-how and knowledge of the business and the customers to handle phone orders and shipping."

- What are the key issues in this case?
- If you were Bill, what would you do?
- If you were Louis, what would you do?

Skill Builder 4—The Case of Helen, Travel Agent

Helen has been working for World Points Travel Agency for about a year. World Point consists of a chain of fifteen travel agencies with a total of about 100 employees. When Helen interviewed for the job, the office seemed perfectly suited to her style. People seemed to like their work and enjoy a little humor. **Franko**, the manager, was very flexible about allowing her to work only twenty-five hours a week and to schedule her hours around her daughter's needs. He hired her on the spot.

Helen was thrilled to get the job: all she wanted was to work part-time so she could spend time with her three-year-old daughter Linda, whom she has just enrolled in a good nursery school. Helen figured that a nice part-time job at a travel agency would give her a chance to get out of the house and meet people and enough money to pay Linda's school expenses.

Everyone was friendly from the beginning, and Helen was invited to join the employee's association, even though part-time workers were technically not eligible for membership. The employee's association didn't negotiate contracts or require dues, but did consult with management in making policies for the agency and the employees. Little did Helen know that the actions of the group would eventually lead to her downfall.

A few weeks ago, the group suggested to management that the company's image needed to be improved. As one of them said, "We sell so many European vacation plans, we need to present a chic, updated European image." Most of the improvements involved changing the names of vacation packages and the office decor. The trouble arose when the group decided to adopt appearance standards for employees; for example: "Employees who deal directly with the public must look attractive and professional and wear outfits that reflect current European high-fashion. Employees must keep their weight within the optimal weight range for their height and bone structure."

Helen is 5'6" tall and weighs about 200 pounds. Last week, two of the women from the employee association committee that drafted the image policy met with Helen. They asked her if she would agree to bring her weight down to 160 pounds within the next six months, saying "That seems reasonable, don't you think." Helen said, "No, I don't think it's reasonable. I gained this weight three years ago when I was pregnant and then nursing my daughter. I've tried to lose it, and it's just not that easy. I'd like to lose it on my own terms and in my own time frame. To make this kind of agreement just puts too much pressure on me."

Marge, the committee chair said, "It was the employee association's idea to do this, and you are a member of our group, so you shouldn't view this as something the company is forcing on you." Helen replied, "Do you think I don't look good enough to sell European vacation plans? Don't I have a right to look the way I want to look, so long as it isn't outrageous or harmful to business?"

Marge replied, "We all know you're a highly professional worker and an attractive representative of the company. But we think the rule should apply to everyone." The others seemed to agree with Marge.

The next day Franko approached Helen and suggested changing her job duties, saying, "Helen, let's try you out at the confirmation desk. You can keep your current salary and hours and it will probably be a better fit for you." Helen objected, "Franko, I love meeting with people and I'm good at it. I don't want a strictly telephone job behind the scenes. All I'll be doing is confirming hotel and flight reservations. It would be boring, and I would go nuts."

- What are the key issues in this case?
- If you were Helen, what would you do?
- If you were Franko, what would you do?

Feedback on Skill Builder 1—The Case of Chris, a Job Applicant

What really happened: The job applicant sued the company, alleging that s/he was illegally rejected because "they regarded me as having a physical handicap, that is, too much weight." A jury ruled unanimously in the company's favor, but a state appeals court reversed the verdict, saying that the trial judge had improperly placed the burden of proof on Chris. In September 1993, the verdict was reversed again by the state supreme court, which unanimously agreed that job applicants turned away because of their weight cannot sue unless there is evidence of a "physiological, systemic basis" for their condition. A person's size alone is not enough to qualify as a physical handicap protected by state discrimination law, the justices ruled. The obesity must be caused by a physiological condition affecting one or more of the basic bodily systems and limit the claimant's ability to participate in major life activities. Still, the court did not specify what medical evidence is required, leaving the rights of obese persons unclear and uncertain.

Two months later, in another case that originated in Rhode Island, a U.S. Appeals Court in Boston ruled that severe obesity over a period of time in itself constitutes a disability, and such persons are protected from discrimination under the ADA. The EEOC filed a brief supporting this view.

Feedback on Skill Builder 2—The Case of Laura, Public Relations Manager

What really happened: Laura was so devastated by the prejudicial and disrespectful treatment that she never wanted to see the place again. Jan and Murray's actions had created an environment in which she felt set apart from other employees and subjected to humiliating comments. She knew that in spite of those obstacles, she had done an outstanding job.

At the time she was fired, Laura had little recourse because "weight is the last bastion of acceptable discrimination." Today she would have a good chance of winning a lawsuit against the medical center. As Laura says, however, "Why would I want to do that to my career?" She was quickly hired by a larger, more prestigious firm that was looking for performance, not thinness. She has been very successful in her new position and has nearly doubled her income.

Feedback on Skill Builder 3—Louis' Career Goals

Key Issues: Appearance discrimination based on weight, and an employer's concern about customer acceptance and company image.

Bill has taken the option that he believes involves the least risk, the safest option, which is to turn down Louis' request for promotion. Bill may have failed to consider that Louis' relationships with customers is a known factor and is definitely a plus. Meanwhile, the person Bill will hire as the new sales rep will be an unknown factor as far as relating to the print shop's clients is concerned. Bill should seriously consider giving Louis a chance in this job. He can cover his bases by giving him the job on a trial basis for a probationary period, with the proviso that Louis will return to his old job if sales goals and standards are not met.

Louis can propose to Bill that he take the job on a trial basis, as mentioned above. If Bill refuses to give him a chance, Louis must consider changing companies if he wants to move out of his current occupation.

Feedback on Skill Builder 4—The Case of Helen, Travel Agent

Key Issues: Appearance discrimination based on weight, and changing the terms of employment in ways that discriminate against an employee.

Helen has done a good job of stating her position. If Franko insists on hiding Helen out at the confirmation desk, Helen can express the belief that this is appearance discrimination and an unfair change of employment terms. She can appeal to his sense of fairness, refer to her track record of producing good results, and question the link of this new approach to the company's bottom line. If Franko sticks to his approach, Helen has little choice but to change jobs and/or file a complaint.

Franko can continue on his present path, of course. He can also look for ways to be flexible and maintain the enthusiasm of all parties. For example, he can view Helen as a "comfortable, motherly type" that certain clients will relate to better than the high-fashion sophisticated types envisioned by the other employees. He can promote the idea of diversity, a staff that many types of customers can relate to.

Chapter Notes

Chapter 1

Chatman, Jennifer A., and S.G. Barsade. "Personality, Organizational Culture, and Cooperation: Evidence from a Business Simulation." *Administrative Science Quarterly* (September 1, 1995): 86–89.

Eisenberger, R., P. Fasolo, and V. Davis-LaMastro. "Perceived Organizational Support and Employee Diligence, Commitment, and Innovation." *Journal of Applied Psychology* 75, no. 1 (1990): 51–59.

Goleman, Daniel. *Emotional Intelligence*. New York: Bantam Books, 1995.

Hecht, M.L., M.J. Collier, and S.A. Ribeau. *African American Communication*. Thousand Oaks, CA: Sage, 1993.

Hinrichs, John R. *Developing Human Resources*. Washington, DC: Bureau of National Affairs, 1991.

Hofstede, Geert. *Cultures and Organization*. New York: McGraw, 1991.

"How to Make Diversity Pay." *Fortune* August 18, 1994, 79–86.

Jackson, S.E. "Team Composition in Organizational Settings." *Group Process and Productivity*. Thousand Oaks, CA: Sage, 1991.

Kanter, Rosabeth Moss. "Transcending Business Boundaries: 12,000 World Managers View Change." *Harvard Business Review* (May/June 1991): 151–164.

Longmore, P.K. "Screening Stereotypes: Images of Disabled People." *Social Policy* (Summer 1985): 32–37.

Marshall, Jonathan. "Education: The President's Apprentices." *Reason* (July 1, 1995): 55–58.

Morrison, Ann (ed.). *The New Leaders: Guidelines on Leadership Diversity in America*. San Francisco: Jossey-Bass, 1992.

"Neighbors Stick Together." *Los Angeles Times* (June 2, 1992).

Sheridan, J.H. "Dividends from Diversity." *Industry Week* (September 1994): 23–26.

Siegal, S., and W. Kaemmerer. "Measuring the Perceived Support for Innovation in Organizations." *Journal of Applied Psychology* 63, no. 5 (1978): 553–562.

Stephens, Gregory K., and Charles R. Greer. "Doing Business in Mexico." *Organizational Dynamics*. New York: American Management Association, 1995.

Tsui, A.S., and L.W. Porter. "A Study of Work Force Diversity in 55 Orange County Companies." Unpublished manuscript, Graduate School of Management, University of California, Irvine, 1993.

Chapter 2

Althen, Gary. *American Ways*. Yarmouth, ME: Intercultural Press, 1988.

Hall, E.T., and M.R. Hall. *Understanding Culture Differences*. Yarmouth, ME: Intercultural Press, 1989.

Hofstede, Geert. *Cultures and Organization*. New York: McGraw, 1991.

Nierenberg, John. "Cross-cultural Management Literature May Be Hazardous." *San Francisco State University School of Business Journal* (Summer 1993): 47–55.

Montagu, Ashley. *Man's Most Dangerous Myth*. Walnut Creek, CA: AltaMira Press, 1997.

Pettigrew, Thomas. *A Profile of the Negro American*. Princeton, NJ: Van Nostrand, 1964.

Ramirez, A. "Racism toward Hispanics." In *Eliminating Racism*, Phyllis A. Katz and Dalmas A. Taylor (eds.) New York: Plenum Press, 1988.

Szapocznik, J., M. Scopetta, and O.E. King. "Theory and Practice in Matching Treatment to the Special Characteristics and Problems of Cuban Immigrants." *Journal of Community Psychology* 6 (1978): 112–122.

Chapter 3

Althen, Gary. *American Ways*. Yarmouth, ME: Intercultural Press, 1988.

Boorstin, D.J. *Americans and the Image of Europe*. New York: Meridian Books, 1960.

Cox, Taylor. *Cultural Diversity in Organizations*. San Francisco: Berrett-Koehler, 1993.

Deal, T.E., and A.A. Kennedy. *Corporate Cultures*. Reading, MA: Addison-Wesley, 1982.

Hall, E.T. and M.R. Hall. *Understanding Culture Differences*. Yarmouth, ME: Intercultural Press, 1989.

Harris, P.R., and R.T. Moran. *Managing Cultural Differences*. Houston, TX: Gulf, 1991.

Hofstede, Geert. *Cultures and Organization*. New York: McGraw, 1991.

Kohls, R.L. *The Values Americans Live By*. San Francisco: LinguaTec, 1988.

Schein, E.H. *Organizational Culture and Leadership*. San Francisco: Jossey-Bass, 1985.

Thomas, Roosevelt. *Beyond Race & Gender*. New York: AMACOM, 1991.

Wheatley, Margaret. *Leadership and the New Science*. San Francisco: Berrett-Koehler, 1992.

Yankelovich Partners, Inc., J. Walker Smith, and Ann Clurman. *Rocking the Ages: The Yankelovich Report on Generational Marketing*. New York: HarperCollins Publishers, 1998.

Chapter 4

Allport. G.W. *The Nature of Prejudice*. Reading, MA: Addison-Wesley, 1954.

Allport, G.W., and J.M. Ross. "Personal Religious Orientation and Prejudice." *Journal of Personality and Social Psychology* 5 (1967): 432–443.

Blanchard, F.A., and F.J. Crosby. *Affirmative Action in Perspective*. New York: Springer-Verlag, 1989.

Catalyst. *Women in Corporate Management*. New York: Catalyst, 1990.

Cox, Taylor. *Cultural Diversity in Organizations*. San Francisco: Berrett-Koehler, 1993.

Elliott, Jane. *A Class Divided* (documentary videotape). Alexandria, VA: PBS Video.

Feagin, Joe. "The Continuing Significance of Race: Antiblack Discrimination in Public Places." *American Sociological Review* 56 (February 1991): 101–116.

Greenhaus, J.H., and S. Parasuraman. "Job Performance Attributions and Career Advancement Prospects." *Organizational Behavior and Human Decision Processes*. Orlando, FL: Academic Press, 1991.

Herek, G.M. "Assessing Heterosexuals' Attitudes." In *Lesbian and Gay Psychology*, Beverly Greene and G.M. Herek (eds.). Thousand Oaks, CA: Sage, 1994.

Ijzendoorn, M.H. "Moral Judgement, Authoritarianism, and Ethnocentrism." *Journal of Social Psychology* 129, no. 1 (1989): 37–45.

McIntosh, Peggy. "White Privilege and Male Privilege." Working paper no. 189, Wellesley, MA: Center for Research on Women, 1988.

Montagu, Ashley. *Man's Most Dangerous Myth*. Walnut Creek CA: AltaMira Press, 1997.

Morrison, Ann, (ed.). *The New Leaders: Guidelines on Leadership Diversity in America*. San Francisco: Jossey-Bass, 1992.

National Opinion Research Center. *Ethnic Images*. GSS Topical Report No. 19. Chicago: University of Chicago, December, 1990.

"Neighbors Stick Together." *Los Angeles Times* (June 2, 1992).

Palmer, Harry. *Living Deliberately*. Palm Beach, FL: Star's Edge, 1994, p. 25.

Ponterotto, J.G., and P.B. Pederson. *Preventing Prejudice*. Thousand Oaks, CA: Sage, 1993.

"SBA Sets New Goals." *Wall Street Journal*, (June 15, 1994): B1.

U.S. Glass Ceiling Commission. *A Report on the Glass Ceiling Initiative*. U.S. Department of Labor, 1991.

U.S. Glass Ceiling Commission. *Good for Business*. U.S. Department of Labor, 1995.

Chapter 5

Allport, G.W. *The Nature of Prejudice*. Reading, MA: Addison-Wesley, 1954.

Bly, Robert. *Iron John: A Book About Men*. New York: Random House, 1992.

Brislin, Richard, and Tomoko Yoshida. *Improving Intercultural Interactions*. Thousand Oaks, CA: Sage, 1994.

Burley-Allen, Madelyn. *Managing Assertively*, 2d ed. New York: John Wiley & Sons, Inc., 1995.

Carr-Ruffino, Norma. *The Promotable Woman*. Franklin Lakes, NJ: Career Press, 1997.

Carr-Ruffino, Norma. "U.S. Women: Breaking through the Glass Ceiling." *Women in Management Review* 6, no. 5 (1991).

Catalyst. Study of dual-earner households. New York: Catalyst, 1998.

Eagly, Alice H. *Sex Differences in Social Behavior*. Hillsdale, NJ: Lawrence Erlbaum Associates, 1987.

Evatt, Chris. *He & She*. Berkeley, CA: Conari Press, 1992.

Farrell, Walter. *The Myth of Male Power*. New York: Simon & Schuster, 1993.

Gates, David. "White Male Paranoia." *Newsweek* (March 29, 1993): 48–54.

Glass Ceiling Commission. *Better for Business*. U.S. Department of Labor, 1995.

Kanter, Rosabeth M. *Men and Women of the Corporation*. New York: Basic Books, 1979.

Keen, Sam. *Fire in the Belly*. New York: Bantam Books, 1991.

Loring, Rosalind K. *Breakthrough: Women Into Management*. New York: Van Nostrand Reinhold, 1972.

Murdock, G.P. "The Common Denominator of Cultures." In *The Personality of Peoples*, R. Linton (ed.). *Scientific American*, 1949.

Naisbett, John, and Patricia Aburdene. *Megatrends 2000*. New York: Wm. Morrow, 1990.

Orenstein, Peggy. *Schoolgirls: Young Women, Self-Esteem, and the Confidence Gap*. New York: Doubleday, 1994.

Peplau, L.A. "Lesbian and Gay Relationships." In *Homosexuality: Research Implications for Public Policy*, J.C. Gonsiorek and J.D. Weinrich (eds.). Thousand Oaks, CA: Sage, 1991.

Rosener, J.B. "Ways Women Lead." *Harvard Business Review* November–December 1990, 199–225.

Sargent, Alice G. *The Androgynous Manager*. New York: Amacom, 1993

Speer, Robert. "What's New with Men?" *Chico News & Review* (April 16, 1993).

Steinem, Gloria. *Moving Beyond Words*. New York: Simon and Schuster, 1994.

Tannen, Deborah. *You Just Don't Understand*. New York: Wm. Morrow, 1990.

U.S. Census Bureau. "We the American . . . Women." U.S. Department of Commerce, 1993.

Wright, John W. *The American Almanac of Jobs and Salaries*. New York: Avon. Updated every three years.

Zilbergeld, Bernie. Berkeley psychologist, expert on men's groups, in interview, April 6, 1993.

Chapter 6

AAUW. *The AAUW Report: How Schools Shortchange Girls*. Washington DC: American Assn. University Women, 1992.

Billingsley, Andrew. *Climbing Jacob's Ladder: The Enduring Legacy of African American Families*. New York: Simon & Schuster, 1992.

"Black Managers Leaving the Fold." *Wall Street Journal* (May 6, 1992): A1.

Blanchard, F.A., and F.J. Crosby. "The Role of Black Psychologists in Black Liberation." In *African American Psychology*, A.K.E. Burlew et al. (eds.). Thousand Oaks, CA: Sage, 1992.

Fraser, George. *Success Runs in Our Race*. New York: Wm. Morrow, 1994.

Hall, E.T. *Beyond Culture*. New York: Doubleday, 1976.

Hecht, M.L., M.J. Collier, and S.A. Ribeau. *African American Communication*. Thousand Oaks, CA: Sage, 1993.

Kochman, Thomas. *Black & White Styles in Conflict*. Chicago: The University of Chicago Press, 1981.

Mauer, Marc. *Young Black Men and the Criminal Justice System*. Washington D.C.: The Sentencing Project, 1990.

Rose, L.F. "Theoretical & Methodological Issues in the Study of Black Culture and Personality." *Humboldt Journal of Social Relations* 10 (1982/1983): 320–338.

Solorzano, Daniel G. "Mobility Aspirations among Racial Minorities, Controlling for SES." *Social Science Review* 75 (July 1991): 182–188.

U.S. Census Bureau, Department of Commerce, *We the African Americans*, 1993.

White, J.L., and T.A. Parham. *The Psychology of Blacks: An African American Perspective*, 2d ed. Englewood Cliffs, NJ: Prentice-Hall, 1990.

Chapter 7

Chow, Esther Ngan-Ling. "Asian American Women at Work." In *Women of Color in U.S. Society*, Maxine Baca Zinn and Bonnie Thornton Dill (eds.). Philadelphia: Temple University Press, 1994.

Dong, Lorraine. Professor of Asian American Studies, San Francisco State University, series of interviews, 1992.

Harris, Philip R., and Robert T. Moran. *Managing Cultural Differences*, 3d ed. Houston, TX: Gulf Publishing Co., 1991.

Hossfeld, Karen. "Hiring Immigrant Women: Silicon Valley's 'Simple Formula.'" In *Women of Color in U.S. Society*, Maxine Baca Zinn and Bonnie Thornton Dill (eds.). Philadelphia: Temple University Press, 1994.

Takaki, Ronald. *A Different Mirror: A History of Multicultural America*. Boston: Little, Brown Co., 1993.

U.S. Census Bureau, Department of Commerce. *We the American . . . Asians*, 1993.

U.S. Census Bureau, Department of Commerce. *We the American . . . Pacific Islanders*, 1993.

Wei, William. *The Asian American Movement*. Philadelphia: Temple University Press, 1993.

Chapter 8

Cohen, R. *Culture, Disease and Stress Among Latino Immigrants*. Washington, DC: Smithsonian Institution, 1979.

Daniel, Clete. *Chicano Workers and the Politics of Fairness: The FEPC in the Southwest, 1941–1945*. Austin, TX: University of Texas Press, 1991.

De Freitas, Gregory. *Inequality at Work: Hispanics in the U.S. Labor Force*. NY: Oxford University Press, 1991.

Gann, L.J., and Peter J. Duignan. *The Hispanics in the United States: A History*. Boulder, CO: Westview Press, 1986.

Grebler, Leo, Joan W. Moore, and Ralph C. Guzman. *The Mexican-American People, the Nation's Second Largest Minority*. New York: Free Press, 1970.

Marin, Gerardo, and Barbara VanOss Marin. *Research with Hispanic Populations*. Newbury Park, CA: Sage 1991.

McWilliams, Carey. *North from Mexico*. New York: Greenwood Press, 1990.

Solorzano, Daniel G. "Mobility Aspirations Among Racial Minorities, Controlling for SES." *Social Science Review* 75 (July 1991): 182–188.

Triandis, H.C., et al. "Simpatia as a Cultural Script of Hispanics." *Journal of Personality and Social Psychology* 47 (1984b): 1363–1375.

Triandis, H.C., et al. *Dimensions of Familism among Hispanic and Mainstream Navy Recruits*. Chicago: University of Illinois, 1982.

U.S. Census, Department of Commerce. *We the Hispanics*, 1993.

U.S. Census, Department of Commerce. *We the American . . . Children*, 1993.

Chapter 9

American Psychological Association. Minutes of the Council of Representatives. *American Psychologist* 30 (1975): 633.

Badget, Lee. "National Random Poll." *Industrial and Labor Relations Review* (July 1995) 23.

Bailey, J. Michael. Northwestern University, see *Archives of General Psychiatry*, March 1993.

"Chicago Research Firm Surveys Gays." *Fortune* December 16, 1992, p.5.

Duberman, Martin. *Stonewall*. New York: Dutton, 1993.

Green, Beverly, and G.M. Herek, eds. *Lesbian and Gay Psychology*. Thousand Oaks, CA: Sage, 1994.

Green, G.D., and F. Bozett. "Lesbian Mothers and Gay Fathers." In *Homosexuality: Research Implications for Public Policy*, J. Gonsiorek and J. Weinrich (eds.). Thousand Oaks, CA: Sage, 1991.

Hamer, Dean, and P. Copeland. *The Science of Desire: The Search for the Gay Gene and the Biology of Behavior*. New York: Simon & Schuster, 1994.

Herek, G.M. In *Homosexuality Research Implications for Public Policy*. Thousand Oaks, CA: Sage, 1991.

Kite, M.D., and K. Deaux. "Attitudes toward Homosexuality." *Basic and Applied Social Psychology* 7 (1986): 137–162.

Michael, Robert T., J.H. Gagnon, E.O. Laumann, and G. Kolata. *Sex in America: A Definitive Survey*. New York: Little, Brown & Co., 1995.

Rich, R. "Compulsory Heterosexuality and Lesbian Existence." *Signs* 5 (1990): 631–660.

Schmitt, P.J., and L.A. Kurdek. "Personality Correlates of Positive Identity, Relationship Involvement in Gay Men." *Journal of Homosexuality* 13, no. 4 (1987).

Seligman, Martin. *What You Can Change and What You Can't*. New York: Knopf, 1994.

Weisner, T.S., and J.E. Wilson-Mitchell. "Nonconventional Family Lifestyles and Sextyping in Six Year Olds." *Child Development* 61 (1990): 1915–1933.

Woods, J.D., and J.H. Lucas. *The Corporate Closet: The Professional Lives of Gay Men in America*. New York: The Free Press, 1993.

Chapter 10

Crew, Nancy M., and Irving Kenneth Zola. *Independent Living for Physically Disabled People*. San Francisco: Jossey-Bass, Inc., 1983.

Cox, Taylor. *Cultural Diversity in Organizations*. San Francisco: Berrett-Koehler, 1993.

Longmore, P.K. "A Note on Language and the Social Identity of Disabled People." *American Behavioral Scientist* 28, no. 3 (January/February 1985a): 419–423.

Longmore, P.K. "Screening Stereotypes: Images of Disabled People." *Social Policy* (Summer 1985b): 32–37

Longmore, P.K. "Uncovering the Hidden History of People with Disabilities," *Reviews in American History* (September 1987): 355–364.

Maloff, Chalda, and Susan Macduff. *Business and Social Etiquette with Disabled People*. Springfield, IL: Charles C. Thomas Publisher, 1988.

"Myths & Facts: About People Who Have Disabilities." Chicago: National Easter Seal Society, 1992.

Potter, Edward E. *A Compliance Guide to the Americans with Disabilities Act*. Washington, DC: Employment Policy Foundation, 1991.

Shapiro, Joseph. *No Pity: People with Disabilities Forging a New Civil Rights Movement*. New York: Times Books, 1993.

Stace, S. "Vocational Rehabilitation for Women with Disabilities." *International Labour Review* 126, no. 3 (1987): 301–316.

Vash, Carolyn. *The Psychology of Disability*. NY: Springer Publishing Co., 1981.

Chapter 11

Cox, Taylor, Jr., and Stella M. Nkomo. "Candidate Age As a Factor in Promotability Ratings." *Public Personnel Management* 2 (Summer, 1992): 197–210.

"Door Ajar to Women of All Ages in Ads." *Advertising Age* October 4, 1993, p. S2.

Friedan, Betty. *The Fountain of Age*. New York: Simon and Schuster, 1993.

Gann, L.J., and P.J. Duignan. *The Hispanics of the United States: A History*. Boulder, CO: Westview Press, 1986.

Gove, Walter R. "The Effect of Age and Gender on Deviant Behavior." In *Gender and the Life Course*, Alice S. Rossi (ed.). New York: Aldine, 1985.

Hushbeck, Judith C. *Old and Obsolete: Age Discrimination and the American Worker, 1860–1920*. New York: Garland, 1989.

Jackson, Susan E. *Diversity in the Workplace*. New York: Guilford Press, 1992.

Menkler, Meredith. "Research on the Health Effects of Retirement." *Journal of Health and Social Behavior* 22 (1981): 117–130.

Mitchell, Olivia S., ed. *As the Workforce Ages*. Ithaca, NY: ILR Press, 1993.

"Older Workers Are Valuable Employees." *Retirement Living* April, 1996.

Rosen, Benson, and Thomas H. Jerdee. *Older Employees: New Roles for Valued Resources*. Homewood, IL: Dow Jones-Irwin, 1995.

Ryff, Carol D. "Subjective Experience of Life-Span Transitions." In *Gender and the Life Course*, Alice Rossi (ed.). New York: Aldine, 1995.

Sandell, Steven H. *The Problem Isn't Age: Work and Older Americans*. New York: Praeger, 1997.

Scripps Howard News Service. "If You're Gray, Sing the Blues." *San Francisco Chronicle/Examiner* May 10, 1998, D–1.

U.S. Census Bureau. *We . . . the American Elderly*. Washington, DC: Department of Commerce, 1993.

Chapter 12

Blair, S., et al. "Physical Fitness and All-Cause Mortality." *Journal of Applied Social Psychology* 18 (1988): 699–719.

Brown, Laura S., and Esther D. Rothblum, eds. *Overcoming Fear of Fat*. Binghamton, NY: Harrington Park Press, 1989.

Burros, Marian. "More Americans Tipping the Scales." *New York Times* (July 15, 1994).

Chernin, Kim. *The Obsession: Reflections on the Tyranny of Slenderness*. New York: Harper & Row, 1982.

Dettmar, Lyn. Chicago clinical psychologist, study conducted in 1990.

Fumento, Michael. *The Fat of the Land*. New York: Viking, 1997.

Gortmaker, Steven, et al. "Social and Economic Consequences of Overweight in Adolescence and Young Adulthood." *New England Journal of Medicine* 329, 14 (September 1993): 1036–1037.

Hirschmann, Jane, and Carol Munter. *When Women Stop Hating Their Bodies*. New York: Fawcett Columbine, 1995.

Jeffrey, R., S. Adlis, and J. Forster. "Prevalence of Dieting Among Working Men and Women." *Health Psychology* 10 (1991): 274–281.

Johnson, Carol A. *Self-Esteem Comes in All Sizes: How to Be Healthy and Happy at Your Natural Weight*. New York: Doubleday, 1995.

Olds, Ruthanne. *Big & Beautiful*. Washington DC: Acropolis Books Ltd., 1992.

Rothblum, Esther D. "Weight and Acceptance on the Job." In *Life Isn't Weighed on the Bathroom Scale*, Laura Rose, S. Brown, and E.D. Rothblum (eds.). Waco, TX: WRS Group, 1994.

Seligman, Martin. *What You Can Change and What You Can't*. New York: Knopf, 1994.

Tisdale, Sally. "A Weight That Women Carry." *Harpers* (May 1993) 54–57.

Wahl, Jan. "Taking a Female Lead." *Radiance* (fall 1994) 35–38.

Wolf, Naomi. *The Beauty Myth: How Images of Beauty Are Used Against American Women*. New York: Doubleday, 1991.